Daniel Van Olmen, Hubert Cuyckens, Lobke Ghesquière (Eds.)
**Aspects of Grammaticalization**

# Trends in Linguistics
# Studies and Monographs

**Editor**
Volker Gast

**Editorial Board**
Walter Bisang
Jan Terje Faarlund
Hans Henrich Hock
Natalia Levshina
Heiko Narrog
Matthias Schlesewsky
Amir Zeldes
Niina Ning Zhang

**Editor responsible for this volume**
Volker Gast

# Volume 305

# Aspects of Grammaticalization

---

(Inter)Subjectification and Directionality

Edited by
Daniel Van Olmen
Hubert Cuyckens
Lobke Ghesquière

DE GRUYTER
MOUTON

ISBN 978-3-11-063502-7
e-ISBN (PDF) 978-3-11-049234-7
e-ISBN (EPUB) 978-3-11-048976-7
ISSN 1861-4302

**Library of Congress Cataloging-in-Publication Data**
A CIP catalog record for this book has been applied for at the Library of Congress.

**Bibliographic information published by the Deutsche Nationalbibliothek**
The Deutsche Nationalbibliothek lists this publication in the Deutsche Nationalbibliografie;
detailed bibliographic data are available on the Internet at http://dnb.dnb.de.

© 2018 Walter de Gruyter GmbH, Berlin/Boston
This volume is text- and page-identical with the hardback published in 2016.
Typesetting: RoyalStandard, Hong Kong
Printing and binding: CPI books GmbH, Leck

♾ Printed on acid-free paper
Printed in Germany

www.degruyter.com

# Acknowledgments

The present volume emanates from the "International Conference on Grammaticalization and (Inter)Subjectification" (GRAMIS), held in Brussels from 11 to 13 November 2010. The conference was organized within the framework of the Interuniversity Attraction Pole (IAP-Phase VI, project P6/44 of the Belgian Science Policy Office on "Grammaticalization and (Inter)Subjectfication", coordinated by Johan van der Auwera (University of Antwerp). The generous financial support of this research project is hereby gratefully acknowledged.

We are very much indebted to Volker Gast, editor of the series "Trends in Linguistics – Studies and Monographs" for having included this volume into the series. Many thanks as well go to Birgit Sievert, Acquisitions Editor at De Gruyter Mouton, for her initial interest in this project.

While we, as editors, are responsible for the final choice of papers, the assessments of the following external referees have been a tremendous help in the selection process: Karin Aijmer, Kersti Börjars, Timothy Colleman, Bert Cornillie, Hendrik De Smet, Dagmar Divjak, Matthias Gerner, Elma Kerz, Svenja Kranich, María José López-Couso, Christian Mair, Tanja Mortelmans, Colette Moore, Maj-Britt Mosegaard-Hansen, Muriel Norde, Helka Riionheimo, Lauren Van Alsenoy, Sophie Van Laer, Alice Vittrant and Ilse Wischer. Furthermore, the reviewers' careful feedback and suggestions have greatly improved the quality of the papers.

Finally, we wish to thank the contributors for developing their study presented at the GRAMIS conference into an article for this volume, for their efficient cooperation and for their patience.

# Table of contents

**Acknowledgments —— v**

Hubert Cuyckens, Lobke Ghesquière and Daniël Van Olmen
Introduction —— 1

## I  Grammaticalization and (inter)subjectification

Heiko Narrog
1   Three types of subjectivity, three types of intersubjectivity, their dynamicization and a synthesis —— 19

Karin Beijering
2   Grammaticalization and (inter)subjectification: The case of the Swedish modals *må* and *måtte* —— 47

Adeline Patard and Johan van der Auwera
3   The French comparative modal constructions *faire mieux de*, *valoir mieux* and *falloir mieux* —— 81

Gijsbert Rutten and Marijke van der Wal
4   Discourse continuity and the written medium: Continuative relative clauses in the history of Dutch —— 113

Hilary Chappell
5   From verb of saying to discourse marker in Southern Min: (Inter)subjectification and grammaticalization —— 139

Thomas Egan
6   The subjective and intersubjective uses of "fail to" and "not fail to" —— 167

## II  Grammaticalization and directionality

Luisa Brucale and Egle Mocciaro
7   Paths of grammaticalization of the Early Latin *per/per-*: A cognitive hypothesis —— 199

Andrzej M. Łęcki and Jerzy Nykiel
8  Grammaticalization of the English adverbial subordinator *in order that* — 237

Björn Hansen
9  What happens after grammaticalization? Post-grammaticalization processes in the area of modality — 257

Helle Metslang
10 Can a language be forced? The case of Estonian — 281

Debra Ziegeler
11 Historical replication in contact grammaticalization — 311

Freek Van de Velde and Béatrice Lamiroy
12 External possessors in West Germanic and Romance: Differential speed in the drift toward NP configurationality — 353

Index — 401

Hubert Cuyckens, Lobke Ghesquière and Daniël Van Olmen
# Introduction

## 1 Grammaticalization

For more than three decades, grammaticalization has attracted great interest in the domains of historical linguistics and typology. The work by Lehmann (1995 [1982]), the collective volumes by Traugott and Heine (1991) and the handbook by Hopper and Traugott (1993) were crucial in the development of the field. They generated a wealth of case studies applying the parameters of grammaticalization laid out in these seminal works to (largely morphosyntactic) diachronic change and cross-linguistic variation studies (Bybee et al. 1994; Ramat and Hopper 1998; Fischer et al. 2000). Following up on some critical assessments, most poignantly voiced in a special issue of *Language Sciences* (Campbell 2001), grammaticalization seemed to have found renewed vigor, with the conference series "New Reflections on Grammaticalization" (Wischer and Diewald 2002; Fischer et al. 2004; López-Couso and Seoane 2008; Seoane and López-Couso 2008; Davidse et al. 2012; Smith et al. 2014);[1] with the publication of such important volumes as Bisang et al. (2004), Stathi et al. (2010), Traugott and Trousdale (2010) and Van linden et al. (2010); with special issues in *Language Sciences* (Norde et al. 2013), *Folia Linguistica* (Von Mengden and Simon 2014) and *Language Sciences* (Breban and Kranich 2015); and with the publication of Heine and Kuteva's *World Lexicon of Grammaticalization* (2002) and Narrog and Heine's *The Handbook of Grammaticalization* (2011). Further, as Traugott (2010b) described and Himmelmann (2004) most clearly articulated, linguists also became aware that grammaticalization should not only be viewed as "reduction", but also as "expansion" (see also Tabor & Traugott 1998). The period after the turn of the century also saw grammaticalization studies spreading out to the generative paradigm (Roberts and Roussou 2003; Van Gelderen 2004) and more recently to construction grammar (Traugott and Trousdale 2013). The importance of grammaticalization studies in nicely summed up in Breban et al. (2012: 1):

---

[1] It is uncertain whether the conference series "New Reflections on Grammaticalization" will be continued, but a new quadrennial series has seen the light "International Conference on Grammaticalization Theory and Data", held in Rouen. Selected papers from the first conference have been published in Hancil and König (2014).

It is unquestionable that the study of grammaticalization and related processes of change has had an enormous impact on the recent linguistic scene. Grammaticalization research in the broad sense has created a meeting ground for approaches as varied as typology, language acquisition, comparative and diachronic study, synchronic language description, usage-based and corpus-based description, and discourse approaches. In about a quarter of a century, it has changed the general assumptions of language *description*, putting awareness of change at the centre of interest, rather than reserving it to specialized historical studies.

## 2 (Inter)subjectification and directionality

The present volume focuses on two dimensions which have been shown to be crucial in grammaticalization research, namely, the interrelation between grammaticalization and (inter)subjectification, and the directionality of grammaticalization. Our definition of grammaticalization is the classical one in Hopper and Traugott (2003: 18):

> [T]he change whereby lexical items and constructions come in certain linguistic contexts to serve grammatical functions, and once grammaticalized, continue to develop new grammatical functions.

The concepts of subjectification and intersubjectification entered the grammaticalization literature after it had been pointed out by Traugott (in such hallmark publications as Traugott 1982, 1989, 1995, 2003; Traugott and König 1991) that semantic change in grammaticalization was not just a matter of semantic reduction,[2] nor that semantic change in grammaticalization could be sufficiently captured in terms of metaphor, as it had been proposed by Claudi and Heine (1986) and Heine et al. (1991a). Additional notable volumes and studies highlighting the relationship between grammaticalization and (inter)subjectification are Stein and Wright (1995), Athanasiadou et al. (2006), Davidse et al. (2010), Brems et al. (2012) and Ghesquière (2014). The relationship between (inter)subjectification and grammaticalization was also at the forefront of the so-called GRAMIS project,[3] from which the present volume emanates.

---

[2] "The general claim that grammaticalization involves loss of meaning (desemanticization, bleaching, etc.) ... ignores that fact that ... there is strengthening of focus on knowledge, belief, and the speaker's attitude toward the proposition" (Traugott 1989: 49).
[3] GRAMIS, short for "Grammaticalization and (Inter)subjectification", was an interuniversity project awarded by the Belgian Science Policy (P6/44) to the universities of Antwerp, Ghent, Hanover, Leuven and Louvain-la-Neuve and the Royal Museum for Central Africa, and was coordinated by Johan van der Auwera.

Traugott (2003: 126) defines subjectification as "the mechanism whereby meanings come over time to encode or externalize the SP[eaker]/W[riter]'s perspectives and attitudes as constrained by the communicative world of the speech event".[4] Intersubjectification, then, is "the development of meanings that encode speaker/writer's attention to the cognitive stances and social identities of addressees" (Traugott 2003: 124). Importantly, intersubjectification "arises out of and depends crucially on subjectification" (2003: 124) (see also the discussion on (uni)directionality below). Other well-known perspectives on (inter)subjectification are Langacker's (1990, 1999, 2003, 2006) and Nuyts' (2001). Langacker looks at subjectification within the framework of cognitive grammar: "a semantic shift or extension in which an entity originally construed objectively comes to receive a more subjective construal" (Langacker 1991: 215). Nuyts (2001) defines subjectivity and intersubjectivity in terms of personal vs. shared responsibility.[5]

As was pointed out in Cuyckens et al. (2010: 6) and Traugott (2010a: 39–41), "([i]nter)subjectification often involves *grammaticalization*, but they are different types of changes which may occur independently of each other." For instance, the semantic shift from *pig* 'animal' to *pig* 'impolite, slobbering eater' is a case of lexical subjectification not accompanied by grammaticalization. Conversely, the development of prepositions such as *to* into an infinitive marker or *by* into a passive marker involve grammaticalization without (inter)subjectification. Still, Traugott (2010a: 39) argues, "subjectification is more likely to occur in grammaticalization than in lexicalization or in semantic change in general, presumably because grammaticalization by definition involves recruitment of items to mark the speaker's perspective".

Another issue that has long concerned grammaticalization researchers is whether grammaticalization is unidirectional or whether it is possible for a grammatical item to *degrammaticalize*, i.e. become less grammatical. In other words, it continues to be a matter of debate whether it is possible for a grammatical item to move from right to left rather than from left to right along Hopper and Traugott's (2003: 7) grammaticality cline: content item > grammatical word > clitic > inflectional affix. Hopper and Traugott's (2003: 18) definition of grammaticalization quoted above suggests that grammaticalization is irreversible (see also Lehmann 1995 [1982]: 19, Bybee et al. 1994 and Haspelmath 1999: 1044 for similar views). This idea of unidirectionality was criticized in, among others,

---

[4] As most of the contributions in this volume take Traugott's perspective as a point of departure, the line of research on subjectivity and subjectification initiated by Langacker and Nuyts will not be pursued further here.

[5] De Smet and Verstraete (2006) present an insightful comparison of Traugott's and Langacker's lines of research. A detailed discussion of various perspectives on (inter)subjectification is also presented in López-Couso (2010).

Newmeyer (1998) and Campbell (2001). Importantly, as Traugott (2010b: 274) points out, "the 'paths' of grammaticalization had for the most part been developed by 'functionalist' linguists who assumed ... that universals are probabilistic tendencies, not absolute". A critical appraisal of unidirectionality has been a recurrent theme at the "New Reflections on Grammaticalization conferences" (see, e.g., Fischer et al. 2004), and has also raised awareness that degrammaticalization should be distinguished from lexicalization, that is, that lexicalization should be seen "as a type of change in its own right, not merely as a counterexample to unidirectionality in grammaticalization" (Traugott 2010b: 275; see also Brinton and Traugott 2005). The most important and comprehensive study of "degrammaticalization" to date is undoubtedly Norde (2009).

The issue of directionality is not confined to morphosyntactic developments but has also been present in discussions of semantic change in grammaticalization. While in Lehmann (1995 [1982]), semantic change in grammaticalization followed a unidirectional path involving increased bleaching, it was pointed out in studies by Heine et al. (1991), Sweetser (1987) and Traugott (1982, 1989) that grammaticalization not only involved the loss of meaning but also the addition of new meaning. According to Heine et al. (1991: 157), the process underlying grammaticalization followed a metaphorically structured cline: PERSON > OBJECT > PROCESS > SPACE TIME > QUALITY. It was Traugott's (1982: 257) insight that, diachronically, lexical items which originate in the propositional domain tend to acquire textual and/or expressive meanings.[6] Later, she replaced the cline ideational > textual > interpersonal by the non-subjective > subjective > intersubjective cline. Modifications to this pathway have been proposed by amongst others Carlier and De Mulder (2010), Ghesquière (2010, 2014), Egan (this volume) and Narrog (2010, 2014, this volume).[7]

## 3 Contributions to this volume

The present volume is divided into two parts, reflecting the two different foci. The papers in the first part center around the relation between grammaticalization and (inter)subjectification. Heiko Narrog, Karin Beijering and Adeline

---

[6] Traugott's terminology builds on Halliday and Hasan's (1976) three-way distinction of the linguistic system into the functional-semantic components referred to as the ideational, the textual and the interpersonal.
[7] It should be noted that in this volume, the notion "directionality" is not problematized, as there is no critical discussion of it. Still, as will be pointed out, directionality is central to a number of the papers.

Patard and Johan van der Auwera examine this relation in the modal domain. Hilary Chappell and Gijsbert Rutten and Marijke Van der Wal study grammaticalization and (inter)subjecfication with an eye on various cohesive devices. Thomas Egan, finally, considers how (inter)subjectification and grammaticalization are relevant to the development of the "fail to" and "not fail to" constructions. The contributions in the second part all relate to directionality in grammaticalization. Some describe developments that are largely in line with the directionality hypothesis. Luisa Brucale and Egle Mocciaro, for instance, analyze the paths of grammaticalization of Early Latin *per/per-* and Andrzej Łęcki and Jerzy Nykiel describe the development of the adverbial subordinators *in order that/to*. The remaining papers in this set propose modifications of the unidirectionality hypothesis. Björn Hansen deals with the processes that already grammaticalized elements can undergo. Both Helle Metslang and Debra Ziegeler look at what happens in contact situations. Finally, in their study of external possessors Freek Van de Velde and Béatrice Lamiroy discuss different speeds of grammaticalization in closely related languages.

At the empirical level, the volume presents data from a range of languages (English, French, Dutch, Swedish, Estonian, Greek, Russian, Polish, Chech, Serbian/Croatian, Greek and Southern Min) and from a variety of areas, but with special attention to modality. At the theoretical level, the book takes a predominantly functional-cognitive position.

## 3.1 Grammaticalization and (inter)subjectification

**Heiko Narrog** focuses on the notions of (inter)subjectivity and (inter)subjectification and then examines their link with grammaticalization. Narrog takes a broad perspective on the topics of (inter)subjectivity and (inter)subjectification, whereby he applies his insights into the synchronic notions of subjectivity and intersubjectivity to his characterization of the dynamic/diachronic concepts of subjectification and (inter)subjectification (mainly exemplified for the field of modality). After discussing different views on subjectivity and intersubjectivity, Narrog suggests a summary of these notions in terms of "speaker-orientation" and "hearer-orientation", respectively. The dynamic notions subjectification and intersubjectification, then, are characterized by increased speaker-orientation and increased hearer-orientation, respectively. Often, however, he points out, the characterization of a grammaticalized item in terms of increased speaker- or hearer-orientation is not sufficient, and requires an additional dimension, namely, "discourse-orientation". Taken together, this triad of "speaker/hearer/discourse orientation" is captured under the cover term "speech-act orientation".

With regard to the relation of the notions of (inter)subjectification and grammaticalization, Narrog tentatively concludes that increased speaker-orientation (subjectification) is compatible with early stages of grammaticalization, while increased hearer-orientation (intersubjectification) and discourse-orientation are more likely to be identified with later stages of grammaticalization. As has been shown by Ghesquière (2014), however, these are just tendencies: in the domain of the noun phrase, for instance, the development of textual functions may precede the development of speaker-oriented evaluative functions.

**Karin Beijering**'s study first addresses the grammaticalization of the Swedish modals *må* 'may, should' and *måtte* 'may, must' and then turns to the relation between these instances of grammaticalization and (inter)subjectification. As Beijering points out, *må* and *måtte* historically derive from the same verb (Old Swedish *magha* 'have the power/strength'), whereby *må* denoted the present tense and *måtte* the past tense. Nowadays, however, they have different distributions, with *må* having specialized into a concessive marker and *måtte* primarily being associated with optative meanings. Beijering then describes the development of *må* and *måtte* as a prototypical case of grammaticalization, also known as "auxiliation" (Heine 1993; Kuteva 2001). In particular, she details essential mechanisms, accompanying primitive changes and side-effects of grammaticalization, which, in her approach, constitute a composite view of grammaticalization (see also Norde and Beijering 2014). In addition, Beijering points out that in the course of their existence, *må* and *måtte* have become increasingly subjective, expressing the speaker's personal views, as well as intersubjective, referring to speaker-writer and addressee-reader interaction in dialogue and exclamations.

**Adeline Patard and Johan van der Auwera** examine the relatively understudied modal comparative constructions in French. They present data on *faire mieux de* 'lit. do better of', *valoir mieux* 'lit. be worth better' and *falloir mieux* 'lit. must/have to better' which are grammaticalizing into semi-modals. The data show that grammaticalization is only incipient: (i) they are creating a new layer within the paradigm of modal verbs in French (see Hopper's 1991 criterion of "layering" as a mark of early grammaticalization); (ii) while modal comparatives can be said to form a paradigm of their own within that of the deontic modals (in particular, a paradigm subordinating deontic assessment to evaluative judgment, which reflects the *persistence* (Hopper 1991) of the original evaluative meaning of the constructions), their integration into the new paradigm is only incipient: the functional specialization of each modal comparative is far from complete, and they do not show uniform morphosyntactic properties. Further, their degree of speaker involvement (subjectivity) differs, with *valoir mieux* instantiating evaluative meaning (weak involvement) only, *falloir mieux* asserting a moral obligation (deontic meaning, stronger speaker involvement) and *faire mieux de* conveying an even stronger speaker involvement (directive meaning, the speaker pressing the addressee to act adequately). It is also *faire mieux de* which carries a potentially greater threat to the hearer's face than the other constructions, and thus instantiates the intersubjective dimension most clearly.

**Gijsbert Rutten and Marijke van der Wal** study the replacement of *d*-relativizers by *w*-relativizers in Dutch as an instance of grammaticalization in which intersubjectivity plays an important part. The change is argued to be a case of grammaticalization in the evolutionary sense of Givón (1979): the interrogative forms are a more explicit marker of subordination than the demonstrative ones. The authors show that the word order in Dutch relative clauses was such that, with *d*-forms, there was the occasional ambiguity between a subclause reading and a declarative main clause or paratactic reading but that, with *w*-forms, relative clauses could only be interpreted as subclauses, never as declarative or interrogative main clauses. The *w*-forms did not spread right across the board, however. Earlier research, which is substantiated here by a study of adverbial relativizers in a collection of 17th-century private letters, indicates that continuative relative clauses lead the way. As Rutten and Van der Wal point out, this is significant in two respects. First, as continuative relative clauses are often considered characteristic of writing, it suggests that written language may in fact have promoted grammaticalization. Second, as this type of relative clause typically conveys new information only loosely connected to the preceding main clause, the use of interrogative forms instead of demonstrative ones can be seen as ensuring discourse coherence and continuity for the reader. This intersubjectivity of the *w*-relativizer is argued to be pragmatic and limited to the context at issue rather than semantic (cf. Traugott 2010a), and to have accelerated the grammaticalization of *d*- into *w*-forms.

**Hilary Chappell** looks at 'say' verbs in Southern Min, a Sinitic language. These 'say' verbs grammaticalized into clause-final discourse markers, thus far an underdescribed process of change. Chappell first provides an overview of the functions of clause-final discourse marker 'say' in Sinitic languages. It is used, among other things, as a marker of evidentiality and mirativity and to form echo questions. Then, the focus is on $kong^1$ 'say' in Southern Min. This clause-final discourse marker is argued to result from the ellipsis of the subject of a postposed quotative 'I say' and from the reanalysis of the preceding quotation as a main clause. This formal change, which the author argues is a case of grammaticalization, is accompanied by an increase in (inter)subjectivity. $Kong^1$ is shown to occur in four types of construction: (i) the first- or second-person imperative with $kong^1$ serves as a suggestion, (ii) the second-person imperative serves as a warning when uttered with a different intonation, (iii) the *wh*-question serves as a rebuttal and (iv) the declarative serves as an assertion in which a contextual presupposition is questioned. In all four constructions, the presence of *kong*[1] is obligatory to convey the specific modality. It is further argued that all four construction types associated with *kong*[1] show subjectification and grammaticalization of the verb 'say' as it develops into a discourse marker as well as the coding of a particular dimension of intersubjectivity: they all involve expression of the speaker's viewpoint or attitude toward the current conversational topic (subjectivity, in line with Traugott's 2010b view), as well as the speaker's "rhetorical reconstruction" of a presupposition made by the addressee (intersubjectivity – a modification of Traugott's 2010b view).

In his study of the "fail to" and "not fail to" constructions (e.g. *In spite of the considerable effort and investment, it* **has** *for many years* **failed to** *pay its way* (BNC); *We will* **not fail to** *witness the rebirth of our nation*; COCA), **Thomas Egan** takes Traugott's notions of subjectification and intersubjectification as a starting point. In line with Traugott's views, he finds support for the fact that intersubjective uses develop later than subjective ones (see, e.g., Traugott 2010b). However, contrary to Traugott, he finds that intersubjective uses do not necessarily develop out of subjective ones. Egan demonstrates that intersubjective uses in "fail to" and "not fail to" develop out of objective uses. With regard to the correlation between grammaticalization and (inter)subjectification, he examines whether the most subjective use of "fail to" ('disappoint speaker's expectation') has developed into a mere grammatical marker of negation 'does not', and so whether there is a process of grammaticalization accompanying the subjectification of "fail to". An example of a candidate for grammaticalization is *When the autism strategy was published in March it* **failed to make** *the establishment of specialist autism teams a requirement for all local authorities* (COCA, 2010). While Egan admits that semantic change to negation is not sufficient evidence for grammaticalization, he suggests that another change is involved that points to grammaticalization: "fail to" is becoming discursively secondary (Boye & Harder 2012). At the same time, "fail to" still occurs with the earlier non-grammaticalized objective, subjective and intersubjective senses. This suggests that if grammaticalization can be observed in "fail to", it is in its early stages (see Hopper's 1991 related notions of layering and divergence as principles of incipient grammaticalization).

## 3.2 Grammaticalization and directionality

**Luisa Brucale and Egle Mocciaro** analyze the grammaticalization path of the preverb *per-* and the preposition *per* in Early Latin. Making use of the Cognitive

Grammar framework, they argue that each of these development paths originates in a common semantic nucleus (spatial configuration), but that their developments differentiate. For *per-* in particular, the shift from the basic spatial meaning to the abstract value of duration/intensification represents a metaphorical-metonymical process (see, e.g., Heine et al. 1991), In some cases a nuance of telicity develops, which can be interpreted as a metonymical shift focusing on the final part of the metaphorical path. Morphosyntactically, the abstract domain of intensification coincides with the grammatical (aspectual) function of *per-*. In other words, *per-* has here acquired a clear-cut grammatical function in the formation of morphologically more complex items (the preverbed verbs), and can therefore be said to have grammaticalized. In the development of its grammatical function, *per-* proceeds along the metaphorically structured path/cline outlined by Heine et al. (1991: 157). Interestingly, the paper also suggests that grammaticalization processes may still be followed by other processes such as lexicalization. In its further development toward 'telicity', *per-* loses its compositionality in combination with a verbal base; it can in the usage [*per-* + verb] therefore be seen as lexicalized. This development of lexicalized usages of an item following its grammaticalized usage ties in with Hansen's discussion in this volume (see below) of lexicalization as a possible post-grammaticalization process.

**Andrzej M. Łęcki and Jerzy Nykiel** examine the grammaticalization of the subordinators *in order that* and *in order to*. They show that the rise of the purposive subordinator *in order to/that* constitutes a regular case of grammaticalization, following a path from lexical to grammatical. In particular, the subordinator *in order to/that* follows a grammaticalization path in which an adverbial of manner becomes a subordinator. On the semantic plane, the prepositional subordinator may have derived from the idea of a desired state of order and gravitated toward purpose. Morphosyntactically, the following processes pertaining to grammaticalization can be observed: renewal, decategorialization, reduction of paradigmatic variability, specialization, obligatorification, decrease in syntactic variability and increase in syntagmatic cohesion.

The paper by **Björn Hansen** adds a new perspective to the unidirectionality literature in that it is the first study to present an account of language change following regular grammaticalization. The paper shows that grammaticalization processes do not have to represent the final stages in the history of a construction. Focusing on the domain of modality in five Slavonic languages, Hansen presents a typology of six post-grammaticalization processes: secondary grammaticalization, marginalization, degrammaticalization, retraction, lexicalization and grammatical word derivation. Some of these post-grammaticalization phenomena are in keeping with the concept of unidirectionality. First, secondary grammaticalization fits within the grammaticalizaton cline (for instance, Hansen discusses the development of the negated modal of possibility *moći* into a prohibitive marker). Second, the process of marginalization, whereby a post-grammaticalized item (e.g. Polish *mieć*) takes up a rather marginal position in the language, is, in principle, also compatible with the notion of unidirectionality. A clear example of degrammaticalization is the change of a modal of necessity (e.g. Czech *nemusim* 'not.must') into a lexical verb meaning 'dislike' (cf. Dutch *Ik **moet** hem niet* [I must him not] 'I don't like him'). A modal auxiliary, i.e. a function word, is reanalyzed as a member of a major word class. Similarly, the process of retraction also challenges the directionality idea, as newer, grammaticalized uses of an item may become obsolete, while older uses may be maintained (see Haspelmath 2004: 33). Finally, the processes of lexicalization (e.g. English *maybe* in English; Russian *možet byt'* 'perhaps') and grammatical word derivation (Russian *moč'* 'can' expressing possibility > *s-moč'* 'manage to do something') point out that the development of a particular construction need not end with grammaticalization.

Another paper challenging common assumptions regarding the teleology of grammaticalization is **Helle Metslang**'s paper on forced grammaticalization. Metslang discusses how a language can contain a product of grammaticalization without having gone through the expected gradual development. This phenomenon, traditionally associated with situations of language contact, is called "forced grammaticalization" and is studied for Estonian here. The author explains how language developers introduced into Old Written Estonian a category of articles, which was modeled after their native language German. They are also held responsible for a number of future markers in Estonian. For *saama* 'get, become' in particular, it is argued that no functional and formal bridging context exists between the lexical verb and the future auxiliary and that the temporal use follows from the polysemy of German *werden* 'become'. In Metslang's view, forced grammaticalization need not be contact-induced, however. She shows that, more recently, native-speaking language reformers have suggested many an innovation not explicitly based on a feature in another language but motivated mainly by a preference for syntheticity to analyticity, the latter being regarded as German influence and the former as Finnish-like and thus more authentic. Their proposals include a synthetic superlative, new cases for one of the types of infinitive and synthetic preterite forms. The aforementioned instances of forced grammaticalization have not all been equally successful. Metslang points out that the actual adoption of an innovation depends on, among other things, the extent to which it fits the structural properties and tendencies of the language as well as the sociolinguistic status of the written/standard variety in which it is introduced.

**Debra Ziegeler** looks at replica grammaticalization in contact situations with New Englishes. Like Metslang, Ziegeler examines how items in a language can grammaticalize without following the stages of the grammaticalization cline. Rather than assuming that the contact "model" language is the substrate or L1 (Heine and Kuteva 2005), the present study proposes replication of diachronic stages in the lexifier. The features Ziegeler looks at are habitual *will* (e.g. *on days i dont have to rush, eg, weekends... I **will** take half an hour and scrub etc shiok*), the specific determiner *one* (e.g. *And I know **one** professor uh ... in Selam who was our professor also*) and the stative progressive (e.g. *Oh maybe I'm not **having** migraine then*). This hypothesis is backed up by data from historically earlier stages of English, revealing a reflection of earlier historical stages in the use of these forms. In other words, a particular directional path is being replicated. Ziegeler further points out that, on the surface, the data also resemble a momentary degrammaticalization, relative to the stages of the same items in the source language, but it is not clear from the available data whether the processes observed will continue to become a counter-directional shift.

Finally, **Freek Van de Velde and Béatrice Lamiroy** discuss how different languages may develop at different speeds along the grammaticalization cline. Specifically, they examine the distribution of external possessors in English, Dutch and German on the one hand and French, Italian and Spanish on the other. The external possessor is shown to be very restricted in English and French but rather productive in German and Spanish. Dutch and Italian occupy a position in-between their respective relatives. Van de Velde and Lamiroy argue that existing accounts are not adequate. They point out, for instance, that attributing the lack of external possessors in English to the nonnuclear status of English in Standard Average European or to its imperfect acquisition by the Vikings fails to explain the position of French, a nuclear member of the Sprachbund which does not have a productive external possessor either and for which an imperfect acquisition hypothesis is hard to maintain. In the authors' view, the distributions are better explained by constructional grammaticalization proceeding at different speeds. The more general structural change in West Germanic and Romance relevant here is increasing noun phrase configurationality: as a tighter structure with, for example, a specific slot for determination develops and floating modifiers decrease, possessors tend to be expressed internally rather than externally. The relative degree of grammaticalization described in this article is then used to show that the increase in configurationality is highest in English and French, lowest in German and Spanish and intermediate in Dutch and Italian. The degree of grammaticalization is thus inversely correlated with the use of external possessors. Although the reason for the general differences in speed of grammaticalization remains unclear, Van de Velde and Lamiroy point to the linguistic contact associated with urbanization as a possible explanation.

## References

Athanasiadou, Angeliki, Costas Canakis & Bert Cornillie (eds.). 2006. *Subjectification: Various paths to subjectivity*. Berlin: Mouton de Gruyter.
Bisang, Walter, Nikolaus P. Himmelmann & Björn Wiemer (eds.). 2009. *What makes grammaticalization: A look from its fringes and its components*. Berlin: Mouton de Gruyter.
Boye, Kasper & Peter Harder. 2012. A usage-based theory of grammatical status and grammaticalisation. *Language* 88(1). 1–44.
Breban, Tine, Jeroen Vanderbiesen, Kristin Davidse, Lieselotte Brems & Tanja Mortelmans. Introduction: New reflections on the sources, outcomes, defining features and motivations of grammaticalization. In Kristin Davidse, Tine Breban, Lieselotte Brems & Tanja Mortelmans (eds.), *Grammaticalization and language change: New reflections*, 1–35. Amsterdam: John Benjamins.
Breban, Tine & Svenja Kranich (eds.). 2015. What happens after grammaticalization? Secondary grammaticalization and other late stage processes. *Language Sciences* 47 (Special issue).
Brems, Lieselotte, Lobke Ghesquière & Freek Van de Velde (eds.). Intersections of intersubjectivity. *English Text Construction* 5 (1) (Special issue).
Brinton, Laurel & Elizabeth Traugott. 2005. *Lexicalization and language change*. Cambridge: Cambridge University Press.
Bybee, Joan, Revere Perkins & William Pagliuca. 1994. *The evolution of grammar: Tense, aspect, and modality in the languages of the world*. Chicago: The University of Chicago Press.
Campbell, Lyle (ed.). 2001. Grammaticalization: A critical assessment. *Language Sciences* 23 (2–3) (Special issue).
Carlier, Anne & Walter De Mulder. 2010. The emergence of the definite article: *ille* in competition with *ipse* in Late Latin. In Kristin Davidse, Lieven Vandelanotte & Hubert Cuyckens (eds.), *Subjectification, intersubjectification and grammaticalization*, 241–275. Berlin: De Gruyter Mouton.
Claudi, Ulrike & Bernd Heine. 1986. On the metaphorical base of grammar. *Studies in Language* 10. 297–335.
Cuyckens, Hubert, Kristin Davidse & Lieven Vandelanotte. 2010. Introduction. In Kristin Davidse, Lieven Vandelanotte & Hubert Cuyckens (eds.), *Subjectification, intersubjectification and grammaticalization*, 1–26. Berlin: De Gruyter Mouton.
Davidse, Kristin, Lieven Vandelanotte & Hubert Cuyckens (eds.). 2010. *Subjectification, intersubjectification and grammaticalization*. Berlin: De Gruyter Mouton.
Davidse, Kristin, Tine Breban, Lieselotte Brems & Tanja Mortelmans (eds.). 2012. *Grammaticalization and language change: New reflections*. Amsterdam: John Benjamins.
De Smet, Hendrik & Jean-Christophe Verstraete. 2006. Coming to terms with subjectivity. *Cognitive Linguistics* 17. 365–392.
Fischer, Olga, Anette Rosenbach & Dieter Stein (eds.). 2000. *Pathways of change: Grammaticalization in English*. Amsterdam: John Benjamins.

Fischer, Olga, Muriel Norde & Harry Peridon (eds.). 2004. *Up and down the cline: The nature of grammaticalization*. Amsterdam: John Benjamins.

Ghesquière, Lobke. 2010. On the subjectification and intersubjectification paths followed by the adjectives of completeness. In Kristin Davidse, Lieven Vandelanotte & Hubert Cuyckens (eds.), *Subjectification, intersubjectification and grammaticalization*, 277–314. Berlin: De Gruyter Mouton.

Ghesquière, Lobke. 2014. *The directionality of (inter)subjectification in the English noun phrase: Pathways of change*. Berlin: De Gruyter Mouton.

Givón, Talmy. 1979. *On understanding grammar*. New York: Academia Press

Hancil, Sylvie & Ekkehard König (eds.). 2014. *Grammaticalization: Theory and data*. Amsterdam: John Benjamins.

Halliday, M. A. K. & Ruqaiya Hasan. 1976. *Cohension in English*. London: Longman.

Haspelmath, Martin. 1999. Why is grammaticalization irreversible? *Linguistics* 37. 1031–1068.

Heine, Bernd. 1993. *Auxiliaries: Cognitive forces and grammaticalization*. Oxford: Oxford University Press.

Heine, Bernd, Ulrike Claudi & Friederike Hünnemeyer. 1991. *Grammaticalization: A conceptual framework*. Chicago: University of Chicago Press

Heine, Bernd & Tania Kuteva. 2002. *World lexicon of grammaticalization*. Cambridge: Cambridge University Press.

Heine, Bernd, Ulrike Claudi & Frederike Hünnemeyer. 1991. From cognition to grammar: Evidence from African languages. In Elizabeth Closs Traugott & Bernd Heine (eds.), *Approaches to grammaticalization*. Vol. 1: *Focus on theoretical and methodological issues*, 149–187. Amsterdam: John Benjamins.

Himmelmann, Nikolaus P. 2004. Lexicalization and grammaticalization: Opposite or orthogonal? In Walter Bisang, Nikolaus Himmelmann & Björn Wiemer (eds.), *What makes grammaticalization: A look from its fringes and its components*, 21–42. Berlin: Mouton de Gruyter.

Hopper, Paul. 1991. On some principles of grammaticization. In Elizabeth Closs Traugott & Bernd Heine (eds.), *Approaches to grammaticalization*. Vol. 1: *Focus on theoretical and methodological issues*, 17–35. Amsterdam: John Benjamins

Hopper, Paul J. & Elizabeth Closs Traugott. 2003. *Grammaticalization*, 2nd edn. Cambridge: Cambridge University Press.

Kuryłowicz, Jerzy. 1964. *The inflectional categories of Indo-European*. Heidelberg: Carl Winter Verlag.

Kuteva, Tania. 2001. *Auxiliation: An enquiry into the nature of grammaticalization*. Oxford: Oxford University Press.

Langacker, Ronald. 1990. Subjectification. *Cognitive Linguistics* 1. 5–38.

Langacker, Ronald. 1991. *Foundations of cognitive grammar*, 2 vols. Stanford, CA: Stanford University Press.

Langacker, Ronald. 1999. Losing control: Grammaticalization, subjectification and transparency. In Andreas Blank & Peter Koch (eds.), *Historical semantics and cognition*, 147–175. Berlin: Mouton de Gruyter.

Langacker, Ronald. 2003. Extreme subjectification: English tense and modals. In Hubert Cuyckens, Thomas Berg, René Dirven & Klaus-Uwe Panther (eds.), *Motivation in language: Studies in honor of Günter Radden*, 3–26. Amsterdam: John Benjamins.

Langacker, Ronald. 2006. Subjectification, grammaticization and conceptual archetypes. In Angeliki Athanasiadou, Costas Canakis & Bert Cornillie (eds.), *Subjectification: Various paths to subjectivity*, 17–40. Berlin: Mouton de Gruyter.

Lehmann, Christian. 1995 [1982]. *Thoughts on grammaticalization*. Munich: Lincom Europe.
Lehmann, Christian. 2002. New reflections on grammaticalization and lexicalization. In Ilse Wischer & Gabriele Diewald (eds.), *New reflections on grammaticalization*, 1–18. Amsterdam: John Benjamins.
López-Couso, María José. 2010. Subjectification and intersubjectification. In Andreas Jucker & Irma Taavitsainen (eds.), *Historical pragmatics*, 127–163. Berlin: De Gruyter Mouton.
López-Couso, María José & Elena Seoane (eds.). 2008. *Rethinking grammaticalization: New perspectives*. Amsterdam: John Benjamins.
Narrog, Heiko & Bernd Heine. 2011. *The Oxford handbook of grammaticalization*. Oxford: Oxford University Press.
Narrog, Heiko. 2010. (Inter)subjectification in the domain of modality and mood: Concepts and cross-linguistic realities. In Kristin Davidse, Lieven Vandelanotte & Hubert Cuyckens (eds.), *Subjectification, intersubjectification and grammaticalization*, 385–429. Berlin: De Gruyter Mouton.
Narrog, Heiko. 2014. Beyond intersubjectification: Textual uses of modality and mood in subordinate clauses as part of *speech-act orientation*. In Lieselotte Brems, Lobke Ghesquière and Freek Van de Velde (eds.), *Intersubjectivity and intersubjectification in grammar and discourse*, 29–51. Amsterdam: John Benjamins.
Newmeyer, Frederick. 1998. *Language form and language function*. Cambridge, MA: MIT Press.
Norde, Muriel. 2009. *Degrammaticalization*. Oxford: Oxford University Press.
Norde, Muriel, Karen Beijering & Alexandra Lenz (eds.). 2013. Current trends in grammaticalization research. *Language Sciences* 36 (Special issue).
Norde, Muriel & Karin Beijering. Facing interfaces: A clustering approach to grammaticalization and related changes. *Folia Linguistica* 48(2). 385–424.
Nuyts, Jan. 2001. *Epistemic modality, language, and conceptualization: A cognitive-pragmatic perspective*. Amsterdam: John Benjamins.
Ramat, Anna Giacalone & Paul J. Hopper (eds.). 1998. *The limits of grammaticalization*. Amsterdam: John Benjamins.
Roberts, Ian & Anna Roussou. 2003. *Syntactic change*. Cambridge: Cambridge University Press.
Seone, Elena & María José López-Couso (eds.). 2008. *Theoretical and empirical issues in grammaticalization*. Amsterdam: John Benjamins.
Smith, Andrew D.M., Graeme Trousdale & Richard Waltereit (eds.). 2015. *New directions in grammaticalization research*. Amsterdam: John Benjamins.
Stathi, Katerina, Elke Gehweiler & Ekkehard König (eds.). 2010. *Grammaticalization: Current views and issues*. Amsterdam: John Benjamins.
Stein, Dieter & Susan Wright (eds.). 1995. *Subjectivity and subjectivisation*. Cambridge: Cambridge University Press.
Sweetser, Eve. 1987. Metaphorical models of thought and speech: A comparison of historical directions and metaphorical mappings in the two domains. *Berkeley Linguistics Society* 8. 446–449.
Tabor, Whitney & Elizabeth Closs Traugott. 1998. Structural scope expansion and grammaticalization. In Anna Giacalone Ramat & Paul J. Hopper (eds.), *The limits of grammaticalization*, 229–272. Amsterdam: John Benjamins.
Traugott, Elizabeth. 1982. From propositional to textual and expressive meanings: Some semantic-pragmatic aspects of grammaticalization. In Winfred P. Lehmann & Yakov Malkiel (eds.), *Perspectives on historical linguistics*, 245–271. Amsterdam: John Benjamins.

Traugott, Elizabeth. 1989. On the rise of epistemic meanings in English: An example of subjectification in semantic change. *Language* 57. 33–65.
Traugott, Elizabeth. 1995. Subjectification in grammaticalisation. In Dieter Stein & Susan Wright (eds.), *Subjectivity and subjectivisation*, 31–54. Cambridge: Cambridge University Press.
Traugott, Elizabeth. 2003. From subjectification to intersubjectification. In Raymond Hickey (ed.), *Motives for language change*, 124–139. Cambridge: Cambridge University Press.
Traugott, Elizabeth Closs. 2010a. (Inter)subjectivity and (inter)subjectification: A reassessment. In Kristin Davidse, Lieven Vandelanotte & Hubert Cuykens (eds.), *Subjectification, intersubjectification and grammaticalization*, 29–71. Berlin: De Gruyter Mouton.
Traugott, Elizabeth. 2010b. Grammaticalization. In Silvia Luraghi & Vit Bubenik (eds.), *Continuum companion to historical linguistics*, 271–285. London: Continuum.
Traugott, Elizabeth Closs & Bernd Heine (eds.). 1991. *Approaches to grammaticalization*, 2 vols. Amsterdam: John Benjamins.
Traugott, Elizabeth Closs & Ekkehard König. 1991. The semantics-pragmatics of grammaticalization revisited. In Elizabeth Closs Traugott & Bernd Heine (eds.), *Approaches to grammaticalization*. Vol. 1: *Focus on theoretical and methodological issues*, 189–218. Amsterdam: John Benjamins.
Traugott, Elizabeth Closs & Graeme Trousdale (eds.). 2010. *Gradience, gradualness and grammaticalization*. Amsterdam: John Benjamins.
Traugott, Elizabeth Closs & Graeme Trousdale. 2013. *Constructionalization and constructional change*. Oxford: Oxford University Press.
Van Gelderen, Ellie. 2004. *Grammaticalization as economy*. Amsterdam: John Benjamins.
Van linden, An, Jean-Christophe Verstraete & Kristin Davidse (eds.). 2010. *Formal evidence in grammaticalization research*. Amsterdam: John Benjamins.
Von Mengden, Ferdinand & Horst Simon (eds). 2014. What is it then, this grammaticalization? *Folia Linguistica* 48(2) (Special issue).
Wischer, Ilse & Gabriele Diewald (eds.). 2002. *New reflections on grammaticalization*. Amsterdam: John Benjamins.

# I Grammaticalization and (inter)subjectification

Heiko Narrog
# 1 Three types of subjectivity, three types of intersubjectivity, their dynamicization and a synthesis

**Abstract:** This paper discusses the three extant concepts of subjectivity and of intersubjectivity in linguistics. It points out their commonalities and the substantial differences between them, which are often overlooked. Furthermore, a synthesis between these concepts is proposed, and then the dynamic (diachronic) dimension of the synthesized concept in terms of increase in speech-act orientation. The paper ends with a short discussion of the relationship between increase in speech-act orientation and grammaticalization.

## 1 Introduction

The topics of subjectivity/subjectification and, more recently intersubjectivity/ intersubjectification, has attracted an enormous amount of interest. It is inevitable that such concepts are also prone to attract criticism, especially for their potential vagueness (see, e.g., Abraham 2005). It is also clear that researchers do not have a uniform understanding or concept of subjectivity, intersubjectivity and their dynamic (diachronic) counterparts. Especially in the area of grammaticalization studies, the contrast between Langacker's and Traugott's concepts has been highlighted by the proponents themselves and by other authors (e.g. Athanasiadou et al. 2006; Cornillie and Delbecque 2006 for the Langackerian concept; Davidse et al. 2010 for the Traugottian concept). Nevertheless, it is not uncommon to see these concepts being used in a rather undifferentiated fashion, as if they were naturally existing categories one can easily tap into by just referring to them. Also, differences between the concepts are often downplayed or ignored, although, as I will show in this paper, they may lead to diametrically opposed results. Another problematic issue is that it is sometimes forgotten that a proper concept of subjectification and intersubjectification presupposes a proper concept of subjectivity and intersubjectivity.

This paper thus aims to (i) analyze current concepts of subjectivity/ subjectification and intersubjectivity/intersubjectification in detail, showing their correspondences and divergences, and (ii) propose a synthesis and further elaboration. The area of grammar used as the means of exemplification is

DOI 10.1515/9783110492347-002

modality. I will proceed as follows. Section 2 will provide a discussion of the concepts of subjectivity and an attempt at synthesis. In Section 3, the concepts of intersubjectivity will be discussed, again followed by a synthesis. Section 4 will be dedicated to subjectification, based on the results of the discussion in Section 2; in a similar fashion, Section 5 will be dedicated to intersubjectification. In Section 6, I will introduce a concept that complements (inter)subjectivity and (inter)subjectification, namely discourse-orientation. Section 7, then, will address the issue of the relationship between (inter)subjectification and grammaticalization, and the last section will provide a short summary of the paper.

Before turning to the actual topic of this paper, I want to get a potential misunderstanding out of the way. Although I use modality as a means of exemplifying approaches to (inter)subjectivity, I do not identify modality with subjectivity or "speaker's stance", as some scholars have done (e.g. Calbert 1975; Bybee et al. 1994). Nor do I believe that certain modal categories, modal markers or modal verbs are by definition subjective (pace, e.g., Larreya and Rivière 1999). Instead, I assume that modality as a grammatical category and subjectivity as a pragmatic (or semantic) concept are independent of each other. Modality is defined in terms of (lack of) factuality (e.g. Kiefer 1997; Palmer 1998; Narrog 2005; Declerck 2009; Portner 2009), and modal expressions can have both objective and subjective uses (e.g. Lyons 1977; Coates 1983; Hengeveld 1987).

## 2 Subjectivity – Three concepts of subjectivity and a synthesis

Although in the English-speaking world subjectivity has become a popular research topic only fairly recently, concepts of subjectivity have already been circulating for a long time in other linguistic traditions. In Japan, the notion of subjectivity in language has a long-standing tradition going back at least to Tokieda (1941) and Kinda'ichi (1953a, 1953b). In the French-speaking world, it has been entertained at least since Benveniste (1971 [1958]), but it is also latently present in earlier work such as Bailly's (1965 [1932]). However, it is fair to say that these pioneers, although sometimes cited with regard to subjectivity, had little direct influence on the development of the concept as it is used today. Merit for today's concept largely belongs to the semanticist John Lyons (1968, 1977, 1995), who became the trailblazer for research on subjectivity in language in the English-speaking countries, and who has had, as we will see below, a huge influence on current thinking on subjectivity. Lyons's concept of subjectivity has two major components, namely (i) speaker commitment/performativity and (ii) accessibility of information. As discussed below (Sections 2.1 and 2.2), each of these components has led to a distinct concept of subjectivity. A third, original concept of subjectivity in terms of "construal", which is less directly related to Lyons's original concept, was later proposed by Langacker (see, e.g., 1990) (Section 2.3)

## 2.1 Subjectivity in terms of speaker commitment/ performativity

### 2.1.1 Terminological issues

As the title of the present section indicates, this approach to "subjectivity" does not appear as a single, clearly delineated concept, but rather as a cluster of concepts, whereby the various terms used to characterize the concept are not clearly distinguished.. At least the following closely related terms are involved: (i) speaker commitment (e.g. Lyons 1977: 797); (ii) speaker involvement in the utterance (e.g. Coates 1983: 32, 36–37); (iii) expression of the speaker (e.g. Finegan 1995: 1; Lyons 1995: 337); and (iv) performativity (e.g. Verstraete 2001: 1517). These terms should be clearly distinguished from each other, but especially "commitment" and "performativity" are often used almost interchangeably. The following definition by Lyons (1982: 102) is probably the most frequently quoted one representing this type of concept of subjectivity.

> The term subjectivity refers to the way in which natural languages, in their structure and their normal manner of operation, provide for the locutionary agent's expression of himself and his own attitudes and beliefs.

Earlier, Lyons (1977: 797) had introduced the notion of subjectivity with respect to epistemic modality, using the example in (1):

(1)  *Alfred may be unmarried.*

Lyons commented as follows: "The speaker may be understood as subjectively qualifying his commitment" (Lyons 1977: 797). Here, he seemed to understand subjectivity not as synonymous with speaker commitment as such, but as a possible qualification of speaker commitment. A few pages down, he elaborated this notion with the following sentence: "Subjective epistemic modality can be accounted for ... in terms of the speaker's qualification of the I-say-so component of his utterance" (1977: 800). That is, subjectivity is viewed as a qualification of a component of speech, formulated as either commitment or as the "I-say-so component" of an utterance.

Coates (1983: 32, 36–37), with reference to Lyons (1977), simply paraphrases subjectivity as the "speaker's involvement in the utterance", and Finegan (1995: 1), similar to Lyons (1982), suggests that subjectivity "concerns expression of self and the representation of a speaker's (or, more generally, a locutionary agent's) perspective or point of view in discourse – what has been called a speaker's imprint".

Verstraete (2001), in a paper dedicated to the issue of subjectivity in modality, also uses the term "commitment", but specifies the decisive element that makes utterances subjective as "performativity". He writes that "taking positions of commitment with respect to the propositional content of the utterance is a distinct aspect of the *performativity* of the utterance" (Verstraete 2001: 1517). Furthermore, according to him, "*performativity* is the key to a semiotic account of the distinction between subjective and objective functions of the modal auxiliaries in English". In this paper, I will adopt Verstraete's (2001) terminology, and label the approach associated with the cluster of concepts introduced in this section as the *speaker commitment/performativity* approach.

### 2.1.2 Subjectivity in terms of speaker commitment/performativity and pragmatics vs. grammar

In Lyons's original conceptualization, subjectivity is clearly not bound to linguistic form but is an essentially non-grammatical, pragmatic concept. Indeed, he pointed out that "it is possible for [subjectivity] to be expressed (for example, prosodically or paralinguistically in speech) without being encoded in the grammatical or lexical structure of the language-system" (Lyons 1995: 340).

However, in the research on subjectivity inspired by Lyons, scholars, from early on, sought to pin down correlations between form and subjective meaning. Hengeveld (1987), for example, set up systematic tests to distinguish between subjective and objective form classes in modality, concluding that modal adverbs were subjective and modal adjectives, in contrast, objective. In the area of modality, more scholars followed who tried to identify certain forms or types of modality categorically with subjectivity. Traugott (2010: 32), then, has tried to identify "expressions [of subjectivity] the prime semantic or pragmatic meaning of which is to index speaker attitude or viewpoint". However, "most frequently, an expression is neither subjective nor objective in itself; rather the whole utterance and its context determine the degree of subjectivity" (Traugott and Dasher 2002: 98). In this view, subjectivity is basically a feature of context, which may in some cases, however, imprint itself on linguistic form, and thus become grammatical. In conclusion, while the view of subjectivity in terms of speaker commitment/performativity is fundamentally pragmatic, it allows for the idea that it may become semanticized in specific linguistic forms over time.

## 2.2 Subjectivity in terms of accessibility of information/ evidentiality

Consider Lyons's (1977: 797) example again of potential subjectivity in modality; it is repeated here as (2).

(2) *Alfred may be unmarried.*

Lyons explains how this utterance could be either subjective or objective. In the latter case, the speaker expresses a quantifiable possibility. This would be a situation where it is known that thirty out of a community of ninety people are unmarried, but the speaker does not know who. If, on the other hand, *may* expresses the speaker's own uncertainty, the reading would be subjective. Thus, the decisive criterion for subjectivity is whether the information about the truth of the proposition is shared across a community of speakers or not.

This analysis was further developed by Nuyts (e.g. 2001a, 2001b), who contrasts "subjective" with "intersubjective" rather than "objective". In the case of a subjective reading, the speaker "suggest[s] that (s)he alone knows the evidence and draws a conclusion from it", while in the case of an intersubjective reading, the speaker "indicate[s] that the evidence is known to (or accessible by) a larger group of people who share the conclusion based on it" (Nuyts 2001a: 34). Nuyts labeled the concept that is decisive for the subjectivity vs. intersubjectivity of an utterance as *evidentiality*.[1] Note that this is not exactly the same concept as Lyons's, since for Lyons the criterion seems to be whether the speaker him-/herself has access to the information, and not whether the information is shared or not. In any case, Lyons's concept is ambiguous between both readings.

Recently, Nuyts's concept has been further developed by Portner (2009), who added a contrast between subjectivity and objectivity to the contrast between

---

**1** I do not think that this is a felicitous label as "evidentiality" is usually not understood as "sharedness of information" but rather as "source of information". I therefore propose the term "interpersonal accessibility" in place of it. However, to the extent that I am discussing Nuyts's concept, I will continue to use his terminology (i.e. also the term "evidentiality").

subjectivity and intersubjectivity. First, following a standard approach to modal semantics based on Kratzer (e.g. 1981), Portner (2009: 165) defines modality as subjective when the modal bases are particular to just one individual. In contrast, intersubjective modality applies to cases where modal bases are shared by more than one individual. Second, modality is subjective when the kind of information that forms the basis of an epistemic judgment is held in relatively low regard in a specific community, whereas it is objective when the information is held in relatively high regard. Note that, for Portner at least, subjectivity is an entirely pragmatic concept, which is not expressed grammatically. Nevertheless, depending on its interpretation, this concept of subjectivity in terms of evidentiality may also be associated with certain linguistic forms. Nuyts (2001a) carried out a detailed corpus study of modal expressions in Dutch, claiming that subjectivity is in this language most frequently associated with mental state verbs, while modal adverbs and auxiliaries, for example, are neutral with respect to subjectivity.

## 2.3 Subjectivity in terms of construal

The third concept of subjectivity was developed by Langacker (1985, 1991, 2002) within his Cognitive Grammar framework. In contrast to pragmatic approaches, which are often based on the study of empirical language data, Cognitive Grammar basically involves a top-down approach to language based on hypotheses about conceptualizations underlying linguistic expressions, and it is therefore labeled here as "conceptualist". Its concept of subjectivity is tightly bound to its specific theoretical framework and does not directly correspond to everyday usage of the term, nor to either of the two more pragmatically oriented concepts discussed above. Since I will not adopt this framework for this paper, and as it is documented in numerous publications, I will confine myself here to the very basics. In short, in Cognitive Grammar, linguistic expressions are viewed in terms of construals involving a conceptualizer (speaker) and an object of conceptualization (an event). A construal is conceived of as subjective if the conceptualizer's perspective is reflected but not explicitly put "onstage" in a linguistic expression. Typical subjective linguistic forms in English include deictic expressions (*here, now, this, the*), tense endings and the modals. Among the expressions of modality, it is the modals that are "grounding predications" because they bear no person endings and incorporate tense. The modals have also experienced loss of subject control, even in their deontic uses (this semantic observation corresponds to raising in traditional syntactic terms). As such, the Cognitive Grammar concept of subjectivity does not require reference to the context but is rather identified with specific linguistic forms and constructions, and thus entirely a matter of grammar.

## 2.4 A comparison of the three approaches

In summary of the brief discussions above, the three concepts of, or approaches to, subjectivity can be contrasted with respect to two salient criteria, namely whether they are essentially pragmatically oriented or grammatically oriented, and whether they contrast subjectivity with objectivity or with intersubjectivity. This leads to the following results, represented in Table 1.

Table 1: The three approaches to subjectivity with respect to two theoretical criteria

|  | Subjectivity as | Subjectivity in contrast with |
|---|---|---|
| Cognitive Grammar approach | Grammatical | Objectivity |
| Approaches based on commitment performativity concept | Pragmatic | Objectivity |
| Approaches based on accessibility of information/evidentiality | Pragmatic | Intersubjectivity (Portner: also objectivity) |

In terms of these two theoretical criteria, each of the concepts appears to have one criterion in common with and one different from each of the other concepts. However, in terms of actual analysis, it turns out that the two pragmatically oriented concepts are more closely related to each other. This can be demonstrated by looking at how specific modal forms are analyzed in terms of degree of subjectivity in each of the three approaches to subjectivity. The results for mental state verbs, modal adjectives and adverbs, and modal auxiliaries are represented in Table 2 (Note that each of the concepts of subjectivity is exemplified by a representative study).

Table 2: Degree of subjectivity in the three concepts of subjectivity

| Degree of subjectivity | Performativity approach (Perkins 1983) (PERF) | Evidentiality approach (Nuyts 2001a) (EVI) | Cognitive Grammar approach (Radden and Dirven 2007) (CONC) |
|---|---|---|---|
| High | Mental state verbs | Mental state verbs | Modal auxiliaries |
| Mid |  |  | Modal adverbs |
| Low | Modal adjectives, modal adverbs | Modal adjectives | Mental state verbs |
| Neutral | Modal auxiliaries | Modal auxiliaries, modal adverbs |  |

The similarities between the performative and the evidential analysis are as striking as their differences with the conceptualist analysis. As was briefly mentioned above, in the conceptualist analysis, the English modals are categorically viewed as subjective. The reason is that they are "grounding predications" which, due to their lack of inflectional endings, are typical "implicit" expressions of the speaker's perspective. Mental state verbs, by comparison, show low subjectivity in that they are not only inflected but also require that the speaker (or a different person) be explicitly expressed onstage as the sentence's subject. The two pragmatic approaches draw almost the opposite conclusion. Here, it is argued that mental state verbs are highly subjective because they most explicitly put the speaker onstage, as they are used to show his or her commitment, and also frequently embed a state of affairs that is the personal opinion of the speaker, the evidence for which is not necessarily shared by others.

There is one big caveat in this comparison, namely the fact that Nuyts (2001a) examines Dutch modal forms, whereas the other authors in Table 2 deal with English. The biggest potential difference concerns the Dutch modal auxiliaries, which have retained distinct singular and plural inflection (see Donaldson 2008: 220–222), and therefore would not necessarily be acknowledged as subjective expressions in Langacker's view. However, other authors from the Cognitive Grammar framework have recently argued for a more general category of "grounding predications" (e.g. Pelyvás 2001a, Pelyvás 2001b, Pelyvás 2006; Cornillie 2005).

Although Table 2 certainly glosses over differences between pragmatically oriented approaches, I do believe that it highlights quite correctly that (very substantial) differences can emerge depending on the choice for a pragmatic vs. conceptualist approach in analyzing subjectivity.[2]

## 2.5 Different notions of subjectivity: A synthesis

In this section, I will try to come up with a viable synthesis of the concepts of subjectivity discussed above, in terms of what I will label *speaker-orientation*. As its basis, I will use the speaker commitment/performativity concept, for three reasons. First, it is unclear how the evidentiality concept should work for linguistic categories other than epistemic modality. Second, as we will see in Section 3, the speaker commitment/performativity concept can be complemented with a concept of hearer-orientation (intersubjectivity) which covers

---

[2] Conversely, there is also research from within the Cognitive Grammar framework that calls for a more differentiated view of the subjectivity of modal auxiliaries and mental state verbs (e.g. Cornillie 2006; Mortelmans 2006; Pelyvás 2006).

cases that are not covered in the evidentiality approach, where intersubjectivity is basically an equivalent of objectivity. Third, it has a clearly defined diachronic dimension (see Sections 4 and 5). I define performativity as follows.

(3) To the extent that a linguistic form qualifies a proposition with respect to the current speech situation (including speaker and hearer), it is used performatively. To the extent that it does not qualify a proposition with respect to the current speech situation, it is used descriptively.

On this definition, performativity is not identical to subjectivity. Rather, it is only those performative meanings which qualify a proposition with respect to the speaker in the current speech situation that are subjective. These probably include most but not necessarily all performative meanings. On the other hand, as the performativity concept by definition lies outside the proposition, it does not cover cases of inner-propositional subjectivity, i.e. mainly subjective meanings of lexical items, or "ideational" subjectivity in the sense of De Smet and Verstraete (2006). The evidentiality concept is useful in that it complements the speaker-orientation concept by covering inner-propositional subjectivity as well. As already mentioned, use of the term "evidentiality" is problematic, as it is usually not understood as "sharedness of information" but as "source of information". I therefore propose a different term, namely, *interpersonal accessibility*, which I define as follows.

(4) To the extent that a linguistic form expresses a qualification which is based on information or evaluations that are accessible or personally linked only to the speaker, it is used in a way which is not interpersonally accessible. To the extent that a linguistic form expresses a qualification which is based on information or evaluations that are accessible or linked to a community of speakers, it is interpersonally accessible.

The aim of this concept is basically to distinguish subjective from non-subjective within non-performative, mostly lexical meanings. Note that this interpersonal accessibility concept not only has a different label from Nuyts's notion of evidentiality, but that it is also broader as it includes evaluations and thus stance. Subjectivity in terms of interpersonal accessibility can be entrenched in the meaning of specific lexical items and idioms (e.g. *gorgeous, idiot, helluva* etc.), which are basically taken as an expression of speaker stance every time they are used. Other lexical items may express the speaker's personal evaluation only in some contexts (e.g. *little, great*), and still others only very rarely in specific contexts. At the same time, interpersonal accessibility is also narrower than Nuyts's concept of evidentiality in that it is explicitly restricted to non-performative meanings. While it may be applicable to performative meanings, this is in fact unnecessary since what is performative is necessarily also personally linked to the speaker's judgment. Consider the paradigm example of subjectivity in terms of "evidentiality" (i.e. interpersonal accessibility) in Nuyts's (2001a, 2001b) research, i.e. mental state verbs expressing propositional attitude, such as *I think* in English:

(5)  *I think you should really go with neon colors.*

*I think* as in (5) is a paradigm case for "evidential" subjectivity in Nuyts's (2001a, 2001b) approach since it makes explicit that the basis for the judgment is the speaker's own evidence (or information/evaluations linked to the speaker). On the other hand, as it expresses the speaker's stance at the time of speech and not a detached description of the speaker's mental state, it is also performative. Conversely, to the extent that it is performative, it is necessarily linked to the speaker and the speech situation. Performativity therefore entails a subjective, i.e. not interpersonally accessible, reading, and no contradiction arises. As soon as the performativity notion is applied, the interpersonal accessibility notion is not necessary anymore to determine the subjectivity of non-propositional meanings, even if it is available. Its basic function is to complement the performativity notion for inner-propositional, mostly lexical meanings, which the performativity notion does not cover.

Finally, despite the insights that it offers, I do not believe that the notion of implicit subjectivity, as proposed in the Cognitive Grammar approach, can be usefully added to the notions of performativity and interpersonal accessibility without leading to considerable contradictions and vagueness. As shown in Section 2.4, the pragmatically based view of explicit subjectivity and the Cognitive Grammar concept of implicit subjectivity have some areas of overlap (especially concerning deixis), but also some areas in which they lead to contradiction. In contrast, there is no conflict between the "performativity" and the "interpersonal accessibility" concepts as defined here.

Speaker-orientation in terms of performativity and interpersonal accessibility can be realized as follows:
(i)  Lexically, especially with lexical items which are inherently subjective (only interpersonal accessibility; no performative reading possible)
(ii) Grammatically,

**Table 3:** Features of speaker-orientation

| | feature | concept | example |
|---|---|---|---|
| i. | Inherently subjective lexical meanings | interpersonal accessibility | Inherently subjective lexical items (e.g. *idiot, gorgeous*) |
| ii. | Constraints on the use of a form in terms of morphosyntactic combinability | performativity | In a language with tense inflection, a modal marker lacks the possibility for past inflection, and thus lacks this specific possibility of descriptive (less subjective) use (e.g. Nitta 1989; Moriyama 2000) |
| iii. | Actual use of a form in a specific syntactic construction | performativity | A deontic modal marker used in the present with a second-person subject is usually performative, and thus more subjective (Coates 1983) |
| | | interpersonal accessibility | Mental state verbs with first-person subject usually indicate that the judgment is personally associated with the speaker, and neither invokes shared knowledge nor a shared judgment (Nuyts 2001a: 122–128) |
| iv. | Discourse- and extra-linguistic context | performativity | Modification of modal markers that indicates distancing, and thus lower performativity (e.g. past tense, negation), may in fact have only a mitigating function. In context, the utterance is actually performative; e.g. *I thought* ... instead of *I think* ... in expressing a counter-argument. The actual subjectivity of a modal judgment in terms of expressing the speaker's stance may merely be veiled by using objectivizing linguistic forms such as the passive (Traugott and Dasher 2002: 126). |
| | | interpersonal accessibility | A deontic judgment can be based on a general rule (more objective) or on the speaker's personal values (more subjective). |

(a) in morphological properties of the linguistic form, as suggested by Kinda'ichi (1953a, 1953b) or Langacker (1990, 1991, 2002) – but not as *the* decisive criterion
(b) in constraints on its use in specific constructions, as reflected in the tests by Lyons (1977), Hengeveld (1987), Verstraete (2001), De Smet and Verstraete (2006), and various Japanese authors (only performativity)
(iii) In actual use in a specific construction, and its linguistic context, as suggested in the criteria by Coates (1983) and Traugott and Dasher (2002) (both performativity and interpersonal accessibility)

(iv) In the broader context including extra-linguistic factors, as suggested by Lyons (1977), Traugott and Dasher (2002), and Portner (2009) (both performativity and interpersonal accessibility)

Features (i) and (ii) are part of linguistic forms, and therefore semanticized (i) and grammaticalized (ii). Features (iii) and (iv) are essentially bound to context, and therefore inherently linked to pragmatics. In short, the idea is that while in both the performativity and in the interpersonal accessibility sense, speaker-orientation is available in the linguistic and extra-linguistic context (iii and iv), only the notion of interpersonal accessibility is relevant for the speaker-oriented features of lexical meanings (i), and only the notion of performativity is relevant for the morphosyntactic features of grammatical items reflecting speaker-orientation (ii). As stated above, "not relevant" does not necessarily mean "absent". Table 3 provides examples of the two types of speaker-orientation in each of the four cases. The criteria and the examples in Table 3 demonstrate that speaker-orientation as conceptualized here is a complex and multi-faceted notion. It is grounded in pragmatics, in the linguistic or extra-linguistic context, but can also be reflected in form.

# 3 Intersubjectivity – Three concepts of intersubjectivity and a synthesis

As in the case of subjectivity, it is possible to identify three concepts of intersubjectivity in language that have substantial influence on the current discussion in the field, namely (i) intersubjectivity as the expression of attention toward the addressee, (ii) intersubjectivity as shared information/evidentiality, and (iii) intersubjectivity as the basic setting of the speech situation. I will introduce these three concepts in Sections 3.1 to 3.3, before comparing them in Section 3.4.

## 3.1 Intersubjectivity as the expression of attention toward the addressee

A major approach to intersubjectivity has been proposed by Traugott, who understands intersubjectivity as "the explicit expression of the SP[eaker]/W[riter]'s attention to the 'self' of addressee/reader in both an epistemic sense (paying attention to their presumed attitudes to the content of what is said), and in a

more social sense (paying attention to their 'face' or 'image needs' associated with social stance and identity)" (Traugott 2003: 128). Intersubjectivity thus "involves SP/W's attention to AD[ressee]/R[eader] as a participant in the speech event, not in the described situation" (Traugott 2003: 128). According to Traugott and Dasher (2002: 23), characteristics of intersubjectivity include the following.
(i) overt social deixis
(ii) explicit markers of SP/W attention to AD/R, e.g. hedges
(iii) predomination of Horn's R-heuristic, i.e. implying more than what is explicitly stated

This idea of intersubjectivity markedly differs from Nuyts's in that it is not the opposite of subjectivity, but complements subjectivity as opposed to objectivity. On the other hand, it is a rather restricted counterpart of subjectivity. In the quotation above, Traugott specifies "attention to presumed attitudes [of addressees/readers]" and their "face or image needs". This narrowing down is even clearer in Traugott (2010: 32), where she states that "expressions of subjectivity and intersubjectivity are expressions the prime semantic or pragmatic meaning of which is to index speaker attitude or viewpoint (subjectivity) and speaker's attention to addressee self-image (intersubjectivity)". That is, while subjectivity is not confined to the attitudes and image needs of the speaker, intersubjectivity is, making it a restricted counterpart to subjectivity. What clearly falls under this definition are (i) social deixis and (ii) hedges, but it is unclear whether other hearer-oriented linguistic expressions, such as questions or commands – to the extent that they are not explicitly polite and thus address the hearer's image needs – or textual devices to guide the attention of the reader – which are clearly hearer-/reader-oriented in a broad sense – are also intersubjective as defined by Traugott. In my view, this is a somewhat problematic aspect of Traugott's concept of intersubjectivity, which also has consequences for the diachronic dimension of intersubjectification.

## 3.2 Intersubjectivity in terms of shared information

Intersubjectivity in terms of shared information holds when the speaker "indicate[s] that the evidence is known to (or accessible by) a larger group of people who share the conclusion based on it", thus leading to "shared responsibility" (Nuyts 2001a: 34). This concept has mainly been applied to epistemic modality, and for the reasons cited above, we would prefer to speak of intersubjectivity in terms of interpersonal accessibility instead of evidentiality. Accordingly, as already mentioned above, Portner (2009: 165) within his formal semantics framework, asserts that intersubjectivity in epistemic modality holds if a modal base is shared by more than one individual.

## 3.3 Intersubjectivity as the basic setting of the speech situation

Langacker did not posit an intersubjective counterpart to his construal concept of subjectivity. However, Verhagen (2005, 2007) has modified Langacker's concept of construal such that intersubjectivity practically replaces subjectivity as the central notion. While Langacker identifies the "ground" in a construal primarily with the speaker (although the hearer is also part of his ground), Verhagen identifies it fundamentally with the presence of two conceptualizers, the speaker and the hearer. The ground as speaker plus hearer then provides the intersubjective basis of a construal. Intersubjectivity, conceptualized in this way, is not opposed to subjectivity but subsumes (or, embeds) it, and is opposed to objectivity. This view of intersubjectivity potentially harmonizes well with recent research on language and social cognition and other research on common ground in language.

## 3.4 Comparison and synthesis

The most striking contrast between these three concepts of intersubjectivity, besides those issues already mentioned in the discussion of subjectivity, consists in how intersubjectivity relates to associated concepts (subjectivity and objectivity). Nuyts (2001a, 2001b) contrasts subjectivity with intersubjectivity, and Portner (2009) with both intersubjectivity and objectivity. Traugott (2003, 2010) contrasts subjectivity and intersubjectivity on the one hand with objectivity on the other hand, and Verhagen (2005, 2007) contrasts intersubjectivity (as including subjectivity) with objectivity. This can be represented as in Table 4.

Table 4: Three different views on the contrast between subjectivity, intersubjectivity and objectivity

| Proponents | Concept(s) 1 | vs. | Concept(s) 2 |
|---|---|---|---|
| Verhagen (2005, 2007) | intersubjectivity (incl. subjectivity) | ↔ | objectivity |
| Traugott (2003, 2010) | subjectivity and intersubjectivity | ↔ | objectivity |
| Nuyts (2001a, 2001b) | subjectivity | ↔ | intersubjectivity |
| Portner (2009) | subjectivity | ↔ | intersubjectivity/objectivity |

It is clear that Traugott's and Nuyts's notions of intersubjectivity are almost each other's antitheses. Traugott's intersubjectivity is derivative of subjectivity, while Nuyts's intersubjectivity is its opposite. Verhagen's intersubjectivity, encompassing subjectivity in the construal sense, is closer to Traugott's than to Nuyts's notion to the extent that it is opposed to objectivity. However, the theoretical premises of Langacker's construal approach are quite different from the other two concepts, and thus it cannot be assumed that Verhagen's notion of intersubjectivity encompasses speaker-orientation in the sense proposed here (i.e. performativity plus interpersonal accessibility). Even more than in the case of subjectivity, a synthesis of the different concepts of intersubjectivity is difficult. Again, one has to choose a basis. In terms of match with the speaker-orientation concept as a synthesis of the subjectivity concepts proposed above, a concept such as Traugott's in which intersubjectivity complements subjectivity, and is opposed to objectivity, provides the best basis. First, like the synthesis of subjectivity proposed in Section 2.5, intersubjectivity then has a pragmatic and not a conceptualist basis (unlike the concept proposed by Verhagen 2005). Second, the hearer-oriented intersubjectivity concept is useful in complementing the subjectivity concept, not only synchronically but also diachronically (unlike the concept of Nuyts 2001a, Nuyts 2001b).

However, unlike Traugott (2010: 32), I do not want to confine intersubjectivity to "attention to the addressee's self-image". In my view, a concept of intersubjectivity that truly complements subjectivity should refer more generally to the speaker's attention toward the addressee. As elsewhere (e.g. Narrog 2012a, Narrog 2012b), I will label this broader concept as *hearer-orientation*, complementing the notion of speaker-orientation. Based on the definition of performativity in (3), I argue that when a linguistic form qualifies a proposition with respect to the hearer in the current speech situation, it is used performatively in a hearer-oriented fashion. While the connection between performativity and hearer-orientation is straightforward, it is difficult to find a counterpart of interpersonal accessibility in hearer-orientation. In my view, if, according to the definition of interpersonal accessibility in (4), a "linguistic form expresses a qualification which is based on information or evaluations that are accessible to or linked to a community of speakers", the appropriate label is "objective". Hearer-orientation on the level of propositional meaning should instead refer to meanings which appeal to the hearer or which serve to establish common ground between speaker and hearer. Examples of hearer-orientation in this sense may include expressions such as *you see, as you will*, etc. (see Brinton 2008), or the secondary determiners in the English noun phrase, as analyzed by Ghesquière (2010, 2011). Even more so than the study of performative hearer-oriented meaning, this is an area which is just emerging in linguistic research, and that I have not yet investigated myself. I am therefore unable to provide more detailed thoughts here.

# 4 Increase in speaker-orientation/subjectification

Although I view speaker-orientation as essentially anchored in context, in some of the pragmatically oriented concepts of subjectivity it is assumed that there are cases in which it eventually becomes associated with linguistic forms. This process of increasing association of a form or construction with subjectivity has been called *subjectification*. It is an evident, yet sometimes forgotten fact, that any notion of subjectification presupposes a specific notion of subjectivity. Among the three major concepts of subjectivity discussed in Section 3, it is primarily the pragmatic one based on speaker involvement/performativity and the conceptualist one which have been associated with a diachronic, processual dimension. Traugott (2003: 125) defines subjectification as follows.

> Subjectification is the mechanism whereby meanings come over time to encode or externalize the SP/W's perspectives and attitudes as constrained by the communicative world of the speech event, rather than so-called 'real-world' characteristics of the event or situation referred to.

Langacker defined subjectification as "the realignment of some relationship from the objective to the subjective axis" (Langacker 1990: 17), and later as "a gradual process of progressive attenuation", in which "an objective relationship fades away, leaving behind a subjective relationship that was originally immanent in it" (Langacker 1998: 75–76). A comparison of these concepts is not necessary here, as this has already been done repeatedly (including by myself in Narrog 2010). Instead, I will briefly outline what subjectification would mean along the lines of the synthesis of subjectivity concepts proposed in Section 3. In keeping with the concept of speaker-orientation developed there, increase in speaker-orientation can take place along the following parameters:

(i) increase in subjective content or meaning associations of a lexical item
(ii) increasing constraints on the use of a form in terms of morphosyntactic combinability
(iii) increasing use in constructions associated with subjectivity
(iv) increasing use in contexts associated with subjectivity

Of primary interest here is an increase in speaker-orientation in grammar (ii to iv). Loss of tense/aspect marking on a grammaticalizing verb is a potential example of parameter (ii). Increasing use with second person subjects in the case of deontic markers would be a potential example of parameter (iii). Parameter (iv) would be reflected in changing frequencies of use in different environments, for example, increasing use in contexts associated with speaker-hearer interaction. Thus, (ii) may be conceptualized in terms of distinct steps that can be identified formally, but (iii) and (iv) are factors primarily associated with changes in frequency. In this manner, subjectification, as it is defined here, is a gradual process.

An often cited case of subjectification, or "speaker-orientation" as defined here, is the functional extension of the English modals to express epistemic meanings in constructions with animate subjects. Consider the following two examples.

(6) *She should go and see the doctor.*

(7) *She should be in Tokyo by now.*

Sentence (6) expresses a deontic or teleological necessity based on physical or social conditions, while (7) expresses a weak epistemic necessity in the speaker's world of reasoning. In the sense of the four criteria named above, the rise of epistemic uses in a modal like *should* corresponds to an increasing use in constructions and contexts associated with subjectivity, even if the immediate formal properties of *should* did not change.

# 5 Increase in hearer-orientation/ intersubjectification

What holds for increase in speaker-orientation also holds for increase in hearer-orientation: (i) the diachronic concept presupposes the existence of a synchronic concept; (ii) hearer-orientation or intersubjectivity, like speaker-orientation or subjectivity, is fundamentally a property of context, but there are cases in which it may become associated with linguistic forms and constructions. It is then possible to speak of an increase in hearer-orientation (or intersubjectification).

Among the three major concepts of intersubjectivity, only one has been explicitly associated with a dynamic dimension of intersubjectification by their proponents, namely Traugott's. Intersubjectification in Nuyts's sense does not show a straightforward direction of language change, as it would conversely entail a decrease in subjectivity. However, I am not aware of any research hypothesizing decrease in subjectivity as a significant directionality of language change. Also, I am not aware of work on intersubjectification within Verhagen's concept.

Verhagen's intersubjectivity involves a constant presupposition of communication, and as such essentially not subject to increase or decrease.

Intersubjectification in the sense of Traugott is designed to complement subjectification rather than being its opposite. Traugott (2003: 129–130) defined it as a "semasiological process whereby meanings come over time to encode or externalise implicatures regarding SP/W's attention to the 'self' of AD/R in both an epistemic and a social sense". This is the concept most suitable to complement the concepts of hearer-orientation in a synchronic sense, as espoused in Section 3.4.

However, as with speaker-orientation/subjectivity (Section 3.4), I wish to understand hearer-orientation as orientation toward the addressee in general, and not as being limited to attention to the addressee's self or image needs. For increase in hearer-orientation (or intersubjectification), then, essentially the same parameters as for increase in speaker-orientation/subjectification hold. It can be reflected either in a change of morphosyntactic properties, or in a change in contexts of use.

A case of intersubjectification in the domain of modality is the development of politeness uses of the modals in specific constructions, as in (8):

(8)  *Could you please stop making that noise?*

An utterance such as (8) presupposes the presence of a hearer and reflects the speaker's consideration of the hearer's face needs. To the extent that this construction emerged at some point in history and then spread to different uses, this is also an example of increasing use in constructions and contexts associated with hearer-orientation.[3]

# 6 Subjectification, intersubjectification and discourse-orientation

Subjectification, as increased orientation toward the speaker, and intersubjectification, as increased orientation toward the hearer, may not be the only tendencies of meaning change in the area of grammar. Consider the following example.

---

[3] According to Visser (1969: 1745), the first examples of this use of *could* date back to the 14th century, as extensions of earlier uses of *could*. I am not aware, though, of research documenting its spread.

(9) *I looked at some of my portraits and grotesque as they may be, they capture some aspects of reality.* (Coates 1983: 135)

*May* as in (9) is known as the concessive use of *may*. This is a usage that can be understood as primarily hearer-oriented/intersubjective. The speaker takes into account an imaginary objection or criticism by the hearer, and presents his or her own counter-argument to it.

However, beyond this strong hearer-oriented/intersubjective component, this use also has a discourse-building component. It marks a concessive proposition, and thus creates textual coherence within a series of propositions associated with different discourse participants. This textual or discourse function may be rather marginal with modal verbs, but it is an important function of discourse markers or modal particles (for instance, in German).

This function can be labeled *discourse-orientation* analogous to subjectivity as speaker-orientation and intersubjectivity as hearer-orientation. Like the latter two concepts, it also has a diachronic dimension, i.e. when linguistic forms develop more discourse-oriented meanings. In the case of *may*, a historical chain of changes as represented in Figure 1 can be assumed (see Narrog 2012b for details).

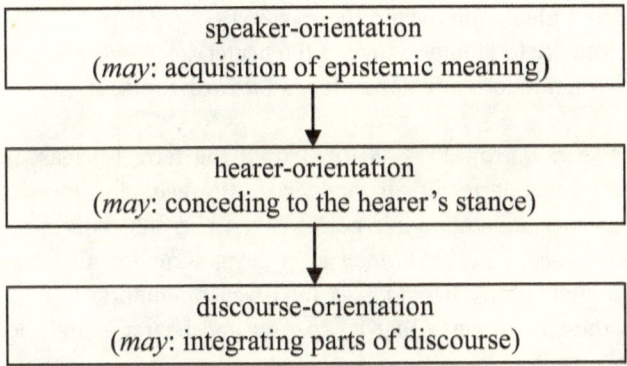

**Figure 1:** A sequence of type changes

An independent tendency toward text/discourse was part of Traugott's (1982, 1989) hypotheses about meaning change, but it has been backgrounded in her more recent work.[4] From the 1990s on, Traugott included the development of

---

4 In Traugott (1980, 1982), the author hypothesized a chain of meaning changes from propositional to textual, and expressive. In Traugott (1989), she hypothesized three tendencies of change, one of which was the tendency of shift toward "textual and metalinguistic" meanings.

textual meanings in subjectification.[5] However, considering a textual or discourse-orientation to be part of the concept of subjectification means that it becomes more stretched and vague. Along with Breban (2006) and Ghesquière (2010), in their research on adjectives, I suggest that this tendency needs to be reconsidered (see also Narrog 2012b). Ghesquière (2010: 286, 309), investigating historical changes in English adjectives, argues that (i) the earlier 1982 pathway "is semantically more fine-grained ... and seems to capture better the semantic development of the adjectives of completeness"; and that (ii) textual meanings can be both subjective and intersubjective. With respect to the development of subordinating functions of mood and modal markers, Narrog (2012b) suggests that referring to this extension in function and meaning simply as subjectification misses the most salient part of this change. Visconti (2013), who is concerned with limiting the concept of subjectification to a clearly definable area, argues that it is advantageous to identify subjectification with change from propositional to non-propositional meaning. This almost inevitably leads to the exclusion of textual meanings, which are, in her opinion, typically extensions from non-propositional to other non-propositional meaning.

In conclusion, I suggest adding (or reviving) change toward textual/discourse functions, and thus positing a triple set of strong tendencies in meaning change, namely:
- increased subjectivity (orientation toward the speaker)
- increased intersubjectivity (orientation toward the hearer)
- increased discourse-orientation (orientation toward text/discourse itself)

In earlier publications (e.g. Narrog 2005, 2010), I used the term (increased) speaker-orientation as a cover term for all tendencies. However, in order to avoid ambiguity with speaker-orientation in a narrower sense as subjectification only, I suggest the term *speech act-orientation* as a cover term for all three tendencies. Speech act-orientation encompasses increased orientation toward all the participants in the speech act – that is, speaker and hearer – and the speech act, or discourse, itself.

## 7 Speech-act orientation and grammaticalization

By grammaticalization, I understand "the development from lexical to grammatical forms, and from grammatical to even more grammatical forms" (Heine

---

[5] Traugott (1995: 47) states that subjectification is "the tendency to recruit lexical material for purposes of creating text and indicating attitudes in discourse situations."

and Narrog 2010: 401). Grammaticalization proceeds along the following four parameters:
- Extension, i.e. the rise of new grammatical meanings when linguistic expressions are extended to new contexts (context-induced reinterpretation)
- Desemanticization (or "semantic bleaching"), i.e. loss (or generalization) in meaning content
- Decategorialization, i.e. loss in morphosyntactic properties characteristic of lexical or other less grammaticalized forms
- Erosion ("phonetic reduction"), i.e. loss in phonetic substance

Irrespective of how grammaticalization is understood, the default assumption is that (inter)subjectification/speech-act orientation and grammaticalization are independent from each other. Traugott (2010: 38) writes that "neither subjectification nor intersubjectification entails grammaticalization". Conversely, not every case of grammaticalization involves (inter)subjectification. Again, to quote Traugott (2010: 40), "not all grammaticalization is equally likely to involve equal degrees of subjectification, and some may involve no subjectification". In fact, I am not aware of a serious claim of a cause–effect relationship between the two, or even of a claim of a strong correlation, although there is likely to be one.

In associating (inter)subjectification with certain stages of grammaticalization, Traugott suggested, as early as in Traugott (1995: 47), that subjectification may be particularly involved in the initial stages of the process. In Traugott (2010: 40), she writes more concretely that: "subjectification is more likely to occur in primary grammaticalization (the shift from lexical/constructional to grammatical) than in secondary grammaticalization (the development of already grammatical material into more grammatical material)". Intersubjectification, in contrast, "intersects less extensively with grammaticalization. In most languages it is grammaticalized only into some discourse markers and interjections. It is strongly grammaticalized… in only a few languages, e. g., Japanese" (Traugott 2010: 41).

Furthermore, Traugott has claimed that subjectification (speaker-orientation) necessarily precedes intersubjectification (hearer-orientation).[6] While initially it was unclear whether this was an empirically testable hypothesis or a matter of definition, more recently it has become clear that Traugott posits this sequence

---

6 She writes: "There cannot be intersubjectification without some degree of subjectification because it is SP/W who designs the utterance and who recruits the meaning for social purposes" (Traugott 2003: 134; cf. also 2003: 129).

of changes quasi by definition.[7] However, if hearer-orientation (intersubjectivity) in its diachronic dimension is conceived of sufficiently broadly, and not as based by definition on speaker-orientation (subjectivity), I believe that the question of the sequence of changes is still an issue open to empirical inquiry. Nevertheless, from the examples in the literature it is clear that hearer-orientation is commonly associated with a later stage in grammaticalization. The same, I would argue, holds for discourse-orientation. I will list here some well-known examples of developments in support of this hypothesis (for more details, see Narrog 2012b).

- As discussed in Section 6, for English *may* it can be assumed that the textual function came last in the modal verb's development.
- In some languages, such as English, Russian, etc., imperatives, the most clearly intersubjective mood constructions in languages (see Fortuin and Boogaart 2009), have assumed a text-building conditional function (e.g. *Make a move and I'll shoot*). These appear to be very late, if not final developments in the lives of such constructions.
- Similarly, imperative constructions in some languages have developed conditional concessive functions, for example in Lithuanian and Japanese (e.g. Ambrazas 1997; Narrog 2012b).[8]
- Subordinating markers indicating logical relations between propositions, discourse markers and final particles are often end points of chains of grammaticalization; see, e.g., Bybee et al. (1994: 240–241) for subordinating functions as end points in the grammaticalization of modal markers; Heine and Kuteva (2007: 111) for subordinating functions as end points in the grammaticalization of a variety of categories; and Abraham (1991) for German modal particles with discourse functions as the end points in grammaticalization.

The interrelationship between speech-act orientation with grammaticalization is an area that has yet to be fully explored, but I tentatively conclude the following:

- As hypothesized by Traugott (2010), speaker-orientation (subjectification) is likely to be identifiable with early stages of grammaticalization from a lexical domain with concrete meanings to a grammatical domain with abstract meanings.

---

[7] "In my view, ... intersubjectification [is] the mechanism by which meanings ... once subjectified may be recruited to encode meanings centered on the addressee (intersubjectification)" (Traugott 2010: 35).

[8] In English, this is apparently less grammaticalized, but see the following example by Haspelmath and König (1998: 583): *Go to Kilkenny, to Dublin or even to London – I won't leave you.*

- Hearer-orientation (that is, intersubjectification in the sense of addressee-orientation and not of shared information) and discourse-orientation are more likely to be identified with later stages of grammaticalization (acquisition of additional, more advanced, grammatical functions).

Furthermore, from my own examples it appears that discourse-orientation is always the very last stage, following speaker- and hearer-orientation (contra Traugott 1980, 1982, 1989). Unlike the early Traugott as well as the more recent Traugott (2003, 2010), however, I do not believe that a fixed order of changes can be established at this stage of research. At least, I doubt that this is possible with a concept of hearer-orientation/intersubjectification that does not already entail a specific order of change (i.e. intersubjectification/hearer-orientation after subjectification/speaker-orientation) *by definition*. Instead, I assume that the above-mentioned tendencies are only tendencies and not absolutes. In fact, other scholars have come up with empirical evidence from areas other than modality that would suggest divergent directionalities. Ghesquière (2010), for example, concludes that in the case of certain adjectives in the English noun phrase (*complete, total, whole*), the development of textual functions is followed by further grammaticalization.[9] It is entirely conceivable that different sequences of semantic change can be found in different domains of grammar. As the papers presented in the conference from which this volume emerged have shown, there is plenty of room for future research in this area.

# 8 Summary

In this paper, I have taken a very broad perspective on the topics of (inter)subjectivity and (inter)subjectification. I have argued that there are three major conceptions both of subjectivity and of intersubjectivity, which despite some superficial similarities in terminology are quite distinct and lead to quite different analyses. With respect to subjectivity, I have suggested that the two pragmatically oriented concepts, i.e. performativity and interpersonal accessibility, which are both in principle further developments of Lyons's subjectivity concept, have

---

**9** Furthermore, Cornillie (2008) posits a sequence of change from intersubjective to subjective meanings with Spanish evidential semi-auxiliaries. However, Traugott (e.g. 2010) has repeatedly identified Cornillie's notion of (inter)subjectivity, which she identifies with Nuyts's, as different from her own, which brings us back to the question of different concepts and definitions leading to different descriptions.

more in common with each other than with the conceptualist notion in Cognitive Grammar. I have suggested a synthesis between them in terms of "speaker-orientation", and I have set up concrete parameters according to which linguistics expressions may vary. I further applied my conclusions about the synchronic concepts of speaker- and hearer-orientation to the diachronic dimension, again favoring a pragmatic concept that allows integration of the two pragmatically oriented concepts. In addition, I suggested that speaker-orientation and hearer-orientation should be complemented by discourse-orientation, thus forming a triad of tendencies of change, which taken together may be covered by the label "speech act-orientation". Lastly, I pointed out that speaker-orientation, hearer-orientation and discourse-orientation do not strictly correlate with grammaticalization. Although it is likely that speaker-orientation is associated with earlier stages of grammaticalization, and hearer-orientation and discourse-orientation with later stages, it seems that some variation is possible, and further research will be necessary to determine actual sequences of change in various areas of grammar.

## Acknowledgments

I wish to thank two anonymous reviewers who helped me enormously in improving this paper. All remaining mistakes are my own. I further wish to thank the organizers of the GRAMIS 2010 conference for their kind invitation, and the editors of this volume for their great support.

## References

Abraham, Werner. 1991. The grammaticization of the German modal particles. In Elizabeth Closs Traugott & Bernd Heine (eds.), *Approaches to grammaticalization*, Vol. 2, 331–380. Amsterdam & Philadelphia: John Benjamins.
Abraham, Werner. 2005. An intersubjective note on the notion of 'subjectification'. In Hans Broekhuis, Norbert Corver, Riny Huybregts, Ursula Kleinhenz & Jan Koster (eds.), *Organizing grammar: Linguistic sudies in honor of Henk van Riemsdijk*, 1–12. Berlin & New York: Mouton de Gruyter.
Ambrazas, Vytautas. 1997. *Lithuanian Grammar*. Vilnius: Baltos Lankos.
Athanasiadou, Angeliki, Costas Canakis & Bert Cornillie (eds.). 2006. *Subjectification: Various paths to subjectivity*. Berlin & New York: Mouton de Gruyter.
Bally, Charles. [1932] 1965. *Linguistique générale et linguistique française*, 4th edn. Bern: Francke.
Benveniste, Emile. [1958] 1971. *Problems in general linguistics*. Coral Gables: University of Miami Press; (English translation of the paper collection *Problèmes de linguistique*

générale. 1966. Paris: Gallimard; originally published in 1958 in the *Journal de psychologie* 55.)

Breban, Tine. 2006. Grammaticalization and subjectification of the English adjectives of general comparison In Angeliki Athanasiadou, Costas Canakis & Bert Cornillie (eds.), *Subjectification: Various paths to subjectivity*, 241–277. Berlin & New York: Mouton de Gruyter.

Brinton, Laurel J. 2008. *The comment clause in English: Syntactic origins and pragmatic developments*. Cambridge: Cambridge University Press.

Bybee, Joan, Revere Perkins & William Pagliuca. 1994. *The evolution of grammar: Tense, aspect, and modality in the languages of the world*. Chicago: The University of Chicago Press.

Calbert, Joseph P. 1975. Towards the semantics of modality. In Joseph P. Calbert & Heinz Vater (eds.), *Aspekte der Modalität*, 1–70. Tübingen: Gunter Narr.

Coates, Jennifer. 1983. *The semantics of the modal auxiliaries*. London: Croom Helm.

Cornillie, Bert. 2005. On modal grounding, reference points, and subjectification: The case of the Spanish epistemic modals. *Annual Review of Cognitive Linguistics* 3. 56–77.

Cornillie, Bert. 2006. Conceptual and constructional considerations on the subjectivity of English and Spanish modals. In Angeliki Athanasiadou, Costas Canakis & Bert Cornillie (eds.), *Subjectification:. Various paths to subjectivity*, 177–205. Berlin & New York: Mouton de Gruyter.

Cornillie, Bert. 2008. On the grammaticalization and (inter)subjectivity of evidential (semi-) auxiliaries in Spanish. In Elena Seoane & María José López-Couso (eds.), *Theoretical and empirical issues in grammaticalization*, 55–76. Amsterdam & Philadelphia: John Benjamins.

Cornillie, Bert & Nicole Delbecque (eds.). 2006. *Topics in subjectification and modalization*. Belgian Journal of Linguistics 20.

Davidse, Kristin, Lieven Vandelotte & Hubert Cuyckens (eds.). 2010. *Subjectification, intersubjectification and grammaticalization*. Berlin & New York: De Gruyter Mouton.

Declerck, Renaat. 2009. 'Nonfactual at t': A neglected modal concept. In Raphael Salkie, Pierre Busuttil & Johan van der Auwera (eds.), *Modality in English: Theory and description*, 31–54. Berlin & New York: Mouton de Gruyter.

De Smet, Hendrik & Jean-Christophe Verstraete. 2006. Coming to terms with subjectivity. *Cognitive Linguistics* 17(3). 365–392.

Donaldson, Bruce. 2008. *Dutch: A comprehensive grammar*, 2nd edn. London: Routledge.

Finegan, Edward. 1995. Subjectivity and subjectivisation: An introduction. In Dieter Stein & Susan Wright (eds.), *Subjectivity and Subjectivisation*, 1–15. Cambridge: Cambridge University Press.

Fortuin, Egbert & Ronny Boogaart. 2009. Imperative as conditional: From constructional to compositional semantics. *Cognitive Linguistics* 20(4). 641–673.

Ghesquière, Lobke. 2010. On the subjectification and intersubjectification paths followed by adjectives of completeness. In Kristin Davidse, Lieven Vandelanotte & Hubert Cuyckens (eds.), *Subjectification, intersubjectification and grammaticalization*, 277–314. Berlin & New York: De Gruyter Mouton.

Ghesquière, Lobke. 2011. The directionality of (inter)subjectification in the English noun phrase: Pathways of change. Leuven: University of Leuven dissertation.

Haspelmath, Martin & Ekkehard König. 1998. Concessive conditionals in the languages of Europe. In Johan van der Auwera and D. P. Ó Baoill (eds.), *Adverbial constructions in the languages of Europe*, 563–640. Berlin & New York: Mouton de Gruyter.

Heine, Bernd & Tania Kuteva. 2007. *The genesis of grammar*. Oxford: Oxford University Press.

Heine, Bernd & Heiko Narrog. 2010. Grammaticalization and linguistic analysis. In Bernd Heine & Heiko Narrog (eds.), *The Oxford handbook of linguistic analysis*, 401–423. Oxford: Oxford University Press.

Hengeveld, Kees. 1987. Clause structure and modality in Functional Grammar. In Johan van der Auwera & Louis Goossens (eds.), *Ins and outs of the predication*, 53–66. Dordrecht: Foris Publications.

Kiefer, Ferenc. 1997. Presidential address – Modality and pragmatics. *Folia Linguistica* 31(3–4). 241–253.

Kinda'ichi, Haruhiko. 1953a. Fuhenka jodōshi no honshitsu 1. Shukanteki hyōgen to kyakkanteki hyōgen no betsu ni tsuite [The essence of uninflecting auxiliaries 1. About the distinction between subjective and objective expressions]. *Kokugo Kokubun* 22(2). 1–18.

Kinda'ichi, Haruhiko. 1953b. Fuhenka jodōshi no honshitsu 2. Shukanteki hyōgen to kyakkanteki hyōgen no betsu ni tsuite [The essence of uninflecting auxiliaries 2. About the distinction between subjective and objective expressions]. *Kokugo Kokubun* 22(3). 15–35.

Kratzer, Angelika. 1981. The notional category of modality. In Hans-Jürgen Eikmeyer & Hannes Rieser (eds.), *Words, worlds, and contexts: New approaches in word semantics*, 38–74. Berlin & New York: Mouton de Gruyter.

Langacker, Ronald W. 1985. Observations and speculations on subjectivity. In John Haiman (ed.), *Iconicity in syntax*, 109–150. Amsterdam & Philadelphia: John Benjamins.

Langacker, Ronald W. 1990. Subjectification. *Cognitive Linguistics* 1(1). 5–38.

Langacker, Ronald W. 1991. *Foundations of cognitive grammar*. Vol. 2: *Descriptive application*. Stanford: Stanford University Press.

Langacker, Ronald W. 1998. On subjectification and grammaticalization. In Jean-Pierre Koenig (ed.), *Discourse and cognition: Bridging the gap*, 71–89. Stanford: CSLI.

Langacker, Ronald W. 2002. Deixis and subjectivity. In Frank Brisard (ed.), *Grounding: The epistemic footing of deixis and reference*, 1–28. Berlin: Mouton de Gruyter.

Larreya, Paul & Claude Rivière. 1999. *Grammaire explicative de l'anglais, Nouvelle edition*. London: Longman.

Lyons, John. 1968. *Introduction to theoretical linguistics*. Cambridge: Cambridge University Press.

Lyons, John. 1977. *Semantics*, Vol. 2. Cambridge: Cambridge University Press.

Lyons, John. 1982. Deixis and subjectivity: Loquor, ergo sum? In Robert J. Jarvella & Wolfgang Klein (eds.), *Speech, place, and action: Studies in deixis and related topics*, 101–124. New York: Wiley.

Lyons, John. 1995. *Linguistic Semantics – An Introduction*. Cambridge: Cambridge University Press.

Moriyama, Takurō. 2000. Kihon johō to sentaku kankei to shite no modariti [Modality as the relationship of basic mood choice]. In Takurō Moriyama, Yoshio Nitta & Hiroshi Kudō (eds.), *Modariti* (Nihongo no Bunpō 3), 3–78. Tōkyō: Iwanami.

Mortelmans, Tanja. 2006. Langacker's 'subjectification' and 'grounding': A more gradual view. In Angeliki Athanasiadou, Costas Canakis & Bert Cornillie (eds.), *Subjectification: Various paths to subjectivity*, 151–175. Berlin & New York: Mouton de Gruyter.

Narrog, Heiko. 2005. Modality, mood, and change of modal meanings – a new perspective. *Cognitive Linguistics* 16(4). 677–731.

Narrog, Heiko. 2010. (Inter)subjectification in the area of modality and mood – concepts and cross-linguistic realities. In Kristin Davidse, Lieven Vandelotte & Hubert Cuyckens (eds.), *Subjectification, intersubjectification and grammaticalization*, 385–429. Berlin & New York: De Gruyter Mouton.

Narrog, Heiko. 2012a. *Modality, Subjectivity and Semantic Change. A Cross-Linguistic Perspective*. Oxford: Oxford University Press.

Narrog, Heiko. 2012b. Beyond intersubjectification – textual uses of modality and mood in subordinate clauses as part of speech-act orientation. *English Text Construction* 5(1). 29–52.

Nitta, Yoshio. 1989. Gendai nihongo-bun no modariti no taikei to kōzō [System and structure of modality in modern Japanese sentences]. In Yoshio Nitta & Takashi Masuoka (eds.) *Nihongo no Modariti*, 1–56. Tōkyō: Kuroshio.

Nuyts, Jan. 2001a. *Epistemic modality, language, and conceptualization*. Amsterdam & Philadelphia: John Benjamins.

Nuyts, Jan. 2001b. Subjectivity as an evidential dimension in epistemic modal expressions. *Journal of Pragmatics* 33. 383–400.

Palmer, Frank R. 1998. Mood and modality: Basic principles. In Keith Brown & Jim Miller (eds.), *Concise encyclopedia of grammatical categories*, 229–235. Oxford: Elsevier.

Perkins, Michael R. 1983. *Modal expressions in English*. Norwood: Ablex Publishing.

Pelyvás, Péter. 2001a. On the development of the category modal: A cognitive view. In Piroska Kocsány & Anna Molnár (eds.), *Wort und (Kon)text*, 103–130. Frankfurt a. M.: Peter Lang.

Pelyvás, Péter 2001b. The development of the grounding predication: Epistemic modals and cognitive predicates. In Enikő Németh & Károly Bibok (eds.), *Pragmatics and the flexibility of word meaning*, 151–174. Amsterdam: Elsevier.

Pelyvás, Péter. 2006. Subjectification in (expressions of) epistemic modality and the development of the grounding predication. In Angeliki Athanasiadou, Costas Canakis & Bert Cornillie (eds.), *Subjectification: Various paths to subjectivity*, 121–150. Berlin & New York: Mouton de Gruyter.

Portner, Paul. 2009. *Modality*. Oxford: Oxford University Press.

Radden, Günter & René Dirven. 2007. *Cognitive English grammar*. Amsterdam & Philadelphia: John Benjamins.

Tokieda, Motoki. 1941. *Kokugogaku Genron. Gengo Kateisetsu no Seiritsu to sono Tenkai* [Principles of National Language Studies: The formation of language processing theory and its expansion]. Tōkyō: Iwanami Shoten.

Traugott, Elizabeth Closs. 1980. Meaning-change in the development of grammatical markers. *Language Sciences* 2(1). 44–61.

Traugott, Elizabeth Closs. 1982. From propositional to textual and expressive meanings: Some semantic-pragmatic aspects of grammaticalization. In Winfred P. Lehmann & Yakov Malkiel (eds.), *Perspectives on historical linguistics*, 245–271. Amsterdam & Philadelphia: John Benjamins.

Traugott, Elizabeth Closs. 1989. On the rise of epistemic meanings in English: An example of subjectification in semantic change. *Language* 65(1). 31–55.

Traugott, Elizabeth Closs. 1995. Subjectification in grammaticalisation. In Dieter Stein & Susan Wright (eds.), *Subjectivity and subjectivisation*, 31–54. Cambridge: Cambridge University Press.

Traugott, Elizabeth Closs. 2003. From subjectification to intersubjectification. In Raymond Hickey (ed.), *Motives for language change*, 124–139. Cambridge: Cambridge University Press.

Traugott, Elizabeth Closs. 2010. (Inter)subjectivity and (inter)subjectification: A reassessment. In Kristin Davidse, Lieven Vandelotte & Hubert Cuyckens (eds.), *Subjectification, intersubjectification and grammaticalization*, 29–71. Berlin & New York: De Gruyter Mouton.

Traugott, Elizabeth & Richard Dasher. 2002. *Regularity in semantic change*. Cambridge: Cambridge University Press.

Verhagen, Arie. 2005. *Constructions of intersubjectivity. Discourse, syntax and cognition*. Oxford: Oxford University Press.

Verhagen, Arie. 2007. Construal and perspectivization. In Dirk Geeraerts & Hubert Cuyckens (eds.), *The Oxford handbook of cognitive linguistics*, 48–81. Oxford: Oxford University Press.

Verstraete, Jean-Christophe. 2001. Subjective and objective modality: Interpersonal and ideational functions in the English modal auxiliary system. *Journal of Pragmatics* 33. 1505–1528.

Visconti, Jacqueline. 2013. Facets of subjectification. *Language Sciences* 36. 7–17.

Visser, Frederik Th. 1969. *An historical syntax of the English language. Part Three, First Half: Syntactical units with two verbs*. Leiden: Brill.

Karin Beijering
# 2 Grammaticalization and (inter)subjectification: The case of the Swedish modals *må* and *måtte*

**Abstract:** This paper reports on a synchronic corpus investigation of the Swedish modals *må* 'may, should' and *måtte* 'may, must'. These modals developed a wide variety of meanings within the modal spectrum, i.e. meanings in the realm of necessity and possibility. The development of modals is a prototypical instance of grammaticalization, also known as auxiliation. The rise of modal and postmodal meanings is a well-attested tendency in semantic change and is generally accompanied by (inter)subjectification. This paper outlines the etymology, semantic distributions and formal properties of *må* and *måtte* and focuses on the relation between grammaticalization and (inter)subjectification. It is shown that *må* and *måtte* are now highly grammaticalized and (inter)subjectified linguistic items.

## 1 Introduction

This paper is concerned with the Swedish modal auxiliaries *må* 'may, should' and *måtte* 'may, must'.[1] These can be seen either as two variants of the same modal, or as two distinct modals (Teleman et al. 1999). Historically, they derive from the same verb (< Old Swedish *magha* 'have the power/strength') – *må* being present tense and *måtte* being past tense – but nowadays they have significantly different semantic distributions (Section 4). In this study, they are treated as two distinct modals as they no longer express present and past tense of the same verb.

In Old Swedish (ca. 1225–1526), *må* and *måtte* were frequently occurring linguistic items that expressed a wide range of meanings in the domain of necessity and possibility (e.g. Björkstam 1919; Andersson 2007; *Svenska Akademiens ordbok* [SAOB]), but they have now largely been replaced by the modal *måste*

---

[1] There is also a lexical verb, *att må* 'to feel', which has the same origin as the modals *må* and *måtte* (see Section 2). Nowadays, *att må* is a full-fledged verb with a regular paradigm: *att må* 'to feel'– *mår* 'feel' – *mådde* 'felt' – *har mått* 'has felt'. Lexical *må* is excluded from this investigation as it has no modal or postmodal meanings.

'must'.[2] At present, *må* and *måtte* are highly grammaticalized forms which are largely restricted to specific constructions and contexts (e.g. Teleman et al. 1999; Wärnsby 2006; Sections 2 and 3). As a consequence, *må* and *måtte* have been largely neglected in synchronic studies of Swedish modals.

The development of the modals *må* and *måtte* is nonetheless interesting. They have reached the final stages of grammaticalization, and their current meanings are highly (inter)subjective, so that their development can be studied and compared in light of attested tendencies in semantic change and hypotheses on the relation between grammaticalization and (inter)subjectification.

The focus of this paper is on the interaction between grammaticalization and (inter)subjectification in the development of the modal and postmodal meanings of *må* and *måtte*, and I will investigate any differences in their development, semantic distributions and formal properties.

In assessing the degree of grammaticalization of *må* and *måtte*, both formal and semantic criteria will be looked at. Indicators of formal change in grammaticalization are the inflectional paradigm (full or defective), syntactic position (fixed or free) and the number of specific constructions and contexts in which a form may occur (few or many). That is to say, when an item has a deficient inflectional paradigm, and it frequently occurs in fixed syntactic positions and specific constructions and contexts, it shows signs of (advanced) grammaticalization. For *må* and *måtte*, the degree to which they have lost verbal characteristics will be essential in determining their degree of auxiliation. As to the semantics of grammaticalization, the proportion of premodal, modal and postmodal meanings for *må* as well as *måtte* will be examined. In line with van der Auwera and Plungian (1998: 80), modal meanings are considered to involve possibility and necessity as paradigmatic variants. This definition applies to the domains of dynamic, deontic and epistemic modality. Postmodal meanings, e.g. optative or concessive meanings, are meanings that originate in either possibility or necessity (van der Auwera and Plungian 1998: 79). Premodal meanings are lexical source concepts (e.g. main verbs) that have the potential to give rise to modal meanings. The development of modal and postmodal meanings is a well-known instance of semantic change that follows predictable developmental paths (Bybee et al. 1994; van der Auwera and Plungian 1998; Heine and Kuteva 2002; Traugott and Dasher 2002). Relations between premodal, modal and postmodal meanings are contiguous as premodal meanings give rise to modal meanings, which in turn may develop further into postmodal meanings.

---

[2] *Måste* is a loanword from Middle Low German (ca. 1100–1600), the lingua franca of the Hanseatic League. It derives from *moste*, which is the imperfect tense of *moten* 'to have permission/ to be obliged' (Wessén 1965: 243).

A well-attested tendency in the development of grammatical items is that their meanings become increasingly (inter)subjective over time (e.g. Traugott 1989, 1995, 2003). With respect to (inter)subjectification, the perspective adopted here builds on Traugott (e.g. 2010). Subjectification is seen as a process of semantic change through which expressions of speaker-reference or speaker-involvement arise. Intersubjectification is taken to be a process of semantic change which gives rise to expressions of speaker–writer and addressee–reader interaction. Subjectification and intersubjectification may affect linguistic items on different linguistic layers (ideational, textual and interpersonal level; see, e.g., Halliday and Hasan 1976; Traugott 1982, Traugott 1989, Traugott 1995) and may, but need not, accompany other processes of change, such as grammaticalization.

It is hypothesized that, in the course of auxiliation, *må* and *måtte* have lost the properties typical of main verbs and that their semantic development follows the well-known path from premodal to modal meaning (and eventually to postmodal meaning). *Må* and *måtte* have then become more subjective over time as they required modal and postmodal meanings. The synchronic status, both formal and semantic, as well as the historical development of these modals will be discussed. Then their development will be analyzed with respect to characteristics of grammaticalization and subjectification to examine how the empirical data match existing theoretical claims and observed tendencies within grammaticalization studies.

This paper is organized as follows. In Section 2, the etymology and development of *må* and *måtte* is sketched from Old Swedish up to now. The sources and methods to the synchronic corpus investigation of *må* and *måtte* are presented in Section 3. In Section 4, the results of the corpus investigation are discussed and illustrated with corpus examples. Grammaticalization and (inter)subjectification and their role in the development of *må* and *måtte* are elaborated on in Section 5. Finally, Section 6 contains an overall summary and concluding remarks.

## 2 Etymology and the rise of modal and postmodal meanings in *må* and *måtte*

In this section, I will first sketch the development of *må* and *måtte* from Old Swedish to the present-day, against the background of cross-linguistic tendencies in semantic change in the domains of possibility and necessity. I will then detail the semantic changes in Swedish *må* and *måtte* on the basis of *Svenska Akademiens ordbok* (SAOB) and Andersson's (2007) study of *må* in legal and religious texts from the Old Swedish period (ca. 1225–1526).

Swedish *må* and *måtte* can be traced back to the Proto-Germanic root *\*mag-*. This is also the case for their Germanic equivalents (English *may*, German *mögen*, Dutch *mogen*, Norwegian *måtte*, Danish *måtte*). These modals belong to a special class of linguistic items, i.e. the so-called preterite-present verbs (Birkmann 1987). Preterite-present verbs were originally strong verbs whose past tense was used as a present tense.

The ancestor of the modern modal "may" in the Germanic languages was a lexical verb with the meaning 'to be strong, to have the power/strength' (e.g. Old English *magan*). The first modal meaning of "may", 'be able to, can', can be situated in the domain of dynamic modality. From very early on, a wide variety of derived meanings were also available, among which 'to have the opportunity' and 'to have permission' (Phillipa et al. 2011). The domain of dynamic modality consists of ability and capacity meanings (= 'be able to/to have the opportunity'). From these dynamic meanings, it is only a small step to deontic possibility 'have permission to'. Over time, necessity meanings may have arisen out of permission meanings. Traugott & Dasher (2002: 124) suggest a plausible scenario in which contexts of denied or negative permission, i.e. 'you may not', gave rise to obligation meanings, i.e. 'you must'. On this view, broadly speaking, the change from negative permission to deontic obligation is driven by scalar strengthening. Since 'you may not' implies 'be obliged to not', the denied permission meaning is strengthened to deontic obligation. Ultimately, the stronger implication of 'you may not', i.e. 'you must', became the conventionalized meaning. This tendency was also noticed by van der Auwera (2001), who found that there seems to be a regular unidirectional shift among modals from 'not necessary that' > 'necessary that not'.

The dynamic modal meaning 'general possibility', which is comparable to 'have the opportunity', may have given rise to epistemic possibility. General possibility indicates in an objective way that something is possible, i.e. without the speaker's evaluation of this possibility, as is the case for epistemic possibility.

Deontic necessity (obligation meanings) is generally assumed to lead to epistemic necessity. A clause like *He must be in the office* is ambiguous, when taken out of context, between a deontic reading (i.e. 'He is obliged to be in the office (because his boss tells him so)') and an epistemic reading (i.e. 'It is necessarily so that he is in the office (I can see the lights are on)'). The transfer, or invited inference, of the obligation meaning is that when something is obligatory it has a high probability of occurring precisely because it is mandatory.

Deontic possibility (permission) may also give rise to optative meanings (wishes and desires). The idea is that "a wish is like an appeal to circumstances (destiny) to allow the realization of a state of affairs" (van der Auwera and Plungian 1998: 107). There is a variety of concessive constructions which are likely to have derived from epistemic meanings. Epistemic possibility may bring about concessive constructions of the type *She may jog, but she sure looks unhealthy to me* (example from Traugott and Dasher 2002: 115). In this construction of the general form "although p, q" (Crevels 2000: 1), the first clause (p) is concessive ('although she may jog, as you say...', paraphrased by Traugott and Dasher 2002: 115), and the speaker draws a conclusion (q) "that does not directly follow from the modalized proposition" (2002: 115) and contrasts with the speaker's own opinion. Another option is a development straight out of dynamic meanings (root possibility). Epistemic and/or root possibility may give rise to concessive constructions in which various latent possibilities are contrasted, for example "whatever X may be, Y", "whether or not X, Y" or "be it X or Y, Z".

Since this study is primarily synchronic in nature, I can only sketch plausible scenarios from the literature for the semantic development of the modal "may" in Germanic languages. It is clear though that from the earliest stages onward a wide variety of co-existing modal meanings were available, which continued to develop more polysemies in – and out of – the domains of necessity and possibility. Figure 2 shows a simplified overview of the contiguous relations between premodal, modal and postmodal meanings in the Germanic modal "may".[3] It is based on work by Bybee et al. (1994), van der Auwera and Plungian (1998), Heine and Kuteva (2002) and Traugott and Dasher (2002).

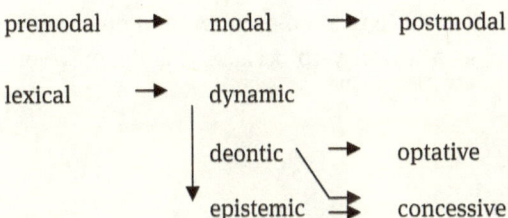

**Figure 1:** Cross-linguistic correlations for premodal, modal and postmodal meanings in the Germanic modal "may"

Let us now turn to the specific development of *må* and *måtte*. As was observed for their Germanic cognates, the semantics of Swedish *må* and *måtte* is a complex matter, whereby notions associated with possibility, necessity and the like are closely related or may be overlapping. Recall that *må* and *måtte* used to be present and past tense of the same modal auxiliary. They have a

---

[3] This view on semantic change is in line with *The Invited Inferencing Theory of Semantic Change*, as proposed by Traugott and Dasher (2002: 34–40). See Andersson (2007: 166–184) for an analysis in terms of *force dynamics* (e.g. Talmy 1988, Talmy 2000; Sweetser 1990).

long common history and I will therefore refer to them as "*må*" in the remainder of this paragraph.

In the earliest Old Swedish texts, lexical and dynamic meanings were most frequent, but they gradually decreased in frequency. *Må* lost its lexical meaning in the course of the Old Swedish period (ca. 1250–1526), while its dynamic meanings can be considered outdated by the Modern Swedish period (1526–1850). On the whole, the dominant meanings in Old Swedish were deontic: permission, freedom of choice and prohibition (= negated permission). In Early Modern Swedish (1526–1750), the ability, capacity and permission meanings of *må* were lost. The modal *kunna* 'can' took over several meanings that used to be associated with *må* (mainly the ability and capacity meanings); as a result, *må* decreased in frequency. Epistemic meanings, which were rare in Old Swedish, spread gradually throughout the Early Modern Swedish period. By this time, epistemic-concessive meanings had arisen and increased in frequency. *Må* came to be restricted to set phrases and specific epistemic, concessive and optative constructions. The following examples illustrate a selection of the many co-existing meanings for *må* up to the end of the Modern Swedish period.

In example (1), the meaning of *må* is close to the original meaning 'have the power/strength/be able to'. It is not easy to discriminate between the lexical meaning 'have strength/power'[4] and the dynamic meaning 'be able/capable' on the basis of semantic criteria, but the auxiliary status of *må* can be defined on syntactic grounds, i.e. whether or not it needs to co-occur with another verb.[5] In example (1), *må (måhr)* is used as a lexical verb because it is the only verb in the clause.

(1) *Hwadh* **måhr** man emot Gudh?
 what empowers one against God?
 'What empowers one against God?' (*Svenska Akademiens ordbok* [SAOB])

Example (2) is an instance of deontic possibility. It illustrates meekness on behalf of the speaker. Here, *må (måge)* expresses a mixture between freedom of choice for the composers (it is up to them to decide) and slight ignorance of the

---

[4] Note that the meaning of the modern lexical verb *att må* 'feel', which has the same origin as the modals *må* and *måtte*, is closely related to the original meaning 'be strong/have the power'. The modern use arose in contexts in which one was inquiring after the power/strength or well-being of someone, as in modern Swedish *Hur mår du?* 'How are you doing?' (Andersson 2007: 67).

[5] It is, however, not possible to trace back exactly when the modals started to behave like auxiliaries since auxiliary uses are found already among the earliest attestations (Diewald 1999; Andersson 2007: 164).

speaker (s/he does not wish to comment on the appropriateness of the verse for music).

(2) *Om ...    (versen)    deri    upfyller Anonymens önskan,*
    whether... (verse-the) therein fulfils   anonymous' wish

   *at vara lämpelig för Musik; derom    **måge** våre*
   to be   suitable for music; thereupon may   our

   *Compositeurer döma.*
   composors    decide.

   'Whether the verse fulfills the wish of Anonymous in that it is suitable for music, that is up to our composers to decide upon.' (SAOB)

In (3), *måtte* expresses inevitable necessity in a conditional context of the form "if X, then I cannot do otherwise than Y".[6] If the person does not get food, it is inevitable that s/he dies. This use is an instance of epistemic necessity; a logical conclusion on the basis of available evidence.

(3) *I   siw    dyngn     har   iagh icke äthit Bröö,/*[7]
    in  seven full.days have  I    not  eaten bread,/

   *Får iagh ey   maat **måtte** iagh döö.*
   get  I   not  food  must    I    die.

   'I have not eaten bread for seven days, if I do not get food I will die.' (SAOB)

To account for the epistemic meaning in *må*, Andersson (2007) identifies and exemplifies a bridging context. He considers conditional clauses with animate subjects and a cognitive verb, as in example (4), to be the main bridging context between root (= dynamic + deontic) and non-root (= epistemic) meanings (Andersson 2007: 205). He postulates that *må* in (4) still expresses root modality. The idea is that the speaker "presents the possibility for the subject-participant (conversational partner) to realize some fact, given some external evidence. When there is no concluding participant present, the concluding becomes associated with the speaker, thereby paving the way for a more speaker-oriented modality" (Andersson 2007: 205; translation KB).

---

6 For *må*, the expression of necessity was fairly restricted in Old Swedish (Andersson 2007: 199). This might have been a reason why Middle Low German *moste* 'to have permission/to be obliged' was borrowed to express deontic, and at a later stage, also epistemic necessity by means of the modal form *måste* 'must'.

7 The slash indicates the end of a strophe.

(4) *Rädhis han glödhina/ oc faklar ey fingrom i rödha*
    fear he ember and put not fingers in red
    *elden tha* **maghin** *i wita at biskopen hawer sant.*
    fire then may you know that bishop has true.
    'If he fears the ember and does not put his fingers in the red fire, then it is possible for you to know (hence conclude) that the bishop was right.'
    (Andersson 2007: 205)

Andersson (2007) also found potential epistemic-concessive readings for *må* in his study. The bridging context for this meaning is found in theological-argumentative contexts in paraphrases of the Old Testament, as in (5). As argued by Sweetser (1990), modals also express a kind of modality which cannot straightforwardly be identified as either root or non-root modality. According to Andersson (2007), (5) is such a case. Here, *må* does not express pure possibility or permission for some men to be frightened, nor does it express the speaker's conclusion about some men's reaction. Rather, "the reaction is presented as hypothetical and reasonable considering the words in the Bible" (Andersson 2007: 206).

(5) *Nw* **magho** *män ther styggias widh/ at en hälgher*
    now may men be frighten at that a holy
    *patriarcha hafdhe fyra husfrwr oc än twa syster...*
    patriarch had four wifes and to that two sisters
    *Än iacob syndar ey mot natwrinne.*
    but Jacob sin not against nature.
    'Now, men may be frightened at the fact that a holy patriarch had four wifes, and in addition to that two sisters, but Jacob does not sin against nature.' (Andersson 2007: 206)

In (6), *må* is part of a concessive construction of the general type "although p, q". Even though the books of Platonis contain some wisdom, it is not adequate when compared to the word of God.

(6) *Så* **må** *nu wäl Platonis böcker... hålla någon wijsdom*
    so may now well Platonis' books hold some wisdom
    *i sig,... men emot den wijsdom..., som är författat*
    in itself men against the wisdom that is written
    *I Gvdz Ord, är hon intet til räknandes.*
    In God's Word, is she not sufficient
    'So Platonis' books may very well contain some wisdom,... but against the wisdom that is written in God's Word, it is not sufficient.' (SAOB)

The use of *må* becomes increasingly bound to the perspective of the speaker and speaker-addressee interaction. *Må* is increasingly used to express emotions and attitudes in set phrases (7a), dialogue (7b) and exclamations (7c). In (7a), *Det må jag säga* 'I must say!' is a set phrase conveying astonishment. The collocation *må veta* 'you know' in (7b) functions as a discourse particle. In (7c), *må* is part of an exclamation in which the speaker proclaims that "the bastard" should not have escaped.

(7) a. *Hå! Det **må** jag säga. Min kära Fröken Mathilda;*
ah! It may I say. My beloved Miss Mathilda
*det här är en högst besynnerlig tête a tête.*
it here is a supreme strange head-to-head
'Ah! I must say, my beloved Miss Mathilda, this is very exquisite private chat.' (SAOB)

b. *Thet bryr folket sig om, **må** veta.*
that worries people.the themselves about may know
'That is what people worry about, you know.' (SAOB)

c. *Han **må** väl inte ha rymt, den karibeln!*
he must well not have escaped the bastard
'He should not have escaped, the bastard!' (SAOB)

In the next sections, I will explore the semantic distribution of *må* and *måtte* in Present-day Swedish.

# 3 Sources and methods

The data for the investigation of *må* and *måtte* in Present-day Swedish were extracted from a subset of Swedish text corpora which were developed and are maintained by *Språkbanken* (the Swedish Language Bank).[8] *Språkbanken*'s corpora can be queried through an online search interface; results from queries take the form of concordances. *Språkbanken* contains modern (e.g. data from blogs, twitter or newspaper texts from the 1990s) as well as historical corpora (e.g. Old Swedish material (ca. 1225–1526), Older Swedish novels from the period 1800–1900), and it includes texts from various sources, such as newspapers,

---

8 http://spraakbanken.gu.se

literature, non-specialist literature, government debates, law texts and historical texts. The entire corpus contains approximately 99 million words.

For the present study, random samples of sentences with *må* and *måtte* were taken from the subcorpora Press 95–98, which all contain newspaper texts (*Arbetet, Dagens Nyheter, Göteborgs-Posten, Svenska Dagbladet* and *Sydsvenskan*) from the 1990s. The total number of words is 33,664,723. The sampling of *må* and *måtte* was part of a larger investigation (Beijering 2011, Beijering 2012), in which samples of 1000 instances of cognate modal verbs in Norwegian (*å måtte*) and Danish (*at måtte*), but also of Swedish *måste*, were examined. Out of a total of 4,782 hits for *må* and only 735 hits for *måtte* in *Språkbankens konkordanser*,[9] the subcorpora Press 95–98 contained only 134 instances of *måtte*, but 1,473 hits for *må*.[10] The sample of *måtte* consists of all 134 instances; the sample of *må* contains 1000 randomly selected cases.

The corpus data was classified according to their different meanings. This coding in terms of semantic categories was based on the meanings listed for *må* and *måtte* in established dictionaries; these include, inter alia, desire/wish (= optative) (8a, 8b), affirmation (8c), probability (epistemic possibility) (8d), permission, generally in legal contexts (deontic possibility) (8e), various concessive expressions (8f, 8g), and ignorance, meekness or slight reluctance on behalf of the speaker/writer (8h, 8i).[11] In addition, there is a petrified adverbial form that may occur in questions and which is similar to the question particle *månne* 'I wonder', but this use is considered to be colloquial (8j).[12] The data, classified on the basis of these dictionary definitions, was then assigned to the broadly defined modal categories: (i) deontic meanings (obligation, necessity, permission and (moral) desirability 'should'), (ii) epistemic meanings (speaker evaluations of degrees of possibility and probability), (iii) concessive meanings (although X, Y) and (iv) optative meanings ([exclamative] wishes).

(8) a. **Må/måtte** *det gå väl!*
may/might it go well
'May it go well!' (SAOL)

---

**9** http://spraakbanken.gu.se/konk/
**10** Note, however, that the majority of these are instances of infinitival forms of the lexical verb *att må* 'feel' (Footnote 1).
**11** The dictionaries consulted are *Svenska Akademiens ordlista* [Wordlist of the Swedish Academy], henceforth SAOL; *Norstedts stora svenska ordbok* [Nordstedt's big Swedish dictionary], henceforth NSSO; and *Folkets Lexicon* [The people's dictionary], henceforth FL (available online at http://folkets-lexikon.csc.kth.se/folkets/folkets.html).
**12** For example: *Månne han kommer ikväll?* 'Is he coming tonight, I wonder?'

b. ... *på det att ingen* **måtte** *komma till skada.*
   ... on it that nobody may come prejudicial
   '... so that no one would get hurt.' (NSSO)

c. *Du* **må** *tro att jag blev förvånad!*
   you have to believe that I was surprised
   'I was surprised, believe me!' (FL)

d. *Han* **måtte** *ha dåligt minne!*
   he must have bad memory
   'He must have bad memory!' (NSSO)

e. *Talan* **må** *ej föras mot styrelsens beslut.*
   appeal may not directed against board.the's decision
   'No appeal may be lodged against the decision of the board.' (FL/NSSO)

f. *(det)* **må** *(så) vara*
   (it) may (so) be
   'be that as it may/so be it' (SAOL)

g. *Jag gillar inte metoden hur effektiv den än* **må** *vara.*
   I like not method-the how effective it ever may be
   'I do not like the method, however effective it may be.' (FL)

h. *Vill någon gå till fots, så* **må** *han göra det.*
   want someone go afoot, so may he do it
   'If someone wants to go afoot, then he may do so.' (NSSO)

i. *Skribenten –* **må** *han förbli anonym – har missuppfattat alltsammans.*
   writer.the – may he stay anonymous – has
   misunderstood all of it
   'The writer – let him remain anonymous – has gotten it all wrong.' (NSSO)

j. **Må** *det?*
   may it?
   'Really?' (SAOL)

Classifying modal meanings is, however, by no means a straightforward task. Especially *må* is an elusive linguistic item, whose exact meaning may be hard to define because of subtle overlaps between the semantic categories of necessity and possibility. In order to determine the most plausible reading for ambiguous instances of *må* and *måtte*, the wider context, paraphrases and clause-internal clues (e.g. modal particles and other modifying elements) were used. For example, epistemic meanings can be paraphrased as 'I deem it possible/probable that X'; a syntactic clue in optative contexts is that *må* and *måtte* predominantly occur in clause-initial position. Native speakers were consulted for contentious cases. The classification of the data was checked by one additional linguist.

The quantified corpus data, i.e. the counts per semantic domain, were checked for statistical significance by means of a Chi-square test. This is a statistical method to verify whether or not there is an association between two categorical variables (Field 2005: 682–702), i.e. in this case, whether there is a statistical relation between the modal (*må* or *måtte*) and the type of meaning (deontic, epistemic, optative, concessive). If such a relation exists, the semantic distributions of *må* and *måtte* will be significantly different (*må* and *måtte* are two different forms). If there is no relation between modal and the type of meaning, the semantic distributions of *må* and *måtte* will not be significantly different (*må* and *måtte* express present and past tense of the same modal).

# 4 Results of the corpus study

This section presents the results of the corpus investigation of the modals *må* and *måtte* in Present-day Swedish. The distribution of the different meanings of *må* and *måtte* is shown in Figure 1 (see Appendix A for an overview of the counts per semantic domain for each modal).

The semantic distributions of *må* and *måtte* differ significantly ($\chi^2$ = 492.9, $df$ = 4 and $p$ = <0.01). This lends support to our suggestion that *må* and *måtte* no longer signal present and past tense of the same modal, but that they have developed into two separate modal markers. Today, the modal *må* is primarily a concessive marker, whereas *måtte* predominantly conveys optative and epistemic meanings. For each modal, postmodal meanings were found to take up a larger share than modal meanings. This points to an advanced stage on the cline from premodal > modal (> postmodal) meanings. The semantic distributions for *må* and *måtte* will be discussed in more detail in Sections 4.1 and 4.2.

## 4.1 The semantic distribution of *må*

As pointed out earlier, 1000 (sampled) instances of *må* were analyzed, the majority of which occur in concessive contexts (53.7%). Deontic (12.1%), epistemic

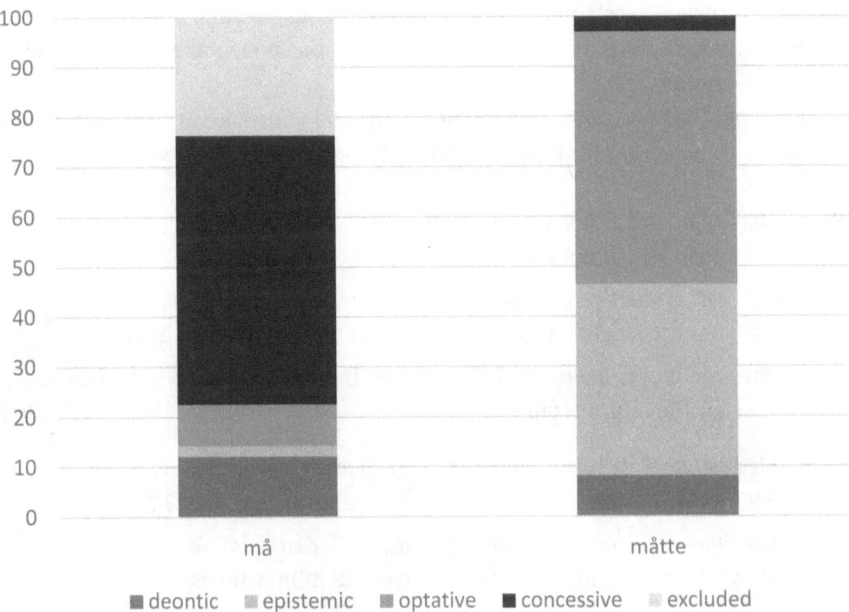

**Figure 2:** Bar chart of the semantic distributions for the Swedish modals *må* and *måtte*

(2.2%) and optative (8.3%) meanings each occur far less frequently than concessive meanings. 23.7% of the examples looked at were excluded from the analysis as they featured non-modal meanings of *må* (23.7%).[13] The different semantic classes are discussed in more detail and illustrated with examples from *Språkbanken*s subcorpora P95–98 in Sections 4.1.1 to 4.1.5 below.

### 4.1.1 Deontic meanings

In this paper, deontic meanings are taken to comprise obligation, necessity, permission and desirability. This is a broader characterization than the traditional definition of deontic modality in terms of permission and obligation: in line with Nuyts et al. (2010), I also include notions of (degrees of) moral acceptability and moral necessity. Unlike Nuyts et al. (2010), I do not distinguish

---

[13] Non-modal instances of *må* include the abbreviation *må* for *måndag* 'Monday' or literal citations of other Mainland Scandinavian language, i.e. Danish or Norwegian. The majority of these cases are infinitival forms of the lexical verb *må*, as in *Det är inte en fråga om att **må** bra, utan om att slippa **må** dåligt* 'It is not about feeling well, but about avoiding feeling bad'.

between "directive uses" (permission, obligation) and "deontic meanings" (moral acceptability and moral necessity). In this study, these meanings are all labeled deontic meanings.

Example (9a) illustrates deontic necessity: the addressee is reminded that it is essential to keep in mind the unusual circumstances of the year 1995.

(9) a. Men man **må** hålla i minnet att 1995 generellt
But one must hold in mind.the that 1995 generally

var ett synnerligen sorgesamt år för hel detaljhandeln.
was a extremely miserable year for entire retail trade.the

'But one has to keep in mind that 1995 in general was a very miserable year for the entire retail trade.' (P97)

b. Med stolthet berättar han om 11 barn och de 34
with pride tells he about 11 children and the 34

barnbarnen och det **må** förlåtas den som är
grandchildren and it must forgive-PAS him who is

95 år (!) att han får söka i minnet en stund
95 years (!) that he gets to seek in memory a while

efter förnamnet på det barnbarn som jobbar på UD.
after first name.the of that grandchild who works at UD

'With pride he reports on 11 children and 34 grandchildren and you must forgive someone who is 95 years (!) that he has to think for a moment about the first name of the grandchild who is employed at (UD).' (P96)

In (9b), we see an instance of moral acceptability/necessity. If you are 95 years old, and you have 34 grandchildren, you should be forgiven if you have to think for a moment about the name of the grandchild who is employed at the Ministry for Foreign Affairs (UD).

### 4.1.2 Epistemic meanings

Speaker judgments and evaluations of degrees of possibility and probability fall under the rubric of epistemic meanings. These occur frequently in constructions of the type *(det) må vara X* '(it) must be X', as in (10a), or *(det) må ha varit X* '(it) must have been X', as in (10b). In example (10a), the modal *må* expresses epistemic necessity. It denotes a logical conclusion or inference on the basis of available evidence: because many previous investigations reached the same conclusions, it can only be inferred that it is about time for political action. In epistemic contexts, *må* often goes together with a modal particle, e.g. *väl* 'well', which emphasizes the high degree of probability of the utterance even more.

(10) a. *Och eftersom det inte är första utredningen som*
and because it not is first investigation.the that

*konstaterar samma sak* **må** *det väl vara dags för*
observes same matter must it well be time for

*politiskt handlande, skriver Konstnärernas riksorganisation.*
political action, writes Artists'national organization

'And since it is not the first investigation that observes the same matter, it must (well) be about time for political action, writes the (Swedish) national organization of artists.' (P98)

b. *Detta kan visa sig mer betydelsefullt än man*
this may manifest itself more significant than one

*i förstone* **må** *ha varit benägen att tro.*
at first may have been inclined to think/believe

'It may manifest itself as more important than one at first sight might have been inclined to think.' (P96)

In (10b), *må* conveys epistemic possibility. The speaker/writer assumes that the addressee may think that X is not that important. This utterance is also close to a concessive reading (see also example (19a)): although one may have been inclined to think that X is not that important, it may nonetheless turn out to be significant. However, since the whole constructions expresses uncertainty, and *må* is part of the construction *(det) må ha varit X* '(it) must have been X', it is classified as epistemic. This is an example that clearly illustrates how difficult it is to deal with cases at the interface of two related categories. Note that epistemic meanings constitute only 2.2% of the sample, whereas concessive meanings take up as much as 53.7%; see Figure 2.

### 4.1.3 Optative meanings

Wishes and desires are grouped under optative meanings. In (11a), the speaker hopes that the party will not be disturbed by rain. In optative expressions, *må* is often the first constituent of the clause.

(11) a. **Må** det inte regna på festdeltagarna.
   may it not rain on partygoers
   'Hopefully it won't rain on the partygoers.' (P97)

b. *Vi joggar och står i      och unnar oss högst*
   we jog   and work-hard and allow us maximal
   *en halv millimeter lättmargarin    på mackan    på*
   a half millimeter light-margarine on sandwich.the on
   *det att vi* **må** *leva för evigt.*
   it that we may live for ever
   'We jog and work hard and allow ourselves at most half a millimeter of low-fat-margarine on our sandwich so that we may live forever.' (P97)

In optative contexts, *må* may also occur in subordinate clauses, such as *på det at X* 'so that X'. In (11b), the speaker ironically comments on a healthy lifestyle in relation to a general desire/wish of mankind to live for ever.

### 4.1.4 Concessive meanings

Concessive constructions involve clauses which "indicate that the situation in the matrix clause is contrary to expectation in the light of what is said in the concessive clause" (Quirk et al. 1985: 1089). They are of the general pattern "although p, q" (Crevels 2000: 1), which subsumes various subtypes.

As is evident from Figure 2, *må* predominantly occurs in concessive constructions and expressions. The most prototypical construction is illustrated in (12a) and (12b), either with or without the adversative connector *men* 'but'. In both examples, the situation in the matrix clause contradicts the expectation raised in the concessive clause. In (12a), with the adversative connector *men*, the looks of a terrorist do not match with the appearance of a grandmother. Likewise in (12b), without the adversative connector *men*, a decayed bourgeoisie is not what one would typically associate with the status of world literature.

(12) a. *Jag* **må** *se ut som en terrorist men jag är en*
   I may look like a terrorist but I am a
   *57-årig    mormor    och när   jag kom till*
   57-year.old grandmother and when I came to
   *rock'n'roll-museet     i Cleveland bad  jag för*
   rock'n'rollmuseum.the in Cleveland asked I for

första gången i livet om en seniorbiljett.
first time.the in life.the for a senior ticket

'I may look like a terrorist but I am a 57-year-old grandmother and when I came to the rock 'n'roll museum in Cleveland it was the first time in my life I asked for a senior ticket.' (P97)

b. *Thomas Mann* **må** *tillhöra en sjunken borgerlighet,*
Thomas Mann may belong to a drowned bourgeoisie,

*hans verk är världslitteratur som aldrig dör.*
his work is world literature that never dies

'Thomas Mann may belong to a decayed bourgeoisie, his work is world literature that never dies.' (P96)

Example (13) is also of the general type "although p, q". Instead of the adversative connector *men*, it contains a *wh*-element, e.g. *hur* 'how', in combination with the adverb *än* 'ever'. In this construction type ("whatever X may be, Y"), the collocation that *må* is part of conveys a latent possibility, which contrasts with the message in the Y-part of the construction.

(13) *Och* **hur** *olika två färger* **än** **må** *vara kan*
and how- different two colours ever may be can

*det aldrig uppstå någon diskussion om att det*
it never arise some discussion about that it

*är färger de är.*
is colors they are

'And however different two colors may be, there can never be any discussion about the fact that they are colors.' (P98)

Another subtype of the general pattern "although p, q" consists of clauses of the type "whether or not X, Y", as in (14). Whether it may please mister Johansson or not, the Swedish lawyers will nonetheless proceed with their task.

(14) *Det är en uppgift som svenska advokater kommer att*
it is a case that Swedish lawyers will to

*fortsätta med,* **må** *det behaga Kurt Ove Johansson eller inte.*
proceed with, may it please Kurt Ove Johansson or not

'Swedish lawyers will continue to work on this case, whether Kurt Ove Johansson likes it or not.' (P97)

In addition to the specific concessive constructions in (12)–(14), *må* is also part of set concessive expressions such as *Må det*, *Må så vara* or *Det må vara hänt*, all meaning 'so be it'/'be that as it may'.

(15) *Somliga kanske vill kalla det indierock.* **Må** *så*
 some maybe will call it indie rock may so
 *vara, jag kommer ändå inte höra er över*
 be, I will anyway not hear you.PL across
 *musiken när jag vridit volymen i topp.*
 music.the when I turned volume.the in top
 'Some may want to call it indie rock. Be that as it may, I will not even hear you over the music when I turn the volume all the way up.' (P98)

By saying *må så vara* 'so be it', the speaker in (15) shows rebellious ignorance about the label "indierock" for his/her favorite music.

## 4.2 The semantic distribution of *måtte*

The sample contains 134 instances of *måtte*. The majority of these instances feature *måtte* in optative (50.7%) and epistemic contexts (38.1%). Deontic (8.2%) and concessive (3%) meanings occur far less frequently. In sections 4.2.1 to 4.2.4 below, the different semantic classes are discussed in more detail and illustrated with corpus examples from Press 95–98.

### 4.2.1 Deontic meanings

Deontic meanings of *måtte*, as with *må*, are not that frequent. Example (16a) is an instance of moral desirability/necessity, in that *måtte* expresses that it is morally desirable that retirement homes be established for chimpanzees that are no longer used as laboratory animals.

(16) a. *Djurskyddsgrupper i USA har föreslagit att*
 animal-protection-groups in USA have proposed that
 *"pensionärshem"* **måtte** *inrättas för de schimpanser*
 pensioner's home must set up for the chimpanzees
 *som inte längre behövs som försöksdjur.*
 who not longer be.needed as laboratory.animal
 'Animal protection organizations in the USA have suggested that "retirement homes" should/must be established for those chimpanzees that are no longer needed as laboratory animals.' (P96)

b. *Man begärde    "att kommissionen    **måtte** undersöka*
   one demanded that commission-the must explore

   *möjligheterna    att sysselsätta denna kategori i    betarbete."*
   possibilities-the to employ    this    category in pasture.labour

   'It was demanded "that the commission must investigate the
   possibilities to employ this category as agricultural laborers".'    (P95)

In some cases, *måtte* even seems to be "redundant" in the sense that it follows verbs of demand, claim or request. In (16b), *måtte* expresses deontic necessity following the verb *begära* 'to demand', which already expresses an obligation.

### 4.2.2 Epistemic meanings

Epistemic meanings constitute the second most frequent use of *måtte*, making up 38.1% of the sample. In (17a), *måtte* expresses epistemic necessity, in that the speaker infers that the giant Hjorten must have been a good-looking guy.

(17) a. *Han **måtte** ha    varit bra snygg,    jätten    Hjorten.*
       he must have been very handsome giant.the Deer.the
       'He must have been very good-looking, the giant Hjorten.'    (P98)

   b. *Hon **måtte** väl ha    insett    till sist vilken gröngöling*
      she must well have realized to last what novice

      *han var, den där    snutfagre charmören    som*
      he was this there pretty    charmer.the who

      *förvred    huvudet på henne förra    våren.*
      distorted head.the of her    previous spring.the

      'Ultimately, she must have realized what a puppy he was, this
      handsome charmer who messed up her head last spring.'    (P97)

Example (17b) also illustrates epistemic necessity. The speaker arrives at a logical conclusion after evaluating the time a woman spent with a man who has a doubtful reputation.

The modal *måtte* occurs mainly in constructions of the type "must$_{PAST}$ have been X", as in (17a), or "must$_{PAST}$ have V$_{PERF}$ X", as in (17b). It is often accompanied by modal particles such as *väl* 'well', as in (17b).

### 4.2.3 Optative meanings

Optative meanings are by far the most common for *måtte*, making up as much as 50.7% of the sample. As for *må* in optative contexts, the first constituent of the clause is also the canonical position for *måtte* (see (18a)). Another peculiarity of these constructions is that they are often exclamative clauses.

(18) a. **Måtte** solen hålla strålarna tillbaka så
may sun.the hold rays.the back so
att inte Ice Globe Theatre smälter!
that not Ice Globe Theatre melts
'May the sun keep its rays back so that Ice Globe Theatre does not melt!' (P97)

b. *Jag önskar att solen* **måtte** *vara hos honom nu.*
I wish that sun.the may be with him now
'I wish that the sun would be with him now.' (P95)

*Måtte* may also occur in subordinate clauses, as in (18b). In this utterance, it co-occurs with the verb *önska* 'to wish' and is somewhat redundant, as the verb 'to wish' does not require the use of *måtte* to express a wish. Here, *måtte* is used in a formulaic expression.

### 4.2.4 Concessive meanings

Concessive meanings are very infrequent in the sample, taking up only 3% of all the modal uses of *måtte*.[14] Example (19a) closely resembles (10b), in which the meaning of *må* is classified as epistemic (although a borderline case). In (19a), the adverb *tvärtemot* 'contrary to' disambiguates the possible ambiguity of this utterance. The construction is of the type "although p, q", which provides another argument in favor for classifying (19a) as concessive.

---

[14] A remarkable difference between Swedish on the one hand, and Danish and Norwegian on the other hand, is that Swedish uses the original present tense form *må* in concessive contexts, whereas Norwegian and Danish use past tense forms in concessive constructions (Beijering 2011).

(19) a. *Tvärtemot vad läsaren   av den här   recensionen*
contrary to what reader.the of this here review.the
***måtte** tro   är han rolig.*
may    think is he funny
'Contrary to what the reader of this review may think, he is funny.' (P97)

b. *Framför allt går   det knappast längre att hålla*
above   all goes it   hardly   longer to hold
*tyskar,    amerikaner, ryssar,   fransmän,   italienare*
Germans  Americans  Russians  Frenchmen  Italians
*och australiensare borta från   den Fornnordiska*
and Australians   away from  the Old.Nordic
*forskningen, vad   än   vikingakongressens brittiska*
research.the what ever Viking.congress    British
*veteraner **måtte**   önska.*
veterans must.$_{PAST}$ wish

'Above all, it can hardly be maintained anymore that Germans, Americans, Russians, French, Italians and Australians should be kept away from Old-Nordic research, whatever the British veterans of the Viking congress may wish.' (P97)

Example (19b) has the same structure as (13). It is a subtype of the general pattern "although p, q" and contains a *wh*-element, i.e. *vad* 'what', in combination with the adverb *än* 'ever'. The collocation that *måtte* is part of conveys a latent possibility which is contrasted with the message in the matrix clause Y ("whatever X may be, Y").

# 5 Grammaticalization, subjectification and intersubjectification

The rise of modals is a classical example of grammaticalization (Hopper and Traugott 2003: 55–58), also known as "auxiliation" (Heine 1993; Kuteva 2001), which is generally accompanied by subjectification (e.g. Traugott 1989). It will be shown that *må* and *måtte* have become highly grammaticalized and (inter)subjectified linguistic items that have reached the final stages of grammaticalization.

The analysis in this paper focuses on the concept of a composite change (Norde and Beijering 2014). A composite change consists of (i) formal reanalysis and semantic reinterpretation, (ii) primitive changes at the levels of phonology, morphology, syntax, semantics and discourse and (iii) the side effects of (i) and (ii).

## 5.1 Grammaticalization

The study of grammaticalization phenomena is concerned with the origin and development of grammatical items or function words. The basic idea is that grammatical elements have their origin in lexical items or content words (Meillet 1912), but grammatical(ized) elements may also be subject to (further) grammaticalization (Kuryłowicz 1965).

Building on the principles, parameters, and characteristics of grammaticalization proposed in the literature (Hopper 1991; Lehmann 1995; Brinton and Traugott 2005) and the usage-based theory of grammatical status and grammaticalization developed by Boye and Harder (2012), I propose the following characterization of grammaticalization:

> Grammaticalization is a composite type of language change whereby lexical or already grammaticalized items, in certain linguistic contexts, undergo both semantic reinterpretation and formal reanalysis. It is accompanied by a subset of correlated primitive changes and side effects. Grammaticalization leads to a grammatical item, i.e. a linguistic item belonging to a minor category, with relational meaning, secondary status, the prime function of which is to regulate grammatical structure and grammatical relations. (Beijering 2012a: 47).

In this study, two types of grammaticalization, viz. "primary grammaticalization" (= Gzn1), from lexical to grammatical status, and "secondary grammaticalization" (= Gzn2), from grammatical to (more) grammatical status, are distinguished.[15]

In what follows, I will discuss the different components of the proposed definition with respect to the development of *må* and *måtte*. First the essential mechanisms of grammaticalization will be discussed (Section 5.1.1), then the accompanying primitive changes will be examined (Section 5.1.2) and, finally, the side effects which may identify potential instances of grammaticalization will be elaborated on (Section 5.1.3).

---

[15] Secondary grammaticalization includes continued or advanced grammaticalization and "intra-categorical shifts" between minor categories (i.e. recategorization within the same domain; see also Joseph 2005 on "lateral shifts").

## 5.1.1 Mechanisms in the grammaticalization of *må* and *måtte*

In essence, grammaticalization is the result of formal reanalysis and semantic reinterpretation. More specifically, in the development of *må* and *måtte*, these essential mechanisms of change are categorical reanalysis and metaphorization/metonymization. Table 1 shows how these mechanisms are at work in the two types of grammaticalization: the "+" sign (in a shaded cell) stands for a key property of grammaticalization; "–" signifies that a particular feature does not apply to grammaticalization.

**Table 1:** Mechanisms in the grammaticalization of *må* and *måtte*

| | | Gzn1 | Gzn2 |
|---|---|---|---|
| Formal reanalysis: Categorical reanalysis | formal reanalysis from major to minor category | + | – |
| | formal reanalysis from minor to minor category | – | + |
| Semantic reinterpretation: Metaphorization and/or metonymization | semantic reinterpretation from referential to relational meaning | + | – |
| | semantic reinterpretation of relational meanings | – | + |

The shift from main verb (Old Swedish *magha*) to modal auxiliary (Present-day Swedish *må* and *måtte*) is an instance of *categorical reanalysis* from a major to a minor category. Successive changes, for example from deontic to epistemic modal, are intra-categorial shifts, i.e. they instantiate categorical reanalysis from grammatical to (more) grammatical(ized) status. In terms of auxiliation, the modals *må* and *måtte* have progressed very far, as they have become grammatical markers which are no longer characterized by properties of main verbs (Section 5.1.2).

The mechanisms by which semantic change is generally considered to take place are *metaphor* and *metonymy* (e.g. Hopper and Traugott 2003). Metaphor is based on a correspondence between different notional domains or paradigms and involves the use of concrete notions to express abstract concepts. Underlying metonymy is the contiguity between related concepts within the same domain. This means that a sign substitutes for another, indexically related sign. Metaphor and metonymy are not mutually exclusive, but complementary, and they may co-occur in grammaticalization.

Metaphor captures a process of semantic change in general, from the beginning to the end. The transition from deontic to epistemic meaning, for instance, has often been analyzed in terms of metaphorical mapping (Sweetser 1982; Bybee and Pagliuca 1985; Heine et al. 1991). The idea is that epistemic meaning results from a metaphorical shift from obligation of a proposition ('X is obliged to Y') to obligation of the truth of a proposition ('X is obliged to be true').

At the micro-level, i.e. at the level of small, gradual steps leading to a single change, semantic change can be described in terms of metonymization. This is reflected by the wide variety of closely related, overlapping meanings in the realm of necessity and possibility. As we have seen in Section 2, premodal, modal and postmodal meanings are synchronically and diachronically related: premodal meanings give rise to modal meanings which, in turn, may, but need not, give rise to postmodal meanings. For example, from the original meaning of *må* 'to be strong/have the power' it only takes a small indexical step to dynamic meanings which denote abilities and capacities.

The development of *må* and *måtte* comprises both "primary" and "secondary" grammaticalization. The change from a major category (verb) to a minor category (auxiliary) and the shift from referential to relational meaning are typical of primary grammaticalization. All subsequent changes, to epistemic modal, optative or concessive marker can be considered continued or advanced grammaticalization, i.e. secondary grammaticalization.

### 5.1.2 Primitive changes in the grammaticalization of *må* and *måtte*

Formal reanalysis and semantic reinterpretation are accompanied by a subset of correlated primitive changes on different linguistic levels which may, but need not, be involved in grammaticalization. Primitive changes (Norde 2009: 36) operate at the levels of phonology, morphology, syntax, semantics and discourse, and tend to form clusters in terms of reduction or expansion (see also Traugott 2010a on grammaticalization as reduction and grammaticalization as expansion). Primitive changes are general linguistic changes (e.g. semantic bleaching versus enrichment, morphological fusion versus separation) and are not restricted to grammaticalization per se.

The accompanying primitive changes in the development of *må* and *måtte* are represented by the shaded cells in Table 2. The sign "+" sign stands for a key property of grammaticalization, and "(+)" represents characteristics that may, but need not, be involved in grammaticalization.

There is loss and change of phonetic substance on the way from the Old Swedish verb *magha* (present tense *ma*, past tense *mat(t)e*) to the Present-day Swedish modal forms *må* and *måtte*. There has been a change to the preterite-present verb paradigm (Section 2). In addition, the infinitive *måtta* and supine *måttat* are newly created forms on the basis of the imperfect form *måtte*

**Table 2:** Primitive changes in the grammaticalization of *må* and *måtte*

|  |  | Gzn1 | Gzn2 |
|---|---|---|---|
| Phonology/phonetics | loss of phonological/phonetic substance (attrition) | (+) | (+) |
| Morphology | loss of morphological compositionality[16] (fusion + coalescence) | (+) | (+) |
|  | loss of morphosyntactic properties (attrition) | + | (+) |
| Syntax | loss of syntactic variability (fixation) | (+) | (+) |
|  | loss of syntactic autonomy (integration) | (+) | (+) |
| Semantics | loss of semantic substance (bleaching) | + | + |
|  | loss of semantic compositionality (demotivation) | (+) | (+) |
| Discourse | gain of speaker's perspective (subjectification) (Section 5.2) | (+) | (+) |
|  | gain of interactive dimensions (intersubjectification) (Section 5.2) | (+) | (+) |

(SAOB). These forms occurred too infrequent, however, to become part of the inflectional paradigm (Table 3).

Loss of phonological/phonetic substance is closely connected to the loss of morphosyntactic properties. As Table 3 shows, the modals *må* and *måtte* have defective inflectional paradigms, consisting of one form only. Their predecessor *magha* had a much more variable and extensive inflectional system (Björkstam 1919; Birkmann 1987; Andersson 2007: 82).

**Table 3:** Inflectional paradigms for *må* and *måtte*

| modal | infinitive | present | past | perfect |
|---|---|---|---|---|
| *må* | – | *må* | – | – |
| *måtte* | – | – | *måtte* | – |

The modals *må* and *måtte* do not inflect for tense, and they lack infinitival, perfect, imperative and passive forms as well as present participles.[17] The loss of morphosyntactic properties comes along with the categorical reanalysis from main verb to auxiliary, whereby *må* and *måtte* gradually lose the prototypical features of lexical verbs, such as inflection. *Må* and *måtte* do not show any

---

**16** Compositionality applies to compositional forms only, not to monomorphemic or polysyllabic items.
**17** In Old Swedish, the participle form *magande* is attested, meaning 'strong, powerful, of age, potent' (Andersson 2007: 83).

changes with respect to their morphological compositionality because they are not compositional forms. Accordingly, changes that affect the morphological compositionality of a form, i.e. fusion and coalescence, do not apply here.

The reanalysis from main verb to auxiliary inevitably leads to a decrease in syntactic variability. Auxiliaries obtain fixed syntactic slots and become more tightly integrated into syntactic constructions. Compared to main verbs in general (and Old Swedish *magha* in particular), auxiliaries (e.g. *må* and *måtte*) lose in autonomy because they cannot (or can no longer) stand on their own: they need a main verb in order to form a predicate, and as such, they are ancillary to the main verb in a clause. In deontic contexts, the modals are free to combine with other verbs. In epistemic contexts, the construction is more constrained in that the prototypical form of epistemic expressions is a stative predicate of the form "must be X/must have been X". For optative contexts, the syntactic position of *må* and *måtte* is either confined to the first position of the clause or to subordinate clauses introduced by a complementizer. As far as concessive contexts are concerned, there are a number of specific constructions in which *må* and *måtte* appear as concessive markers.

With respect to semantic changes affecting *må* and *måtte*, it can be observed that there is loss of referential meaning, but gain of relational and meta-linguistic meaning on the way from lexical verb meaning 'have the power/strength' to auxiliary form with ability, permission, possibility and necessity meanings. The meanings of these modals become increasingly dependent on the context in which they occur. Over time, the correlations between the different possible meanings may fade so that an item becomes opaque. This applies especially to *må*, the exact meaning of which may be hard to describe (for example the borderline cases in Section 4).

As regards the discourse level, there is an increase in subjective and intersubjective meanings for *må* and *måtte* (see also the examples in Section 2). The role of (inter)subjectification in the development of *må* and *måtte* will be discussed in more detail in Section 5.2.

### 5.1.3 Side effects in the grammaticalization of *må* and *måtte*

The side effects of categorical reanalysis, semantic reinterpretation and their accompanying primitive changes can serve as diagnostics to identify potential cases of grammaticalization, in that they are observable signs of ongoing change. These concomitant changes are called side effects because they are not properties of the change proper, but basically the result of formal reanalysis, semantic reinterpretation and their accompanying primitive changes. The side effects in the grammaticalization of *må* and *måtte* are shown in the shaded cells in Table 4 below.

**Table 4:** Side effects of grammaticalization in *må* and *måtte*

|  | Gzn1 | Gzn2 |
|---|---|---|
| paradigmaticization (= increase in paradigmaticity) | + | + |
| obligatorification (= decrease of paradigmatic variability) | (+) | (+) |
| condensation (= structural scope reduction) | + | + |
| layering (synchronic variation of a given form), divergence (split), specialization, persistence | + | + |
| productivity (= context expansion) | + | + |
| frequency (= increased type and token frequency) | + | + |
| typological generality (= cross-linguistic replicated patterns) | + | (+) |

*Paradigmaticization*, i.e. the degree to which a linguistic item is part of a paradigm, correlates with *productivity* (context expansion) and *frequency* (increased type and token frequency). That is, when a linguistic item enters another grammatical paradigm, it can be used in more and different contexts. This phenomenon is also known as "host-class expansion" (Himmelmann 2004). For *må* and *måtte*, it can be observed that, once they entered the paradigm of modal auxiliaries, and their status as modals was established, they continued to develop more modal and postmodal meanings. However, since *må* and *måtte* ultimately specialized into concessive and optative markers, they did not become more frequent simply because concessive and optative are in general less frequent than deontic and epistemic meanings or than dynamic meanings. These are now encoded by the deontic and epistemic modal *måste* 'must' and and by the dynamic modal *kunna* 'can', respectively.

*Condensation* and *obligatorification* are two parameters that are often mentioned in relation to formal change. The degree to which modals are grammatically obligatory in expressing modal and postmodal meanings is hard to establish as there are many alternative ways of expressing these meanings (e.g. by means of adverbs, predicative adjectives or nouns). Recall that in some corpus examples the presence of the modal even seemed to be redundant (Section 4). Condensation – a decrease in syntactic scope and increased dependency – involves syntactic integration and leads to a decrease in syntactic autonomy of a linguistic item. The structural scope of *må* and *måtte* is reduced as they have become ancillary to the main verb of the clause and acquired fixed syntactic slots.

The synchronic coexistence of more and less grammaticalized variants of a given form is called *layering*.[18] Over time, *må* and *måtte* developed a wide variety of meanings within the realm of necessity and possibility. The newly emerged and older forms (= layers) may coexist for hundreds of years; some layers may in the long run disappear.

*Divergence* or split is a subtype of layering, in which the source construction of a grammaticalized construction continues to exist and may undergo the same changes as ordinary lexical items. This is the case for Swedish *må*, which, besides its modal variant, also has a full-fledged lexical variant meaning 'to feel'.[19]

*Specialization*[20] is a general type of semantic change that involves narrowing of meaning. In Old Swedish *må* could express all kinds of modal meaning, which were subsequently encoded by other modals. The modal *kunna* 'can' took over the dynamic meanings, and the modal *måste* came to denote obligation and deontic and epistemic necessity. In addition, there was some overlap and confusion with the now obsolete auxiliary *månde* 'may, might', which developed into the epistemic question particle *månne* 'I wonder' (Beijering 2012b). The modal *må* specialized into a concessive marker, and *måtte* is primarily used in optative contexts.

*Persistence* relates to the observation that a linguistic item or construction retains traces of the linguistic item or construction from which it emerged. All the correlated semantic changes in *må* have led to the extremely polysemous and opaque linguistic item that it was during the Old Swedish period. But also today it is not always easy to define the exact sense of *må* (Section 4). Although previous meanings may persist, it is not the case that premodal meanings persevere all the way up to postmodal meanings. Premodal (lexical) meanings develop into modal meanings which in turn may develop postmodal meanings. This is an incremental development, whereby some meanings get lost whilst

---

**18** This is not what Hopper (1991) originally meant by "layering", but how the notion is now generally applied in grammaticalization studies (Van Bogaert 2010).

**19** This development has been claimed to be an instance of degrammaticalization by van der Auwera and Plungian (1998: 105, 116). However, the lexical variant derives from one of the earliest meanings of *må*, and developed simultaneously with – and not out of – the modal meanings of *må*. Therefore, its development cannot be an instance of degrammaticalization. See Andersson (2007, 2008) for more arguments against a degrammaticalization analysis.

**20** As defined by Hopper (1991), *specialization* applies to a situation, where a variety of near-synonyms compete for expressing a particular meaning, and where, in the end, only one form becomes the prominent one in expressing this meaning.

others persist. A remnant of their verbal origin is that, despite their defective inflectional paradigms, *må* and *måtte* are still the tense markers in a clause, as main verbs occur as non-finite forms.

Finally, the principle of *typological generality* stands for the tendency that grammaticalization paths have a propensity for cross-linguistic replication. As pointed out in Section 2, the development of modal and postmodal meanings is a well-known tendency in semantic change. Developments similar to those described for *må* and *måtte* can also be observed in the other Germanic languages.

## 5.2 Subjectification and intersubjectification

The terms subjectification and intersubjectification have already been mentioned with respect to grammaticalization and semantic change. In this study, the general perspective on (inter)subjectivity and (inter)subjectification is in line with Traugott (e.g. 2010). That is, subjectification is the tendency that "meanings come to express grounding in the SP[eaker[/WR[iter]'s perspective explicitly" and intersubjectification pertains to the observation that "meanings come to express grounding in the relationship between speaker/writer and addressee/reader explicitly" (Traugott and Dasher 2002: 6).

In this paper, I return to the original insights by Halliday and Hasan (1976) and Traugott (1982, 1995) and assume that the following linguistic levels may be subject to (inter)subjectification. The ideational level (words and expressions with referential meaning, i.e. the "lexicon") and the textual level (grammatical functions and structural dependencies, i.e. the "grammar") belong to the propositional level, which is composed of lexical and grammatical items that are syntagmatically related. As such, lexical items may have primary status and grammatical items have secondary status (Boye and Harder 2012). The interpersonal level (communicative comments toward the proposition, i.e. the "discourse") contains extra-propositional, i.e. syntactically and semantically externalized, elements such as various types of discourse markers.

```
ideational > ([textual]   >    [interpersonal])
[      propositional      ]   [ extra-propositional ]
```

Both (inter)subjectification and different types of language change (e.g. grammaticalization) apply to these different components of language.[21] For

---

[21] See Beijering (2012a) and Norde and Beijering (2014) for the relation between lexicalization, grammaticalization, pragmaticalization and (inter)subjectification, and their interfaces.

instance, grammaticalization is a shift from the ideational to the textual level (primary grammaticalization) or a shift within the textual level (secondary grammaticalization). It is important to bear in mind that subjectification and intersubjectification are particular types of semantic change, not composite changes like grammaticalization. Processes of subjectification and intersubjectification may accompany grammaticalization, but they are in principle independent of one another (e.g. Traugott 2010). That is, (inter)subjectification may affect ordinary lexical and grammatical items without being involved in grammaticalization, and grammaticalization may take place without (inter)subjectification. This means that both lexical(ized) and grammatical(ized) items may have subjective and/or intersubjective meanings.

The modals *må* and *måtte* express a variety of modal and postmodal meanings with different degrees of (inter)subjectification. Traditionally, dynamic and deontic modality (= root modality) are distinguished from epistemic modality because they do not convey speaker judgments. That is, the rise of these meanings does not involve (inter)subjectification. However, in the broader definition of deontic modality as adopted in this paper, the domain of deontic modality also includes permission and obligation meanings. These directive uses do have (inter)subjective dimensions as they are directly directed toward the addressee.

Epistemic meanings are characterized by the speaker's subjective evaluation of the likelihood of a state of affairs. The speaker judges from his/her own perspective that something is likely or must be the case. The rise of epistemic meaning always involves subjectification, i.e. "the development of a grammatically identifiable expression of speaker belief or speaker attitude to what is said" (Traugott 1995: 32).

Optative meanings concern the speaker's personal or collective wish, which are clearly (inter)subjective. As shown by the examples in Section 4, optative *må* and *måtte* occur predominantly in exclamations and dialogue.

Concessive meanings are (inter)subjective because the speaker evaluates his/her statement in light of contrasting opinions or general accepted truths. As such, concessive contexts involve an interaction between speaker/writer and addressee/reader in that the speaker's opinion is in contrast with the view of the interlocutor (e.g. although p, as you say, I think q).

Table 5 illustrates subjectification and intersubjectification in the development of *må* and *måtte*.

In sum, the development of *må* and *måtte* is an instance of grammaticalization, defined in terms of categorical reanalysis and semantic reinterpretation from the ideational to the textual level, which is accompanied by subjectification and intersubjectification at the textual level. On the cline from premodal to modal and then to postmodal meanings, we see that deontic directive meanings and

**Table 5:** Subjectification and intersubjectification in *må* and *måtte*

|    | | må/måtte |
|----|---|---|
| I. | Subjectification:<br>[increased speaker perspective, attitude and judgment]<br>textual level: epistemic, concessive, optative | + |
| II. | Intersubjectification:<br>[increased focus on interaction with interlocutor]<br>textual level: directive meanings (permission, obligation), concessive, optative | + |

epistemic modal meanings involve subjectification. Premodal, dynamic and deontic necessity meanings are not affected by subjectification. The postmodal meanings concessive and optative involve both subjectification and intersubjectification.

As regards *må* and *måtte*, an advanced stage of semantic change in the (post)modal domain corresponds to high degrees of (inter)subjectification.

# 6 Concluding remarks

In this paper, significant semantic differences have been found with respect to the development of modal and postmodal meanings in the Swedish modals *må* and *måtte*. This supports the idea that these modals diverged into two separate modal markers.

Throughout their history, the modals *må* and *måtte* have been characterized by polysemy. A wide variety of meanings in the realm of possibility and necessity was lost and gained. At present, the modal *kunna* 'can' conveys the former dynamic meanings of *må* and *måtte*. Deontic and epistemic necessity are currently expressed by *måste* 'must', which has replaced *må* and *måtte*. *Må* specialized into a concessive marker, whereas *måtte* primarily has epistemic and optative meanings.

Over the course of their existence, the meanings of *må* and *måtte* have become increasingly subjective, expressing the speaker's personal views, emotions and attitudes as well as more intersubjective, referring to speaker-writer and addressee-reader interaction in dialogue and exclamations.

In the development of *må* and *måtte*, grammaticalization and (inter)subjectification go hand in hand. Today, the modals *må* and *måtte* live on as highly grammaticalized and intersubjectified linguistic items, primarily in concessive and optative contexts. They have reached the final stages of grammaticalization.

## Acknowledgments

I would like to thank the two anonymous reviewers and the editors for feedback on an earlier version of this paper. Especially the detailed comments by "reviewer 2", Lobke Ghesquière and Hubert Cuyckens have been very useful in revising and refining the paper. I thank Lena Kjellström for having a look at the Swedish examples and their translations. Finally, I am grateful to Muriel Norde and Jack Hoeksema for comments and suggestions on this topic during my time as a PhD researcher at the University of Groningen. Work on the final version of this paper was supported by a postdoctoral fellowship (grant number 12L7715N) awarded by the Research Foundation-Flanders (FWO).

## References

Andersson, Peter. 2007. *Modalitet och förändring: En studie av må och kunna i fornsvenska* [Modality and change: A study of *må* and *kunna* in Old Swedish]. Göteborg: Göteborgs Universitet.

Andersson, Peter. 2008. Swedish må and the degrammaticalization debate. In Elena Seoane & María José López-Couso (eds.), *Theoretical and empirical issues in grammaticalization*, 15–32. Amsterdam: John Benjamins.

Beijering, Karin. 2011. Semantic change and grammaticalization: The development of modal and postmodal meanings in Mainland Scandinavian *må*, *måtte* and *måste*. *Nordic Journal of Linguistics* 34(2). 105–132.

Beijering, Karin. 2012a. *Expressions of epistemic modality in Mainland Scandinavian: a study into the lexicalization-grammaticalization-pragmaticalization interface*. Groningen: University of Groningen dissertation.

Beijering, Karin. 2012b. From modal auxiliary to adverb: The development of Mainland Scandinavian MONNE/MON. In Van der Liet, Henk & Muriel Norde (eds.), *Language for its own sake: Essays on language and literature offered to Harry Perridon*, 287–312. Amsterdam: Scandinavisch Instituut.

Benveniste, Emile. 1966. De la subjectivité dans le langage. In Emile Benveniste (ed.), *Problèmes de Linguistique Générale*, Vol. I, 258–266. Paris: Gallimard.

Birkmann, Thomas. 1987. *Präteritopräsentia: Morphologische Entwicklungen einer Sonderklasse in den altgermanischen Sprachen*. Tübingen: Niemeyer.

Björkstam, Harald. 1919. *De modala hjälpverben i svenskan: Tör, lär, mon, må, måtte och vill* [The modal auxiliaries in Swedish. Tör, lär, mon, må, måtte and vill]. Lund: Håkan Ohlssons Boktryckeri.

Boye, Kasper & Peter Harder. 2012. A usage-based theory of grammatical status and grammaticalization. *Language* 88(1). 1–44.

Brinton, Laurel J. & Elizabeth Closs Traugott. 2005. *Lexicalization and language change*. Cambridge: Cambridge University Press.

Bybee, Joan & William Pagliuca. 1985. Cross-linguistic comparison and the development of grammatical meaning. In J. Fisiak (ed.), *Historical semantics, historical word formation*, 59–83. The Hague: Mouton.

Bybee, Joan, William Pagliuca & Revere Perkins. 1994. *The evolution of grammar: Tense, aspect, and modality in the languages of the world*. Chicago: University of Chicago Press.
Crevels, Emily I. 2000. *Concession: A typological study*. Amsterdam: University of Amsterdam dissertation.
Diewald, Gabriele. 1999. *Die Modalverben im Deutschen*. Tübingen: Max Niemeyer Verlag.
Field, Andy. 2005. *Discovering statistics using SPSS*. London: Sage.
Halliday, Michael. A. K. & Ruqaiya Hasan. 1976. *Cohesion in English*. London: Longman.
Heine, Bernd. 1993. *Auxiliaries: Cognitive forces and grammaticalization*. Oxford: Oxford University Press.
Heine, Bernd, Ulrike Claudi & Friederike Hünnemeyer. 1991. *Grammaticalization. A conceptual framework*. Chicago: University of Chicago Press.
Heine, Bernd & Tania Kuteva. 2002. *World lexicon of grammaticalization*. Cambridge: Cambridge University Press.
Himmelmann, Nikolaus P. 2004. Lexicalization and grammaticalization: Opposite or orthogonal? In Walter Bisang, Nikolaus P. Himmelmann & Björn Wiemer (eds.), *What makes grammaticalization? A look from its fringes and components*, 21–42. Berlin: Mouton de Gruyter.
Hopper, Paul J. 1991. On some principles of grammaticization. In Elizabeth Closs Traugott & Bernd Heine (eds.), *Approaches to grammaticalization*, Vol. 1, 17–35. Amsterdam: John Benjamins.
Hopper, Paul J. & Elizabeth Closs Traugott. 2003. *Grammaticalization*, 2nd edn. Cambridge: Cambridge University Press.
Joseph, Brian D. 2005. How accommodating of change is grammaticalization? The case of "lateral shifts". *Logos and Language* 6. 1–7.
Kuryłowicz, Jerzy. 1965. The evolution of grammatical categories. *Diogenes* 51: 55–71. (Reprinted in: Jerzy Kuryłowicz, 1975. *Esquisses linguistiques II*. München: Fink, 38–54.)
Kuteva, Tania. 2001. *Auxiliation: An enquiry into the nature of grammaticalization*. Oxford: Oxford University Press.
Langacker, Ronald W. 1985. Observations and speculations on subjectivity. In John Haiman (ed.), *Iconicity in Ssyntax*, 109–150. Amsterdam: John Benjamins.
Langacker, Ronald W. 1990. Subjectification. *Cognitive Linguistics* 1. 5–38.
Lehmann, Christian. 1995. *Thoughts on grammaticalization*. München: LINCOM Europa.
Meillet, Antoine. 1912. L'Évolution des formes grammaticales. *Scientia* 12(6): 384–400. (Reprinted in Antoine Meillet, 1958. *Linguistique historique et linguistique générale*. Paris: Champion, 130–148.)
Norde, Muriel. 2009. *Degrammaticalization*. Oxford: Oxford University Press.
Norde, Muriel & Karin Beijering. 2014. Facing interfaces: A clustering approach to grammaticalization and related changes. *Folia Linguistica*, 48(2). 385–424.
Nuyts, Jan, Pieter Byloo & Janneke Diepeveen. 2010. On deontic modality, directivity, and mood: The case of Dutch *mogen* and *moeten*. *Journal of Pragmatics* 42. 16–34.
Nuyts, Jan. 2012. Notions of (inter)subjectivity. *English Text Construction* 5(1). 53–76.
Palmer, Frank. 1986. *Mood and Modality*. Cambridge: Cambridge University Press.
Philippa, Marlies, Frans Debrabandere, Arend Quak, Tanneke Schoonheim & Nicoline van der Sijs (eds.). 2011. *Etymologisch woordenboek van het Nederlands* [Etymological dictionary of Dutch. Amsterdam: Amsterdam University Press. http://www.etymologie.nl/ (accessed on 10 January 2015).
Quirk, Randolph, Sidney Greenbaum, Geoffrey Leech & Jan Svartvik. 1985. *A comprehensive grammar of the English language*. London: Longman.

SAOB = *Svenska Akademiens ordbok*. Available online at http://g3.spraakdata.gu.se/saob/.
Sweetser, Eve. 1982. Root and epistemic modals: Causality in two worlds. In Macaulay, Monica, Orin D. Gensler et al. (eds.), *Proceedings of the Eighth Annual Meeting of the Berkeley Linguistics Society*, 484–507. Berkeley, CA: Berkeley Linguistics Society.
Sweetser, Eve. 1990. *From etymology to pragmatics: The mind-body metaphor in semantic structure and semantic change*. Cambridge: Cambridge University Press.
Talmy, Leonard. 1988. Force dynamics in language and cognition. *Cognitive Science* 12(1). 49–100.
Talmy, Leonard. 2000. *Toward a cognitive semantics*. Vol. 1: *Concept structuring systems*. Cambridge, MA: The MIT Press.
Teleman, Ulf, Staffan Hellberg, Erik Andersson & Lisa Christensen (eds.). 1999. *Svenska Akademiens Grammatik*. Stockholm: Svenska Akademien/Norstedts Ordbok.
Traugott, Elizabeth Closs. 1982. From propositional to textual and expressive meanings: Some semantic-pragmatic aspects of grammaticalization. In Winfred P. Lehmann & Yakov Malkiel (eds.), *Perspectives on historical linguistics*, 245–271. Amsterdam: John Benjamins.
Traugott, Elizabeth Closs. 1989. On the rise of epistemic meanings in English: An example of subjectification in semantic change. *Language* 65(1). 31–55.
Traugott, Elizabeth Closs. 1995. Subjectification in grammaticalisation. In Dieter Stein & Susan Wright (eds.), *Subjectivity and subjectivisation*, 31–54. Cambridge: Cambridge University Press.
Traugott, Elizabeth Closs. 2003. From subjectification to intersubjectification. In Hickey, Raymond (ed.), *Motives for language change*, 124–139. Cambridge: Cambridge University Press.
Traugott, Elizabeth Closs. 2010. (Inter)subjectivity and (inter)subjectification: A reassessment. In Kristin Davidse, Lieven Vandelanotte & Hubert Cuyckens (eds.), *Subjectification, intersubjectification and grammaticalization*, 29–74. Berlin & New York: Mouton de Gruyter.
Traugott, Elizabeth Closs. 2010a. Grammaticalization. In Silvia Luraghi & Vit Bubenik (eds.), *The Continuum companion to historical linguistics*, 271–285. London: Continuum Press.
Traugott, Elizabeth Closs & Richard B. Dasher. 2002. *Regularity in semantic change*. Cambridge: Cambridge University Press.
Van Bogaert, Julie. 2010. A constructional taxonomy of *I think* and related expressions: Accounting for the variability of complement-taking mental predicates. *English Language and Linguistics* 14(3). 399–427.
van der Auwera, Johan. 2001. On the typology of negative modals. In Jack Hoeksema, Hotze Rullmann, Victor Sanchez-Valencia & Ton van der Wouden (eds.), *Perspectives on negation and polarity items*, 23–48. Amsterdam: John Benjamins.
van der Auwera, Johan & Vladimir A. Plungian. 1998. Modality's semantic map. *Linguistic Typology* 2. 79–124.
Wessén, Elias. 1965. *Svensk språkhistoria*. Vol. I: *Ljudlära och ordböjningslära* [History of the Swedish language. Vol. 1: Phonetics and morphology]. Stockholm: Almqvist & Wiksell.
Wärnsby, Anna. 2006. (De)coding modality – The case of *must, may, måste* and *kan*. Lund: University of Lund dissertation.

Adeline Patard and Johan van der Auwera
# 3 The French comparative modal constructions *faire mieux de*, *valoir mieux* and *falloir mieux*

**Abstract:** In the recent literature, a number of articles have been dedicated to the study of comparative modal constructions (CMCs) in Germanic languages such as English, Dutch and German. However, CMCs are not restricted to the Germanic area. The present paper presents original data from a Romance language, namely French, in which (at least) three CMCs are attested: *faire mieux de* 'lit. do better of', *valoir mieux* 'lit. be worth better' and *falloir mieux* 'lit. must better'. The aim of this paper is twofold. It intends to offer the first linguistic description of CMCs in French. Making use of several corpora, it presents a synchronic structural characterization of CMCs in Modern French, it investigates their diachronic development and describes their semantics. In addition, the paper seeks to define the degree of grammaticalization of French CMCs. This will enable us to specify their status as semi-auxiliaries within the paradigm of French modals.

## 1 Introduction

In recent years, comparative modal constructions (henceforth CMCs), such as English *had better* (e.g. *You had better shut up*), have become a popular topic of research. According to a number of studies, CMCs are attested in various Germanic languages such as Dutch (Byloo et al. 2010), English (Mitchell 2003; Denison and Cort 2010; van der Auwera and De Wit 2010; van der Auwera et al. 2013), German (Vanderbiesen 2011; Vanderbiesen and Mortelmans 2011), Yiddish and West Frisian (Byloo et al. 2010: 107). However, CMCs are not restricted to the Germanic area and are also found in a number of Romance languages such as Italian (e.g. *Faresti meglio a tacere*), Romanian (e.g. *Ai face (mai) bine să taci*), Spanish (e.g. *Harías mejor en callar*) and French (e.g. *Tu ferais mieux de te taire*).[1]

---

[1] The Romance sentences are translations of English *You had better shut up*.

The present study focuses on French, which exhibits three principal CMCs, each involving the comparative adverb *mieux* 'better': (i) *faire mieux de* 'lit. do better of', (ii) *valoir mieux* 'lit. be worth better' and (iii) *falloir mieux* 'lit. must/ have to better'. Its aim is twofold. First, the paper wants to contribute to remedying the lack of studies in the field, especially in the Romance domain, by providing the first linguistic description of CMCs in French, both from a synchronic and a diachronic perspective; second, it seeks to explore the grammaticalization of these constructions, i.e. "the proces[s] whereby items become more grammatical through time" (Hopper and Traugott 1993: 2), which encompasses both a shift from a lexical to a grammatical status and from a less to a more grammatical status. To capture the degree of grammaticalization of French CMCs, we make use of Lehmann's (2002 [1995]) seminal work, which describes the characteristics of grammaticalizing items. However, we will not discuss all of the six parameters suggested by Lehmann, but only consider those that seem to us most relevant to grasp the modal-like status of French CMCs. One such parameter is the syntagmatic *variability* of French CMCs which concerns "the positional mutability" of the constituents making up the construction (Lehmann 2002: 140). In other words, we seek to determine whether the ordering of the different constituents within the construction is fixed (*syntagmatic fixation*) or whether the constituents may easily be shifted or separated from each other (*syntagmatic variability*). In the case of modal auxiliaries, syntagmatic fixation is expected to be high, with an intimate connection between the modal verb and the non-finite verb. On the semantic side (Section 4), we will consider the *semanticity* or *semantic integrity* of CMCs, i.e. their "possession of a certain [semantic] substance which allows [them] to maintain [their] identity" (Lehmann 2002: 112). The grammaticalization of an item usually goes hand in hand with a decrease in semanticity (*desemanticization* or *semantic bleaching*), which is reflected in the loss of semantic features. In addition to these two parameters, we will also consider the parameter of *decategorialization* (e.g. Heine 1993, Heine 2003; Heine and Kuteva 2007; Lamiroy and Drobnjakovic 2009), which corresponds to the tendency shown by grammaticalizing items "to lose morphological and syntactic properties characterizing [their] earlier use but being no longer relevant to [their] new use" (Heine and Kuteva 2007: 40). In the case of modal verbs, decategorialization is manifested in the loss of the verbal morphosyntactic features of the lexical source (most often a lexical verb) from which they developed. Finally, the degree of grammaticalization of French CMCs may also be captured by examining the evolution of their frequency. As underlined in a number of studies (e.g. Bybee and Hopper 2001; Bybee 2003, Bybee 2006), a significant rise in frequency may constitute both a trigger for, and a result of, grammaticalization. Looking at these different parameters, we will argue that French CMCs should be taken as semi-modals that have experienced a modest degree of grammaticalization.

To give a synchronic and diachronic description of French CMCs and examine their degree of grammaticalization, we resort to corpora extending from Old French up to Modern French. The synchronic analyses of Modern French CMCs are carried out using four corpora, covering the period from 1960 to the 2000s: the more recent texts (from 1960 to 2009) of the written corpus *Frantext*, which is mainly composed of literary texts and essays; and three corpora of spoken French (*Elicop*, *Corpus de Langue Parlée en Interaction* (CLAPI) and *Corpus de Français Parlé Parisien des années 2000* (CFPP2000)). The diachronic analyses are conducted on a corpus covering the period from the 12th century to the 2000s. The diachronic corpus includes the texts of *Frantext* and *Frantext Moyen Français*, ranging between 1180 and 1999. Detailed information about these corpora is provided in a separate section at the end of the paper.

The paper is organized as follows. Section 2 first provides a synchronic description of French CMCs. The aim is to characterize the structural properties of these constructions in Modern French. Section 3 then investigates the history of French CMCs and their development from their source constructions. Finally, we explore the semantics of French CMCs, focusing on the extent to which their interpretations in Modern French reflect a semantic evolution or mirror some features of the source constructions.

## 2 Synchronic analysis

### 2.1 The three constructions and their variants

The three most frequent CMCs in French consist of the combination of a verb (*faire* 'do', *valoir* 'be worth' or *falloir* 'must, have to') and the comparative adverb *mieux* 'better'. Two types of French CMCs can be distinguished. The first is the personal construction *faire mieux*, which patterns as follows: [*faire mieux de* + infinitive], as in (1). The second type comprises the impersonal constructions *valoir mieux* and *falloir mieux*, as in (2) and (3) respectively.

(1) Tu **ferais**     **mieux de** dormir!
    you do.COND.2SG better of sleep.INF

    '**You'd better** sleep.'          (*Frantext*, Louis-Ferdinand Céline, *Rigodon*)

(2) *Je crois qu' il **vaut** **mieux que** je laisse la parole*
I think that it be.worth.PRS.3SG better that I let the word

*à mon collègue.*
to my colleague

'I think that **I'd better let** my colleague speak.' (Elicop)

(3) ***Faut** **mieux** continuer à pied.*
have.to.PRS.3SG better continue.INF on foot
'**We'd better** go on on foot.'
(*Frantext*, Frédéric Lasaygues, *Vache noire, hannetons et autres insectes*)

Unlike *faire mieux*, *valoir mieux* and *falloir mieux* have several variants: they may combine with an infinitive, as in (3), or with a complement clause in the subjunctive mood, as in (2); further, they do not require the presence of a dummy subject, as in (3). *Valoir mieux* also allows two different word orders, i.e. [*valoir mieux*] and [*mieux valoir*]. The second (impersonal) type thus comprises the following variants:
- [*(il) valoir mieux* + infinitive]
- [*(il) valoir mieux que* + subjunctive]
- [*mieux valoir* + infinitive]
- [*mieux valoir que* + subjunctive]
- [*(il) falloir mieux* + infinitive]
- [*(il) falloir mieux* + subjunctive]

According to Lehmann's (2002) inventory of grammaticalization criteria, the syntagmatic variability of the [*valoir mieux*] and [*falloir mieux*] constructions would indicate a rather low degree of fixation and hence grammaticalization. The [*faire mieux de* (+INF)] construction, in contrast, is more firmly fixed and shows less positional mutability.

Syntagmatic variability may also be measured in terms of the separability of the inflected verb and *mieux*. In this regard, the two types of CMC exhibit a moderate degree of grammaticalization. They are only loosely tied as the sequence [verb + *mieux*] can be interrupted by negation, as in (4), or by an adverbial, as in (5) and (6).

(4) *Est- ce qu' il **ne** **faudrait** **pas mieux** retrouver*
Is it that it NEG have.to.COND.3SG NEG better find.INF

*des mathématiques plus utilisables?*
of.the mathematics more usable

'Wouldn't it be better to find more usable mathematics?' (CLAPI)

(5) *Il **vaut**  beaucoup **mieux** pour toi que tu restes ici*
    It be.worth.PRS.3SG much    better  for  you that you stay here
    *seul et nu devant Dieu, à méditer sur tes péchés.*
    'You'd much better stay here, alone and naked in front of God,
    meditating on your sins.'        (*Frantext*, Zoé Oldenbourg, *Les Cités charnelles*)

(6) *Je **ferais**   peut-être **mieux de** présenter*
    I  do.COND.1SG maybe     better  of  present.INF
    *tout de suite Candie.*
    immediately Candie
    'I'd maybe better present Candie to you at once.'
                        (*Frantext*, Roger Vrigny, *La Nuit des Mougins*)

## 2.2 Frequencies

When we compare the frequencies of the CMCs in the Present-day French corpora (Table 1), *valoir mieux* is by far the most frequent construction, both in written and in spoken French. *Faire mieux* comes second and *falloir mieux* comes third.

**Table 1:** Absolute frequencies (n) and normalized frequencies (per million words) of *faire mieux*, *valoir mieux* and *falloir mieux* in the Present-day French corpora

|              | spoken | | written (*Frantext*) | | total | |
|---|---|---|---|---|---|---|
|              | n  | n/million | n    | n/million | n    | n/million |
| faire mieux  | 7  | 3.55      | 358  | 7.60      | 365  | 7.43      |
| valoir mieux | 65 | 33.02     | 1384 | 29.34     | 1449 | 29.49     |
| falloir mieux| 13 | 6.60      | 5    | 0.11      | 18   | 0.37      |
| total CMC    | 85 | 43.19     | 1747 | 37.04     | 1832 | 37.29     |

Increase in frequency is known to play an important role in the process of grammaticalization, both as a trigger and as a result (see, for instance, Bybee and Hopper 2001; Bybee 2003, Bybee 2006). CMCs are much less frequent (approximately 37.29 tokens per million words) than modal verbs such as *devoir* 'have to' (1082.22 tokens per million words) or than highly grammaticalized constructions such as *venir de* 'come from' + infinitive expressing near/recent past (335.92 tokens per million words) and *aller* 'go' + infinitive expressing future

(1065.50 tokens per million words).[2] Accordingly, one could expect that French CMCs have not reached an advanced stage of grammaticalization.

Furthermore, it is noteworthy that *falloir mieux* is far more common in spoken French than in written French (approximately 66 times more frequent). A likely explanation is that the use of *falloir mieux* is still considered incorrect in normative grammars.[3] As a consequence, *falloir mieux*, which is quite common in spoken language (even more so than *faire mieux*, according to the data), is rarely used in written texts.

What Table 1 does not reveal, but what immediately strikes the eye when looking at the written corpus is that the overwhelming majority of CMCs occur in represented speech, i.e. in direct or indirect speech. Table 2 presents the distribution of CMCs in represented speech. It shows that in the written corpus 75.31% of the CMCs occur in reported speech. Van der Auwera et al. (2013) found similar results for English.

**Table 2:** Percentages of reported vs. unreported speech in the synchronic written corpus (*Frantext*) (based on samples of 200 if total n > 200 in Table 1)[4]

|  | unreported | reported | | total |
|---|---|---|---|---|
|  |  | direct | (free) indirect |  |
| *faire mieux* | 17 | 63.50 | 18.50 | 83 |
| *valoir mieux* | 32 | 37 | 31 | 68 |
| *falloir mieux* | 40 | 40 | 20 | 60 |
| total CMC | 24.29 | 50.12 | 25.19 | 75.31 |

## 2.3 Combination with tenses

As can be seen from Table 3, French CMCs exhibit defective conjugations. The more restricted choice of tense forms may be seen as signaling grammaticalization in at least two respects. First, it may be indicative of a lesser degree of syntagmatic variability of the constructions (Lehmann 2002: 140–143), as it imposes a higher degree of fixation at the constructional level. Second, by allowing fewer tense inflections, CMCs are in a way "losing" the morphosyntactic properties of

---

[2] Frequencies are calculated on the basis of the texts from the POS-tagged French database "Frantext catégorisé", which includes texts from 1960 onward.
[3] The *Nouveau dictionnaire des difficultés du français moderne* (Hanse 1989: 973) stipulates for instance: "Se garder de dire ou écrire : ... [*il faut mieux*] au lieu de **il vaut mieux**: *Il vaut mieux se taire.*" (Avoid saying or writing: ... [*il faut mieux*] instead of **il vaut mieux** : *Il vaut mieux se taire.*)
[4] See Table 4 in the appendix for the n values corresponding to the percentages for indirect and free indirect speech.

lexical verbs and resemble fully-fledged modals, a process which could be subsumed under the notion of *decategorialization* (e.g. Heine 1993, Heine 2003; Heine and Kuteva 2007; Lamiroy and Drobnjakovic 2009), i.e. the loss of the morphosyntactic properties of the source construction.

**Table 3:** Choice of tense forms (percentages based on samples of 200 if total n > 200 in Table 1)

| | | *valoir mieux* | | *faire mieux* | | *falloir mieux* | |
|---|---|---|---|---|---|---|---|
| present tense (*présent*) | present perfect (*passé composé*) | 62 | 0.5 | 0 | 0 | 72 | 0 |
| present conditional (*conditionnel présent*) | past conditional (*conditionnel passé*) | 18 | 2.5 | 71 | 27.5 | 5.5 | 5.5 |
| imperfect (*imparfait*) | pluperfect (*plus-que-parfait*) | 14 | 0 | 0 | 0 | 17 | 0 |
| future tense (*futur simple*) | future perfect (*futur antérieur*) | 0.5 | 0 | 0.5 | 0 | 0 | 0 |
| imperfect subjunctive (*subjonctif imparfait*) | pluperfect subjunctive (*subjonctif plus-que-parfait*) | 0 | 2.5 | 0 | 1 | 0 | 0 |
| total simple form | total compound form | 94.5 | 5.5 | 71.5 | 28.5 | 94.5 | 5.5 |

Interestingly, the two constructional types mentioned earlier – *faire mieux de* and *valoir/falloir mieux* – show two clearly distinct patterns. *Faire mieux de* occurs almost exclusively in the conditional tense (present or past), as in (7), while *valoir mieux* and *falloir mieux* mostly combine with the present tense (as in (8)), although they also occur with other tenses, such as the past imperfect tense (as in (9)). Note that, unlike *faire mieux de* (28.5%), *valoir mieux* and *falloir mieux* do not easily admit compound tenses (only 5.5%).

(7) Le jour… où   j' ai    croisé le regard de votre
     The day   when I have crossed the look  of your

  fille,     j' **aurais**        **mieux fait**      de me
  daughter I have.COND.1SG better do.PPTCP of to.me

  casser les  deux jambes.
  break the two  legs

  'The day when I crossed the eyes of your daughter, I had better have broken my two legs.'
        (*Frantext*, Frédéric Lasaygues, *Vache noire, hannetons et autres insectes*)

(8) On pense qu' il **faut**           **mieux** garder
  one thinks that it have.to.PRS.3SG better keep.INF

  l'  ascenseur client là.
  the lift      client there

  'We think that we'd better keep the client lift there.'         (CLAPI)

(9) **Mieux valait** ne pas y penser, certes,
better be.worth.IMP.3SG NEG NEG about.it think.INF sure
mais j' y pensais quand même.
but I about.it think.IPFV.1SG anyway

'I'd better not think about it, sure, but I was thinking about it anyway.'

(Frantext, Léo Malet, *Sueur aux tripes*)

One possible explanation for these facts is the diachrony of the two types of construction. As we will see in Section 3, *faire mieux de* probably originated from an irrealis conditional of the type [*faire*.COND *mieux si* X.IMP] 'would do better if X'. This would explain why *faire mieux de* is almost always in the conditional tense. By contrast, *valoir mieux* (and consequently *falloir mieux*, see Section 3.2) do not have this kind of origin and thus allow a freer choice, and may combine with the present tense as well as with other tenses (mainly the conditional tense and the imperfect).

These patterns could also be related to the *Aktionsart* or actionality of the lexical verb. *Faire* is typically an activity verb describing a bounded situation which may easily be viewed as accomplished. That is why it can be used with the perfect form of the conditional (*conditionnel passé*). In contrast, *valoir* refers to a stative unbounded situation which cannot normally be viewed as terminated. *Valoir mieux* is therefore less compatible with perfect tenses than its counterpart based on *faire*.

A third determining factor could be the distinct functional domains that the two types *faire mieux de* and *valoir/falloir mieux* bear on (Sections 4.1 and 4.2). *Faire mieux de* tends to be used more to express directive meaning (advice, threat, command) than *valoir/falloir mieux*, which rather express a subjective (deontic and evaluative) meaning. On the one hand, *faire mieux* involves a potentially greater threat for the hearer's face (an intersubjective dimension, in Traugott's 2003 view). As a consequence, the speaker uses the conditional tense to soften a possibly "threatening act" and preserve the hearer's face (Brown and Levinson 1987). On the other hand, the subjectivity of *valoir/falloir mieux* represents a smaller threat to the hearer's face and does not require the use of a mitigating form such as the conditional – although the speaker may still decide to use it (20.5% and 11% of the uses of *valoir mieux* and *falloir mieux* have the conditional tense).

## 2.4 Syntactic properties

As far as their syntactic behavior is concerned, French CMCs resemble more grammaticalized modals like *pouvoir* 'can' or *devoir* 'must' in certain respects, but in other respects, they still resemble plain verbs.

According to Chu (2008: 25–28, 31–32), when the verb phrase includes an inflected modal like *pouvoir* and *devoir*, it is not the modal but the infinitival verb which is the head of the verb phrase, i.e. the element that carries the central information about the denoted situation. As a consequence, it is the infinitive which determines the argument structure of the verb phrase, i.e. the number and the characteristics of the complements. In the case of CMCs, the argument structure is (at least partly) determined by the infinitival verb. On the one hand, *faire mieux de* imposes no constraints on the number of arguments; rather, it adopts the argument structure of the infinitival verb. This indicates that the infinitival verb is the head in the verb phrase, as is the infinitival verb in the case of *pouvoir* and *devoir*. On the other hand, *valoir mieux* and *falloir mieux* seem to retain some elements of their argument structure. They are characterized by the deletion of the subject (which is replaced by a dummy *il*) due to their impersonal nature, and, in formal genres, they may license an additional argument (typically a dative clitic) in addition to the arguments of the non-finite verb. In (10a) and (10b), for instance, *valoir mieux* and *falloir mieux* possess what superficially look like indirect objects (*me* and *te*), while the infinitival verbs have their own indirect objects (*aux dieux* 'to the gods', *à la fibre* 'to fibre optics'). It follows, then, that *valoir mieux* and *falloir mieux* behave more like lexical verbs with regard to argument structure.

(10) a. *Il me vaut mieux obéir aux dieux qu'*
It DAT.1SG be.worth.PRS.3SG better obey to the gods than

*aux hommes.*
to.the men

'I'd better obey to gods than to men.'
(*Le semeur*, newspaper, 1835, Google books, accessed on 26 January 2012)

b. *Il te faut mieux passer à la fibre.*
it DAT.2SG have.to.PRS.3SG better switch to the fibre
'You'd better switch to fibre optics.'
(Google, accessed on 26 January 2012)

Furthermore, CMCs impose constraints on the status of the participants. In contrast to *pouvoir* and *devoir*, they require that the subject be animate; compare in this respect (11a) with (11b) and (11c). This suggests that, even in the case of *faire mieux de*, CMCs still have a certain influence on the argument structure. In conclusion, unlike with *pouvoir* and *devoir*, the infinitival verb cannot be fully regarded as the head of the verb phrase, especially when it is combined with *valoir mieux* and *falloir mieux*.

(11) a.  La   table  **pourrait/devrait**  être  là.
         the  table  could/should          be    there
         'The table could/should be here.'

   b.  ??*La  table  **ferait**        mieux    d'   être  là.
       the    table  do.COND.3SG       better   of   be    there
       'The table had better be here.'

   c.  *Il  **vaut/faut**              mieux   être  là    (pour la table).
       It   be.worth/have.to.PRS.3SG   better  be    there (for the table)
       'The table had better be here'.⁵

Then again, there is another fact which suggests that the infinitival verb is not a complement of the CMC, which makes CMCs more similar to modals like *pouvoir* and *devoir*. According to Chu (2008: 35–36), the impossibility to pronominalize the infinitival verb shows that the latter is not governed by the finite verb. In the case of CMCs, the picture is rather clear-cut: the infinitival verb cannot normally be replaced by an anaphoric pronoun (such as *le* 'it'). Like *devoir* and *pouvoir* (12a), it rather prefers a null anaphoric complement (see 12b, 12c).⁶

(12) a.  *Doit- il/peut- il  acheter    le   journal?*
         must he/can he      buy.INF    the  newspaper?

         ?*Oui, il  le  **doit/peut**.*
         yes,  he  it  must/can

   vs.  *Oui, il  **doit/peut**.*⁷
        yes, he   must/can
        'Does he have to/can he buy the newspaper?
        lit. 'Yes, he has to/can it.' vs. 'Yes, he has to/can.'

---

**5** When no source is given in the rest of article, the example is constructed, as is the case for examples (11) to (14).

**6** No such occurrences are found in *Frantext*, but an exploratory Google search revealed that the combination is possible with *valoir mieux*. These cases are, however, considered to be very formal. e.g. *La jeune femme est honnête et ne mentira jamais, même s'il LE **vaudrait mieux**, parfois.* 'The young woman is honest and will never lie, even though she'**d better** IT, sometimes' (Google, accessed on 26 January 2012)

**7** The combination of *pouvoir* and *devoir* with an anaphoric pronoun also sounds very formal.

b. *Ferait           -il mieux d' acheter le   journal?*
   do.COND.3SG he better of buy.INF the newspaper

   *?Oui, il <u>le</u> ferait        mieux.*
   yes  he it do.COND.3SG better

vs. *Oui, il ferait         mieux.*
    yes he do.COND.3SG better
    'Had he better buy the newspaper?
    lit: Yes, he'd better it. vs. Yes, he'd better.'

c. *Vaut/faut           -il mieux acheter le   journal?*
   be.worth/have.to.PRS.3SG it better buy   the newspaper

   *?Oui, il <u>le</u> vaut/faut           mieux.*
   yes  it it be.worth/have.to.PRS.3SG better

vs. *Oui il vaut/faut           mieux*
    yes it be.worth/have.to.PRS.3SG better
    'Had he better buy the newspaper?
    lit: Yes, he'd better <u>it</u>. vs. Yes, he'd better.'

A final property of CMCs is the *syntagmatic fixation* of the sequence [CMC + infinitive]. For Chu (2008: 27), the modal verb and the infinitival verb form a cohesive syntactic entity. This is why *devoir* and *pouvoir* require the use of the verbal proform *faire* in (pseudo-)cleft constructions and questions, so as not to be separated from the infinitival verb. And so does *faire mieux* (see 13b, 14b), which thus behaves like a modal verb. By contrast, with *valoir/falloir mieux*, the verbal proform is optional, as in (13c) and (13d); these verbs thus occupy an intermediate position on the cline between ordinary verbs and modal verbs, as in (13c) and (14c).

(13) a. *\*Ce qu' il  doit/peut,  c'  est   partir.*
        what  he must/can   it  is   leave.INF

   vs. *Ce qu' il  doit/peut faire,  c'  est  partir.*
       what  he must/can  do.INF  it is  leave.INF
       'lit. What he must/can is to leave. *vs.* What he must/can do is to leave.'

   b. *\*Ce qu' il  ferait         mieux, c'  est   partir.*
      What  he do.COND.3SG better    it  is   leave.INF

   vs. *Ce qu' il  ferait         mieux de faire,  c'  est  partir.*
       What  he do.COND.3SG better    of do.INF  it is  leave.INF
       'lit: What he had better is to leave. *vs.* What he had better do is to leave.'

    c. *Ce qu' il **vaut/faut** **mieux** (pour lui)*
       what it be.worth/have.to.PRS.3SG better for him
       *c' est (de) partir.*
       it is of leave.INF

   vs. *Ce qu' il **vaut/faut** **mieux** <u>faire</u>*
      what it be.worth/have.to.PRS.3SG better do
      *(pour lui), c' est (de) partir.*[8]
      for him it is of leave.INF
      'lit: What he had better is to leave. *vs.* What he had better do is to leave.'

(14) a. **Que doit/peut* -il?*
      What must/can he

   vs. *Que **doit/peut** -il <u>faire</u>?*
      What must/can he do
      'lit: What must/can he? *vs.* What must/can he do?

   b. **Que ferait -il mieux?*
      what do.COND.3SG he better

   vs. *Que **ferait** -il **mieux** de <u>faire</u>?*
      what do.COND.3SG he better of do.INF
      'What had he better? *vs.* What had he better <u>do</u>?'

   c. *Que **vaut/faut** -il **mieux**?*
      what be.worth/have.to.PRS.3SG it better

   vs. *Que **vaut/faut** -il **mieux** <u>faire</u>?*
      what be.worth/have.to.PRS.3SG it better do.INF
      'lit: What had he better? *vs* What had he better do?'

In sum, *faire mieux de* is more firmly connected to the infinitive (just like the modals *devoir* and *pouvoir*) than *valoir mieux* and *falloir mieux*, which allow for more syntagmatic variability.

Concluding this section on syntactic properties, we want to note that with French CMCs, as with modal verbs, the non-finite verb is not a complement

---

**8** Another possibility based on *ce qu'* (instead of *ce qu'il*) is also attested in less formal registers:

(i) <u>*Ce qui* **vaut mieux**</u> *(faire), c' est partir.*
   what be.worth.PRS.3SG do.INF it is leave.INF
   'What is better (to do) is to leave.'

governed by the CMC (it cannot be pronominalized). At the same time, CMCs, and more specifically *valoir mieux* and *falloir mieux*, also resemble lexical verbs in that they still exert some influence on the argument structure. In the following section, we will investigate whether these properties may be interpreted as a sign of decategorialization (e.g. Heine 1993, Heine 2003; Heine and Kuteva 2007; Lamiroy and Drobnjakovic 2009).

One may further distinguish between *faire mieux* on the one hand, which resembles modals in forming a close unit with the infinitive, and *valoir mieux* and *faire mieux*, on the other hand, which may still be separated from it. This confirms what we noted in Section 2.1, namely the higher degree of syntagmatic variability of *valoir mieux* and *falloir mieux* compared to *faire mieux de*, which exhibits greater fixation to the main verb. It follows that *faire mieux de* is best seen as a structurally more grammaticalized construction than *valoir mieux* and *falloir mieux*.

The next section will explore the diachrony of CMCs and seek to establish to what extent the source constructions determine the structural properties observed in Present-day French.

# 3 The development of French CMCs

## 3.1 Some diachronic data

*Valoir mieux* is the oldest of the three constructions, with attestations from the second half of the 13th century onward (15). *Faire mieux de* (16) and *falloir mieux* (17) are first attested in the 15th century.

(15) **Miex** li **vauroit** chi demourer
 better it be.worth.COND.3SG here stay.INF
 *Que prendre la crois d'outremer, S'il ne se paie netement.*
 'He had better stay here than go on a crusade overseas (...).'
 (*Frantext*, Ruteboeuf, *Œuvres complètes*, ca 1249–1277)

(16) *Et* **eusses** **mieulx fait** *de non parler dudit*
 and have.SBJV.2PL better do.PPTCP of not talk about.said
 *traictié que tu appelles traictié de paix.*
 treaty that you call treaty of peace
 'And you had better not talk about the aforementioned treaty that you call peace treaty.'
 (*Frantext moyen français*, Jean Juvenal des Ursins, *Audite celi*, 1435)

(17) *Neantmoins* **faut-** *il [**mieulx**] premièrement avoir*
nevertheless have.to.PRS.3SG it better first have

*du malheur que de l' heur,*
of.the bad.luck than of the luck

*et doit-on prendre en pascience les choses ameres et les diversitez de fortune, qui vuelt parvenir à hault estat.*

'Nevertheless it is better to be first unfortunate than fortunate (...).'
                (*Frantext moyen français*, Jean de Bueil, *Le Jouvencel*, 1461–1466)

The existence of *falloir mieux* in Middle French is quite surprising given the fact that today it is still considered incorrect in normative grammars.

The diachronic data suggest that the crucial period for the grammaticalization of *valoir mieux* is the 14th century, during which the construction shows an important increase in frequency (Figure 4). From this period onward, the overall frequency remains relatively high, with between 22 and 53 occurrences per million words.

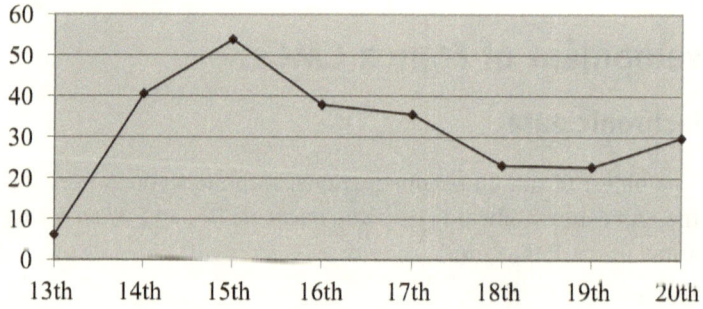

**Figure 4:** *Valoir mieux*: frequency (number of occurrences per million words)

No such striking rise in frequency has been observed for *faire mieux de* or for *falloir mieux*, but both constructions seem to have gradually increased in frequency from the 15th century onward.[9] Their more modest increase points toward a less advanced grammaticalization of *faire mieux de* and *falloir mieux*, as compared to *valoir mieux*, which rapidly gained in frequency after its emergence in Middle French.

---

[9] *Falloir mieux*'s higher frequency in the 15th century is only due to two occurrences that were found in the corpus, which was quite small (approximately 3,295,023 words).

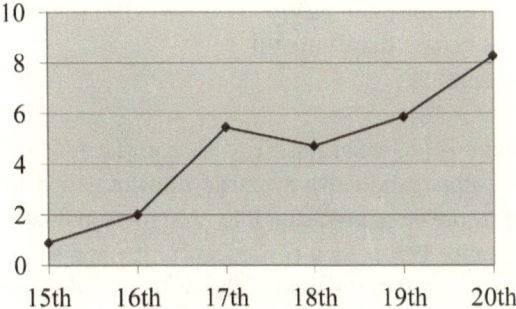

**Figure 5:** *Faire mieux de*: frequency (number of occurrences per million words)

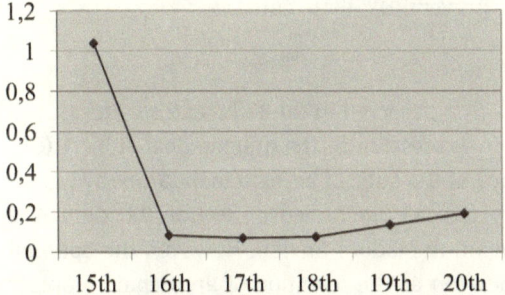

**Figure 6:** *Falloir mieux*: frequency (number of occurrences per million words)

The next section investigates the constructional origins of French CMCs and tries to emphasize how the source constructions from which they derive account for some of the synchronic properties that we have discussed in Section 2.

## 3.2 Hypotheses on the origin of French CMCs

### 3.2.1 *Valoir mieux:* Two constructional origins

*Valoir mieux* developed from the lexical verb *x valoir y* 'x be worth y', where x was in most cases a noun phrase. *Mieux* was then used to compare the value of x with an element z, which did not need to be made explicit: *x vaut mieux (que z)* 'lit. x is worth better (than z)'. As in other languages, the slot of the grammatical subject can be occupied by an infinitive verb (or a subordinate clause), as in (18). We argue that sentences such as these were the source construction of the *valoir mieux* construction.

(18) *Prévenir*　　**vaut**　　　　　　　*mieux (que guérir).*
　　　prevent.INF　be.worth.PRS.3SG　better　than　cure.INF
　　　'To prevent is better (than to cure).'

The first constructional subtype – [*(il) valoir mieux* + INF (or *que* + SUBJ)] (Section 2.1) – is the result of a rather productive syntactic transformation in French, which allows turning an intransitive predicate into an impersonal construction (e.g. Gaatone 1970; Legendre 1990). As a consequence, the subject x, whether infinitival or clausal, is extraposed to the right of the verb and a dummy *il* 'it' takes the position of the subject.

(19) *(Il)* **vaut**　　　　　*mieux* *prévenir*　　*(que guérir).*
　　　It　be.worth.PRS.3SG　better　prevent.INF　than　cure.INF
　　　'To prevent is better (than to cure).'

When this transformation was first observed in the 13th century, French still allowed a null subject, i.e. the non-expression of the grammatical subject (e.g. Vance 1988). However, the presence of the subject became mandatory by Classical French (from the 16th century on). As mentioned in Section 2.1, dummy *il* seems to have become optional again in Modern French. However, the optional non-expression of *il* should not be seen as the retention of an archaic property due to high frequency (Bybee 2003, Bybee 2006); rather, it should be considered a consequence of the tendency in colloquial French to delete, with certain verbs, the impersonal *il* which is uninformative (see Blanche-Benveniste 2010).

The second constructional subtype – [*mieux valoir* + INF (or *que* + SUBJ)] – originates in the syntax of Old French, which was characterized by a verb second (V2) word order (Marchello-Nizia 1995: 61–67; Buridant 2000: 741–756), that is, the verb mostly occurred in second position and could be preceded by any kind of constituent. This feature progressively disappeared during Middle French and gave way to the stricter subject–verb order (XXX)SV(XXX), which is characteristic of Modern French.[10] In line with the V2 feature, still present in Middle French, *mieux* could occur in preverbal position while the infinitival or clausal subject could take postverbal position, as in (20).

(20) **Mieux vaut**　　　　　*prévenir*　　*(que guérir).*
　　　better　be.worth.PRS.3SG　prevent.INF　than　cure.INF
　　　'To prevent is better (than to cure).'

---

**10** X refers to a constituent that is neither subject nor verb.

This means that the construction [*mieux valoir x*] was not originally impersonal. It is therefore to be distinguished from the first subtype [*(il) valoir mieux x*], which is the result of an impersonal transformation.

The fact that this second construction was maintained up to Modern French (Section 2.1) clearly is indicative of the retention of archaic properties of the syntax of Medieval French, in particular, that this subtype was entrenched enough (and sufficiently grammaticalized) to maintain conservative features into the modern language (Bybee 2003, 2006).

### 3.2.2 *Faire mieux de:* A conditional origin?

At the time of its emergence in the 15th century, *faire mieux de* coexisted with another (less frequent) variant which seems to have disappeared after the Classical period.[11] This variant combined with a *si*-clause instead of the prepositional phrase introduced by *de*: [*faire mieux si* + FINITE CLAUSE], as in (21).

(21) *Et   ainsi je diray,   qu'  il   eust                    mieux fait,*
and  so   I  say.FUT that he have.SBJV.3SG better do.PPTCP
*s'il eust employé sa plume à rimer comme Du-Bartas.*[12]
'And so I will say that he had done better to use his quill to rhyme like Du-Bartasil (lit. would have better done, if he had used his quill to rhyme like Du-Bartas).'
(*Frantext*, Pierre de Deimier, *L'académie de l'art poétique*, 1610)

In this construction, *faire* was a dummy verb with a proform function: its role was to refer (anaphorically or cataphorically) to the situation denoted in the conditional clause. So in (21), dummy *faire* refers to the situation *il eust employé sa plume à rimer comme Du-Bartas*, which was deemed to be a better alternative for the agent *il* 'he'.

It is noteworthy that in most cases, the conditional sentence is an irrealis conditional. As a consequence, the conditional tense and the imperfect are the tenses that are most commonly used [*faire*.COND *mieux si* X.IMP], along with the pluperfect subjunctive [*faire*.PLU.SBJV *mieux si* X.PLU.SBJV], as in (21), which was

---

[11] Seven occurrences were observed in the 15th and 16th centuries (against 15 occurrences of *faire mieux de* for the same period).
[12] *S'* is the contracted form of *si*.

functionally equivalent to the past conditional.¹³ We saw in Section 2.3 that the conditional tense was used as a politeness device to mitigate the speech act of the speaker and preserve the face of the addressee: by presenting a piece of advice as unreal, the speaker allows the addressee to see it as a mere supposition and disregard it. By using an imperfect subjunctive or the past conditional, the speaker rather refers to what should have been done and thus expresses regret.

We hypothesize that *faire mieux de* is a simplified version of this conditional construction. For (21), this simplification would give rise to example (21').

(21') *Et    ainsi je diray,     qu'  il   **eust**                **mieux fait**        **d'***
and so    I    say.FUT that he have. SBJV.3SG better do.PPTCP of
*employer sa plume à rimer comme Du-Bartas.*

'And so I will say that he'd better have used his quill to rhyme like Du-Bartas.'

We may now wonder why *faire mieux de* combines with the preposition *de* (*faire mieux de* + INF) instead of a bare infinitive (*faire mieux* + INF), as do the two other CMCs *valoir mieux* and *falloir mieux*. One possible reason is the frequent use of *de* in French to introduce an alternative situation in expressions such as (*plutôt*) *que de* (22), or *au lieu de* 'instead of'.

(22) *Si par dextérité tu n'en peux rien tirer,*
*Accorde    tout        **plutôt que de** plus    différer.*
accept.IMP everything rather than    more postpone

'If you did not manage, using your skills, accept everything instead of postponing more.'

(Frantext, Pierre Corneille, La Veuve ou le Traître trahi, 1634)

As a consequence, the use of *de* may have developed to allow for a morphological parallel to the expression of the standard of comparison [*faire mieux* DE X (*plutôt*) *que/au lieu* DE Y)].

---

**13** That is why the pluperfect subjunctive is sometimes called *conditionnel passé deuxième forme* 'second form past conditional'. The pluperfect subjunctive may still be used in Modern French but sounds very archaic.

(23) "Il me semble, monsieur, que vous en avez assez faict pour ceste heure,
et que vous **ferez** **mieulx** DE penser à saulve
and that you do.COND.2PL better of think.INF of save

vostre vie, **_que de_** la vouloir oster à aultres."
your life than it want.to take to others

'It seems to me, sire, that you have done enough so far, and that you'd
better think about saving your life than willing to take it from others.'
(*Frantext*, Marguerite de Navarre, *L'Heptaméron*, 1550)

The hypothesis that *faire mieux de* developed out of *irrealis* conditionals may explain why the conditional tense is predominant with *faire mieux de* (Section 2.3). This, then, would be a feature inherited from the source construction [*faire*.COND *mieux si* X.IMP].

Finally, we may note that *faire mieux de* could also be used in the future tense, and that this use was fairly frequent up to Classical French (23).[14] This indirectly confirms the conditional origin of the CMC. Even though we found no attestations, it is plausible that the future tense variant developed out of *potentialis* conditionals (and not irrealis conditionals), which are formed with the future tense and the present tense. Accordingly, the source construction would be [*faire*.FUT *mieux si* X.PRS]. From Classical French onward, the future tense is used less, in favor of the conditional tense, which is now almost obligatory. As we noted in Section 2.3, this can be viewed as a sign of grammaticalization in at least two respects: an increasingly defective conjugation implies a rigidification (or increased fixation) of the construction and it indicates the loss of the morphosyntactic properties of plain verbs (or decategorialization) and the adoption of more modal-like characteristics.

### 3.2.3 *Falloir mieux*: Confusion with *valoir mieux*

The emergence of *falloir mieux* in the 15th century plausibly stems from the confusion with the already grammaticalized *valoir mieux* construction, the only difference between the constructions being the initial labio-dental consonant of the verb (voiced in the case of *valoir mieux* and unvoiced in the case of *falloir mieux*). This confusion may have led to the reanalysis of the existing sequence [[*falloir*][*mieux* X]], in which *mieux* modifies the non-finite verb X (24), as the

---

[14] We observed 9 occurrences in the future tense between 1500 and 1639 (against 32 occurrences in the conditional tense or in the pluperfect subjunctive).

sequence [[*falloir mieux*][x]], in which *falloir mieux* forms a linguistic entity associated with the non-finite verb (25). In principle, both readings are possible, and it is the context which determines the correct interpretation.

(24) *Attendez Abonde, ne veuillez courrir si furieusement:*
    *il* **nous** *en*     **faut**             *mieux informer.*
    it us    about.it have.to.PRS.3SG better inform.INF

'Wait Abonde, don't run so furiously: we have to get better informed about it.'             (*Frantext*, Jean de La Taille, *Le Négromant*, 1573)

(25) *Mais que finallement lesdits comtes et luy arresterent que pour le bien du royaume...,*
    *il* **falloit**             *mieux couronner Charles.*
    it have.to.IPFV.3SG better crown.INF Charles

'... it was better to crown Charles.'
            (*Frantext*, Claude Fauchet, *Declin de la maison de Charlemagne*, 1602)

However, when *falloir mieux* is followed by a subjunctive clause, its interpretation as a CMC is the only one possible as *mieux* cannot modify an object clause. This implies that the construction with the subjunctive clause [*falloir mieux que* + SUBJ] necessarily appeared in a second step, after the construction with the infinitive [*falloir mieux* + INF] was reanalyzed as a CMC. Unfortunately, the diachronic data on *falloir mieux* are too scarce to confirm this hypothesis.

The proposed hypothesis on the origin of *falloir mieux* explains many of its observed synchronic characteristics. First, the confusion with *valoir mieux* accounts for the morphosyntactic similarities between the two constructions. They can both be construed either with a bare infinitive or with a subjunctive clause, they exhibit the same tense distribution (e.g. the predominance of the present tense), and they are very similar in terms of syntactic behavior (Section 2.4). As well, the development of *falloir mieux* in the 15th century, when French had turned to the stricter subject–verb order, explains why *falloir mieux*, unlike *valoir mieux* ([*mieux valoir* x]), cannot normally occur with *mieux* in the preverbal position ([?*mieux falloir* x]). The verb second feature, which had previously favored the emergence of the *mieux*-initial construction, had almost disappeared by the time *falloir mieux* came into being.[15]

---

[15] We found no such examples in our corpus. However, an exploratory Google search revealed that this word order is possible, albeit characteristic of very informal register. e.g. *Quand ça va,* **mieux faut** *aussi le dire.* 'When everything is ok, one **had better** also say it.' (Google, accessed on 26 January 2012)

## 3.3 On the grammaticalization of French CMCs

To conclude this diachronic section, we want to stress that historical data are essential to properly assess the grammaticalization of linguistic items. In the case of the French CMCs, it has been shown that some of the synchronic morphosyntactic properties do not reflect a particular stage of grammaticalization, but rather mirror features of the source constructions.

Crucially, the modal-like syntactic properties of French CMCs (Section 2.3) do not in all cases result from decategorialization. Actually, this is only the case for *valoir mieux*, which developed out of the lexical verb *valoir*. By contrast, *faire mieux de* probably derives from the conditional construction [*faire*.COND *mieux si* X.IMP], in which *faire* functions as a verbal proform. If this is the case, the source construction already exhibited a defective conjugation (only the tenses allowed in conditional sentences were possible) and there was no constraint on the argument structure (since the proform *faire* could refer to any kind of predicate). Consequently, there was probably no decategorialization in the case of *faire mieux de*. *Falloir mieux* exhibits the same argument structure as modal *falloir*, from which it is derived.[16] It follows that there was presumably no decategorialization in the case of *falloir mieux* either.

However, the diachronic data also allow us to confirm some aspects of grammaticalization suggested by by the synchronic data. First, the historical data support the claim that *faire mieux de* gained in syntagmatic fixation when grammaticalizing (through reduction and through obligatorification of the conditional tense). The data also partly explain why *valoir mieux* shows synchronic syntagmatic variability. One reason could be that *valoir mieux* is actually based on two distinct constructions, which were maintained up to Modern French.

As a final remark, we would like to underline that French CMCs seem to instantiate two types of moderate grammaticalization. On the one hand, *valoir mieux* showed a drastic increase in frequency when it emerged in Middle French and, at that time, it became sufficiently entrenched for features from the medieval language to be maintained. However, in Modern French, the construction still has a high degree of syntagmatic variability and is only loosely fixed to the main verb. On the other hand, *faire mieux de* has grammaticalized to a higher degree of syntagmatic fixation, but the construction still remains moderately infrequent (although it seems to be gaining in frequency). This illustrates that entrenchment on the one hand and syntagmatic fixation on the other hand do not necessarily go hand in hand in cases of moderate grammaticalization.

---

**16** Modal *falloir* also requires an animate agent (e.g. *\*Il **faut** pleuvoir* 'It must rain'), which may be expressed by a dative clitic (e.g. *Il te* [DAT.2SG] ***faut** rentrer* 'You must go back home.').

# 4 The semantics of CMCs

This final section returns to the synchronic use of French CMCs, with a focus on their semantics. The section aims to determine more precisely to what extent CMCs in Modern French are influenced by their source constructions and to what extent they is the result of grammaticalization and semantic change.

## 4.1 From evaluation to deonticity and directivity

French CMCs can be said to convey "modal" meanings in the broad sense, pertaining to the expression of subjective attitude or judgment of the speaker toward the expressed state of affairs. As the three CMCs all involve the comparative adverb of superiority *mieux* 'better', their source meaning can be viewed to be *evaluative*, i.e. it expresses value judgments. The situation denoted is evaluated as preferable and more suitable, possibly in comparison to another situation given in the context. This "evaluative" meaning is still quite common in Modern French, as in (26).

(26) *Pour qui exerce un métier sans doute*
for who practices a craft without doubt
**vaut-** *il* **mieux** *être "en forme".*
be.worth.PRS.3SG it better be in shape
'For someone who practices a craft, it **is** no doubt **better** to be "in shape".'
(*Frantext*, Jean-Bertrand Pontalis, *Fenêtres*)

The analysis of the synchronic corpora shows that, besides evaluation, CMCs may carry additional modal interpretations.[17] They may convey *deonticity* and express a participant-external necessity (van der Auwera and Plungian 1998: 81). In such examples, the CMC refers to an obligation related to certain ethical or social norms, as in (27).

(27) *Il* **faut** *mieux parler comme tout le monde.*
It have.to.PRS.3SG better talk.INF like whole the world
'It is better to talk like everybody else.' (*Elicop*)

---

[17] The proposed classification is solely based on semantic criteria, i.e. the interpretation associated with the observed CMCs.

CMCs may also convey *directivity*. In contrast with deontic modality, directivity involves some "action" plan (see Nuyts et al. 2005: 9) and resembles senses conveyed by mood markers such as the imperative as the addressee is incited to engage in the state of affairs. In directive uses, the CMCs typically express an advice, a threat, a command, etc., as in (28).

(28) Tu **ferais** **mieux** de préparer le souper
you do.COND.2SG better of prepare.INF the dinner

que de discutailler sur l' histoire contemporaine.
than of discuss on the history contemporary

'You'd better prepare dinner than discuss contemporary history.'
(*Frantext*, Raymond Queneau, *Les fleurs bleues*)

CMCs may also occasionally occur in *optative* contexts, as in (29), in which they serve to formulate a wish, a hope or (most often) a regret.

(29) Ah! Les blancs. Ils **feraient** bien **mieux**
ah! the whites they do.COND.3PL much better

de rentrer chez eux, tous.
of return.INF with them all

'Ah! The whites! They'd better go back home, all of them.'
(*Frantext*, René Maran, *Batouala, véritable roman nègre*)

Figure 7 represents the distribution (in percentages) of the different interpretations of CMCs in the synchronic corpora.

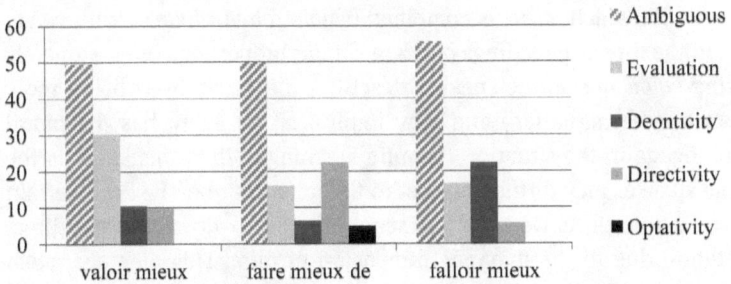

**Figure 7:** Interpretations of French CMCs (in percentages)

The data show several things. First, in most cases, the interpretation of the CMCs is ambiguous and cannot be said to be clearly evaluative, deontic or directive (or optative). This indicates that the context is crucial to determine the precise interpretation of the CMCs. Second, all the CMCs may receive one of the three modal interpretations evaluation, deonticity or directivity, whereas the optative interpretation seems to be available only for *faire mieux de*. Interestingly, each CMC also tends to be specialized to some extent in expressing one of the different modal meanings. *Valoir mieux* is more inclined to convey evaluation (30%). *Faire mieux de* is more directive (22%), although it also often serves to give an evaluative judgment (16%). Finally, *falloir mieux* is more inclined toward deonticity (22%), but it also quite often conveys evaluation (almost 17%).

These results clearly reflect the compositionality of the source constructions. In the case of *valoir mieux*, the two components of the construction – *valoir* 'be worth' and *mieux* 'better' – have an intrinsic evaluative meaning. This semantic synergy explains why evaluative interpretations are by far the most frequent, even though *valoir mieux* may also receive non-evaluative (deontic and directive) readings. With the other two CMCs, the association of the verbs *faire* and *falloir* with the comparative *mieux* more easily gives rise to other modal interpretations, due to the semantics of those verbs. The evaluative sense conveyed by *mieux* still surfaces in 16 to 17% of the cases, but in 22% it is the meaning of the verb that seems to take precedence. As *faire* refers to a dynamic situation (which is typically performed by an agent), directive interpretations are favored: the addressee is expected to act in an adequate manner. With *falloir*, which is a deontic auxiliary, the dominant reading is, unsurprisingly, deontic: the construction serves to express a moral obligation.

These non-evaluative interpretations of the CMCs may be viewed as modal readings derived from the compositional meaning of each construction via *pragmatic inferencing* (Heine 2002; Traugott and Dasher 2002). More precisely, the modal inferences may be triggered by the evaluative meaning of *mieux*, with the deontic or directive (or optative) interpretations being preferred depending on the verb with which *mieux* is combined (*valoir*, *faire* or *falloir*). With *valoir*, the deontic and the directive readings occur in similar proportions (approximately 10%). By using *valoir mieux*, the speaker describes the situation as being more suitable (than another situation) and may imply that an agent has the moral obligation to engage in the situation (deontic meaning). When this agent is the addressee, the speaker may further suggest to the latter that he/she act a certain way (directive meaning). As we have just seen, *faire mieux de* prefers the directive interpretation due to the dynamic dimension of *faire*. This may also stem from the fact that *faire mieux* is used more in the second person than in the other persons, which often triggers the inference of a directive speech act. Finally, in the case of *falloir mieux*, the deontic meaning is not the result of an inferential process, but rather reflects the semantics of the construction and the intrinsic deonticity of *falloir*. The evaluative meaning of *mieux* then reinforces this dimension (instead of causing it) as the moral obligation is explicitly said to rest upon the social norm of "what is better". Note that, in some contexts (17%), *falloir mieux* is interpreted evaluatively, as the evaluative sense of *mieux* is emphasized at the expense of the semantics of *falloir*.

The fact that the different interpretations of the CMCs still reflect the semantics of their components points toward the *persistence* (Hopper 1991) of the original meaning of the constructions (most notably in the case of *valoir mieux* and *falloir mieux*). However, CMCs have developed additional deontic and directive interpretations via the triggering of pragmatic inferences. Note that this semantic evolution does not manifest any desemanticization. First, the acquisition of a new meaning – whether deontic, directive or optative – is clearly not completed. The evaluative component of the source constructions is still available, although it may yield further modal inferences. Second, the semantic shift toward a deontic, directive or even optative meaning does not reflect the loss of semantic substance but rather corresponds to a semantic enrichment on top of the positive evaluation carried by *mieux*. Some contexts allow for additional deontic or directive (or optative) meanings which provide further information about the subjective attitude or judgment of the speaker toward the state of affairs. One must conclude that the grammaticalization of French CMCs has operated at the structural level but not at the semantic level.

## 4.2 The expression of a standard of comparison

The CMCs contain the comparative adverb *mieux* 'better', which entails that the denoted situation is compared with a standard of comparison (henceforth SoC), namely another situation. To further assess the weight of the comparative meaning in the semantics of each CMC, we have examined the expression of SoCs in the synchronic corpora. The results are given in Figure 8.

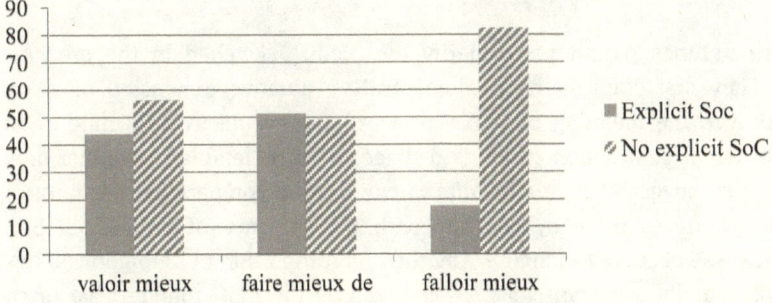

**Figure 8:** French CMCs and the expression of a standard of comparison (SoC) (in percentages)

We can observe that *valoir mieux* and *faire mieux de* are still frequently used with an explicit SoC (respectively 44% and 51% of the occurrences). Sometimes the SoC is introduced by means of a connector, e.g. *au lieu de* in (30), but most often it is simply given in the textual context without any grammatical marker connecting it to the verb phrase containing the CMC, as in (31). By contrast, in the majority of cases (82%), *falloir mieux* does not require the expression of an SoC, as in (32).

(30) Vous **feriez** mieux de m' aider,
you.PL do.COND.2PL better of me help.INF
*au lieu de* vous prélasser.
instead.of REFL take.a.rest
'You'd better help me, instead of taking a rest.'
(Frantext, Irène Monési, *Nature morte devant la fenêtre*)

(31) *Mais si le service civil n'est ... que l'occasion de profiter à bon compte d'une masse de main d'œuvre,*
**mieux vaut** alors qu' il ne voie jamais le jour.
better be.worth.PRS.3SG then that it not sees ever the day
'But if the service civil is only the occasion to easily use a huge workforce, it **is** better that it never comes into being.'
(Frantext, *Service militaire et réforme de l'armée, par le Groupe d'étude des problèmes du contingent*)

(32) **Faut mieux continuer** à pieds
have.to.PRS.3SG better continue.INF on foot
*à cause qu'on sait jamais c'qu'y nous attend.*
'Better go on by foot because you never know what's going to happen.'
(Frantext, Frédéric Lasaygues, *Vache noire, hannetons et autres insectes*)

These findings permit us to clarify the picture sketched in the previous section. They first confirm the predominantly evaluative dimension of *valoir mieux*. Due to the meaning of *valoir* 'be worth', *valoir mieux* still quite often serves to denote a situation which is deemed to be preferable to another one. Figure 8 also suggests that, with *faire mieux de*, the comparative meaning of *mieux* still surfaces in many contexts with the presence of an explicit SoC (51%). This was obscured in Figure 7 by the high proportion of ambiguous interpretations. Finally, we learn that *falloir mieux* is the CMC that is least often accompanied by the expression of an SoC. This result is not surprising given that the construction, which is based on the modal *falloir*, is inherently deontic. Deontic interpretations of *falloir mieux* are consequently not the result of desemanticization, but rather of the persistence of features of the source construction.

To complete the picture, we may now compare the situation of Present-day French to that of Renaissance French (from 1500 to 1599). Given the very limited number of hits for *falloir mieux* in Renaissance French, we only present the results for *valoir mieux* (Figure 9) and *faire mieux* (Figure 10).

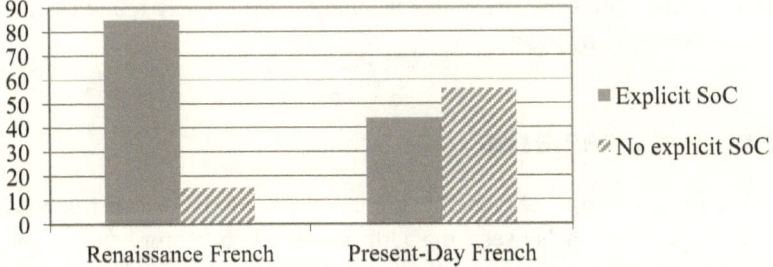

**Figure 9:** *Valoir mieux* and the expression of standard of comparison (SoC) in Renaissance and Present-day French (in percentages)

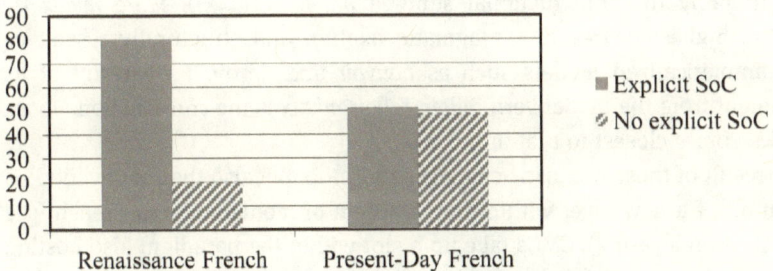

**Figure 10:** *Faire mieux de* and the expression of a standard of comparison (SoC) in Renaissance and Present-day French (in percentages)

Figures 9 and 10 show that *valoir mieux* and *faire mieux de* require the expression of an SoC less in Present-day French than in Renaissance French. This demonstrates that, although *valoir mieux* and *faire mieux de* retain a clear comparative dimension in Present-day French, they have also moved away from this evaluative meaning to develop other, modal (deontic and directive) senses. In the case of *valoir mieux*, these modal readings are nevertheless peripheral and evaluation remains central due to the evaluative lexical meaning of *valoir* (Section 4.1).

In conclusion, French CMCs have semantically evolved since they emerged in the 14th and 15th century, but this evolution has been rather modest. Whereas the semantics of the source constructions was evaluative due to the adverb *mieux*, the CMCs have developed new modal (mainly deontic and directive) interpretations. However, as pointed out in Section 4.1, this development is not the result of semantic bleaching. Indeed, the evaluative interpretations are still prominent in the case of *valoir mieux* and *faire mieux de* (with a relative presence of SoC ranging between 43% and 51%). The interpretation of *falloir mieux* is more independent of the comparative meaning of *mieux* but, in this construction, evaluation is not the source meaning, *mieux* merely reinforces the deontic sense conveyed by *falloir*.

# 5 Concluding remarks

French CMCs are an example of moderate grammaticalization. The constructions emerged in Middle French between the 13th and the 15th century from three different source forms – a lexical verb, a verbal proform, and an auxiliary – and have accordingly followed different paths of grammaticalization to end up, in Modern French, as semi-modals. *Valoir mieux* is the most entrenched of the three constructions and it retains, for this reason, some features of Medieval French (notably the constructional subtype [*mieux vaut* x]). *Faire mieux de* shows the highest degree of syntagmatic fixation and structurally resembles more grammaticalized modals such as *pouvoir* and *devoir*. As a result of its development from the modal verb *falloir*, *falloir mieux* is the construction whose semantics comes closest to that of modals.

The result of these linguistic changes (and probably also their motivation) is the creation of a new layer within the paradigm of modal verbs in French (see Hopper 1991 on layering). CMCs take up a slot within the paradigm also hosting the deontic *devoir* and *falloir* and the epistemic *pouvoir*. More precisely, they introduce a new category of deontic modals which subordinate the deontic assessment to an evaluative judgment (because of the adverb *mieux*).[18]

French CMCs can also be said to form a paradigm of their own within that of deontic modals. Within this CMC paradigm, each construction differs as to the degree of speaker involvement: *valoir mieux* instantiates weak involvement, which takes the form of a comparison between two states of affairs (evaluative meaning); *falloir mieux* implies a stronger involvement, with the speaker asserting a moral obligation (deontic meaning); and *faire mieux de*, finally, carries an even stronger involvement with the speaker pressing the addressee to act adequately (directive meaning). However, the integration into the new paradigm,

---

[18] Lehmann (2002) also talks about paradigmaticization.

or paradigmaticization (Lehmann 2002), is only incipient. CMCs still exhibit a large degree of paradigmatic variability, both on the semantic side – the functional specialization of each construction is far from being complete – and on the structural side – CMCs do not show any uniform morphosyntactic properties.

## Acknowledgments

The authors wish to thank the two anonymous reviewers for their useful comments.

## Abbreviations

1/2/3 = first/second/third person; COND = conditional; DAT = dative; FUT = future; IMP = imperative; IPFV = imperfective; NEG = negation; PL = plural; PLU.SBJV = pluperfect.subjunctive; PPTCP = past participle; PRS = present; REFL = reflexive; SG = singular

## Corpora

|  | Dates | Number of words |
|---|---|---|
| SYNCHRONIC CORPORA<br>*Frantext* (written texts)<br>http://www.frantext.fr/<br>(last accessed on 8 December 2011) | 1960–2009 | 46 026 672 |
| *Elicop* (oral texts)<br>http://bach.arts.kuleuven.be/elicop/<br>(last accessed on 22 September 2010) | 1961–1976 | 1 164 000 |
| CLAPI (oral texts)<br>http://clapi.univ-lyon2.fr/<br>(last accessed on 22 September 2010) | 1984–2007 | 442 513 |
| CFPP2000 (oral texts)<br>http://clapi.univ-lyon2.fr/<br>(last accessed on 22 September 2010) | 2007–2008 | 361 724 |
| DIACHRONIC CORPORA<br>*Frantext* (written texts)<br>http://www.frantext.fr/<br>(last accessed on 31 January 2012) | 1180–2009 | 240 038 096 |
| *Frantext moyen français* (written texts)<br>http://www.frantext.fr/<br>(last accessed on 22 October 2010) | 1330–1579 | 6 851 879 |

# References

Blanche-Benveniste, Claire. 2010. Où est le *il* de *il y a* ?. *Travaux de linguistique* 61(2). 137–153.
Brown, Penelope & Stephen C. Levinson. 1987. *Politeness: Some universals in language usage.* Cambridge: Cambridge University Press.
Buridant, Claude. 2000. *Grammaire nouvelle de l'ancien français.* Paris: Sedes.
Bybee, Joan & Paul Hopper. 2001. *Frequency and the emergence of linguistic structure.* Amsterdam & Philadelphia: John Benjamins.
Bybee, Joan. 2003. Mechanisms of change in grammaticization: The tole of frequency. In Brian D. Joseph & Richard D. Janda (eds.), *The handbook of historical linguistics*, 602–623. Oxford: Blackwell.
Bybee, Joan. 2006. From usage to grammar: The mind's response to rpetition. *Language* 82(4). 711–733.
Byloo, Pieter, Jan Nuyts & Johan van der Auwera. 2010. *Beter* en *best*. In Johan de Caluwe & Jacques Van Keymeulen (eds.), Voor Magda: Artikelen voor Magda Devos bij haar afscheid van de Universiteit Gent, 93–109. Gent: Academia Press.
Chu, Xiaoquan. 2008. *Les verbes modaux du français.* Paris: Ophrys.
Denison, David & Alison Cort. 2010. *Better* as a verb. In Kristin Davidse, Lieven Vandelanotte & Hubert Cuyckens (eds.), *Subjectification, intersubjectification and grammaticalization*, 349–383. Berlin & New York: De Gruyter Mouton.
Gaatone, David. 1970. La transformation impersonnelle en français. *Le Français Moderne* 38(4). 389–411.
Hanse, Joseph. 1989. *Nouveau dictionnaire des difficultés du français moderne.* Paris & Louvain-la-Neuve: Duculot.
Heine, Bernd. 1993. *Auxiliaries: Cognitive forces and grammaticalization.* Oxford: Oxford University Press.
Heine, Bernd. 2003. Grammaticalization. In Brian D. Joseph & Richard D. Janda (eds.), *The handbook of historical linguistics*, 575–601. Blackwell: Oxford.
Heine, Bernd. 2002. On the role of contexts in grammaticalization. In Ilse Wischer & Gabriele Diewald (eds.), *New reflections on grammaticalization*, 83–101. Amsterdam & Philadelphia: John Benjamins.
Heine, Bernd & Tania Kuteva. 2007. *The genesis of grammar.* Oxford: Oxford University Press.
Hopper, Paul J. 1991. On some principles of grammaticalization. In Elizabeth Closs Traugott & Bernd Heine (eds.), *Approaches to grammaticalization*, Vol. I, 17–35. Amsterdam & Philadelphia: John Benjamins.
Hopper, Paul J. & Elizabeth Closs Traugott. 1993. *Grammaticalization.* Cambridge: Cambridge University Press.
Lamiroy, Béatrice & Ana Drobnjakovic. 2009. Auxiliaries and grammaticalization: A case study of Germanic and Slavonic languages. In Corinne Rossari, Claudia Ricci & Adriana Spiridon (eds.), *Grammaticalization and pragmatics: Facts, approaches, theoretical Issues*, 19–34. Bingley: Emerald Group.
Legendre, Géraldine. 1990. French impersonal construction. *Natural Language and Linguistic Theory* 8(1). 81–128.
Lehmann, Christian. 2002 [1995]. *Thoughts on Grammaticalization*, 2nd revised edn. Erfurt: Seminar für Sprachwissenschaft der Universität.

Marchello-Nizia, Christiane. 1995. *L'évolution du français: Ordre des mots, démonstratifs, accent tonique*. Paris: Armand Colin.
Mitchell, Keith. 2003. *Had better* and *might as well*: On the margins of modality?. In Roberta Facchinetti, Frank Palmer & Manfred Krug (eds.), *Modality in contemporary English*, 129–149. Berlin & New York: Mouton de Gruyter.
Norde, Muriel. 2009. *Degrammaticalization*. Oxford: Oxford University Press.
Nuyts, Jan, Pieter Byloo & Janneke Diepeveen. 2005. On deontic modality, directivity, and mood: A case study of Dutch *mogen* and *moeten*. *Antwerp Papers in Linguistics* 110. 1–56.
Vance, Barbara. 1988. L'évolution de Pro-drop en français médiéval. *Revue québécoise de linguistique théorique et appliquée* 7(3). 85–109.
van der Auwera, Johan & Vladimir Plungian. Modality's semantic map. *Linguistic Typology* 2. 79–124.
van der Auwera, Johan & Astrid De Wit. 2010. The English comparative modals – a pilot study. In Bert Cappelle & Naoaki Wada (eds.), *Distinctions in English grammar offered to Renaat Declerck*, 127–147. Tokyo: Kaitakusha.
van der Auwera, Johan, Dirk Noël & An Van linden. 2013. *Had better, 'd better* and *better*: Diachronic and transatlantic variation. In Juana I. Marín-Arrese, Marta Carretero, Johan van der Auwera & Jorge Arús Hita & (eds.), *English modality: Core, periphery and evidentiality*, 119–153. Berlin & New York: De Gruyter Mouton.
Vanderbiesen, Jeroen. 2011. 'Welches Outfit sollte man am besten anziehen?' A corpus study of comparative modal constructions in German. Leuven: University of Leuven MA thesis.
Vanderbiesen Jeroen. & Tanja Mortelmans. 2011. 'Welches Outfit sollte man am besten anziehen?' Eine Korpusstudie komparativer Modalkonstruktionen im Deutschen. *Germanistische Mitteilungen* 37(2). 65–85.
Traugott, Elizabeth Closs. 2003. From subjectification to intersubjectification. In Raymond Hickey (ed.), *Motives for language change*, 124–139. Cambridge: Cambridge University Press.
Traugott, Elizabeth Closs & Richard B. Dasher. 2002. *Regularity in semantic change*. Cambridge: Cambridge University Press.
Trousdale, Graeme. 2010. Issues in constructional approaches to grammaticalization in English. In Katerina Stathi, Elke Gehweiler & Ekkehard König (eds.). *Grammaticalization: Current views and issues*, 51–72. Amsterdam & Philadelphia: John Benjamins.

# Appendix

**Table 4:** Reported vs. unreported speech in the synchronic written corpus (*Frantext*) (based on samples of 200 if total n > 200 in Table 1)

| | unreported | | reported | | | | | | total | | total |
|---|---|---|---|---|---|---|---|---|---|---|---|
| | | | direct | | indirect | | free indirect | | | | |
| | n | % | n | % | n | % | n | % | n | % | n |
| *faire mieux* | 34 | 17 | 127 | 63.50 | 27 | 13.50 | 12 | 6 | 166 | 83 | 200 |
| *valoir mieux* | 64 | 32 | 74 | 37 | 26 | 13 | 36 | 18 | 136 | 68 | 200 |
| *falloir mieux* | 2 | 40 | 2 | 40 | 0 | 0 | 1 | 20 | 3 | 60 | 5 |
| total CMC | 100 | **24.29** | 203 | 50.12 | 53 | 13.09 | 49 | 12.10 | 305 | **75.31** | 405 |

Gijsbert Rutten and Marijke van der Wal
# 4 Discourse continuity and the written medium: Continuative relative clauses in the history of Dutch

**Abstract:** The paper discusses the significant relativization change from *d*-forms into *w*-forms in the history of Dutch. Focusing on relative adverbs and relative pronominal adverbs in particular, we examine 17th-century data taken from the Leiden *Letters as Loot Corpus*, a collection of private letters written by men and women of all social ranks. It is shown that one specific type of relative clause appropriates *w*-forms at a remarkably fast rate, i.e. continuative relative clauses. Against the background of an evolutionary perspective on grammaticalization, the *w*-preference of continuative relative clauses is treated as an example of the syntactic coding of discourse continuity and in particular as an intersubjective effort to create coherence. Since continuative relative clauses are often considered typical of written language, the paper also provides evidence that the written medium may promote grammaticalization.

## 1 Introduction

Like other Germanic languages, Dutch has undergone a change from *d*- to *w*-relativization, whereby relative adverbs, relative pronominal adverbs and relative pronouns change from a *d*-form to a *w*-form. *Het huis daar ik woon* 'the house there I live' becoming *het huis waar ik woon* 'the house where I live' is a case in point. For relative adverbs and relative pronominal adverbs, the 17th and 18th centuries constitute the crucial stage in this change. Rutten (2010) studied it from the perspective of diachronic construction grammar (see Fried 2009), using diaries from the period.[1] He claims that the change proceeds from construction to construction and suggests that so-called continuative relative clauses attract *w*-relativizers at a remarkably fast rate. This is in line with the history of English, in which this type of relative clause also adopts *wh*-relativizers early on (see Rissanen 1999: 293, 295). In the present study, we continue this line

---

[1] See Rutten (2010) for a review of the literature, which includes Van der Horst and Storm (1991), Schoonenboom (1997), De Schutter and Kloots (2000) and Van der Wal (2002). Part of the research presented here has also been discussed in Rutten and van der Wal (2014: Ch. 8).

of research by focusing on continuative relative clauses in historical Dutch to find out whether they were truly forerunners in the appropriation of w-relativizers. After establishing that continuative relative clauses indeed prefer w-forms, we argue that this phenomenon enables language users to secure discourse continuity. We also argue that the change from d- to w-relativizers constitutes an instance of grammaticalization co-occurring with intersubjectification. In doing so, we join in on recent discussions on the interplay of grammaticalization and intersubjectification (e.g. Cuyckens et al. 2010; Traugott 2010).

Continuative relative clauses are characterized by a discrepancy between form and function. They typically convey new information, which is normally presented in a main clause. Sentence (1) is an example from Modern English. Sentence (2) shows that it is possible to paraphrase (1) by means of a coordinated clause or an independent main clause.

(1) *She was found face down in the water and airlifted to hospital, where she died hours later.* (Loock 2007: 340)

(2) *She was found face down in the water and airlifted to hospital, and she died there hours later. / She died there hours later.* (Loock 2007: 342)

In the history of the Germanic languages, continuative (or sentential) relative clauses are often considered typical elements of written language or even latinisms (e.g. Van der Wal and Van Bree 2008: 271–272). However, it has been pointed out that this type of construction occurs long before the influence of Latin-style models may be assumed (Von Polenz 1994: 279). Still, the remarkable increase of continuative relative clauses in both postmedieval English and German is generally associated with the influence of Latin prose style (Von Polenz 1994: 279; Rissanen 1999: 295–296). With regard to the change from d- to w-relativization, this would mean that continuative relative clauses, taking on w-forms early on, are marked by w-forms at a time when d-forms are still common in texts closer to the oral mode of discourse. There is some evidence from the history of English and Dutch that this is in fact the case (Rissanen 1999: 293; Rutten 2010). If continuative relative clauses are indeed more closely associated with written language, at least in postmedieval times, and if they take up w-relativizers at a remarkably fast pace, we have evidence that written language may promote the change of d-forms into w-forms. Moreover, since we consider the change from d- into w- a case of grammaticalization, as will be explained in Sections 2 and 3, this is proof that the written medium may promote grammaticalization.

In Sections 2 and 3, we explain the concept of grammaticalization used in the present study and discuss the change from *d-* to *w-*relativization in Dutch as a case of grammaticalization. Section 4 presents a case study of relative clauses in 17th-century Dutch, which focuses on the distribution of *d-* and *w-*relativizers across different constructions and, most importantly, in continuative relative clauses. The latter will be shown to prefer *w-*relativizers. In Section 5, we interpret this result from the perspective of discourse continuity. Section 6 summarizes the main results.

## 2 Grammaticalization from an evolutionary perspective

The basic working hypothesis of evolutionary linguists is that syntax developed later than simple signs and words (e.g. Bickerton 1990; Jackendoff 1999; Nowak and Krakauer 1999; Nowak et al. 2000; Tomasello 2008). This is reminiscent of Givón's (1979: 208) well-known dictum that language develops from discourse into grammar, a development which he termed "syntacticization". By this, Givón (1979: 209) meant, first, that human pragmatic and semantic operations, including meaning-making through words, precede encoding into syntactic structures, and second, that basic syntactic structures may become more syntactic over time, even though syntactic structures may, in their turn, erode over time. Givón (2009: 10) presents a three-step evolutionary model:
(i) single words > simple clause;
(ii) simple clause > clause chains (parataxis);
(iii) clause chains > complex/embedded clauses (syntaxis).

Steps (ii) and (iii), which Givón labels as the transition from parataxis to syntaxis, have also been described as a development from parataxis through hypotaxis to subordination (Hopper and Traugott 2003: 177). Here, parataxis refers to independent and unembedded clauses, hypotaxis to dependent but unembedded clauses and subordination to dependent and embedded clauses (Hopper and Traugott 2003: 178). These changes constitute a popular topic in historical linguistics and they are also central to the present study. We will henceforth regard them as instances of grammaticalization, this being a less specific and more widely used term than syntacticization (Tomasello 2003: 8). In a similar vein, Heine and Kuteva (2007: 210–261) provide a fine-grained description of the evolution of subordinate clauses within a grammaticalization framework. The evolutionary perspective on grammaticalization sketched here is corroborated by research into child language acquisition (Tomasello 2003) and by computational models of language evolution (Steels 2005).

With this brief overview we do not want to create the impression that increasing complexity is a general trait of human language evolution. Simplification occurs as well, but typically involves verbal and nominal deflexion rather than the reversal of evolved syntactic structures (Dahl 2004; Sampson et al. 2009; Trudgill 2011). Deflexion often co-occurs with syntacticization: as is well known, when Dutch and English lost most of their cases, more prepositional phrases developed and word order became more rigid (e.g. Lass 1999: 138–140).

For the history of Dutch, the following view of grammaticalization has been taken by Burridge (1993). She argues that many of the changes characterizing the transition from Middle Dutch to Modern Dutch are due to the grammaticalization of word order, i.e. the stabilization of syntactic patterns, where previously pragmatic considerations allowed more syntactic flexibility. The changes she discusses include the fixation of verb-second (or V2) in main clauses and of verb-final (or V-final) in subclauses, the development from bipartite to single negation and the rise of dummy subjects and of expletive *er* 'there' in presentative constructions. The change under discussion in the present paper, i.e. the change from *d-* to *w-*relativizers, will be treated as another such case of grammaticalization.

Importantly, the development from parataxis to hypotaxis/subordination, though a general trend in linguistic systems, may well be socially and/or culturally motivated, especially from an evolutionary perspective (Croft 2000). When we consider language as an evolutionary system that adapts to social/cultural circumstances, the development of literacy must have had an enormous impact on languages. Thirty years ago already, Pawley and Syder (1983: 552) formulated their "adaptation hypothesis" (see Ellis et al. 2009 as well):

> Our principal hypothesis is that in the history of English certain usages have developed or gained preference in a given system because they are advantageous in the circumstances. We are dealing with an ecology of grammar, in which forms of construction are molded to suit the constitutive conditions and purposes of face-to-face talk, on the one hand, and impersonal written communication on the other.

The basic idea is that the social/cultural context in which a language is used influences its grammar. One of the most significant aspects of this context is mode: is the language spoken or written? Pawley and Syder (1983: 557–558) list systematic differences between written and spoken communication, which are also well known from the work of Chafe (1985, 1994) and which are central to corpus-based research into genre differences (Biber and Conrad 2009; see also

Koch and Oesterreicher 1985). Discourse phenomena may be coded in gestures, pauses, intonation and facial expressions, but the written mode needs other means to code pragmatic meanings. As will be demonstrated by means of a case study of relativization in Dutch, one such means is syntax.

## 3 The grammaticalization of Dutch relatives

The change from *d-* to *w*-forms in relative (pronominal) adverbs in Dutch is part of a significant series of changes in the relativization system, with relative pronouns, adverbs and pronominal adverbs all changing from a *d*-form into a *w*-form. The change from *d-* to *w*-relativization constitutes a major shift in the grammar of Dutch, as in other Germanic languages (Rissanen 1999: 292–301; Von Polenz 1994: 278–279). The change affects any kind of relative clause (restrictive and appositive relative clauses, including continuative relative clauses), any kind of relativizer (pronouns, adverbs and pronominal adverbs) and any kind of syntactic/semantic context (dependent and independent or free relative clauses). In Dutch, the change began somewhere in the Late Middle Dutch period, in the 14th or 15th century (Van der Horst 2008: 603, 703) and is not yet complete: relative pronouns are still widely used with *d*-forms and prescribed in many positions in Present-day Standard Dutch. With relative adverbs and relative pronominal adverbs, the change has now been completed, though. In this paper, we focus on the variation and change in relative (pronominal) adverbs, for which the crucial period was the 17th and 18th centuries (Van der Horst and Storm 1991; De Schutter and Kloots 2000; Van der Wal 2002; Van der Horst 2008). The case study in Section 4 focuses on the 17th century in particular.

A few examples, taken from the literature and the Internet, will illustrate the foregoing. The as yet incomplete changes in the pronominal system are shown with free relatives in (3) and (4) and with nominal antecedents in (5) and (6). The (a) examples are Middle Dutch, the (b) ones Modern Dutch. In (3) and (5), the antecedent is inanimate, in (4) and (6) it is animate. The change represented by (3) and (4) is complete. The change in (5) is in progress, with the *w*-form being common in many colloquial varieties of Dutch, while the *d*-form is preferred in the written standard. Only few speakers would accept (6b) but *w*-forms are attested in this position, also in written language.

(3) a. *had ic ghevonden **dat** ic zoeck*
  had I found that I seek
  'had I found what I was looking for'
  (Van der Horst 2008: 603; 14th century)

b. *Na 5 weken had ik gevonden **wat** ik zocht.*
   after 5 weeks had I found what I sought
   'After five weeks, I had found what I had been looking for.'
   (http://www.datingwebsites.nl/reviews/second-love/?page=23; accessed 9 June 2015)

(4) a. ***Die*** *sine cuusheit uerlieset, die uerlieset sine siele.*
       That his chastity loses that loses his soul
       'He who loses chastity, loses his soul.'
       (Van der Horst 2008: 603; ca. 1400)

   b. ***Wie*** *zijn KUISHEID bewaakt mag door elk deur die*
      who his chastity guards may through each door that
      *hij/zij wil het paradijs binnentreden!*
      he/she wants the paradise enter
      'He who guards his chastity, may enter paradise through any door he/she wants to.'
      (http://forums.marokko.nl/archive/index.php/t-1459274%2520%253C/t-1703877-p-3.html; accessed 9 June 2015)

(5) a. *dat woordt **dat** die heilighe man job sprac*
       that word that that holy man Job spoke
       'the word that the holy man Job spoke'
       (Van der Horst 2008: 377; 14th century)

   b. *Neger, ja, dat is het woord **wat** Totti tegen mij zei.*
      negro yes that is the word what Totti to me said
      'Negro, yes, that is the word that Totti said to me.'
      (http://www.voetbalzone.nl/doc.asp?uid=105236; accessed 9 June 2015)

(6) a. *vrouwen, **die** ter merct brengen wouden eyer ende botter*
       women that to.the market bring would eggs and butter
       'women, who wanted to bring to the market eggs and butter'
       (Van der Horst 2008: 601; 15th century)

   b. *het aantal single vrouwen, **wie** veelal de persoonlijke*
      the number single women who often the personal
      *financiën zelf moeten regelen*
      finances self must arrange
      'the number of single women that often have to take care of their personal finances themselves'
      (http://geldzaken.afaspersonal.nl/2014/geld-een-vrouwending/; accessed 9 June 2015)

Similar changes have affected free relative adverbs as in (7), relative adverbs as in (8) and pronominal adverbs as in (9), all originating from locative expressions. The changes exemplified here are complete.

(7) a. *Sine es niet **daer** si was tevoren.*
 she is not there she was before
 'She is not where she was before.' (Van der Horst 2008: 477; 13th century)

 b. *dat had ze ook niet **waar** ze eerst was.*
 that had she also not where she before was
 'She didn't have that where she first was.'
 (http://www.dekattensite.nl/phpBB2/viewtopic.php?t=26880&p=558449; accessed 9 June 2015)

(8) a. *tot Bruesel, **daer** sy hoer antwoort kreghen*
 in Brussels there they their answer got
 'in Brussels, where they got their answer'
 (Van der Horst 2008: 703; 15th century)

 b. *te Brussel, **waar** zij haar debuut maakte*
 in Brussels where she her debut made
 'in Brussels, where she made her debut'
 (http://www.401dutchdivas.nl/nl/belgische-zangers/446-raymonde-serverius.html; accessed 9 June 2015)

(9) a. *den viere / **daer** die bouc in bernende lach*
 the fire there the book in burning lay
 'the fire in which the book lay burning'
 (Van der Horst 2008: 498; 12th century)

 b. *het vuur **waarin** ze branden zal niet doven*
 the fire wherein they burn shall not smother
 'the fire in which they burn will not smother'
 (http://www.allaboutworldview.org/dutch/bestaat-de-hel.htm; accessed 9 June 2015)

In (3) to (9), *d*-relativizers are giving or have given way to *w*-forms. Generally speaking, interrogatives replace demonstratives as the main means of relativization. In Middle Dutch main clauses, the finite verb is usually in second position while it is mostly in third or a subsequent position in subordinate clauses (Burridge 1993: 26, 46–47; Van der Horst 2008: 536–537). This syntactic difference would distinguish (8a) from its constructed main clause alternative (10). It also implies that *daer* 'there' in (8a) is already a grammaticalized use of the original locative expression, which has taken up the function of clause linker while maintaining its locative function.

(10) tot Bruesel, **daer** kreghen sy  hoer antwoort
     in  Brussels  there got        they their answer
     'in Brussels, there they got their answer'

It should be noted that V2 in main clauses was merely a tendency in Middle Dutch, as was the position of the finite verb further on in subclauses. What characterizes the transition to Modern Dutch is, first, the stabilization of both tendencies (with V2 becoming obligatory in declarative main clauses and V-final in subclauses)[2] and, second, the replacement of *d*-relativizers by *w*-forms. Both developments strengthen the difference between main and subordinate clauses. Interrogatives are the source of *w*-relativizers, but when these forms are used as interrogatives, as in the constructed dialogue in (11), the finite verb appears in second position from the earliest Dutch onward (Van der Horst 1981: 43; Quak and Van der Horst 2002: 60–61).

(11) **waer** kreghen sy  hoer antwoort? tot Bruesel
     where  got      they their answer?  in  Brussels
     'Where did they get their answer? In Brussels.'

In other words, a *w*-form with the finite verb in third position or later has always ruled out an interrogative reading, as in (8b), whereas a *d*-form left some room for either a main clause demonstrative reading, as in (10), or a subclause relative interpretation, as in (8a). Table 1 schematizes the relevant features (V2, V-final, *d*-form and *w*-form) for all three contexts (declarative main clauses, interrogatives and relative subclauses).

**Table 1:** Word order and the distribution of *d*- and *w*-forms in declarative main clauses, interrogative clauses and relative subordinate clauses

|         | Declarative main clause | Interrogative | Relative subclause | |
|---------|------------------------|---------------|--------------------|---|
|         | Modern Dutch           | Modern Dutch  | Middle Dutch       | Modern Dutch |
| V2      | +                      | +             | –                  | – |
| V-final | –                      | –             | +/–                | + |
| *d*-form| +                      | –             | +                  | – |
| *w*-form| –                      | +             | –                  | + |

---

[2] In Modern Dutch, it is mainly prepositional phrases that can still occur after the final verb in subordinate clauses.

Without assuming any inherent teleology, we note that, with regard to word order and *d/w*-forms, the make-up of relative clauses has changed into the exact opposite of declarative main clauses. In addition, *d*-forms in main clauses are demonstratives while *w*-forms in relative clauses are relatives. So there seems to be a strong tendency toward functional specialization, with main clauses and subclauses adopting their own characteristics with regard to both word order and *d/w*-forms. Finally, the redistribution of *d*- and *w*-forms, with *w*-forms taking over the relative function previously fulfilled by *d*-forms, may very well have been catalyzed by the fact that demonstratives appear to have been much more frequent, at least in historical written Dutch (Rutten 2010). Similarly, Rissanen (1999: 294) notes that there is "little doubt that the spread of the *wh*-forms was supported by the heavy functional load of *that*". The functional specialization described here amounts to marking the difference between main and relative clauses even more explicitly than before and it is for that reason that we view it as an instance of grammaticalization.

# 4 Continuative relative clauses in historical Dutch

Our case study concerns the change from *d*- to *w*-relativizers in adverbial relative clauses, as in (7) to (9), in the 17th century, a crucial stage for the shift. In Section 4.1, we will briefly discuss our hypotheses, based on previous research, and introduce the corpus. In Section 4.2, the different types of relative clause will be discussed which are at the heart of the corpus study reported on in Section 4.3.

## 4.1 Hypotheses and corpus

Bergs (2005: 151) shows that the 15th-century Paston letters exhibit a remarkable distribution of *that* and *wh*-relativizers: whereas restrictive relative clauses use *that* in 83.3% of all instances, non-restrictive relative clauses prefer the new *wh*-relativizers in 90.3% of the cases. Rissanen (1999: 293) notes that "in the discussion of the spread of the *wh*-forms [in the history of English] it has proved useful to distinguish a special type of non-restrictive clause called 'continuative'". He also points out that when *wh*-forms spread throughout the language, the old form *that* was mainly found in texts representing the oral mode of discourse (Bergs 2005: 181). This interesting observation appears to be in line with the evolutionary perspective discussed in Section 2: if *wh*-forms are stronger markers of hypotaxis and subordination than, for instance, *that*, one would expect the spread of *wh*-forms to be promoted in the written language and, conversely, the older forms to be preserved in the spoken language.

Furthermore, it has been argued that continuative relative clauses play an important role in the spread of *w*-forms in the history of Dutch. Rutten (2010), a case study of 17th- and 18th-century diaries, reveals that continuative relative clauses employ *w*-forms far more frequently than *d*-forms. They promote the use of *w*-forms and therefore the grammaticalization of *w*-relatives. The study is based on a fairly small number of diaries, however. Its line of research is continued and improved upon in the present paper by taking into account a larger collection of texts so as to establish the validity of the claims in Rutten (2010), and to see whether the type of relative clause (e.g. restrictive/nonrestrictive) influences the distribution of *d*- and *w*-forms. In particular, our hypothesis is that continuative relative clauses are ahead of other constructions in the appropriation of *w*-relativizers.

The texts used for the present study are 17th-century private letters from the so-called *Letters as Loot Corpus* compiled at Leiden University for historical-sociolinguistic research.[3] The corpus comprises letters from the 1660s–1670s,[4] which have all been transcribed from the original manuscripts and digitized within the project. For the present study, a selection was made of 210 letters, totaling 109,000 words. Although the corpus is socially stratified and contains letters by men as well as women, we will only focus on so-called internal factors here. Note, however, that *w*-forms are more widely used by upper (middle) class members than by lower (middle) class members and more widely by men than by women (Rutten and Van der Wal 2014: 296–302). This too suggests that the written language promoted the use of *w*-forms, as upper (middle) class men were far more involved in the written culture than lower (middle) class men and than women in general.

## 4.2 Types of adverbial relative clause

Before we present the results of our case study, we will briefly discuss the types of relative clause that we distinguish. Since continuative relative clauses are said to promote *w*-forms, we suspect that the choice of relativizer depends on

---

[3] Letters as Loot (*Brieven als Buit*) is a research project funded by the Netherlands Organisation for Scientific Research (NWO) (see www.brievenalsbuit.nl). The corpus is available online at http://brievenalsbuit.inl.nl.

[4] The letters were part of ships' cargo confiscated by the English during the Anglo-Dutch wars of the 17th century, when privateering was a legitimate activity. The letters are kept in the National Archives in Kew, London.

the degree of integration of the relative clause into the matrix clause. Syntactically, the relative clause's degree of integration is determined by its position: embedded or clause-final. Its semantic integration depends on it being restrictive or appositive. This leaves us with four options.

We consider the relative clause as an expansion of something that has already been mentioned (the antecedent), an expansion being a syntactic slot added and linked to an existing syntactic projection (Auer 2009). Adopting a linear approach to syntax (Sinclair and Mauranen 2006; Auer 2009), we first look at the syntactic position at which the relative clause is inserted. Two possible positions are attested: either immediately following the constituent it expands or postponed to clause-final position, as in (12) and (13) respectively. In the examples, taken from the corpus, the antecedents and the relativizers are in boldface.

(12) *dese gaende met* **een cleen scheepje, waer op** *neeff Cornelis*
 this going with a little ship.DIM where on cousin Cornelis

 *Meppelen gaet als assistent, sal alleen dienen* ...
 Meppelen goes as assistant, will only serve

 'this [one, letter], sent with a little ship on which cousin Cornelis Meppelen works as an assistant, will only serve...'

(13) *dat zeij* **een poort** *hadden toe gesloeten* **waer doer** *dat*
 that they a gate had closed where through that

 *de hollanders moesten pasceren*
 the Hollanders had.to pass

 'that they had closed a gate the Hollanders had to pass through'

In (12), the relative clause immediately follows the antecedent. The main clause continues with the finite verb *sal* 'will', the subject of which is *dese* 'this [one, letter]'. In Lehmann's (1984: 49) typology, this is an example of an embedded postnominal relative clause. In (13), the predicate *hadden toe gesloeten* 'had closed' with the subject *zeij* 'they' precedes the relative clause attached to *een poort* 'a gate'. According to Lehmann (1984: 49), this is a relative clause in postposition. We will call examples such as (12) "embedded" and examples such as (13) "final".

As regards the semantics, we adopt the common distinction between restrictive and appositive relative clauses. The relative clause in (12) is restrictive. It would be pointless to state that the letter is sent with some little ship. It is the fact that it is the ship on which the mutual acquaintance Cornelis Meppelen works as an assistant that is significant here. A syntactically similar construction from the corpus is given in (14), which favors an appositive interpretation, however.

(14) uE      schrivens wegens **mijn lossicheyt int**      **vrije**    **daer** ul
     your    writing   about   my    looseness   in.the  wooing  there you

   naer mijn oordeel al      vrij wat  gelooff in slaedt maeckt
   to   my   opinion  already quite some belief  in hits  makes

   mijn      gans        geen onsteltenisse af.
   me.DAT    completely  no   dismay       off

   'Your writing about my moral laxity, to which you give quite some credit in my opinion, does not at all nullify my dismay.'

So (12) contains an embedded restrictive relative clause, (13) a final restrictive relative clause and (14) an embedded appositive relative clause. The fourth possibility, i.e. a final appositive relative clause, is exemplified in (15).

(15) Zal    hem  wel  doen betaelen **waermede** Blijve  met  haest
     Shall  him  well do   pay       where.with  remain  with hurry

   Waerde Moeije UEDW:D:                en   Neef    Alexander Batij.
   beloved aunt  your.obedient.servant  and  nephew  Alexander Batij

   '[I] shall make him pay. With which I remain, [while I'm] in a hurry, beloved aunt, your obedient servant and nephew Alexander Batij.'

The antecedent of *waermede* in (15), if there is one, is the entire previous stretch of discourse. The relative clause is in final position, or in the first position of a new clause, but, in any case, it is not embedded.

Example (15) is an instance of a continuative relative clause, which is a subtype of final appositives. According to Loock (2007), appositive relative clauses come in three subtypes: continuative appositives, relevance appositives and subjectivity appositives. The first subtype is mainly characterized by a discrepancy between form and function. Continuative relative clauses convey new information typically presented in a main clause. In conversation, they tend to have their own intonation contour. They belong to what are often called glue-ons or increments (Couper-Kuhlen and Ono 2007): pieces of discourse which are prosodically distinct but syntactically, and sometimes also semantically, linked to the material they immediately follow. Continuative relative clauses create coherence with the preceding discourse by employing subordinating syntax where the information structure would canonically trigger a new main clause. The other two subtypes described by Loock (2007) are both used for detailing information in the main clause which the speaker/writer deems necessary on second thought. Relevance appositives are a "repair strategy" (Loock 2007: 346): adding the appositive repairs what may not have been sufficiently specified in the main clause. Subjectivity appositives verbalize the speaker/writer's opinion, judgment or comment (Loock 2007: 353).

Bergs (2005: 136), discussing relative clauses in the history of English, notes how difficult it sometimes is to distinguish between restrictive and appositive clauses in actual practice. It can be equally difficult to distinguish between continuative, relevance and subjectivity appositives. But because research into final appositives is necessary to find out whether continuative relative clauses promote *w*-relativizers more strongly, we restricted ourselves to final appositives which could unambiguously be assigned to one of the subtypes of appositive clauses. We managed to assign 166 out of 183 appositive clauses (see Section 4.3) to one of the subtypes distinguished by Loock (2007). Example (15) is a clear case of a continuative relative clause. Another continuative appositive is given in (16): the writer routinely confirms that s/he has received a letter and goes on to indicate what was in it, which brings new information into the discourse – information that is, arguably, more important than the preceding statement. Example (17) contains a relevance appositive: the ship, not sufficiently identified by its name, is specified further by mentioning the name of its commander. Example (18) features a subjectivity appositive, indicating the writer's evaluation of the situation communicated in the preceding discourse.

(16) *Soo ijst dat ick naer datto van dien een houder van datto uijt*
so is.it that I after date of that an older of date from
*Cap$^t$ Tange hebbe ontfangen* **waer uijt** *verstaen ue*
captain Tange have received where out understood you
*grootelijcx verwondert zijt ick soo weijnich rettour ben zendende.*
greatly surprised are I so little return are sending
'So it is [the case] that after the date of that letter I received a [letter] of an older date through captain Tange, from which I have understood that you are greatly surprised that I am returning so little.'

(17) *desen bryef aen den eersammen man ijan wijllemse luijtenant op*
this letter to the honourable man IJan Wijllemse lieutenant on
*het schep de spijegel* **daer op** *komder menheer menheer*
the ship De Spijegel there on commands Mr Mr

*fijes amarael de ruijter*
vice admiral De Ruijter

'this letter to the honorable man IJan Wijllemse, lieutenant on the ship De Spijegel, on which the vice-admiral Mr De Ruijter commands'

(18) ende sal  op donderdagh den 26 maijus begraven worden
    and will on Thursday  the 26 May    buried  be

    **daer** Ick seer bedroeft om    ben
    there I very sad    about am

'and [he] will be buried on Thursday 26 May, about which I am very sad'

Building on the above categorization of relative clauses, we investigated the distribution of *d*- and *w*-relativizers in our corpus.[5] For this, we needed two more categories, however. Free or headless relative clauses such as the idiom in (19) cannot readily be analyzed in terms of the present classification and will be considered a separate category here. Another category was created for relativizers that have grammaticalized into conjunctions, fulfilling an argumentative function as in (20).

(19) **Daer** men hovden daer  vallen spander.
    there one chops there fall    chips
    'You cannot make an omelette without breaking eggs.'

(20) god ... dancken ende loeuen voor de  genaede die  heij aen ons
    god    thank   and praise  for  the mercy  that he  to us

    bewcijst **daer** woij sulcke kinderen van verderf sijn
    shows    there we such children of doom are

'[we should] thank God and praise him for the mercy which He shows to us there where / while / even though we are such children of doom'

## 4.3 Corpus results

We extracted all relative clauses introduced by an adverb or a pronominal adverb from the corpus by searching for forms such as *waer*, *waar*, *daer* and *daar*. This led to 269 tokens of *d*- and *w*-forms, including both bare adverbs

---

[5] Examples (15) to (17) are instances of epistolary formulae, i.e. expressions frequently occurring in and presumably even restricted to the language of letters. Note, however, that these formulae are not necessarily conservative vis-à-vis language change, as illustrated by (15) and (16).

(e.g. *daer, waer*) and pronominal adverbs (e.g. *daer* + preposition). The prepositions, which are mostly graphically separated from the *d*- and *w*-forms, include a wide variety of types such as *van* 'from', *uit* 'out, from', *over* 'over', *na* 'to, after', *op* 'on', *voor* 'for', *in* 'in' and *achter* 'after'. All 269 tokens were then allocated to one of the six categories described in Section 4.2: restrictive and appositive embedded relative clauses, restrictive and appositive final relative clauses, free relatives and grammaticalized relatives with an argumentative function. For five tokens, no final decision could be made for lack of context. The absolute numbers of *d*- and *w*-forms in our corpus are presented in Table 2.

**Table 2:** The distribution of *d*- and *w*-forms over six categories of relative clauses

|  |  | *d*- | *w*- |
|---|---|---|---|
| Embedded | Restrictive | 7 | 1 |
|  | Appositive | 9 | 0 |
| Final | Restrictive | 17 | 11 |
|  | Appositive | 87 | 96 |
| Free relative |  | 9 | 10 |
| Argumentative function |  | 17 | 0 |
| Undecided |  | 3 | 2 |
| Total |  | 149 | 120 |

We will first discuss the distribution of *d*- and *w*-forms in the four main categories in Table 2, viz. embedded, final, free relatives and argumentative functions, and then zoom in on the embedded and final relative clauses and on restrictive and appositive relative clauses. Figure 1 gives the proportion of *d*- and *w*-relativizers in the main categories.

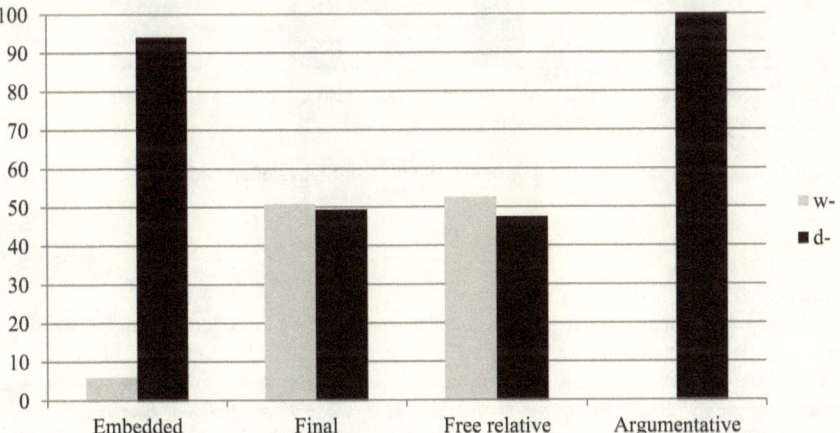

**Figure 1:** The proportion of *d*- and *w*-forms in the main categories of relative clauses

Two things stand out in Figure 1: *d*-forms are preferred both in embedded relative clauses and in argumentative functions. As to the relatives with an argumentative function, it should not come as a surprise that these retained the older *d*-forms. Rutten (2010) argues that one reason why *w*-forms took over the function of relativizer from the *d*-forms is the latter's polyfunctionality. *D*-forms served not only as relativizers but also as demonstratives in assertive clauses and they grammaticalized into argumentative connectives as well.[6] Figure 1 also shows that final relative clauses distribute *d*- and *w*-forms quite evenly while free relatives favor *w*-forms just slightly. The preference for *w*-forms in free relative constructions is in line with earlier studies as summarized by Van der Horst (2008: 1392–1392). For the present purposes, we will refrain from an extensive discussion of the argumentative and free relative uses and focus on embedded and final relative clauses instead.

For the difference between restrictives and appositives, consider the results in Figure 2, which gives the proportion of *d*- and *w*-relativizers in each of the subcategories.

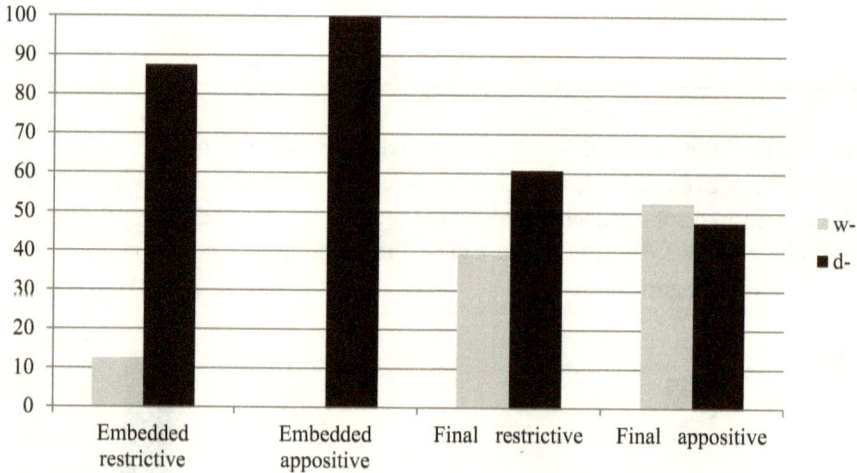

**Figure 2:** The proportion of *d*- and *w*-forms in the different types of embedded and final relative clause

---

6 *W*-forms have grammaticalized into argumentative connectives in Modern Dutch. The development may be fairly recent, as the examples in the extensive historical dictionary of Dutch, the WNT, only date back to the 19th and 20th centuries. The following sentence is a case in point: *Alle banden des maatschappelijken levens worden losgerukt, waar de eerbied voor beiden verloren is* [1837] 'All the ties of social life are torn loose, if deference to both is lost' (WNT s.v. *waar* VI).

Figure 2 shows that the semantic difference between restrictive and appositive embedded relative clauses does not influence the choice of relativizer. In both cases, *d*-forms are widely used. There is in fact only one embedded clause with a *w*-form (see Table 2). In final position, there does seem to be a small difference between restrictive and appositive clauses. Recall that, in general, final relative clauses distribute *d*- and *w*-forms quite evenly (see Figure 1). Restrictive relative clauses in final position appear to behave somewhat more conservatively, in that just over 60% retain the old *d*-form. Final appositives, however, turn out to be a modest *w*-promoting context – like free relatives (see Figure 1), they constitute the only context where *w*-forms actually outnumber *d*-forms. While the difference between final restrictives and final appositives is not statistically significant ($\chi^2 = 1.69$, $df = 1$, $p = 0.194$), the results in Figure 2 still suggest that both the syntactic and the semantic degree of integration may determine the form of the relativizer. Possible semantic differences are overruled by syntax in the case of embedded clauses, where *d*-forms largely outnumber the one attestation of a *w*-form. In final position, however, the semantic difference might be more important: appositives seem to prefer *w*-relativizers. In any case, this supposed preference calls for further investigation of the different types of final appositives.

Of the 183 final appositives, we were able to assign 166 instances to one of the three subtypes of appositive clause and to either *d*- or *w*-. Table 3 presents the results.

**Table 3:** The distribution of *d*- and *w*-forms in the different types of final appositive clause

|  | d- | w- | Total |
|---|---|---|---|
| Relevance | 29 | 12 | 41 |
| Subjectivity | 38 | 23 | 61 |
| Continuative | 11 | 53 | 64 |

Relevance and subjectivity appositives mostly combine with *d*-relativizers whereas continuative relative clauses prefer *w*-relativizers. This is even more clear in Figure 3, which presents the proportion of *d*- and *w*-forms per type of appositive. The observed difference between continuative relative clauses as opposed to relevance and subjectivity appositives is statistically significant ($\chi^2 = 37.8$, $df = 2$, $p < 0.001$).

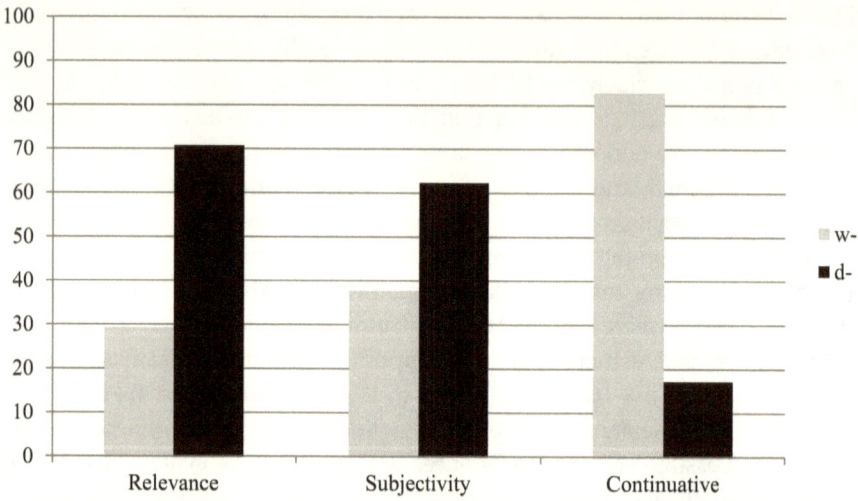

**Figure 3:** The proportion of *d*- and *w*-forms in the different types of final appositive clause

Relevance and subjectivity appositives occur with *d*-forms in 71% and 62% of the cases respectively, but this pattern is reversed for continuative relative clauses. These occur with *w*-forms in no less than 83% of the cases. This implies that the slight preference of final appositives for *w*-forms (see Figure 2) is mainly due to continuative appositives triggering the *w*-variant. The pattern for relevance and subjectivity appositives, with 60 to 70% of *d*-forms, resembles that for final restrictive relative clauses much more closely (see Figure 2). Summing up, continuative relative clauses constitute the sole context where *w*-forms are unambiguously preferred in the corpus.

## 5 Discourse continuity

Having established the *w*-preference of continuative relative clauses in Section 4, we now turn to the interpretation of this result against the background of the evolutionary perspective discussed in Section 3. Section 5.1 argues that continuative appositives introduced by *w*-forms secure discourse continuity by creating coherence, Section 5.2 argues that this is a reader-oriented or intersubjective move.

## 5.1 Creating coherence

Continuative relative clauses are only loosely integrated into the matrix or preceding clause, both syntactically and semantically. We argue that this explains why they adopt *w*-relativizers early on. Consider (15) again, repeated here as (21).

(21) Zal    hem  wel  doen betaelen **waermede** Blijve  met  haest
     Shall  him  well do   pay      where.with  remain with hurry

  Waerde   Moeije UEDW:D:                   en  Neef    Alexander Batij.
  beloved  aunt   your.obedient.servant and nephew Alexander Batij

  '[I] shall make him pay. With which I remain, [while I'm] in a hurry, beloved aunt, your obedient servant and nephew Alexander Batij.'

In the first part of (21), the writer states that he will try his best to make a third party disburse. This is the final message he wanted to communicate to the addressee. There is in this part of the discourse no explicit linguistic material signaling to the reader that the discourse is going to be ended. In other words, the reader may have imagined many following statements, for instance, on the expected success of making this third party disburse or on a date by which the payment will have to be made, perhaps even a complaint on this third party's reluctance to disburse. No such statement follows, however. Instead, the writer continues with the closing formula *Blijve*... '[I] remain...' and thus finishes the discourse altogether. To avoid the disjoint transition from his final message to the closing formula, the writer inserts the relative pronominal adverb *waermede* 'with which', thereby creating a continuative relative clause. The relativizer *waermede* is anaphorically related to the preceding clause, which functions as its syntactic antecedent. Semantically, however, *waermede* favors a cataphoric interpretation: it introduces a whole new topic, viz. the end of the discourse, for which one would canonically expect a new main clause.[7] What the *w*-form in (21) does is create coherence between two informationally distinct messages. They are glued together by the *w*-form, not necessarily at the semantic but at least at the syntactic level. This feature sets continuative relative clauses apart from relevance and subjectivity relative clauses, which are always semantically linked to the preceding discourse.

---

[7] In (21), the writer could have opted for a *d*-form and a main clause (e.g. *daermede blijve ik*... 'with that I remain...'). Since the subject is lacking (as is fairly common both in letter writing and in diary style), a *d*-form would in fact have left the clause type ambiguous (either a main clause or a subordinate relative clause).

By avoiding a disjointed transition between two separate stretches of discourse, continuative relative clauses code discourse coherence and continuity syntactically where no obvious semantic or informational coherence exists. As such, they create what Mithun (2008: 69) calls "dependency beyond the sentence". Continuative relative clauses may be analyzed as new sentences (for their semantic orientation) but also as part of a matrix sentence (for their syntactic structure). We will consider them primarily as new clauses, which happen to have the form of a subclause. This is in line with the traditional view of continuative relative clauses as constructions that code new information in subclauses. It is also in line with recent research into insubordination, which focuses precisely on autonomous subclauses, i.e. on the conventionalized main clause use of what appear to be formally subordinate clauses (Evans 2007: 367). If we consider continuative relative clauses as new clauses and assume that grammaticalized *w*-relativizers mark subordination more strongly than *d*-forms, then these *w*-relativizers enable continuative relative clauses to become more explicitly connected to the preceding discourse. This is why continuative relative clauses adopt *w*-relativizers at the fastest pace. The *w*-relativizers introducing continuative relative clauses code a pragmatic function syntactically by creating discourse coherence and continuity where a semantic clash of two distinct statements threatens to occur. As such, they represent a textbook example of the grammaticalization pattern summarized in Givón's (1979: 208) well-known slogan "from discourse to grammar".

Example (21) is the most extreme situation of semantic incoherence, as the clause starting with *waermede* introduces an entirely new topic. Other continuative relative clauses too are semantically less connected to the preceding discourse than relevance and subjectivity appositives but they do not change the topic altogether. Rather, in examples such as (22) (see also 16), the continuative appositive introduces a new subtopic within the current discourse topic.

(22) twijfele niet of sal in Jndie wel voort geracken. soo hy hem
doubt not if will in India well further get so he him

als vooren wel comporteert. ende oock de gonst van eenige
as before well behaves and also the favor of some

vrinde moght bekomen. **waer op** ick oock uwe goede gonst
friends may come where on I also your good favor

voor hem versoeke
for him request

'[I] do not doubt whether [he] will go a long way in the Dutch East Indies, if he behaves himself well as before and may also find the favor of some friends. Whereupon I also request your good favor toward him'

Example (22) is taken from a passage about a young man. In the final clause, introduced by *waer op* 'where on, whereupon', the young man is still under discussion, but the perspective has changed. He is not the central figure anymore, as the writer now draws attention to what he would like the addressee to do, viz. help the young man. The first part of (22) comprises fairly descriptive prose on the young man's characteristics and career. The final part is a request directed toward the addressee. Although there is some continuity from the first part to the final part, i.e. the discourse is still about the young man in a broad sense, the request also constitutes a new piece of information that could have been packed in a new main clause. As in (21), however, the writer ensures discourse continuity by using subordinate syntax.

It should also be clear that continuative relative clauses are somewhere in between parataxis and subordination, with parataxis referring to independent and unembedded clauses and subordination to dependent and embedded ones (Hopper and Traugott 2003: 178). They are not however clear cases of Hopper and Traugott's (2003) intermediate stage of hypotaxis, which refers to dependent but unembedded clauses. Whereas relevance and subjectivity appositives are indeed semantically dependent and may even be embedded (Hopper and Traugott 2003: 182), continuative relative clauses can be semantically independent while their syntax at least formally allows for dependency, as in the case of insubordination. As such, they offer an alternative interpretation of hypotaxis as well as an alternative to well-researched examples of the opposite, i.e. semantic subordination with syntactic coordination (e.g. Culicover and Jackendoff 1997; Fortuin and Boogaart 2009). Obviously, this does not imply that continuative relative clauses are necessarily moving along a cline toward subordination (see Hopper and Traugott 2003: 199).

## 5.2 Grammaticalization and intersubjectification

When the locative adverb *daer* 'there' and pronominal adverbs with *daer*- grammaticalized into relativizers, they took up a textual, clause linking function. Relativizers, like other items operating in the textual domain, may be said to display subjectification, since they can be used to mark the speaker's perspective on how utterances are connected to each other (see Traugott 2010: 40). As explained in Sections 2 and 3, we consider the subsequent change from *d*- into *w*-relativization as another instance of grammaticalization, which underlines the subordinate function of the relative clause. While the change from *d*- to *w*-forms was in full swing, it was – ironically – continuative relative clauses which appropriated *w*-forms at the fastest pace. This may be unexpected: continuative relative clauses can be semantically independent from the preceding clause, so why would their (syntactic) subordinate form need to be underlined? As argued in Section 5.1, continuative relative clauses employ the new *w*-forms to establish coherence and discourse continuity. They code a pragmatic meaning syntactically, in that they signal to the reader that the discourse is coherent despite the fact that the new clause is informationally incoherent with the preceding clause. In (21), for instance, the form *waermede* 'with which' centers on the addressee, for it is primarily in the interest of the reader that discourse coherence and continuity are signaled. Traugott (2010: 35) defines intersubjectivity as "the mechanism by which ... meanings ... may be recruited to encode meanings centered on the addressee", and we argue that this is exactly what is at stake here.[8] Because of this focus on the reader, the change from *d*- to *w*-relativizers in continuative relative clauses may qualify as an example of intersubjectification. Traugott (2010: 35) also stresses that we need to distinguish between two types of (inter)subjectivity, since "(inter)subjective" may indicate that a form "has pragmatic (inter)subjective meanings in relevant contexts" but also that it "has a newly coded (inter)subjective meaning". We will argue that it is the first type of intersubjectivity which applies to continuative relative clauses in the history of Dutch.

Recall example (21). When the reader reaches the relative pronominal adverb *waermede* 'with which', there is no formal sign as to what will follow. The adverb may introduce a relevance appositive (e.g. 'with which I mean that I will take care of this'), a subjectivity appositive (e.g. 'with which I will certainly enjoy myself') or even a restrictive appositive (e.g. 'with which he always pays me'). It is only when the informationally completely new *Blijve* ... 'remain ...' follows that it becomes apparent that *waermede* introduces a continuative relative clause, confronting the reader with a new proposition, which in itself is not connected to the preceding discourse in any meaningful way. It is at this point that s/he is invited to infer that the discourse is coherent, as signaled by the morphosyntax of the relative adverb. Put differently, it is only in this specific context that *waermede* codes an intersubjective meaning morphosyntactically. In a different context, the same relative might have coded another, possibly more objective meaning. Building on Auer (2009) and Fried (2010), we can say that *waermede* itself in (21) only opens up a new syntactic slot, the interpretation of which depends on the discourse frame selected by the reader. As soon as s/he notices the semantic incoherence of the two clauses linked by *waermede*, s/he

---

[8] We need to distinguish the (inter)subjective function of the relative clause as coded by the relativizer and the relative clause's actual propositional contents, which may also be subjective, as in the case of subjectivity appositives (see Section 4.2).

will understand its pragmatic/intersubjective function as a coherence creator and exclude other interpretations.

This analysis of intersubjectivity as a pragmatic by-product of grammaticalization is in line with the view that grammaticalization does not necessarily imply or co-occur with (inter)subjectification (see Cuyckens et al. 2010: 6; Traugott 2010). In certain contexts, viz. when introducing continuative relative clauses, Dutch w-relativizers may fulfill an intersubjective function. It so happens that these intersubjective w-relativizers heavily promote the spread of w-forms and thus speed up the grammaticalization process. But it appears to be the frequency of continuative relative clauses rather than their pragmatic/ intersubjective function in certain contexts as such that fuels the spread of w-forms (see Table 2). The w-forms do not code a new intersubjective meaning by themselves and since the change from d- to w-relativization is in progress in the period represented in our corpus, continuative relative clauses are not necessarily formally distinguished from other relative clauses. All adverbial relative clauses occur with both d- and w-forms (and all have changed to w-forms only). In sum, the pragmatic/intersubjective function of continuative relative clauses accompanies and speeds up the grammaticalization into w-forms but is not inherently connected to it.

# 6 Conclusions

One of the major changes in 17th- and 18th-century Dutch is the change from d- to w-relativization, whereby relative (pronominal) adverbs such as *daar* 'there, where' and *daarmee* 'therewith, with which' changed into *waar* 'where' and *waarmee* 'with which'. In this paper, we have treated this change as an example of grammaticalization. The new w-relativizers mark (syntactic) subordination more strongly than the old d-forms. A corpus study of 17th-century private letters reveals that, as in English, insubordinate continuative (or sentential) relative clauses take up the new w-forms at a significantly faster pace than other relative constructions, including other final appositives. By using the w-forms, continuative relative clauses, which may be semantically completely independent from the preceding clause, become more strongly attached to the preceding discourse. As a result, coherence and discourse continuity are secured. This pragmatic move is primarily reader-oriented and therefore an example of intersubjectification.

We have taken an evolutionary view of grammaticalization. Central to this view is the concept of syntacticization, i.e. the idea that pragmatic meanings may become encoded in the grammar over time. Continuative relative clauses, adopting subordinate w-forms at the fastest pace, exemplify this development from discourse to grammar. Furthermore, it is part of the evolutionary perspective that social/cultural circumstances may influence the form of the language. One of these circumstances concerns the mode of communication: is the language spoken or written? Seeing that continuative relative clauses have often been considered as characteristic of the written language, our results provide evidence that the written medium may promote grammaticalization.

# Acknowledgments

We wish to thank two anonymous reviewers for their comments on an earlier draft.

# Abbreviations

DIM = diminutive

# References

Auer, Peter. 2009. On-line syntax: Thoughts on the temporality of spoken language. *Language Sciences* 31(1). 1–13.
Bergs, Alexander. 2005. *Social networks and historical sociolinguistics: Studies in morphosyntactic variation in the Paston letters (1421–1503)*. Berlin: Mouton de Gruyter.
Biber, Douglas & Susan Conrad. 2009. *Register, genre and style*. Cambridge: Cambridge University Press.
Bickerton, D. 1990. *Language and species*. Chicago: University of Chicago Press.
Burridge, Kate. 1993. *Syntactic change in Germanic: Aspects of language change in Germanic with particular reference to Middle Dutch*. Amsterdam: John Benjamins.
Chafe, Wallace. 1985. Linguistic differences produced by differences between speaking and writing. In David R. Olson, Nancy Torrance & Angela Hildyard (eds.), *Literacy, language and learning: The nature and consequences of reading and writing*, 105–123. Cambridge: Cambridge University Press.
Chafe, Wallace. 1994. *Discourse, consciousness, and time: The flow and displacement of conscious experience in speaking and writing*. Chicago: The University of Chicago Press.
Couper-Kuhlen, Elizabeth & Tsuyoshi Ono. 2007. 'Incrementing' in conversation: A comparison of practices in English, German and Japanese. *Pragmatics* 17(4). 513–552.
Croft, William. 2000. *Explaining language change: An evolutionary approach*. Harlow: Pearson.
Culicover, Peter W. & Ray Jackendoff. 1997. Semantic subordination despite syntactic coordination. *Linguistic Inquiry* 28(2). 195–217.

Cuyckens, Hubert, Kristin Davidse & Lieven Vandelanotte. 2010. Introduction. In Kristin Davidse, Lieven Vandelanotte & Hubert Cuyckens (eds.), *Subjectification, intersubjectification and grammaticalization*, 1–26. Berlin: De Gruyter Mouton.

Dahl, Östen. 2004. *The growth and maintenance of linguistic complexity*. Amsterdam: John Benjamins.

De Schutter, Georges & Hanne Kloots. 2000. Relatieve woorden in het literaire Nederlands van de 17e eeuw [Relative words in 17th-century literary Dutch]. *Nederlandse Taalkunde* 5(4). 325–342.

Ellis, Nick C., Clay Becker, Richard Blythe, Joan Bybee, Morten H. Christiansen, William Croft, John Holland, Jinyun Ke, Diane Larsen-Freeman & Tom Schoenemann. 2009. Language is a complex adaptive system: Position paper. *Language Learning* 59(1). 1–26.

Evans, Nicholas. 2007. Insubordination and its uses. In Irina Nikolaeva (ed.), *Finiteness: Theoretical and empirical foundations*, 366–431. Oxford: Oxford University Press.

Fortuin, Egbert & Ronny Boogaart. 2009. Imperative as conditional: From constructional to compositional semantics. *Cognitive Linguistics* 20(4). 641–673.

Fried, Mirjam. 2009. Construction Grammar as a tool for diachronic analysis. *Constructions and Frames* 1(2). 262–291.

Fried, Mirjam. 2010. Constructions and frames as interpretative clues. *Belgian Journal of Linguistics* 24. 83–102.

Givón, Talmy. 1979. *On understanding grammar*. New York: Academia Press.

Givón, Talmy. 2009. *The genesis of syntactic complexity: Diachrony, ontogeny, neuro-cognition, evolution*. Amsterdam: John Benjamins.

Heine, Bernd & Tania Kuteva. 2007. *The genesis of grammar: A reconstruction*. Oxford: Oxford University Press.

Hopper, Paul J. & Elizabeth Closs Traugott. 2003. *Grammaticalization*. Cambridge: Cambridge University Press.

Jackendoff, Ray. 1999. Possible stages in the evolution of the language capacity. *Trends in Cognitive Sciences* 3(7). 272–279.

Koch, Peter & Wulf Oesterreicher. 1985. Sprache der Nähe – Sprache der Distanz: Mündlichkeit und Schriftlichkeit im Spannungsfeld von Sprachtheorie und Sprachgeschichte. *Romanistisches Jahrbuch* 36. 15–43.

Lass, Roger. 1999. Phonology and morphology. In Roger Lass (ed.), *The Cambridge history of the English language*. Vol. 3: *1476–1776*, 56–186. Cambridge: Cambridge University Press.

Lehmann, Christian. 1984. *Der Relativsatz: Typologie seiner Strukturen, Theorie seiner Funktionen, Kompendium seiner Grammatik*. Tübingen: Narr.

*Letters as Loot / Brieven als Buit Corpus*. Leiden University. Compiled by Marijke van der Wal (Programme leader), Gijsbert Rutten, Judith Nobels and Tanja Simons, with the assistance of volunteers of the Leiden-based *Wikiscripta Neerlandica* transcription project, and lemmatized, tagged and provided with search facilities by the Institute for Dutch Lexicology (INL). 2013 & second release 2015.

Loock, Rudy. 2007. Appositive relative clauses and their functions in discourse. *Journal of Pragmatics* 39(2). 336–362.

Mithun, Marianne. 2008. The extension of dependency beyond the sentence. *Language* 84(1). 69–119.

Nowak, Martin A. & David C. Krakauer. 1999. The evolution of language. *Proceedings of the National Academy of Sciences of the United States of America* 96(14). 8028–8033.

Nowak, Martin A., Joshua B. Plotkin & Vincent A. A. Janssen. 2000. The evolution of syntactic communication. *Nature* 404. 495–498.

Pawley, Andrew & Frances H. Syder. 1983. Natural selection in syntax: Notes on adaptive variation and change in vernacular and literary grammar. *Journal of Pragmatics* 7(5): 551–579.

Quak, Arend & Joop M. van der Horst. 2002. *Inleiding Oudnederlands* [Introduction to Old Dutch]. Leuven: Universitaire Pers Leuven.

Rissanen, Matti. 1999. Syntax. In Roger Lass (ed.), *The Cambridge history of the English language*. Vol. 3: *1476–1776*, 187–331. Cambridge: Cambridge University Press.

Rutten, Gijsbert. 2010. Vroegmoderne relativa: Naar een diachrone constructiegrammatica [Early modern relative words: Toward a diachronic construction grammar]. *Nederlandse Taalkunde* 15(1). 1–32.

Rutten, Gijsbert & Marijke van der Wal. 2014. *Letters as loot: A sociolinguistic approach to seventeenth- and eighteenth-century Dutch*. Amsterdam: John Benjamins.

Sampson, Geoffrey, David Gil & Peter Trudgill. 2009. *Language complexity as an evolving variable*. Oxford: Oxford University Press.

Schoonenboom, Judith. 1997. De geschiedenis van *dat, wat* en *hetgeen* in bijbelvertalingen [The history of *dat, wat* and *hetgeen* in bible translations]. *Nederlandse Taalkunde* 2(4). 343–369.

Sinclair, John M. & Anna Mauranen. 2006. *Linear unit grammar: Integrating speech and writing*. Amsterdam: John Benjamins.

Steels, Luc. 2005. The emergence and evolution of linguistic structure: From lexical to grammatical communication systems. *Connection Science* 17(3/4). 213–230.

Tomasello, Michael. 2003. *Constructing a language: A usage-based theory of language acquisition*. Cambridge, MA & London: Harvard University Press.

Tomasello, Michael. 2008. *Origins of human communication*. Cambridge, MA: MIT Press.

Traugott, Elizabeth Closs. 2010. (Inter)subjectivity and (inter)subjectification: A reassessment. In Kristin Davidse, Lieven Vandelanotte & Hubert Cuyckens (eds.), *Subjectification, intersubjectification and grammaticalization*, 29–71. Berlin: De Gruyter Mouton.

Trudgill, Peter. 2011. *Sociolinguistic typology: Social determinants of linguistic complexity*. Oxford: Oxford University Press.

Van der Horst, Joop M. 1981. *Kleine Middelnederlandse syntaxis* [Small Middle Dutch syntax]. Amsterdam: Huis aan de Drie Grachten.

Van der Horst, Joop. 2008. *Geschiedenis van de Nederlandse syntaxis* [History of Dutch syntax]. Leuven: Universitaire Pers Leuven.

Van der Horst, Joop M. & Reinder Storm. 1991. Over de geschiedenis van het betrekkelijk voornaamwoordelijk bijwoord [On the history of the relative pronominal adverb]. *Tijdschrift voor Nederlandse Taal- en Letterkunde* 107(2). 105–119.

Van der Wal, Marijke. 2002. Relativisation in the history of Dutch: Major shift or lexical change? In Patricia Poussa (ed.), *Dialect contact and history on the North Sea Littoral*, 27–36. Munich: Lincom.

Van der Wal, Marijke & Cor van Bree. 2008. *Geschiedenis van het Nederlands* [History of Dutch]. Utrecht: Spectrum.

Von Polenz, Peter. 1994. *Deutsche Sprachgeschichte vom Spätmittelalter bis zur Gegenwart*. Band II, *17. und 18. Jahrhundert*. Berlin: Walter de Gruyter.

WNT = *Woordenboek der Nederlandsche Taal* [Dictionary of the Dutch Language]. http://gtb.inl.nl/?owner=WNT

Hilary Chappell
# 5 From verb of saying to discourse marker in Southern Min: (Inter)subjectification and grammaticalization

**Abstract:** The main topic of this paper is the clause-final discourse marker *kong*[1] 講 in Taiwanese Southern Min, a Sinitic language. This marker is compatible with several construction types, each of which expresses a distinct type of modality. Differing in terms of syntax and prosody, these constructions code assertions, suggestions, warnings and rebuttals. Discourse data are used to describe the semantic, pragmatic and structural features of each construction. The marker *kong*[1] 講 is also examined in terms of its pathway of grammaticalization from its lexical source, a verb of saying, and with respect to the notions of subjectivity and intersubjectivity. The grammaticalization of 'say' verbs into discourse markers is briefly illustrated for several other Sinitic languages.

## 1 Introduction

The present analysis concentrates on a grammaticalization pathway for 'say' verbs whereby they develop a modal use as discourse markers in clause-final position. The main focus is on the verb *kong*[1] 講 'say' in Southern Min, with brief references to 'say' verbs in several other Sinitic languages. It will be argued that a range of different intersubjective inferences is possible, depending on the modality of the given syntactic construction. Four types of construction are discerned on the basis of syntactic form, intonation and pragmatic meaning. These are assertions, suggestions, warnings and rebuttals. All involve some kind of correction or challenging of a presupposition on the part of the speaker.

### 1.1 Subjectivity and intersubjectivity

In this analysis, we adopt the definition of subjectivity posited by Lyons (1982: 102) and further developed by Traugott (2007, 2010) mainly in relation to grammaticalization, but also in its relation to intersubjectivity. Subjectivity is essentially considered to be speaker-oriented in its reference to mechanisms which express speakers' attitudes, viewpoints and their evaluation of a situation, whereas intersubjectivity refers to addressee-oriented expressions reflecting the speaker's attention to the addressee and his or her self-image (Traugott and Dasher 2002: 20–22; Traugott 2010).

However, Traugott (2007, 2010) has defined intersubjectivity in a narrower manner than it will be in this analysis, limiting it mainly to social deixis and considerations of "face", in which pragmatic meanings inferable from the context have been "semanticized" (or "intersubjectified") and become formally coded. This is adeptly exemplified by the use of honorifics and verbal forms appropriate for polite speech levels in Japanese. Included under this concept are also discourse markers, interjections and illocutionary types such as tag questions and imperatives (Traugott 2007: 303, Traugott 2010: 37).[1]

In this paper, I adopt a broader view on the notion of intersubjectivity as being intrinsic to the communicative process, whereby pragmatic features of context that provide the conditions of use for a particular syntactic structure are necessarily coded as part of the constructional meaning. This approach is more aligned with that of Benveniste (1958: 258–266), who saw this special property of language as being of primary importance in enabling linguistic communication to take place.

Hence, intersubjectivity can be related more broadly to linguistic mechanisms which code many different kinds of interaction between the speaker and the addressee, through the speaker's attribution of subjectivity to the other interlocutor. As aptly explained by Fitzmaurice (2004: 429), the same resources used for the speaker's rhetorical self-positioning (modal verbs, parentheticals, mental verbs and their complements, etc.) may be "marshaled for the speaker's rhetorical reconstruction of the interlocutor's perspective or attitude. In pragmatic terms, intersubjectivity has to do with the representation of speaker stance as addressee stance".[2]

## 1.2 Mood, modality and Sinitic languages

In Sinitic languages, there are no morphological distinctions for mood in terms of the classic definition, which involves marking by verbal inflection (see Chappell and Peyraube 2016). The traditional categories of mood can,

---

[1] In Traugott (2003: 128), however, a more elaborated view of intersubjectivity is proposed as having two facets: (i) the epistemic one of the speaker's attention to the presumed attitudes of the addressee toward the content of communication and (ii) the social one of paying attention to the face needs of the addressee. This approach is somewhat closer to the definition adopted here.

[2] The term "stance" refers to the social construction of meaning, including the expression of the viewpoints, commitment and beliefs of interlocutors. It is a term frequently used in research analyzing discourse data, spoken and written.

however, be *structurally* distinguished, for example, through the grammatical patterns which code the four basic, prototype moods of the declarative, interrogative, imperative and exclamative. In this paper, terms such as "imperative mood" are thus used to refer to entire syntactic configurations in Sinitic languages which serve to express this kind of constructional meaning. In contrast to this, the term "modality" refers more broadly to any linguistic mechanism used to code semantic and pragmatic values, the three main types being epistemic, deontic and dynamic.

The expression of modality consequently encompasses a large number of grammatical categories including modal auxiliary verbs (*can, must*), sentential adverbs (*apparently, of course*), ossified phrases from which parentheticals develop (*I think, you know*), clause-final particles that function as discourse markers and even special prosodies such as a final, high rising question intonation on declaratives in certain varieties of English. Although not the only ones, mood and modality are hence important vehicles through which subjectivity and intersubjectivity are manifested.

### 1.3 A note on Sinitic languages in China

The most prominent member of the Sinitic languages (Sino-Tibetan) is undoubtedly Mandarin or Standard Chinese, known as *pǔtōnghuà* 普通話 'the common language' in China. Notwithstanding this, the present analysis is principally concerned with the development of a discourse marker in a Sinitic language which is not a variety of Mandarin, specifically, the variety of Southern Min spoken in Taiwan. Southern Min dialects may be more familiar to westerners under the appellation of "Hokkien". They are not mutually intelligible with Standard Mandarin in their oral register.[3]

## 2 Clause-final uses of 'say' verbs as discourse markers in Sinitic

In an earlier study of the reanalysis of 'say' verbs as complementizers in Sinitic serial verb constructions (Chappell 2008), I argued that the colloquial varieties of Taiwanese Southern Min and Beijing Mandarin have already reached an

---

3 Taiwanese Southern Min is closely related to the Xiamen 厦门话, Quanzhou 泉州话 and Zhangzhou 漳州话 dialects of Southern Min spoken just across the Taiwan Strait in Fujian Province on the mainland of China. The relationship is due to migration from these areas in Southern Fujian, which began in the late Ming dynasty (1368–1644).

advanced stage of grammaticalization. I also argued that several different outcomes of grammaticalization can be identified for 'say' verbs, including hearsay evidential markers, topic and conditional markers, in addition to the formation of other kinds of composite conjunctions expressing purpose, consequence and concession.

Discourse markers, generally known under the name of *yǔqìcí* 語氣詞 'rhetorical/sentence-final particles' in Chinese linguistics, serve to express the illocutionary force associated with different kinds of speech acts including admonitions, orders, suggestions, threats, compliments and warnings.[4] In Sinitic languages, they are principally found in clause-initial and clause-final position, that is, on the left and right periphery of the clause, in preference to the clause-medial position (see Huang 2000 for Chinese languages; Traugott 2007 on cross-linguistic correlates). They serve as major markers of mood and modality to build questions, warnings, directives and hortatives, not to mention even more subtle functions that have not always been recognized as solid modal types – coded by miratives, counter-expectation and hearsay markers.

In this analysis, the focus is on clause-final discourse markers that are the outcome of grammaticalization, subjectification and intersubjectification of verbs of saying. In the present section, I provide a brief overview of 'say' verbs in several Sinitic languages which have grammaticalized into clause-final discourse markers, illustrating this phenomenon with both historical and contemporary data from Hakka, Hong Kong Cantonese and Shanghai Wu. While the most highly grammaticalized and generalized sentence-final particles are well-described for Standard Mandarin and other major Chinese languages, little is known about those derived from 'say' verbs in Sinitic. In the subsequent sections, I focus on clause-final *kong*[1] 講 in Southern Min, which is used to express assertions, as well as suggestions, warnings and rebuttals in different syntactic constructions.

In Sinitic languages, there is a variety of different construction types formed by the use of a clause-final discourse marker derived from a 'say' verb, which determines the modality of the entire construction. Once grammaticalized, the discourse marker takes scope over a new construction which may code evidentiality or epistemic modality, form an echo question prompting the addressee to

---

[4] The notion of "illocutionary force" is subsumed under the broader notion of "modality" in the framework used in this paper. The terms may sometimes be used interchangeably in the present article, but only where this does not lead to any ambiguity. Illocutionary force, needless to say, is irrevocably linked with speech act theory, specifically, the speaker's intention in pronouncing an utterance, whereas modality is a more general term, referring to a semantic subfield of the wider domain of qualificational categories and is on a par with tense and aspect (see Nuyts 2016).

repeat earlier information or code a mirative meaning in combination with other elements of the clause. Several illustrative examples are provided below from a variety of Sinitic languages.[5]

In (1), from Sin-on Hakka, the speaker warns the addressee of the possibility that someone might take revenge on them if they engage in the act of mocking, overall a kind of epistemic modality. In (2), the Meixian Hakka example shows a hearsay evidential use of a 'say' DM, coding that it would be unwise to eat a certain kind of food.

(1) Sin-on dialect of Hakka
你唔好給佢, 佢噲報口仇話...
ngi² m¹ hau³ thoi⁴ ki², ki² woi⁴ pau⁴ nya¹ šu² **wa⁴**...
2SG NEG.IMP mock 3SG 3SG will take 2.POSS revenge PRT$_{WRNG<SAY}$
'Don't mock him, or else he might revenge himself on you...'
(Chappell and Lamarre 2005: 132)

(2) Meixian dialect of Hakka
食裏噲頭哪痛話.
chĭt ê voé t'eoûnâ t'oúng **và**
eat PRT.NOM will head ache PRT$_{EVD<SAY}$
'Apparently, eating it gives you a headache.' (Rey 1988 [1926]: xxvii)[6]

In the Cantonese example in (3), an echo question is formed by the discourse marker wa⁵ < wa⁶ 話 'say' found in the clause-final position of speaker V's turn. Speaker V asks the interlocutor to repeat information she has missed regarding the price of a barbecue grill, which was however stated earlier in the conversation (discussion and more examples can be found in Chui 1994, Matthews and Yip 2011: 367–369 and Kwok 1984).

(3) Hong Kong Cantonese
K: yiga jikhai giu nei lo BBQ yatbak man jek.
now that.is ask 2SG pay BBQ 100 dollar PRT
'That is, (we're) now asking you to pay one hundred dollars for the BBQ.'
[59 turn takings later]

---

[5] Unless indicated otherwise, the examples in this paper are from Southern Min. Examples without any details on the source have been taken from my own set of data. Apart from Lien (1988), all other examples have been glossed, translated and in some cases, transcribed, by the present author.
[6] The discourse markers và and wa⁴ represent the pronunciation of 'say' using different transcription systems. They refer nonetheless to the cognate forms for this clause-final discourse marker in Hakka.

V: *Winnie a go BBQ geido chin* **wa⁵?**
   Winnie PRT that BBQ how.much money PRT_ECHO<SAY
   'Winnie, how much (should I pay for) that BBQ, as you said?'

(Chui 1994: 5–6)

Two further clause-final markers in Hong Kong Cantonese code, respectively, reported speech and surprise. The first marker, *wóh* 喎 (low rising tone), can be used to signal reported speech and acts as a device for disclaiming responsibility (Kwok 1984: 67–69, 104–105). In (4), the speaker reports that a certain film is worth seeing. The second marker, *wo* (mid-level tone), which functions as a mirative (Matthews 1998; Wang 2013), is illustrated in (5): a TV interviewer shows surprise at how tealeaves quickly change color after being soaked in hot water.

(4) Hong Kong Cantonese
幾好睇嘅喎.
*géi hóu tái ge* **wóh.**
quite good see PRT.ASST PRT_EVD<SAY
'(I'm) told it's quite good.'

(Kwok 1984: 67)

(5) Hong Kong Cantonese
同埋啲顏色唔同咗喎.
*Tùhng-màaih dī ngàahnsīk m̀h tùhng-jó* **wo.**
and           CL.PL color      NEG same-PFV PRT_MIR<SAY
'And the colors are not the same!'
(Line 132, *The Art of Tea Appreciation*, author's recording and transcription of interview broadcast on TVB Jade, Hong Kong)

These two discourse markers, *wo* and *wóh*, possibly derive from a combination of the verb *wáh* 話 (= *wa⁶*) 'say' in Cantonese with the sentence-final particle *a¹* 啊 (Chao 1947: 121), again with tone sandhi taking place on what are its more grammaticalized uses.

The Meixian Hakka imperative usage in (6) appears to share, with Cantonese echo questions as in (3), the semantic feature of repetition of an utterance. However, unlike Hakka *và* 話 < 'say', Cantonese *wa⁵* is only found in information questions, and not in imperatives (Chui 1994). The Hakka imperative in (6) acts as a prompt, as in the context of a doctor's surgery.

(6) Meixian Hakka
舌麻拉出來話.
*chăt   mâ   laî   tch'oût loî   **và**.*
tongue NOM pull out   come PRT_SAY
'Just stick out your tongue (I said).'           (Rey 1988 [1926]: xxvii)

In a study on mirativity in southeastern Sinitic languages, Wang (2013) discusses a variety of 'say' verbs for the Wu dialect group, including *jiào* 叫, *huà* 话, *dào* 道 or *jiăng* 讲, which form composite discourse markers.[7] These develop from reported speech and hearsay markers into miratives expressing surprise. Most markers can occur freely in either clause-initial or clause-final position as well as between the subject and predicate. Nonetheless, overall, clause-final position appears to be the position most clearly favored for the grammaticalized mirative use. For example, in the Shanghai Wu dialect, for *ɦi⁵²-kã²¹* 伊讲 < '3SG speak', only the clause-final position is available for this function. In (7), the first occurrence of this phrase in clause-initial position expresses the original lexical meaning, and the clause-final occurrence, the mirative meaning. These uses are further distinguished by tone sandhi, which occurs only on the more grammaticalized mirative form with respect to the third person singular pronoun: *ɦi¹³* > *ɦi⁵²*.

(7) Shanghai Wu
伊讲伊戆伊讲!
*ɦi¹³ ka⁴⁴ ɦi¹³ ga¹³   **ɦi⁵²-ka²¹**!*
3SG say 3SG stupid  PRT_MIR<3SG SAY
'S/he even said he's really stupid!'           (Wang 2013: 114)

Hence, the construction type determines which modality or, more precisely, which illocutionary force is coded by these clause-final discourse markers derived from 'say' verbs: a warning, a hearsay evidential, a request to repeat information, a prompt, or a mirative meaning.

Similarly, in Taiwanese Southern Min, several constructions can be distinguished which use a clause-final discourse marker *kong¹* 講, based on the main verb of saying. I will propose that *kong¹* 講 is a truncated version of the postposed quotative index, '1SG say', and that it has undergone semantic and

---

[7] For the convenience of quoting, the Mandarin romanization is given here for these 'say' verbs, lacking in many cases the IPA transcription in the article by Wang (2013).

pragmatic change from a quotative index to a discourse marker coding at least four different modalities, according to the construction type in which it occurs. In Section 3, I examine and discuss data from Taiwanese Southern Min and attempt to account for the semantic, pragmatic and discourse features of *kong*[1] 講. In Section 4, its development is examined. Section 5 presents the conclusion.

## 3 Semantic, pragmatic and discourse features of clause-final *kong*[1] in Taiwanese Southern Min

The discourse marker *kong*[1] is found at the end of an intonation group in clause-final position with the polysemous function of expressing assertions, warnings, suggestions or rebuttals.[8]

The frequency of *kong*[1] as a clause-final discourse marker tends to be low in the various colloquial databases consulted,[9] even though it is well illustrated and described in several earlier studies on this and other markers in Southern Min. These include Lien (1988: 226–227), Cheng (1997 [1991]), Liu (1996), Hwang (1998), Chang (1998) and Tseng (2008), who all treat *kong*[1] as belonging to the paradigm of sentence-final modal particles in Southern Min.

In this study, I refer principally to examples from the computerized database of contemporary Southern Min materials (National Tsing Hua University, Taiwan) as well as from several smaller corpora of conversational data including those

---

[8] The clause-final discourse marker *kong*[1] 講 is invariably used in its tone sandhi form. This tonal change from high falling to high level is discussed in Chappell (2008) as an important phonological correlate of the grammaticalization process.

[9] For example, just two were found in my corpus of Southern Min oral texts totaling 58:17 minutes. The low frequency in my sample of texts may be due to the fact that two of the transcriptions contained narratives with long monologic passages, apart from occasional questions and interpolations from the interviewer and other family members who were present. The third, though a lively family conversation, was directed at a family member, not present at the recording, for whom they were taping their news. As such, it did not contain the kind of interaction or confrontation that might have provoked the use of assertions, imperatives and rebuttals, or the context appropriate for newsworthy assertions between two speakers. Just a handful of examples was found by the author in the National Tsing Hua University database of contemporary Southern Min materials. For similar data in Taiwanese Mandarin, concerning the clause-final discourse marker *shuō* 说, Su (2004) found zero examples in the Sinica database (0/1992 instances of *shuō* 说) and just two in her spoken corpus (2/1536).

assembled in Liu (1996), Chang (1998), Tseng (2008) and my own. These extracts from spoken data are indispensable for discussing the semantic and pragmatic features of *kong*[1], given their clearly defined discourse contexts.

In two studies of the clause-final use of *kong*[1] in Southern Min, Lien (1988) proposes that this polysemous discourse marker has two main uses, namely, a directive and an assertive one. Liu (1996) adds a third, interrogative category (*yíwèn* 疑問). In a study based on conversational discourse data, Chang (1998) proposes to explain the clause-final usage in terms of counter-expectations, while more recently Wang (2013) treats it as a mirative usage. In the present paper, I propose and argue for four main syntactic constructions that contain the clause-final discourse marker *kong*[1], each associated with a different modality determined by the type of subjectivity and intersubjectivity at play. These are:
(i) declaratives, coding assertions in which the speaker challenges a presupposition from the surrounding context;
(ii) imperatives in the first or second person, coding suggestions;
(iii) imperatives in the second person, coding warnings – accompanied by a different intonation than (ii);
(iv) *wh*-questions, coding rebuttals in the form of a rhetorical question.

The pragmatic and semantic features of each type of modality will now be discussed for each of these four construction types.

## 3.1 Assertions in declarative form: NP$_{SUBJ}$ – Verb – (X) – *kong*[1]

In declarative constructions, clause-final *kong*[1] is used to make an assertion that contradicts a presupposition, inherent in the speech context. Its use involves, more specifically, a semantic component of counter-expectation. The presupposition could be: (i) a commonly held opinion; (ii) the viewpoint implied or overtly expressed in the prior conversational turn of the other interlocutor; or (iii) something implicit in the external speech situation. This presupposition is then contradicted in the speaker's reply, using assertive *kong*[1] in a declarative syntactic form.

In the first example of the assertive modality, (8), the speaker has just upbraided the addressee in the immediately preceding context for not listening properly to his account about the strange odor in the area, possibly due to the presence of a corpse. The addressee initially misunderstood the situation, thinking that Fuzhou Bo wanted him to go and find out in person where the odor was coming from, to which Fuzhou Bo replies (8).

(8) [Immediately preceding context: I didn't mean that at all. You should listen more carefully. I was saying that the American soldier has a strange smell. Didn't you notice?]

牽一只軍用狗去共鼻出來，就怀是叫你去鼻講，你敢是狗？

| Khan¹ | chit⁸ | chiah⁴ | kun¹-iong⁷ | kau² | khi³ | ka⁷ | phinn⁷-chhut⁸-lai⁵, |
|---|---|---|---|---|---|---|---|
| lead | one | CL | military | dog | go | OM.3SG | sniff-out-come.DIR |

| chiu⁷ | m⁷ | si³ | kio³ | li² | khi³ | phinn⁷ | **kong¹**, |
|---|---|---|---|---|---|---|---|
| then | NEG | be | CAUS | 2SG | go | sniff | DM_SAY |

| li² | kam² | si³ | kau². |
|---|---|---|---|
| 2SG | how | be | dog |

'Why don't you bring a military dog along to sniff it out? *After all, it isn't up to you to go and find out by sniffing* (at what is on the ground) [*kong¹*]. You're not a dog, are you?'
(Line 14437, *Hou Shan Wan Zhao* 後山晚照, Tsing Hua database)

[Illocutionary force: I'm saying that I know this is true (i.e. you do not have to go and search) and that what you thought is not true (i.e. that you have to do it)]

In (9), the speaker, Granny Qin (秦婆婆), tries to allay any fears about her health, explaining that quite a few people are keeping an eye on her. Furthermore, she points out that the addressee's uncle was very relieved to see her in a good state of health during a recent visit, contrary to expectations.

(9) [Immediately preceding context: A: How have you been lately? – Granny Qin: I'm well. You don't need to worry about me.]

恁阿舅呼頂個月嘛來，啊佇遮住三工啊，伊看了嘛足放心的講。

| Lin² | A⊦ku⁷ | honnh¹ | ting² | ko³ | gueh⁸ | ma⁷ | lai⁵, |
|---|---|---|---|---|---|---|---|
| 2PL | uncle | PRT | last | CL | month | also | come |

| a¹ | ti⁷ | chia¹ | tua³ | sann¹ | kang¹ | a¹. |
|---|---|---|---|---|---|---|
| PRT | at | here | stay | three | day | PRT |

| yi¹ | khuann³-liau³ | ma⁷ | chiok⁴ | hong³sim¹ | e⁵ | **kong¹**. |
|---|---|---|---|---|---|---|
| 3SG | see-finish | also | very | relieved | PRT | DM_SAY |

'Your uncle came last month and stayed for three days here. After he'd seen (me), *he was extremely relieved* [*kong¹*].'
(Line 11608, *Si Chong Zou* 四重奏, Tsing Hua database)

Example (10) is extracted from a narrative concerning the history of Japan and the rise of General Toyotomi. Here, the newsworthy value lies in the fact that a manservant has been promoted to the position of chief foreman in the army. This goes against the usual presupposition that it would have been hard to change one's position in life in Medieval Japan.

(10) 彼共儂^拿^拿^拿 ₁su-li-pa₁ 的 ho$^n$ , \ 喔 = ^提升起來講, -做^總 - 總工頭呢！
hit$^4$ kang$^5$     theh$^8$ theh$^8$ theh$^8$ ₁su-li-pa₁ e$^5$    ho$^n$,
that for.people fetch fetch fetch slippers NOM PRT
oh   the$^5$-seng$^1$ khi$^2$-lai$^5$ **kong$^1$**,
PRT promoted INCH     DM$_{SAY}$
cho$^3$   chong$^2$ chong$^2$-kang$^1$-thau$^5$ ne.
do    chief    chief-foreman       PRT
'The one who fetched – fetched slippers (for the general) – oh – *turned out to get promoted* [*kong$^1$*] *to chief – chief foreman.*'
(Lines 1128–1130, *Japanese History*, author's recording and transcription)

The corpus of conversational data assembled by Chang (1998) contains several revealing examples of this counter-expectation use of clause-final *kong$^1$*, one of which is reproduced here as (11). As Chang (1998) similarly claimed, the discourse marker *kong$^1$* corrects a previously held opinion or presupposition. In (11), Speaker A gives praise for someone's fluency in Japanese. Speaker B retorts that the person in question has just returned from living in Japan and so obviously, it follows that they should have a good level of Japanese, a view which thus challenges the implicit presupposition.

(11) A: 伊日語講甲真好。
     i$^2$    jit$^8$gi$^2$     kong$^2$ kah$^4$ chin$^1$ ho$^4$.
     3SG Japanese speak EXT very good
     'He speaks Japanese really well.'

    B: 伊對日本回來的講。
     i$^2$    ui$^3$    Jit$^8$pun$^2$ tng$^3$ai$^5$ e$^5$   **kong$^1$**.
     3SG from Japan     return   PRT DM$_{SAY}$
     'Well, he's just returned from Japan [*kong$^1$*].'      (Chang 1998: 621)

Below is a final example of the assertive use of *kong$^1$*, showing that it is also used in monologues. Lien (1988) describes a context where what appears to be a nail on the wall to a near-sighted speaker moves all of a sudden, whereupon the speaker realizes that it is an insect, as it flies away:

(12) A    (goân-lâi) sī hōu-sîn **kong**.
INTERJ (ADV)    be  fly   PRT
'It was a fly after all.'                                      (Lien 1988: 226)

This modal construction with assertive *kong*[1] is the best described of the four types under discussion for Southern Min. Moreover, there appears to be a general consensus that this discourse marker is used to express the meaning of counter-expectation (see, inter alia, Liu 1996; Chang 1998; Lien 1988) We can further elaborate on these insightful studies by formulating *kong*[1]'s use in terms of the two parameters of subjectivity and intersubjectivity.

The assertive *kong*[1] construction is clearly subjective in its expression of the speaker's viewpoint on the current conversational topic: the speaker challenges a presupposition by asserting his or her own belief ("I'm saying that I know this is true"). It is also intersubjective in having attributed an incorrect presupposition to the addressee ("I'm saying that what you thought is not true"). In (8), for example, the false presupposition at this point of the conversation is the belief that the addressee has to go and search out the source of a strange odor. Having projected this viewpoint onto the addressee, the speaker, Fuzhou Bo, then disagrees with it, stating that this is not the case and that a military dog should do the work. This holds even in the case of a supposed monologue, as in (12), where the speaker realizes that his own presupposition about the black spot on the wall was incorrect. Since he is talking to himself, he in fact acts assumes both roles of speaker and addressee.

## 3.2 Suggestions in imperative form: (NP$_{SUBJ}$) – Verb – (X) – *kong*[1]

Clause-final *kong*[1] can in Southern Min also be used in imperative constructions with the prototypical second person addressee, either overt or understood, as shown in the syntactic configuration (NP$_{SUBJ}$) – Verb – (X) – *kong*[1].[10]

The construction does not, however, have the illocutionary force typically associated with the imperative, i.e. a directive speech act such as a command, a prohibition or an order (Wierzbicka 1987: 37–49). It codes instead a suggestion and, as such, is perfectly compatible with an amicable, non-hierarchical relationship between speaker and addressee, one of its pragmatic conditions of use.

---

[10] Note that there is no morphological marking on the verb for the imperative mood, as observed in Section 1.2.

(13) Suggestion to addressee to leave
去講!
Khi³ **kong¹**.
go   DM_SAY
'How about you go.'
[Illocutionary force: I'm saying that I think it's a good idea for you to do it]

In (13), the speaker is encouraging the addressee to think about leaving. Hence, one presupposition compatible with the pragmatic meaning is that the addressee might have been hesitating to do so. The speaker is, however, of the opinion that it would be good for the addressee to undertake this action, for example, to leave at the given point in time so that they will not be late (see Wierzbicka 1987: 187 on suggestions in English for a similar feature of pragmatic meaning).

This construction is equally well suited to the imperative form with a first person plural inclusive addressee, 'let's X'. The speaker utters (14) to show agreement with a prior suggestion to leave. In addition, he or she simultaneously implies readiness to leave, as opposed to what the addressee may have believed (see also Lien 1988: 226).

(14) Suggestion to addressee to leave together
去講!
(Lai⁵)        khi³ **kong¹**!
(come.PURP) go   DM_SAY
'Let's go then!'
[Illocutionary force: I'm saying this to you: I think it's a good idea for us to go]

The brusqueness of the pure imperative with its bare verb form khi³! 去 'leave!', denuded of any softening discourse markers, basically results in a somewhat rude and impolite way of addressing another person. The imperative form does not take the addressee's "face" into consideration at all. This is because directive speech acts, including orders, commands and instructions, have roughly the following illocutionary force: "I'm telling you: do it!". Directives are evidently associated with an unequal status between interlocutors, where one person is obliged, for reasons of social or political convention, to do what the other has asked.

The same contrast is found for the minimal pair of a suggestion in (15) and an order in (16).

(15) Suggestion
   緊做講!
   *Kin² cho³ **kong¹**!*
   quickly do DM<sub>SAY</sub>
   'How about you do it quickly?'

(16) Order
   緊做!
   *Kin² cho³!*
   quickly do
   'Hurry up and do it!'

Example (15) may be used in a context where the speaker believes that the addressee has a tendency to be rather slow to get his or her work done. Hence, it would be a positive event, if he or she could do it more quickly. The use of the discourse marker *kong¹* softens an order into a suggestion and can thus be felicitously translated as an English whimperative, as in (13), (15) and (17).

(17) 無你四點半來講.
   *Bo⁵ li² si³ tiam² puann³ lai⁵ **kong¹**.*
   NEG 2SG four o'clock half come DM<sub>SAY</sub>
   'Why not come at 4.30 pm then?' (Liu 1996: 12)[11]

The presupposition in (17) is that the meeting had originally been planned for another time, which is no longer possible. As with (15) and (16), if the discourse marker *kong¹* is omitted, then (17) is far less polite and does not respect the addressee's face needs.

In examples discussed by Tseng (2008), we find *kong¹* in a complex conditional clause, where it is nonetheless being used as a suggestion, as in (18).

(18) 你若卜食, 我就分你食講.
   *Li² na⁷ beh⁷ chiah⁸, gua² chiu⁷ pun¹ li² chiah⁸ **kong¹**.*
   2SG if want eat 1SG then share 2SG eat DM<sub>SAY</sub>
   'If you want to eat it, then how about I share it with you?'
   (*ho²-ko¹-po⁵* 虎姑婆, Tiger Aunty) (Tseng 2008: 45)

---

**11** Both Frajzyngier (1991: 227) and Hopper and Traugott (1993: 14) point out that *say* or *let's say* can be used as a conditional formant in English to introduce the hypothetical mood. Example (17) could also be translated more literally as 'say, couldn't you come at 4.30 pm?', i.e. not as a directive but as a suggestion in the form of a proposal to the addressee (in both the Southern Min original and in the English translation).

This example is from the rather gruesome story of Tiger Aunty, a tiger demon that disguises itself as an elderly woman to gain entry into a house and snare the children, who are on their own. Its plan is to eat them up, a prerequisite for becoming fully human. While the tiger demon is eating the younger sister, the brother looks for her. He wonders what it is that the "aunty" is actually eating. The aunty, feasting away, then offers to share her food with him, which is somewhat surprising in the circumstances. Pragmatically, this has the illocutionary force of a suggestion, albeit sinister in nature: "say I share it with you (against all expectations)?"

The final example of this type, in (19), is from the narrative *Jesse's stories*: the speaker talks about the time when he was a young boy, penniless, and was offered summer work. He humorously relates his decision to take up this otherwise rather poorly remunerated part-time waitering job, giving two reasons in its favor: first, free meals were provided and, second, the work was not at all unpleasant. The utterance is thus a suggestion aimed at the speaker himself in this case, on the basis of his reasoning, and clearly contrary to expectations in the given context.

(19) 彼 陣仔着去! 去講喔!
$hit^8$ $chun^1$-$a^2$ $toh^8$ $khi^3$!
that time    then go
'So then I went!'

$khi^3$ **$kong^1$** oh!
go   $DM_{SAY}$  PRT
'Why not go?!'

(Lines 187–188, *Jesse's stories*, author's recording and transcription)
[Illocutionary force: I'm saying: I think it is a good idea for me to do this]

Importantly, this imperative-form construction is polysemous. With a different prosody and context, it can also be construed as a warning, as in (20), a salient feature that has also been observed by Lien (1988: 227) and Liu (1996).

## 3.3 Warnings in imperative form: ($NP_{2P\text{-}SUBJ}$) – Verb – (X) – $kong^1$

A third use of clause-final $kong^1$ is in warnings. This pragmatic function is found in contexts where the speaker does not want the addressee to perform a certain action, and indirectly forbids it by the use of $kong^1$. Example (20), which is structurally identical to (19), could be felicitously interpreted as a warning when used in a different context from (19) and pronounced with a different, threatening intonation.

(20) 去講！
 Khi³ **kong¹**!
 go  DM_SAY
 'Just you dare go!'

 [Illocutionary force: I say: If you go, you'll find out the consequences!
 (I think you know that I don't want you to go. If you do go, something bad could happen to you)]

Note that, in the suggestion in (13), the speaker actually wants the addressee to consider leaving in the belief that it would be good for him or her to do so. In contrast, in the warning in (20), the speaker does not want the addressee to go at all, since this action could lead to some kind of undesirable or unfortunate situation for him/her. The speaker thus means the opposite of what he or she says literally. Hence, a rhetorical effect is produced which leads to the construal of a warning. It seems that 'say'-derived discourse markers invite a hypothetical inference which could be paraphrased as follows: (i) condition: if you do it (action of the verb, e.g. 'you go'); (ii) implied (unspoken) consequence: it could be bad for you.

Example (21) similarly has two possible interpretations and could be understood as either a suggestion or a challenge in the form of a warning.

(21) 試看覓講.
 Chhi³ khuann³ mai³ **kong¹**.
 try  see   TENT  DM_SAY
 'Let's give it a try and see! (Don't be afraid.)' [suggestion]
 'Just you try it and see!!' [warning]

On the one hand, in the suggestion interpretation, a possible context could be the lifting of a dauntingly heavy object. This situation would be accompanied by a presupposition on the speaker's part that the addressee might not be able to do it, and is possibly even afraid to try. On the other hand, a possible context for the warning construal could be the case of two adversaries, one of whom has already issued a challenge to the other by stating or implying that he or she is weak and lacks the courage to fight. A possible response could thus be to use (21) with clause-final *kong¹* from which it can be inferred that the speaker refutes any such presupposition of weakness in issuing the challenge. This reading could be felicitously used in a context where the speaker wants to imply that he or she may turn out to be surprisingly stronger than the addressee believes.

Consequently, the same component of intersubjectivity is arguably present in the warning *kong*¹ construction as the one that we claimed is present in declarative form assertions with *kong*¹: the speaker challenges the presupposition he or she believes that the addressee holds, from which the opposite viewpoint can be inferred. A final example of this category shows the same opposition between speaker's and addressee's points of view:

(22) 好胆你就去講.
Hao² tann²   li²   tioh⁴  khi³  **kong**¹.
good courage 2SG  then   go    DM$_{SAY}$
'If you're brave enough, then go and do it.'        (Chang 1998: 621)

As in the previous examples, contrary to the literal reading of the utterance, the speaker does not in fact want the addressee to undertake the action. Moreover, the consequences of such an action are in the unspoken implication that it could be dangerous in some way for the addressee to do so.

The use of *kong*¹ in warnings also appears to be semantically closely related to the use of *kong*¹ in wh-questions coding rebuttals, in that a presupposition is similarly overturned. Rebuttals are discussed in the following section.

## 3.4 Rebuttals in *wh*-interrogative form: NP$_{SUBJ}$ – *wh*-pronoun – Verb – (X) – *kong*¹

Liu (1996: 12) points out that *wh*-interrogative questions may take clause-final *kong*¹ to produce utterances that express scorn or contempt and can be used to mock the addressee. They are interpreted, however, as rhetorical questions, not as literal ones. This has the end-effect of coding a rebuttal to the preceding assertion made by the other interlocutor.[12]

Example (23), taken from Liu (1996), contains a *wh*-question formed with *kui*² 幾 'how many'. In this example, A is mocking B for apparently obtaining a low grade in the exams, despite an enormous revision input. B retorts with a question challenging the very presupposition upon which A's utterance rests, namely, A's evaluation of B's exam result as poor. B simply turns the tables on A by asking her about her own performance.

---

[12] By interrogatives, the type that uses *wh*-pronouns is intended (and not the alternative or A-not-A polar question types).

(23) A: 你讀暝讀日才考60分喔！
Li² thak⁸ mi⁵　thak⁸ jit⁸ chiah⁴ kho² lak⁴chap⁸ hun¹ o!
2SG study night study day only　test 60　　　point PRT
'You were studying night and day, but only got 60 in your exams!'
[= P1]

B: 你考幾分講？
Li² kho² kui²　　hun¹ **kong¹**.
2SG test how.many point DM$_{SAY}$
'(So don't make fun of me:) How high a grade did you get then?' [= P2]
[Illocutionary force: if you say this (P1) to say something bad about me, then I can ask you the same in return (P2). I think it will be difficult for you to answer]　　　　　　　　　　　　　　(Liu 1996: 12)

The second example, in (24), carries the presupposition that A is on a strict diet and cannot eat treats such as chocolate. The offer therefore challenges the actual state of affairs, i.e. A's determination to stick to her diet, whence the rebuttal in the form of a rhetorical question:[13]

(24) CM: 你慾愛 ₘ巧克力ₘ 無？
Li² beh⁴ ai³ ₘqiǎokèlìₘ bo⁵?
2SG want like chocolate Q$_{<NEG}$
'Would you like some chocolate?'

A: 無在痟講。
bo⁵ teh⁴ siao² **kong¹**!
NEG PROG crazy DM$_{SAY}$
'You think I'm crazy!'　　　　　　　　　　　　　　　　(Chang 1998: 620)

A final example involves the rebuttal, in this case, of any sympathy in (25), in which a tall person hits his or her head on a doorway. The rhetorical question with *siang⁵* 誰 'who' implies that it is the fault of the victim for growing so tall.

(25) 誰叫你生彼高講？
Siang⁵ kio³ li² sing¹ hiah⁴ kuainn⁵ **kong¹**?
who make 2SG be.born so tall DM$_{SAY}$
'Well, who told you to grow so tall?'

In a similar manner to assertions and warnings with *kong¹*, rebuttals allow for the expression of the speaker's viewpoint (the parameter of subjectivity), more

---

[13] Note that the clause-initial negator *bo⁵* means 'otherwise' or 'it's not the case that' here and together with *kong¹* transposes the clause into a rhetorical question.

precisely, they allow for the denial of the addressee's point of view. They also allow for the rhetorically reconstructed viewpoint of the addressee (intersubjectivity) to be deduced – in other words, the presupposition which has been challenged: for example, the view that someone must be a poor scholar in (23) or that it is acceptable to eat chocolate in (24) or even the situation where someone has been "unwise" enough to grow too tall in (25).

## 3.5 Interim summary

Taiwanese Southern Min possesses four different construction types formed with clause-final *kong*[1]. It is used to code the different modalities of assertions, suggestions, warnings and rebuttals, which are distinguished by the syntactic construction in which they occur, by the appropriate intonation for suggestions and warnings and by the form of the presupposition.

Chang (1998) provides an interesting discussion of this clause-final usage and sets out to treat all types – regardless of their different illocutionary forces – as examples of the use of *kong*[1] as a counter-expectation marker, as do Lien (1988) and Liu (1996). Yet, this one label does not and cannot possibly account for all the relevant semantic and pragmatic features that we have described.

I would therefore like to suggest that all four clause-final uses of *kong*[1] specifically involve the correction of a presupposition attributed to the other interlocutor. It is this correction of a presupposition which is shared by all four constructions and not the vaguer notion of counter-expectations. Further, all these discourse uses are clearly based on the meaning of *kong*[1] as a 'say' verb and its lexical use to introduce a proposition, even as a kind of hypothetical in the case of suggestions and warnings: "Say you go now ...". These usages of *kong*[1] are cases of intersubjectivity *par excellence*, through which the speaker rhetorically reconstructs the subjectivity of the addressee (or his or her stance/perspective) and then goes on to refute this point of view, the presupposition which initially triggers the use of *kong*[1].

# 4 Development of clause-final *kong*[1] in Taiwanese Southern Min

## 4.1 Syntactic features, grammaticalization and (inter)subjectivity

In this section, I discuss six features of clause-final *kong*[1] that are connected with its syntax, syntactic reanalysis and grammaticalization.

First, in terms of syntactic features, what is striking about this function of *kong*¹ is that it displays its sandhi (or changed) tone [55] rather than its citation tone [51]. The sandhi tone is typically used in a non-final position within a tone group and is aptly described as its "context" or "combination" tone. When *kong*¹ occurs at the end of the clause, we would thus expect the citation or isolation tone in this position, i.e. high falling [51]. I suggest that there is a discourse reason for this: if tone sandhi applies, then this normally indicates that there is more speech to come, such as a quotation or a reported clause (i.e. indirect speech) introduced by the quotative marker *kong*¹. In the wake of the grammaticalization and subjectification of the quotative verb *kong*¹ into a discourse marker with metalinguistic value, the sandhi tone maintains its function to indicate that there is more speech to come. In this case, however, it signals the omitted speech, whose value and import the interlocutors need to infer. The change described here can be represented as the shift from (i) to (ii):

(i) clause₁ – *gua*⁵¹ – *kong*⁵⁵ 'I say'[QUOTATIVE INDEX] >

(ii) clause₁ – Ø – *kong*⁵⁵_DM ... (inferred context)

If this suprasegmental feature becomes invariant with the use of the discourse marker, as it appears to be doing, it reflects the erosion which is typically associated with grammaticalization, realized in this case as a phonological reduction and "obligatorification" of tonal possibilities (see Heine 2002 and Hopper and Traugott 1993 on obligatorification).[14]

Second, *kong*¹'s ability to refer to the immediately preceding context gives it a clause-linking function: it anaphorically evokes the prior clause(s) and its associated context and presuppositions. This points to the development of a metalinguistic textual function, as defined in Traugott (1995) and Traugott and Dasher (2002). The discourse marker *kong*¹ does not describe a real world event of speaking but serves to link parts of the discourse and set up the coding of an intersubjective meaning, as argued in Section 3.

Third, there is a category change from a quotative verb ("X said:" + quotation) to a discourse marker at the periphery of the clause. In this new function, *kong*¹ has completely lost all its verbal functions, being unable to take aspect, be negated or form questions.

Fourth, the use of *kong*¹ as a discourse marker does not seem to be entirely optional: when *kong*¹ is omitted, the constructional meaning changes completely, as is particularly clear in the case of suggestions versus orders (see

---

**14** This phenomenon is pointed out as early as in the seminal work of Cheng (1997) on complementizers in Southern Min, and it is also discussed in Simpson and Wu (2003) and Tseng (2008), among others.

Section 3.2). Compare also *lai⁵-khi³ kong¹* 來去講 'come-go DM_SAY' with *lai⁵-khi³ la¹* 'come-go PRT' 來去啦 'let's go!'. While both have the same denotation, the first utterance is used when the speaker is ready to leave, taking up the suggestion of his or her interlocutor (see example (14) as well). The second utterance could be suitably used when the addressee is reluctant to go, as the particle or discourse marker *la¹* 啦 has the function to insist and to cajole (Lien 1988: 214).

Fifth, the discourse marker *kong¹* can be used in a monologue. Two examples of lone speakers have been presented above in (12) and (19), where the speaker is reasoning with him- or herself and thus assumes the role of the addressee as well.

Sixth, none of the four constructions may be used in a polar A-not-A question form, as (26) shows.

(26) *阿張是不是台北人講?
    *A¹ Tiong¹   si³-m⁷-si³   Tai⁵pak⁴   lang⁵   **kong¹**?
    A-Tiong      be-NEG-be    Taipei     person  DM_SAY
    'Is A-Tiong from Taipei?'                               (Hwang 1998: 7)

This points to the semantic incompatibility of an interrogative form, which requires either a yes or a no answer, with clause-final *kong¹*. They are at semantic cross-purposes: *kong¹* builds a modally marked construction involving a different presupposition to that in a polar question. This restriction on co-occurrence helps demonstrate that *kong¹* has scope over the entire utterance – it is not merely a tag at the end of the clause. This brings us back to where we started: the constructions with clause-final *kong¹* rhetorically reconstruct the addressee's viewpoint, in particular, an incorrect presupposition, which is then challenged, "corrected" and overturned by the speaker. This applies to all four syntactic constructions which *kong¹* builds: assertions, suggestions, warnings and rebuttals.

## 4.2 Grammaticalization pathway for clause-final *kong¹*

Grammaticalized outcomes of the lexical verb *kong²* 講 'say' point to a case of complex polyfunctionality. At least three separate grammaticalization chains would be required to account for all its synchronic uses in Southern Min: (i) a complementizer arising from an earlier serial verb construction where the quotative sense of 'say' is coded by $V_2$ in a verb complex: say_quotative > $V_1$ speech act – $V_2$ say_quotative > $V_1$ (host expansion) – complementizer (see Chappell 2008 for details); (ii) a topic marker and conditional conjunction in clause-initial position from the transitive use of 'say' which means 'talk about (X)': say$_{\text{talk about}}$ X > say$_{\text{topic marker}}$ + clause 1 > say$_{\text{conditional marker}}$ + clause 1 (= protasis) (see also Haiman 1978) and (iii) the discourse marking function in clause-final position discussed in this paper.[15]

I have suggested that the development of the discourse marker is intimately associated with the reduction of a complex sentence to a simplex clause, in which the first clause containing a quotation is embedded under a following quotative clause: *gua² kong²* 我講 'I say'. The reduction first involves truncation and reanalysis of the original postposed clause in the complex sentence. Through ellipsis of the subject pronoun in *gua² kong²* 我講 'I say', this postposed quotative clause is truncated to just the bare 'say' verb form (see Güldemann 2008: 397–439 for a detailed discussion of this phenomenon) and appended to the remaining clause which, in its turn, is subsequently reanalyzed as the main clause. The discourse marker derived from the verb 'say' is now in clause-final position, and evidently no longer codes its literal, propositional meaning but rather has a metalinguistic function, challenging a presupposition of the interlocutor. This new metalinguistic function results from the (inter)subjectification which has accompanied the grammaticalization process for *kong¹* from (i) to (ii):

(i) complex sentence incorporating a matrix quotative clause:

   [clause$_1$]$_{\text{QUOTATION}}$ + clause$_2$ [*gua² kong¹* 我講 'I say']$_{\text{QUOTATIVE INDEX}}$

(ii) reanalysis as a simplex clause via truncation of the first person singular subject pronoun: [clause$_1$] + [*kong¹* 講]$_{\text{DM<SAY}}$

The syntactic reanalysis in stage (ii) is accompanied by semantic and pragmatic changes which involve generalization of the clause type to any kind of proposition. The concomitant invariable use of the tone sandhi value for *kong¹* represents a type of phonological reduction or "erosion" in terms of Heine (2002). The specific semantic and pragmatic values grammatically coded by each of the four main constructions have been described in the main part of this article.

At this stage, the account of the proposed stages for grammaticalization and inter/subjectification is a mere hypothesis for the development of this clause-final discourse marker. Unfortunately, we do not have the necessary diachronic data needed to support such a hypothesis. Further cross-linguistic research is needed to verify whether such a hypothesis may be upheld.

---

[15] These three pathways evidently do not account for how clause-initial discourse markers developed, nor for several other compound conjunctions formed with 'say' verbs. For this more research is needed.

## 5 Conclusion

I have argued that the grammaticalization of *kong*[1] from a verb of saying into a clause-final discourse marker has led to the formation of four distinct constructions, each with its own structure and modality. Furthermore, it has been argued that all four construction types associated with *kong*[1] show subjectivization and grammaticalization of the verb 'say' upon its development into a discourse marker and the coding of a particular dimension of intersubjectivity: they all involve expression of the speaker's viewpoint or attitude toward the current conversational topic as well as the speaker's "rhetorical reconstruction" of a presupposition made by the addressee (intersubjectivity).

More specifically, the modal meanings of the four new constructions can no longer be linked with the basic lexical use of the verb 'say', which originally denotes an event in the external world, i.e. the act of speaking. The case of *kong*[1] presents a clear illustration of Traugott and Dasher's (2002) notion of the capacity of subjectification to pre-empt material in the speech event for the speaker's own uses – in this case, from the lexical form associated with a 'say' verb to a metalinguistic discourse marker.

Furthermore, in building modally marked constructions in which it has scope over the entire utterance, *kong*[1] is clearly a fully integrated constituent used to form these four modal constructions. It is not a mere "optional tag" at the end of the clause, shown clearly by loss of pragmatic meaning, that is, the particular intersubjective value, upon its omission. At this simple level of comparison, the semantic contrast is evident in the difference between suggestions formed with *kong*[1] and "bare verb" orders that do not use this discourse marker in Southern Min. At a more elaborate level of comparison, *kong*[1] is closely connected with the denial of certain presuppositions which trigger its use. The grammaticalization and (inter)subjectification of *kong*[1] in clause-final position thus leads to new metalinguistic functions, forming constructions which can code assertions and suggestions, or express warnings and rebuttals in Southern Min.

## Acknowledgments

This paper was first read at GRAMIS, the *Conference on Grammaticalization and (Inter)Subjectification*, held at the Royal Flemish Academy of Belgium for Science and the Arts in Brussels, November 11–13, 2010. I would like to thank the organizers, Johan van der Auwera and Jan Nuyts for this windfall opportunity to present my research on 'say' verbs and their grammaticalization pathways in Sinitic languages from the perspective of intersubjectivity.

Research leading to these results has received funding from the European Research Council under the European Community's Seventh Framework Programme (FP7/2007–2013) / ERC Advanced Grant agreement n° 230388 *The Hybrid Syntactic Typology of Sinitic Languages (2009–2013)* and from the Agence Nationale de la Recherche in France for the project *Diachronic Change in Southern Min* (DIAMIN) (n° ANR-08-BLAN-0174 CSD 9, 2009–2011).

I would also like to thank Professor Chinfa Lien 連金發 for his comments on earlier versions of this paper, not to mention his generosity in making available the computerized database of Southern Min materials at National Tsing Hua University to the French DIAMIN project as part of our collaboration with his National Science Council team in Taiwan. I gratefully acknowledge the research assistance of Chien Tang Su 蘇建唐 and Jang-ling Lin 林徵玲 on the Taiwanese Southern Min data, as well as many valuable questions and comments received from the editors and reviewers of this volume and from the ERC-SINOTYPE and ANR-DIAMIN team members in Paris – Manjun Chen 陳曼君, Yujie Chen 陳玉潔, Hilario de Sousa, Xuping Li 李旭平, Sing Sing Ngai 倪星星 and Wang Jian 王健, from colleagues in the audience at the Brussels conference and colleagues in our partner NSC-DIAMIN team at National Tsing Hua University, Hsin Chu, Taiwan, during a workshop on Reflections of Diachronic Change Mirrored in Early Southern Min Texts, held in November 2011 in Taiwan.

## Abbreviations

1/2/3 = first/second/third person; ADV = adverb; ASST = assertive; CAUS = causative verb; CL = classifier; COMPR = comparative marker; COND = conditional marker; CRS = currently relevant state; DEM = demonstrative; DIMN = diminutive; DIR = directional; DM = discourse marker; ECHO = echo question; EVD = evidential; EXT = extent 'so X that'; IMP = imperative; INCH = inchoative; INTERJ = interjection; J = Japanese; LIG = marker of ligature; LOC = locative; M = Mandarin; MIR = mirative; NEG = negative; NOM = nominalizer; OM = object marker; PFV = perfective; PL = plural; POSS = possessive; PROG = progressive; PRT = particle; PURP = purpose; Q = question marker; SG = singular; SUBJ = subject; TENT = tentative aspect; WRNG = warning

## References

Benveniste, Emile. 1958. *Problèmes de linguistique générale*, Vol. 1. Paris: Editions Gallimard.
Chang Miao-Hsia. 1998. The discourse functions of Taiwanese *kong* in relation to its grammaticalization. In Shuanfan Huang (ed.), *Selected papers from the Second International Symposium on Languages in Taiwan*, 111–128. Taipei: Crane.

Chao Yuen Ren. 1947. *Cantonese primer*. Cambridge, MA: Harvard University Press.
Chappell, Hilary. 2008. Variation in the grammaticalization of complementizers from *verba dicendi* in Sinitic languages. *Linguistic Typology* 12(1). 45–98.
Chappell, Hilary & Christine Lamarre. 2005. *A grammar and lexicon of Hakka: Historical materials from the Basel Mission Library*. Paris: École des Hautes Études en Sciences Sociales.
Chappell, Hilary & Alain Peyraube. 2016. Modality and mood in Sinitic languages. In Johan van der Auwera & Jan Nuyts (eds.), *Oxford handbook of mood and modality*, 296–329. Oxford: Oxford University Press.
Cheng, Robert L. 鄭良偉. (1997) [1991]. Taiyu yu Taiwan Huayu-li de ziju jiegou biaozhi 台語與台灣華語裏的句結構標誌"講"與"看" [The complementation markers *kóng* 'say' and *khuàⁿ* 'see' in Taiwanese and Taiwanese Mandarin]. In Robert L. Cheng (ed.), *Tai, Huayu de jiechu yu tongyi yu de hudong* 台,華語的接觸與同義語的互動 [Contact between Taiwanese and Mandarin and restructuring of their synonyms], 105–132. Taipei: Yuanliu Publishers.
Chui Kawai. 1994. Grammaticization of the saying verb *wa* in Cantonese. *Santa Barbara Papers in Linguistics* 5. 1–12.
Douglas, Carstairs. 1990 [1873]. *Chinese-English dictionary of the vernacular spoken language of Amoy, with the principal variations of the Chang-Chew and Chin-Chew dialects*. Supplement by Thomas Barclay. Taipei: Southern Materials Center.
Du Bois, Jack, Stephan Schuetze-Coburn, Danae Paolino & Susanna Cumming. 1993. Outline of discourse transcription. In Jane Edwards & Martin Lampert (eds.), *Talking data: Transcription and coding in discourse research*, 45–89. Hillsdale, NJ: Lawrence Erlbaum.
Fitzmaurice, Susan. 2004. Subjectivity, intersubjectivity and the historical construction of interlocutor stance: From stance markers to discourse markers. *Discourse Studies* 6(4). 427–448.
Frajzyngier, Zygmunt. 1991. The *de dicto* domain in language. In Elizabeth Closs Traugott & Bernd Heine (eds.), *Approaches to grammaticalization*, Vol. 2, 219–251. Amsterdam & Philadelphia: John Benjamins.
Güldemann, Tom. 2008. *Quotative indexes in African languages: A synchronic and diachronic survey*. Berlin: Mouton de Gruyter.
Haiman, John. 1978. Conditionals are topics. *Language* 54(3). 564–589.
Heine, Bernd. 2002. On the role of context in grammaticalization. In Ilse Wischer & Gabriele Diewald (eds.), *New reflections on grammaticalization*, 83–101. Amsterdam: John Benjamins.
Hopper, Paul J. & Elisabeth Closs Traugott. 1993. *Grammaticalization*. Cambridge: Cambridge University Press.
Huang Shuanfan. 2000. The story of heads and tails: On a sequentially sensitive lexicon. *Language and Linguistics* 1(2). 79–107.
Huang Shuanfan. 2003. Doubts about complementation: A functionalist analysis. *Language and Linguistics* 4(2). 429–455.
Hwang Jya-Lin. 1998. A comparative study on the grammaticalisation of saying verbs in Chinese. In Chaofen Sun (ed.), *Proceedings of the 10th North American Conference on Chinese Linguistics*, 574–584. Stanford: Stanford University.
Kwok, Helen. 1984. *Sentence particles in Cantonese*. Hong Kong: Centre of Asian Studies, University of Hong Kong.
Lien Chinfa. 1988. Taiwanese sentence-final particles. In Robert L. Cheng & Shuanfan Huang (eds.), *The structure of Taiwanese: A modern synthesis*, 209–233. Taipei: Crane.
Liu Hsiu-ying 劉秀瑩 1996. Minnanhua shuo-hua dongci *kóng* zhi gongneng yanbian ji yuyi tantao 閩南話說話動詞講之功能演變及語義探討 [Exploration of the functional develop-

ment and semantics of the speech act verb *kóng* 'say' in Southern Min]. Manuscript. Hsinchu: Institute of Linguistics, National Tsing Hua University.

Lyons, John. 1982. Deixis and subjectivity: *Loquor, ergo sum?* In Robert J. Jarvella & Wolfgang Klein (eds.), *Speech, place and action: Studies in deixis and related topics*, 101–124. New York: Wiley.

Matthews, Stephen. 1998. *Evidentiality and mirativity in Cantonese: Wo5, wo4, wo3!* Manuscript. Hong Kong: University of Hong Kong.

Matthews, Stephen & Virginia Yip. 2011. *Cantonese: A comprehensive grammar*. London: Routledge.

Nuyts, Jan. 2016. Analyses of the modal meanings. In Jan Nuyts & Johan van der Auwera (eds.), *Oxford handbook of mood and modality*, 31–49. Oxford: Oxford University Press.

Rey, Charles. 1988 [1926]. *Dictionnaire chinois–français: Dialecte Hakka*. Taipei: Southern Materials Center.

Simpson, Andrew & Zoë Wu. 2002. IP-raising, tone sandhi and the creation of S-final particles: Evidence for cyclic spell-out. *Journal of East Asian Linguistics* 11(1). 67–99.

Su, Lily I-Wen. 2004. Subjectification and the use of the complementizer *SHUO*. *Concentric: Studies in Linguistics* 30(1). 19–40.

Traugott, Elizabeth Closs. 1995. Subjectification in grammaticalization. In Dieter Stein & Susan Wright (eds.), *Subjectivity and subjectivisation*, 31–54. Cambridge: Cambridge University Press.

Traugott, Elizabeth Closs. 2003. From subjectification to intersubjectification. In Raymond Hickey (ed.), *Motives for language change*, 124–139. Cambridge: Cambridge University Press.

Traugott, Elizabeth Closs. 2007. (Inter)subjectification and unidirectionality. *Journal of Historical Pragmatics* 8(2). 295–309.

Traugott, Elizabeth Closs. 2010. Revisiting subjectification and intersubjectification. In Kristin Davidse, Lieven Vandelanotte & Hubert Cuyckens (eds.), *Sugjectification, intersubjectification and grammaticalization*, 29–70. Berlin: De Gruyter Mouton.

Traugott, Elizabeth Closs & Richard B. Dasher. 2002. *Regularity in semantic change*. Cambridge: Cambridge University Press.

Tseng Ming-hua. 2008. The multifunction of Taiwanese Southern Min *kong*[2]. Hsinchu: National Tsing Hua University MA thesis.

Wang Jian. 2013. Yīxiē nánfāng fāngyán zhōng láizì yánshuō dòngcí de yìwài fànchóu biāojì 一些南方方言中来自言说动词的意外范畴标记 [From 'say' verbs to mirative markers in several Southern Sinitic languages]. *Fangyan (Dialects)* 2. 111–119.

Wierzbicka, Anna. 1987. *English speech act verbs: A semantic dictionary*. Sydney: Academic Press.

# Appendix: Southern Min transcription conventions

The modified Church Romanization is used in all the transcriptions of the Taiwanese Southern Min data with tone numbers, unless I am quoting from an article where tone diacritics have been used. The modifications of the Church Romanization devised by Carstairs Douglas (1990 [1873]) are as follows: the symbols *ts* and *ts^h* are not used since they represent sounds which are no longer phonemically distinct from the sounds represented by *ch* and *chh* respectively in modern Southern Min; open *o* and closed *o* are represented as *ou* and *o*; vocalic nasalization is indicated by a double *n*; an empty box ☐ is used where the Chinese character is not known, which is not infrequent in the case of the special Southern Min lexemes.

For the convenience of the reader, the tones are represented by tone numbers in the transcription known as the modified Church Romanization, as indicated in Table 1. The tone sandhi values are given in italic numbers below the citation values in the table, and, in general, will not be given in the transcription of examples used in the present description.

**Table 1:** Tone inventory of Southern Min

|  | Level tone 平聲 | Ascending tone 上聲 | Departing tone 去聲 | Entering tone 入聲 |
|---|---|---|---|---|
| Upper register | Tone 1 High level 55 *33* | Tone 2 High falling 51 *55* | Tone 3 Low falling 21 *51* | Tone 4 Low checked 2 *5* |
| Lower register | Tone 5 Mid rising 25 *21/33* |  | Tone 7 Low level 33 *21* | Tone 8 High checked 5 *2* |

The transcription of my recordings in Southern Min follows the system devised for natural conversation and oral narratives by Du Bois and colleagues at the University of California at Santa Barbara (see Du Bois et al. 1993) for the Santa Barbara Corpus of Spoken American English. The intonation unit is treated as the basic unit of conversation, a unit of discourse with prosodic, syntactic and cognitive ramifications.

Thomas Egan
# 6 The subjective and intersubjective uses of "fail to" and "not fail to"

**Abstract:** It is virtually a commonplace in grammaticalization studies that intersubjective senses of lexical or grammatical items develop later than, and as extensions of, subjective senses. The two constructions examined in this chapter, "fail to" and "not fail to", provide further support for the assertion that intersubjective senses develop later than subjective ones. However, their development challenges the assumption that intersubjective senses always constitute extensions of subjective senses. In fact, both in the case of the "not fail to" construction in Early Modern English (EModE) and the "fail to" construction in Late Modern English (LModE), the intersubjective senses are independent extensions of objective senses, rather than contemporary subjective ones. Moreover, whereas the objective and subjective senses of positive and negative polarity "fail to" code semantic opposites (contraries), their intersubjective senses are completely unrelated to each other. The development of each of these intersubjective senses is first described in detail and then related to the current discourse on intersubjectivity and intersubjectification. Finally, the question of whether positive polarity "fail to" is in the process of grammaticalizing as a marker of negation is addressed.

## 1 Introduction

The "fail to" construction (shorthand for [NP *fail to*-INFINITIVE]) is unusual among English verb + complement constructions in having twice shown a development from non-subjective to intersubjective senses, as these notions are described, for instance, by Traugott and Dasher (2002). In the first several centuries after its appearance in English, the matrix verb *fail* was negated, as in (1) and (2).

(1) *For she hath taught hym how he* **shal not fayle**
 *The Fles* **to wynne.**
 'For she has taught him how he cannot fail to win the fleece.'[1]
 (Chaucer, *The Legend of Good Women*, 1646–1647)

---

**1** All translations are the author's.

DOI 10.1515/9783110492347-007

(2) ***I will not faile***, *upon knowledge of your pleasure and desire herin,* ***to procure*** *the same to be dispatched with expedition.*
(CEECS, *Walsyngham to the Earl of Leycester*, 1586)

In (1), "not fail to" is to be understood objectively: the agentive subject is making a conscious effort to win the fleece. In (2), on the other hand, "not fail to" is used intersubjectively, to encode a promise on the part of the letter writer to the Earl of Leicester.

The non-negated form of the construction surfaces in the 16th century and gradually supersedes the negated form, in the process tracing a path from non-subjectivity to intersubjectivity, similar to that of its negated counterpart several centuries earlier.

(3) *Thrice she attempted to speak, and thrice her voice* ***failed to penetrate*** *the folds of the heavy door.*
(CLMET, Bulwer-Lytton, *The Last Days of Pompeii*, 1834)

(4) *"I* ***fail to see*** *the connection," said Leonard, hot with stupid anger.*
(CLMET, Forster, *Howards End*, 1910)

The sentence in (3) represents the more objective reading of "fail to": the owner of the voice is making a patent, though unsuccessful, effort to make herself heard. Sentence (4), on the other hand, has an intersubjective reading, in that the speaker implies obtuseness or ill-faith on the part of his interlocutor.

In this chapter, I trace the evolution of both the negated and non-negated forms, with a particular emphasis on the development of the intersubjective senses. In Section 2, I touch briefly on some theoretical issues that are relevant to the development of intersubjective meanings. Details of the corpora investigated are provided in Section 3, while Section 4 presents the semantics of the various "fail to" constructions. Section 5 is devoted to the earlier construction with the negated matrix verb and Section 6 to its later non-negated counterpart. In Section 7, I relate both subjective and intersubjective senses of the two constructions to current theory on subjectivity, intersubjectivity and intersubjectification. In section 8, Boye and Harder's (2009, 2012, 2014) theory of grammaticalization in terms of primary and secondary information focus is applied to the now dominant non-negated form of the construction in an effort to ascertain the extent to which this form can be said to have grammaticalized. Finally, Section 9 contains a summary and conclusions.

## 2 Theoretical issues

With the aim of this chapter in mind, namely to trace the evolution of the "fail to" and "not fail to" constructions with a special emphasis on the development of intersubjective readings, I will briefly introduce the theoretical concepts at issue here.

First, I go along with Goldberg's (2006: 3) definition of constructions as "conventionalized pairings of form and function". Constructions may vary in size from individual words to phrases of varying length (Goldberg 2006: 5). They may occur at various levels of abstraction (see, for instance, the micro-, meso- and macro-level distinguished by Traugott 2007 and Traugott 2008) and, correspondingly, contain one or more open slots. The construction mentioned at the outset of this paper, [NP *fail to*-INFINITIVE], contains at least two slots that are not lexically specified (with the *fail to* slot possibly constituting a third open slot, as it offers the choice between *fail to* and *not fail to*). Then again, the construction [*I will/shall not fail to* V] contains four slots that are lexically specified, one slot that offers the user a choice between two lexemes, and just one, the infinitive, that is open. This construction fits the definition of "phraseologism" adopted by Gries (2008: 5): "the co-occurrence of a form or lemma of a lexical item and any other kind of linguistic element".

Second, any discussion of the emergence in a language of new lexemes or constructions, or new uses/senses of existing items, is bound to tacitly or explicitly assume a theoretical stance about the point at which the new item or sense may be said to have become established in the language in question. This point must necessarily come later than the point at which it is established in the internal grammar of some speakers of the language. I will not address the question here of how many speakers it takes before a construction is to be considered part of the language (rather than being merely idiolectal), but I will touch on this issue in Section 7.

The process by which a linguistic item becomes established in the grammar of an individual speaker is called "entrenchment" by Langacker, according to whom:

> Every use of a structure has a positive impact on its degree of entrenchment, whereas extended periods of disuse have a negative impact. With repeated use, a novel structure becomes progressively entrenched, to the point of becoming a unit; moreover, units are variably entrenched depending on the frequency of their occurrence (*driven*, for example, is more entrenched than *thriven*). (Langacker 1987: 59)

I will refer to entrenchment in Section 7, when discussing whether the intersubjective constructions discussed in Sections 5 and 6 may be said to have undergone intersubjectification in the sense of Traugott (2010). By intersubjectification is meant the process whereby intersubjective senses of a construction become entrenched in the grammar of a cross-section of the speakers of a language.

A final issue relates to the notion of "grammaticalization", whose relevance for the development of "fail to" is taken up in Section 8. According to Trousdale (2010: 58), "the grammaticalization of constructions requires changes at both the form and meaning poles, a view consistent with standard work on grammaticalization (see e.g. Hopper & Traugott 2003)". In the present study, a question that must be addressed deals with the sort of changes at the form pole we might expect to see if "fail to" is grammaticalizing. Since "the process of grammaticalization is a process whereby linguistic items gain grammatical function while reducing their lexical-descriptive function" (Diewald 2010: 18), we should see a change whereby "fail to" displays an increase in functional as opposed to lexical content. There remains the question of how it can be determined whether such an increase in functional load has actually taken place. According to Boye and Harder (2009), the assumption of functional category status by a full lexical item is a change in which "lexical elements go from being used to convey primary information to being used predominantly to encode secondary information.... Grammaticalization resides basically in the coding of secondary information status" (Boye and Harder 2009: 32). I operationalize this definition of Boye and Harder's in Section 8 in considering the possible grammaticalization of "fail to".

## 3 Corpora

A wide selection of corpora was examined, as it was necessary to find evidence of non-subjective, subjective and intersubjective uses of the "fail to" constructions (in this respect, for instance, the intersubjective senses required including sources containing dialogue, either face-to-face or epistolary).

To begin with the historical corpora, evidence for Middle English was provided by the *Helsinki Corpus*, Chaucer's complete works and Gower's *Confessio Amantis*.[2] For Early Modern English, the *Helsinki Corpus of English Texts* (Helsinki) was again used, as were the *Corpus of Early English Correspondence Sampler* (CEECS), the *Lampeter Corpus* and the complete works of Shakespeare. The first (shorter) version of the *Corpus of Late Modern English Texts* (CLMET) and the *Corpus of Historical American English* (COHA) provided data for the Late Modern period.

---

[2] In the case of Chaucer, the actual text searched was the one in Project Gutenberg with modernized spelling. The tokens returned were checked against the Riverside Chaucer.

For Present-day English, a number of recent or contemporary corpora were examined. These included six corpora available on the ICAME CD-Rom, LOB and FLOB for British English, Brown and Frown for American English and the ACE and Wellington corpora for Australian and New Zealand English, respectively. Recourse was also had to the much larger *British National Corpus* (BNC), from which a random sample of one thousand tokens of the lexeme *fail* was downloaded. This sample included 729 tokens of the constructions with the *to*-infinitive. The *Corpus of Contemporary American English* (COCA), like its historical sister corpus, was mostly consulted for tokens conveying the intersubjective senses. Finally, in order to get an impression of how the constructions were being used in the twenty-first century, I conducted a search of the internet using *WebCorp*.

Except for COCA, COHA and *WebCorp*, all corpora were searched, using WordSmith, for *fail* in its various forms and spelling variants, followed by *to* within a context search horizon of five words to the right. COCA and COHA were mainly searched, using their custom-built search engine, for tokens of the intersubjective senses, using search queries such as *I will not fail to*. Because of the limited number of returns per query provided by the custom-built *WebCorp* search engine, when using it I searched separately for all forms of *fail* followed either directly or after one or two wild cards by *to*. I also used *WebCorp* to search for tokens of *failed*, followed by up to five wildcards and then *did*, *so* and *neither*, in order to obtain tokens relevant to the discussion of grammaticalization in Section 8.

## 4 The senses of the "fail to" constructions

The two constructions that are investigated in this chapter, the "fail to" construction and the "not fail to" construction, are both polysemous. According to the *New Oxford Dictionary of English*, which is corpus-based, there are three main senses of the verb *fail* followed by the *to*-infinitive in Present-day English. These are, firstly, 'to be unsuccessful in achieving one's goal'; secondly, 'to neglect to do something'; and thirdly, to 'behave in a way contrary to hopes or expectations by not doing something'. I will refer to these three senses as the 'effort' sense, the 'duty' sense and the 'expectation' sense, respectively. They are exemplified by (5)–(7), taken from the British National Corpus (BNC).

(5) Detectives searched the area with a helicopter and tracker dogs but **failed to catch** the man.   (BNC, K1W 1645)

(6) To add insult to injury the hypnotist claimed Kylie **had failed to pay** the consultation bill.   (BNC, ADR 655)

(7) But, in spite of the considerable effort and investment, it **has** for many years **failed to pay** its way.   (BNC, BNS 1684)

Whereas (5) and (6) respectively convey that the subject has made an effort or has neglected a duty, in (7) it is not the expectations of the grammatical subject that remain unfulfilled. Rather, it is the expectations of the speaker (which, for the sake of convenience, I take to also denote "the writer"), or at least expectations of which the speaker is aware, that are not met. Accordingly, (7) may be said to be more subjective than either (5) or (6). Note that I am using the terms "objective" and "subjective" in the Traugottian sense of connoting the absence or presence of an attitude on the part of the speaker to the content of the predication, rather than in the Langackerian sense of construal (see, for example, Traugott 2010: 33 and Langacker 2008: 77). The three senses may be placed on a cline from least subjective to more subjective, as illustrated in (8).

(8) Cline of objectivity – subjectivity for "fail to"
*try and not succeed → neglect a duty → fail to meet speaker's expectations*

When "*fail*" is negated, the polarity of these three senses is reversed, yielding the three meanings 'succeed in one's efforts', 'fulfill one's duty' and 'meet one's expectations', where "one" in the two more objective senses again refers to the grammatical subject and in the expectation sense to the speaker. These three senses are exemplified by (9)–(11), taken from the *Corpus of Contemporary American English* (COCA).

(9) *Toward that goal, we may try and fail, but* **let's not fail to try.**
(COCA, Khosla, Vinod, *Newsweek*, 2008)

(10) *Congress* **did not fail to do** *its job when it deliberately ignored right-wingers' concerns when extending long overdue civil rights to the deaf and disabled.*
(COCA, Letter to the Editor, *San Francisco Chronicle*, 1993)

(11) *I have chosen to be guided by hope and if you join me in this, we* **will not fail to witness** *the rebirth of our nation.*
(COCA, Baldauf, Scott, *Christian Science Monitor*, 2008)

The three negated senses may also be situated on a cline of objectivity-subjectivity, as in (12):

(12) Cline of objectivity – subjectivity for "not fail to"
*try and succeed* → *fulfill a duty* → *meet speaker's expectations*

In addition to the non-subjective and subjective uses of these two constructions, particular attention will also be paid to intersubjective uses, in which the slot(s) preceding *fail* are specified for lexical content. Thus, in the 'promise' sense, to be discussed in Section 5, *not fail* is always preceded in direct speech by modal *will* or *shall*, which in turn is preceded by the first-person singular pronoun. The construction is thus "I will/shall not fail to". As I pointed out in Section 2, these constructions can be seen as phraseologisms (Gries 2008: 5).

# 5 The history of "not fail to"

The "fail to" construction is first recorded in English in the late 14th century. The English verb *fail* was borrowed from the French verb *faillir*, which was soon to split into *falloir* denoting epistemic or deontic necessity, and *faillir* denoting an 'almost-but-not-quite' realization of the situation in the complement clause. In most of the early occurrences of "fail to" in English, the matrix verb is negated, as in the example from Chaucer in (1).[3] There is one other instance of the construction in Chaucer (in *The Merchant's Tale* IV (E) 1631–1632), also negated, and six negated tokens in Gower, three of which resemble the Chaucerian tokens in being non-subjective in meaning. One of these is cited as (13).

(13) *Such wepne also for him sche dighte,*
*That he be reson **mai noght faile***
***To make an ende** of his bataile;*
'She also made such a weapon for him that there was no way he could fail to bring his combat to a successful conclusion.'
(*Confessio Amantis*, Book 5, 5352–5354)

The "fail to" construction in (13) conveys a non-subjective meaning in that the subject is understood to be making an effort to succeed in some endeavor. The

---
[3] The Helsinki Corpus contains 14 tokens of its negated "fail to" and just one non-negated token, cited as (28). All 24 tokens of "fail to" in the *Corpus of Early English Correspondence Sampler* (CEECS) are negated. All 14 tokens in the Lampeter Corpus are negated.

remaining three negated tokens in Gower, exemplified here by (14), are more subjective in meaning.

(14)  Bot what man that his lust desireth
      Of love, and therupon conspireth
      With wordes feigned to deceive,
      He **schal noght faile to receive**
      His peine, as it is ofte sene.
      'But any man with an appetite for love, who conspires with lies to deceive, shall not fail to receive his just desserts, as has often been seen.'
      (*Confessio Amantis*, Book 1, 1206–1209)

In (14), there is no implication that the deceitful subject is in search of punishment for his falsehood. Rather, it is the narrator who voices his subjective opinion that the subject will necessarily get his comeuppance. There is evidence in French from the early 14th century of both non-subjective and more subjective uses of *faillir*, suggesting that both uses were borrowed at the same time.[4]

In Late Middle English, the negated construction developed two intersubjective uses. Firstly, from the mid-15th century it is used to encode injunctions, as in (15).

(15)  And that ye **faille not thus to doo** as ye tendre our pleasure.
      (CEECS, Henry VII to Sir Gilbert Talbot, ca. 1500)

In (15), the writer imposes an obligation on the addressee. The negated construction as used here carries deontic force, in much the same manner as its non-negated impersonal French cognate *Il faut que vous...*. The second intersubjective use surfaces in the data around a century later. Pragmatically, it is the mirror image of the injunction sense. When used with first-person subjects and the modals *will* or *shall*, "not fail to" codes a promise on the part of the speaker. There are 12 such tokens in the CEECS, represented here by (16).

(16)  According to my promise, **I will not faile** to let you understand of my proseedings last week.
      (CEECS, Anne Lady Meautys to Jane Lady Bacon, 1632)

The expression *will not faile to* in (16) could be paraphrased 'I promise to', and indeed the writer actually uses the word *promise* to refer to a previous commitment to keep the addressee informed of her actions. Moreover, the same

---

4 For some examples of the construction in Old French, see Egan (2010: 124).

writer, in correspondence with the same person, uses the "will not fail to" construction in reported speech with the reporting verb *promise*. She does so in two separate letters, (17) and (18), written three years apart.

(17) They have both promised me seriously **they will not faile to performe** all that they can for me.
(CEECS, Anne Lady Meautys to Jane Lady Bacon, 1633)

(18) Sister, her Majestie doth use you with much fauor, and hath promised me that what soeuer doth lie in her power to doe mee good **shee will not faile to perform** it.
(CEECS, Anne Lady Meautys to Jane Lady Bacon, 1636)

There can be no doubt that in examples such as (2) and (16)–(18) the "will not fail to" construction is used to intersubjectively encode a commitment on the part of the (actual or reported) speaker. Moreover, the fact that (18) was produced three years after (17) shows clearly that the "will not fail to" construction is entrenched in the grammar/lexicon of this particular writer. Whether the construction can be said to be intersubjectified as opposed to merely intersubjective is a question which will be addressed in Section 7.

We can see in (19)–(20), taken from the 1710–1780 subperiod of the *Corpus of Late Modern English Texts* (CLMET), that both injunction and promise senses continue to be used in the 18th century.

(19) *I* **will not fail to make** *your compliments to the Pomfrets and Carterets.*
(CLMET, letter from Robert Walpole to Horace Mann, 1744)

(20) *I desire, therefore, that one of you two* **will not fail to write** *to me once a week.*
(CLMET, letter from Chesterfield to his son, 1748)

Example (19) resembles (16) in encoding a promise on the part of the speaker, while (20) resembles (15) in encoding an injunction on the addressee.

The first half of the 19th century witnessed a decrease in the use of the intersubjective construction, as of other uses of "not fail to" (see Section 6 for details of this decrease). There are only four tokens of the intersubjective senses in the 1780–1850 period of the CLMET, (two of which are cited as (21) and (22).

(21) *"I* **shall not fail to do so**, *madam," replied Suffolk. "Your majesty will have strict justice."*
(CLMET, Ainsworth, *Windsor Castle*, 1843)

(22) "Your grace acts as beseems a loyal gentleman," replied Surrey. "Hereafter I **will not fail to account** to you for my conduct in any way you please."
(CLMET, Ainsworth, *Windsor Castle*, 1843)

It is perhaps worth mentioning that the texts in which (21) and (22) occur are works of historical fiction. It is quite possible therefore that the authors employed what they felt to be a somewhat archaic mode of expression in order to lend their narratives a period feel. Whether or not this is the case, the construction was certainly in its dying throes by the 1840s. In the 1850–1920 period of the CLMET, the construction is not attested. There are, however, a few later examples in the much larger *Corpus of Historical American English* (COHA). Details of the incidence of the intersubjective construction in the century 1820–1919 can be seen in Figure 1.

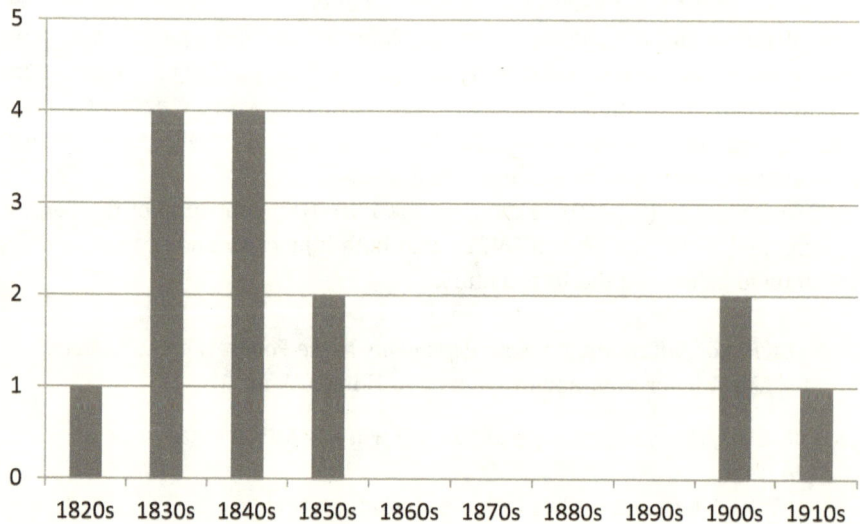

**Figure 1:** Raw frequencies for the intersubjective sense of "will not fail to" in COHA, 1820–1919

In what sort of texts do we find intersubjective "will not fail to" in American English? Typical examples are (23)–(25):

(23) *"Nevertheless,"* continued Amador, *"I **will not fail to** make thy petition, backed with my own request, to the seor Narvaez".*
(COHA, Robert M. Bird, *Calavar: Or The Knight of the Conquest, A Romance of Mexico*, Vol. 1, 1834)

(24) *"I **will not fail to wait** on thee, my liege."*
(COHA, Horatio N. Moore, *Orlando*, 1835)

(25) *"My lady, go to thy tiring room and make thee ready. I **will not fail to wait** thee."*
(COHA, Beulah M. Dix, *Road to Yesterday*, 1906)

It would not be necessary to know the titles of these works to assign them to the genre of historical fiction. For example, all three texts employ the archaic form of the second-person singular pronoun. Other vocabulary items not in current use in 19th-century America include *liege* and *tiring room*. There can be little doubt that first-person "will not fail to" is considered archaic, or at least exotic, by these authors. More evidence lending an exotic tinge to a narrative may be seen in (26).

(26) *"I am called Master Anseau, and am the goldsmith of our seigneur, the king of France, at the sign of St. Eloi. Promise me to be in this field the next Sabbath, and I **will not fail to come**, though it were raining halberts."*
(COHA, Maturin M. Ballou, *The Sea-Witch Or, the African Quadroon: A Story of the Slave Coast*, 1855)

Like (21)–(25), (26) is clearly the product of an author attempting to recreate what he takes to be the dialogue of a previous age: witness the title *Master*, the description of the French king as *seigneur*, the address *at the sign of*, the use of *the next Sabbath* as the date for an appointment, and the raining, French style, of *halberts* instead of the more usual English *cats and dogs*. Embedded in these archaic and/or exotic expressions, we find the equally archaic "will not fail to". This use of "will not fail to" to lend an exotic air to the dialogue of historical fictional texts peters out in the course of the 19th century. The second half of the 19th century also sees a progressive decline in the use of negated "fail to" as a whole, as we shall see in Section 6.

Before looking at the rise of positive polarity "fail to", let us sum up the story thus far. Both non-subjective and subjective uses of "not fail to" date from the late 14th century. Intersubjective uses of "not fail to" begin to surface in the 15th century, in the first place with second-person subjects, encoding injunctions. From the 16th century, we find first-person "will/shall not fail to" used to encode promises. This soon develops into a fixed formula, which in the 19th century is felt to be archaic. Whether it may be said to be intersubjectified (in sense of Traugott 2010) and not just intersubjective is a question I will return to in Section 7.

## 6 The history of "fail to"

At the time when "fail to" first appeared in English, it already occurred with both positive and negative polarity in French. However, I have only come across two positive polarity examples in Middle English, reproduced here as (27) and (28).

(27) And wel sche wiste, if he ne spedde
Of thing which he hadde undertake,
Sche mihte hirself no porpos take;
For if he deide of his bataile,
Sche **moste thanne algate faile
To geten him**, whan he were ded.
'And she well knew that if he did not succeed in his endeavour, she would herself lose out, for if he died in combat, she would certainly fail to win him, him being dead.'
(*Confessio Amantis*, Book 5, 3426–3431)

(28) As, gif monye men baron a weyghte, and eche schulde helpe othur therto, he that **fayluth to helpe** oon, mut nedys fayle aghenys hem alle.
(Helsinki Corpus, Wycliffe?, ca 1380?)
'As, if many men are carrying a heavy object, and they are meant to help one another, he that fails to help one of them, must needs let them all down.'

Examples (27) and (28) both fall towards the objective end of the objective-subjective cline, with (27) coding the effort sense and (28) the duty sense. Despite the evidence in these two examples of the early availability of the positive polarity construction, it nevertheless does not seem to have taken root in Middle English. Several centuries pass before it resurfaces in the Early Modern period. There is one example in Shakespeare (29), as opposed to five negated examples. This is a subjective example in that her *homely stars* have made no effort to favor Helena.

(29) Helena.   *Sir, I can nothing say,*
              *But that I am your most obedient servant.*
     Bertram.  *Come, come, no more of that.*
     Helena.   *And ever shall*
              *With true observance seek to eke out that*
              *Wherein toward me my homely stars* **have fail'd**
              **To equal** *my great fortune.*
              (*All's Well that Ends Well*: ll: v: 74–79)

The positive polarity construction initially made slow progress and throughout the 18th century, as seen from the 1710–1780 subperiod of the CLMET, it was still thin on the ground, accounting for only 6 tokens compared to 81 for the still dominant negated form. However, in the second CLMET period, 1780–1850, it accounts for a quarter of the total number of tokens of "fail to", and in the third period, 1850–1920, it is the dominant form, accounting for just over 75% of all tokens. It has continued to advance ever since, as shown in Figure 2.

The progress of the positive polarity construction at the expense of its negative counterpart, shown in Figure 2, is global. The two American English corpora, Brown from the 1960s and Frown from the 1990s, each contain fewer than 10% negative polarity tokens, as do the ACE and Wellington corpora, representing Australian and New Zealand English, respectively. The figures for the BNC also bear witness to this trend. Moreover, the negated construction would appear to be even rarer in Present-day English. Only five of 380 tokens of "fail to" downloaded from the World Wide Web were negated.[5] Moreover, all five were quotations from the bible, a work which typically displays conservative language use on the part of its translators.

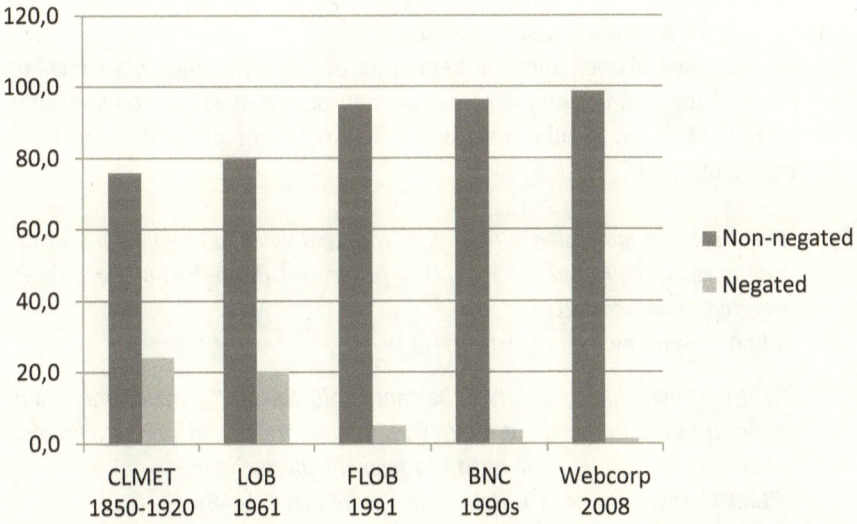

**Figure 2:** Percentages of tokens of non-negated and negated '*fail to*' in a selection of corpora from 1850 to the present day

---

5 The tokens were downloaded on 27 May 2008 using the WebCorp search engine.

The handful of non-negated tokens attested in the 18th century convey non-subjective (30) as well as subjective meanings (31).

(30)  *In the administration of governments, my lords, many measures reasonable and just, planned out in pursuance of a very exact knowledge of the state of things then present, and very probable conjectures concerning future events,* **have yet failed to produce** *the success which was expected.*
(CLMET, The Duke of Newcastle, cited by Johnson in *Parliamentary Debates*, 1740)

(31)  *But Otway* **failed to polish or refine**,
*And fluent Shakespeare scarce effaced a line.*
(CLMET, Pope, First epistle of second book of Horace, 1734)

The "fail to" construction in (30) is non-subjective in that the measures adapted by governments to achieve a certain goal are seen as falling short of that object. In (31), on the other hand, it is clearly subjective, in that there is no suggestion of Otway making any effort to polish his texts. One can infer that Pope, an inveterate polisher himself, expects a poet to make such revisions and that these subjective expectations are disappointed.

As mentioned above, from the beginning of the 19th century, an increase in the use of the non-negated construction can be observed: 25 non-subjective tokens, as in (32), and 11 subjective tokens, as in (33), are attested in the 1780–1850 period of CLMET.

(32)  *These petty tyrants ruled with an iron rod; and when at any time a patriot rose to resist their oppressions, if they* **failed to subdue** *him by force they resorted to assassination.*
(CLMET, Southey, *Life of Nelson*, 1813)

(33)  *"Is it that they think it a duty to be continually talking," pursued she; "and so never pause to think, but fill up with aimless trifles and vain repetitions, when subjects of real interest* **fail to present** *themselves?"*
(CLMET, Anne Brontë, *The Tenant of Wildfell Hall*, 1848)

In the final sub-period of CLMET (1850–1920), when the non-negated form outnumbers its negated counterpart by approximately three to one (see Figure 2), not only are numerous examples of both non-subjective and subjective uses attested, but the period also sees the first instances of "fail to" conveying an intersubjective sense. In these latter cases, "fail to" combines with a verb of comprehension, such as *see* or *understand*, as illustrated by (34) and (35).

(34) *After rather an unpleasant pause, Cummings, who had opened a cigar-case, closed it up again and said: "Yes – I think, after that, I SHALL be going, and I am sorry **I fail to see** the fun of your jokes."*
(CLMET, Grossmiths, *The Diary of a Nobody*, 1892)

(35) *"I **fail to see** the connection," said Leonard, hot with stupid anger.*
(CLMET, Forster, *Howards End*, 1910)

The intersubjective use of "fail to see/understand/follow..." invites the inference that not only is the putative landmark of the seeing impossible to actually discern, but that no amount of effort on the part of the speaker would allow him/her to access it. *I fail to see the fun of your jokes* in (34) does not just mean 'I do not see the fun of your jokes'. It carries the additional implication that the jokes in question are not in the least bit funny. The construction normally signals both stupidity on the part of the addressee and irritation or even anger on the part of the subject, signaled in (35) by the phrase *hot with stupid anger*.

The intersubjective use of "fail to see" also appears in American English in the second half of the 19th century. Figure 3 contains raw figures for the incidence of "I fail to see" in COHA for 1850–1919, paralleling the third subperiod of CLMET. Typical examples from this period are (36)–(38).

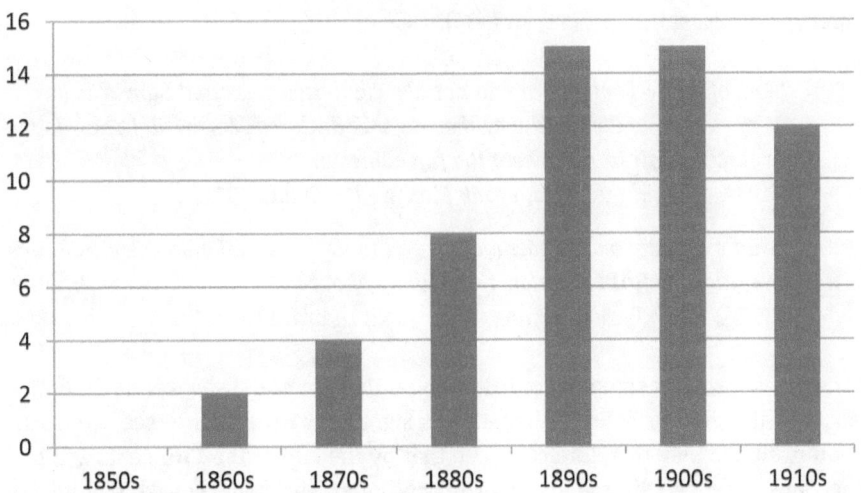

**Figure 3:** Raw figures for "I fail to see" in COHA 1850–1919

(36) "I confess **I fail to see** it," said Arthur, a little sharply. Graeme had hardly time to notice his tone.
(COHA: Margeret M. Robertson, *Janet's Love and Service*, 1869)

(37) "Yes," he went on, hastily, "Perle r-rhymes with Erle – that means an alder-tree – and that r-reminds me of you." "I must say **I fail to see** the resemblance," came an injured voice from behind the chair.
(COHA: Mabell S.C. Smith, *A Tar-Heel Baron*, 1903)

(38) "**I fail to see** the similarity between a buckwheat cake and a porous plaster," said the School-master, resolved, if possible, to embarrass the Idiot.
(COHA: John K. Bangs, *Coffee and Repartee*, 1893)

Examples (36) and (37) resemble (35) in so far as both contain explicit evidence in the form of an adverb (*sharply*) or an adjective (*injured*) of irritation on the part of the speaker. The same expression is employed in (38), on the other hand, not so much to express irritation on the part of the speaker as to provoke embarrassment on the part of his addressee. One may infer that the desire to provoke such embarrassment is prompted by irritation, but this is not stated explicitly in the co-text.

In (34), we saw that humor is one of the things that one can fail to see. Indeed it would appear to be one of the more common objects of lack of comprehension, as shown by (33) and (34).

(39) "Lots of fellows smoke who do not like cigarettes," assured Sam Winslow. "Well, I can't understand why they do so," declared Merriwell. "They do it for fun." "**I fail to see** where the fun comes in."
(COHA, Burt L. Standish, *Frank Merriwell's Chums*, 1902)

(40) "That's a funny one!" Maizie appeared to derive signal enjoyment from this revelation. "**I fail to see** anything funny about it."
(COHA, Edith Bancroft, *Jane Allen: Right Guard*, 1918)

There is no explicit signaling of irritation on the part of the speaker in either (39) or (40). Rather, this sense of irritation is signaled by the "fail to see" construction itself. We may therefore conclude that by the end of the 19th century it had become entrenched in the grammar/lexicon of at least some speakers/writers of the language as a means of expressing irritation at the obtuseness or ill-faith of their addressees.

# 7 Subjectivity, intersubjectivity and intersubjectification

In this section, I look more closely at the terms "subjectivity", "intersubjectivity" and "intersubjectification" and discuss how the various "fail to" constructions presented in Sections 5 and 6 may be related to these. The diachronic process of "subjectification" will not be discussed, since the subjective sense is found among the earliest examples of the "fail to" construction(s) in English. The process of subjectification must therefore have taken place prior to the borrowing of the construction(s) from French. Indeed, it must have taken place quite early since, according to the OED, Old French *faillir* developed from vulgar Latin *\*fallīre* which meant 'to disappoint expectation, be wanting or defective'.

Let us consider subjectivity first. A succinct description of it (along with a description of intersubjectivity) is provided by Traugott (2010).

> [E]xpressions of subjectivity and intersubjectivity are expressions the prime semantic or pragmatic meaning of which is to index speaker attitude or viewpoint (subjectivity) and speaker's attitude to addressee self-image (intersubjectivity). At issue is the development of semantic (coded) polysemies that have to be learned with subjective or intersubjective meanings, and how these come into being. (Traugott 2010: 32)

Two questions are raised by this definition. First, how does one go about calibrating the "prime" meaning of an expression? As soon as we make reference to something in the world outside ourselves, however colored this reference may be by our own attitudes, we are including a certain objective element in the predication. Consider example (14), repeated here for the sake of convenience.

(14) *Bot what man that his lust desireth*
*Of love, and therupon conspireth*
*With wordes feigned to deceive,*
**He schal noght faile to receive**
*His peine, as it is ofte sene.*
'But any man with an appetite for love, who conspires with lies to deceive, shall not fail to receive his just desserts, as has often been seen.'
(*Confessio Amantis*, Book 1, 1206–1209)

I have unequivocally labeled (14) as subjective on the grounds that it is the speaker rather than the grammatical subject that predicts that the latter will be punished. In the imagined world in which this lustful generic character is situated by the speaker, he is nevertheless profiled objectively as suffering punishment. The point is that there is a mixture of subjective and objective elements in the predication. Moreover, this is the case with many, if not most, predications. As Kranich (2010) puts it:

> If we take it that subjective meaning components are based on the speaker's belief state or attitude, while objective meaning components are based on properties of situations in the reference world, we must see that real-life utterances often contain both elements. But this does not mean that investigations into the question are hopeless to begin with. Rather one can work with the concept of clines of objectivity and subjectivity. (Kranich 2010: 103)

The point at issue here is just where a predication must be situated along this cline for us to conclude that its "prime" meaning is speaker-related.

The second question raised by Traugott's definition is how we are to identify an element as indexing speaker attitude. Despite the attention paid to subjectivity in recent years, no consensus has emerged on this issue. As De Smet and Verstraete (2006: 366) put it, "both concepts [subjectivity and subjectification] remain surprisingly ill-defined: there is a lack of good formal criteria to detect subjectivity in a particular item, i.e. to measure how and why the item relates to the speaker". The type of formal criteria that may be applicable will necessarily vary according to the linguistic item under investigation. In the case of "fail to", one such criterion is the degree of agency exhibited by the grammatical subject. The most objective sense of "fail to" is 'try and not succeed'. The very act of trying presupposes agency on the part of the person trying. In example (1), for instance, the subject is engaged in a conscious, willed, self-driven effort to win the Golden Fleece. In (14), on the other hand, the subject is profiled as the future recipient of punishment, unconscious of the fact that his deceitful behavior is leading him in that direction. We can apply the same diagnostic test for subjectivity to the non-negated construction. The tyrants in (32) are agents in the repression of the patriots. In (33), on the other hand, the grammatical subject is not only non-agentive, it is non-animate.

Although lack of agency on the part of the grammatical subject is an indication of subjectivity, this does not mean that the presence of agency is a clear indication of objectivity (indeed it is a precondition for the intersubjective senses of both "fail to" and "not fail to", as we shall see below). Consider in this respect (28), in which there is no implication that the subject has made an effort to help his fellow carriers. The subject is, however, agentive is the sense that the action he is accused by the speaker of not performing, namely, helping to carry a weight, is one he could have carried out consciously and willingly. The predication does not satisfy the definition of the most objective sense of "fail to", which is 'try and (not) succeed'. Indeed, the whole point of the speaker is that the subject has neglected to realize a situation that was within his power to bring about. In Section 4, I proposed clines of subjectivity for both "fail to" and "not fail to", both of which are repeated here for convenience.

(8) Cline of objectivity – subjectivity for "fail to"
*try and not succeed* → *neglect a duty* → *fail to meet speaker's expectations*

(12) Cline of objectivity – subjectivity for "not fail to"
*try and succeed* → *fulfill a duty* → *meet speaker's expectations*

Predications to the left of the clines are clearly objective, while predications to the right are clearly subjective. But what of the duty-related predications, such as (28)? A duty may be objective; for example, it may follow from a legally binding contract. On the other hand, a process presented as a duty may also be more subjective, insofar as it exists mainly in the eye of the beholder. It may merely follow from the moral code of the speaker, for instance. Indeed, it may be both subjective and objective, as in the case of a speaker who feels very strongly about obligations to fulfill legally binding contracts. Moreover, in all three cases the grammatical subject must be agentive. Otherwise it would make no sense to speak of success or failure in carrying out a duty.

The fact that it may be difficult to reach firm conclusions about the degree of subjectivity in the case of the duty sense of "fail to" does not mean that the senses to the left and right of it on the cline in (8) are equally indeterminate. Indeed, if we accept that subjectivity is a matter of degree, it should not be surprising that some expressions fall mid-way between the two extremes. Moreover, even though (8) and (12) are intended to represent synchronic polysemies, the clines may also represent a plausible hypothesis for the diachronic development of the subjective senses. In order to test this hypothesis, however, one would have to consult Old French or Latin corpora.

The duty sense of "not fail to" is the semantic source of both intersubjective senses of "not fail to", i.e. the injunction sense and the promise sense. Traugott (2010: 34) points out that "diachronic work has shown repeatedly that for some lexical item or construction X,... intersubjectified polysemies of that item or construction arise later than subjectified ones (intersubjectification)." Leaving aside, for the moment, the question of whether the injunction or promise senses of "not fail to" may properly be described as intersubjectified, rather than merely pragmatically intersubjective, it should be pointed out that while these two senses certainly occur later in English than either the objective or subjective senses, they do not represent meaning extensions of the subjective sense. Rather, they represent extensions from the less subjective duty sense, which is situated in the middle of the objectivity–subjectivity cline in (12). Thus the imperative "do not fail to" means 'I impose a duty on you' and the first-person "I will not fail to" means 'I impose a duty on myself'. Moreover, both senses can be related, through the mediation of the duty sense, to the maximally objective sense of 'try and succeed'. Thus the injunction sense means 'you must try and succeed' and the promise sense 'I will try and succeed'.

Of the two intersubjective senses of "not fail to", the promise sense is by far the most common. This may be due to reluctance on the part of speakers to employ the face-threatening injunction sense, as pointed out by Narrog (2010).

> ... obligation markers and constructions are absent in a large number of languages. This may be due to the fact that they are associated with marked and socially problematic scenarios. Obligations potentially put human relationships at risk, since non-compliance is associated with all kinds of sanctions. Talking directly about obligations may be face-threatening or even menacing, and consequently, if the speaker is not in a position of full authority, puts the speaker her- or himself at risk. (Narrog 2010: 409)

The fact that all five instances of injunction "not fail to" in my data are the products of figures of substantial authority, such as a king addressing a subject in (15) or a father his sons in (20), might tend to lessen their face-threatening impact, orders being more palatable when promulgated by someone whose authority is unchallengeable. Unlike the injunction sense, the much more common promise sense can be used to address one's equals, inferiors or superiors on the social scale. A subject may make a promise to a monarch, as in (18), but a monarch may also make a promise to a subject, as in (21).

While there can be no doubt that both the injunction and the promise senses of "not fail to" may be described as pragmatically intersubjective, this does not necessarily mean that they have been intersubjectified in the sense of being part of the grammar/lexicon in their own right. As Traugott (2010: 35) puts it, "we need to distinguish between the intersubjectivity that may pragmatically accompany the use of a form from its development into a coded meaning". There are too few instances of the injunction sense in my material on which to base firm conclusions about its degree of entrenchment, at least with respect to the language as a whole and not just the grammar of individual speakers. We do, however, have almost thirty examples of the promise sense. Moreover, as pointed out already, the fact that the parallel expressions in (17) and (18) are produced three years apart by one and the same speaker, shows that this usage of "will not fail to" is entrenched in the grammar/lexicon of this particular person's idiolect. I have written "grammar/lexicon" because I believe it impossible to make a strict categorical distinction between the two (see Langacker 1987: 449). However, if we think of the grammatical end of the lexicon/grammar cline as containing more abstract(ed) elements and the lexical end as containing more substantive elements, the development of the 'promise' sense of "not fail to" would seem to partake of some of the features of lexicalization, as described by Trousdale (2010).

> As [a] new construction emerges, it becomes more unit-like, more distinctive as a construction: in other words, it is the product of an entrenched routine in the minds of a network of language users, a routine which has emerged through pragmatic inferencing in contexts of language use, and which has been conventionalized by those language users. By contrast, in lexicalization, the direct link between a more substantive and a more schematic construction is lost, and what becomes entrenched is the more substantive construction. (Trousdale 2010: 54).

The promise sense is more substantive than the more general "not fail to" construction, in that it always contains both a first-person subject and modal *will/shall*, at least in direct speech. Further testimony to its assimilation into the language is provided by its use in historical fiction, as in examples (21)–(25), after it ceased to be used in other genres.

Turning now to the intersubjective use of positive polarity "fail to", as exemplified by (34)–(40), it too appears later than the objective and subjective senses at the two extremes of the cline in (8). It is even more substantive than the promise sense in that it always contains a complement predicate coding comprehension, most often *see*. That the "I fail to see" construction is used to signal obtuseness or ill-faith on the part of the addressee and/or irritation on the part of the speaker was clearly shown in Section 6. Like its negated counterpart several centuries earlier, it is not a semantic extension of the subjective sense which codes disappointed speaker expectations. Quite the contrary in fact: *I fail to see your point* means something like 'I have tried hard but, no matter the amount of effort I put into it, I cannot for the life of me find any point whatsoever'. In other words, it implies that there is no point at all. It is thus an extension of the more objective sense of 'try and not succeed'.

It is no doubt the contribution of the semantic component of disappointed effort that makes "I fail to see" intersubjectively antagonistic to a greater extent than a mere "I do not see", although the latter may also be face-threatening, coding as it does explicit disagreement with one's addressee. Is the "I fail to see" construction then intersubjectified, or does the hearer/reader infer the antagonism anew every time he or she is exposed to it? How many times does a construction have to be experienced with similar implications by a cross section of speakers who draw the requisite inferences from it, before we can conclude that it is lexicalized with these meanings in the language? Examples (34)–(40) are from 1869 to 1918. Examples (41)–(43) are from the BNC and COCA.

(41) *Harding was looking at him now all right, voice shaking as he fought for control: "Firstly ... Lawrence, isn't it? Yes, it is. Firstly, Lawrence, you do not use language when addressing a school monitor – remember that, will you. Secondly, Lawrence,* **I fail to see** *what your ... problem has to do with me."* (BNC, G02 2851)

(42) *Johnny sliced through her words with icy civility. "I'm obliged to Teddy Hargreaves, but his opinion is of supreme indifference to me. As he rarely lifts his head off the pillow – yours usually, I believe, my sweet –* **I fail to see** *how he's qualified to judge."* (BNC, G1S 2808)

(43) *"It's different," Paul said. "Really?" Laurie questioned. "***I fail to see*** how it's different." Paul stared back at Laurie. His face had reddened.*
(COCA, Robin Cook, *Vector*, 1999)

Just as (35)–(37) contained explicit descriptions of the attitude of the first-person subject in the form of *hot with stupid anger* (35), *sharply* (36) and *injured* (37), in (41) the subject is explicitly described as *shaking as he fought for control* and in (42) as evincing *icy civility*. In (43), we can divine the attitude of Laurie by the effect her utterance has on Paul. In (41)–(43), the same form, the lexical chunk *I fail to see*, is being used with the exact same intersubjective connotations as in (35)–(37), some five or six generations earlier. In distinguishing between the merely pragmatically intersubjective and the intersubjectified proper, Traugott places special emphasis on the extent to which the meaning may be deduced from the context:

> What may look like a case of intersubjectification actually may not be. If it is derivable from the context, it is only a case of increased pragmatic intersubjectivity. In other words, there may be more addressee-oriented uses, but unless a form-meaning pair has come to code intersubjectivity, we are not seeing intersubjectification (-*ation* being the important item here). (Traugott 2010: 37)

There is no doubt that the intersubjective sense of irritation/antagonism can be derived from the context in most of the examples of "I fail to see", whether they be from the 19th or the 21st century. But does this necessarily mean that the form–meaning pair has not come to code intersubjectivity? I see no reason to adopt the standpoint that coded meanings may not also be inferred. Indeed, at some point in the transition from pragmatically inferable to semantically coded, there must have been a period of overlap. Moreover, when we find a construction like "I fail to see" being used with the same intersubjective pragmatic meaning over a period of a century and a half, it would be surprising if it had not become sufficiently codified to warrant the label of "intersubjectification".

I noted in Section 6 that humor was one of the things people often had difficulty detecting. The same thing applies a hundred years on, as attested by (44)–(45).

(44) *Jacoby Sarto laughed. It was an ugly, contemptuous sound, delivered by a man who had spent decades using his voice to wither other men's courage. The commander glared at him. "**I fail to see the humor** in any of this, Lord Sarto."* (COCA, Karl Schroeder, *Queen of Candesce*, 2007)

(45) *I still can feel the effects of the spray on my face, like a sunburn, and taste the foulness in my throat from breathing the noxious gas. It was and remains a very painful and traumatizing incident that **I fail to see as a joke**.* (COCA: *San Francisco Chronicle*, LETTERS TO DATEBOOK, 1997)

Tokens such as (44) and (45) constitute evidence for the continued existence of the lower-level substantive construction "I fail to see x" where "x" codes some form of expression for amusement. Having been around for over a hundred years, this construction must also be judged to have become lexicalized.

To round off this discussion of the "I fail to see" construction, it should be pointed out that not all tokens of "I fail to see" instantiate the antagonistic interactive sense. The verb *see* may also combine with the subjective "fail to" construction at the right of the cline in (8), rendering a subjective reading, as in (46) and (47), rather than an intersubjective one.

(46) *Now she usually hurries home after school, tackles her homework and turns in by 6 or 6:30. When friends invite her out, she begs off. "I just don't want to do anything," she said. "**I fail to see** the point. I don't want to be outside my house too much."*
(COCA: *N. R. KLEINFIELD,* In Nightmares and Anger, Children Pay Hidden Cost of 9/11, New York Times, 2002)

(47) *Very often **I fail to see** that something is on its way to birth, and tax myself with totally useless questions as to what the matter might be. Then, at some point, the idea is ready to emerge, and, as it does so, all the tension disappears.* (BNC CCN 1443)

One may wonder why the use of *I fail to see* in contexts such as those of (46) and (47) is not pre-empted by the existence of the lexicalized "I fail to see" construction. One possible answer is that in these examples the expression is not used in dialogue with a particular addressee. Although it occurs in direct speech in (46), it is used to report an attitude rather than to assert one. Another possible answer is that *fail to* in contexts such as these is bleached of all connotations of effort, which we have seen underlines the antagonistic interpretation of the intersubjective construction. Indeed, it may also be bleached of connotations of duty or even expectation, in which case it is merely functioning as a marker of negation. Whether or not this may be the case is the topic of the next section.

## 8 The possible grammaticalization of "fail to"

In (8) and (12), I sketched synchronic clines of objectivity/subjectivity for both "fail to" and "not fail to". I also mentioned that these might represent possible diachronic clines for the evolution of the more subjective sense, noting, at the same time, that this development must have taken place prior to the borrowing of the constructions in English. The question addressed in this section is whether there has been a further semantic development in the case of the positive polarity construction from 'disappoint speaker's expectation', the most subjective sense in (8), to 'does not'. In other words, has the element of speaker expectation become so bleached, at least in certain contexts, that what is left is a mere negation marker? Representative examples where this sort of interpretation would seem plausible are (48)–(50).

(48) *When the autism strategy was published in March it **failed to make** the establishment of specialist autism teams a requirement for all local authorities.*
(COCA, Jeremy Dunning, Evidence grows for specialist teams, *Community Care*, 2010)

(49) *Social support appeared to be only modestly associated with psychological distress in the bivariate analysis. When included in multivariate analyses, it **failed to achieve** statistical significance.*
(COCA, Barbara Kilbourne, Sherry M. Cummings & Robert S. Levine, The influence of religiosity on depression among low-income people with diabetes, Health & Social Work 34(2), 2009)

(50) *The Cold War is also an excellent example of a war that ended at a time and in a way that most people living through it **failed to foresee** – and had even stopped trying to foresee.*
(COCA, Philip H. Gordon, Can the war on terror be won?, *Foreign Affairs* 86(6), 2007)

The writer of (48) does not imply that the *autism strategy* (metonymically) made an effort to require the establishment of autism teams, or that it had a duty to do so. Nor is there any suggestion that the speaker had expected them to do so. *It failed to make* in (48), shorn as it is of the senses of disappointed effort, duty and expectation, boils down semantically to the mere negation of *make*; in other words, it just means 'did not make'. Similarly, (49) could be aptly paraphrased 'did not achieve' and (50) 'did not foresee'. Indeed, in (50) the objective sense is explicitly excluded in the final clause by the writer.

(48)–(50) are just three of many examples which exhibit bleaching of the element of expectation on the part of the speaker denoted by the subjective sense of "fail to". A semantic change like this is not usually considered sufficient, however, to conclude that a process of grammaticalization has taken place. As pointed out in Section 2, we need a means of ascertaining an increase in functional load on the part of the items in question. We can apply Boye and Harder's (2009) formulation, introduced in Section 2, in terms of primary and secondary information to the "fail to" construction, by looking at examples where *did* follows a *fail to* phrase and functions as an anaphoric pro-form. Depending on the referent of *did* we can ascertain whether *failed to* is discursively primary or secondary. Consider in this respect examples (51)–(53), downloaded from the internet with the aid of *WebCorp*.

(51) When they launched it, everyone from engineers to Communist Party big shots **failed to realize** its importance. Only Korolyov **did**.
(http://www.columbiamissourian.com/stories/2007/10/07/Space-remains-a/, accessed on 1 June 2015)

(52) The simpler N,N'-bis(salicylidene)-ethylenediaminocobalt(II) [Co(Salen)2] **failed to catalyze** deoygenations in THF but **did** in DMF
(http://www.ingentaconnect.com/content/els/00404039/1999/00000040/000|00050/art01880, accessed on 1 June 2015)

(53) What he **failed to mention** (and neither **did** Dimbleby) was that this principled Nazi perjured himself in that "trial" to try and "convict" an innocent man.
(http://a-place-to-stand.blogspot.com/2011/05/ratko-mladic-arrested.html, accessed on 1 June 2015)

In each of these three examples, *did* refers to the complement clause predicate rather than the matrix verb *fail*. Thus the second sentence in (51) must (on account of contrastive *Only*) be read "Korolyov *did realize* its importance" and not "Korolyov *failed to realize* its importance". The expression *failed to realize* does not imply unsuccessful effort, dereliction of duty or disappointed expectation. It is employed by someone who could equally well have written *did not realize*. In other words, "fail to" is here just another means of encoding negation. This usage of "fail to" instantiates semantic attrition of the element of speaker expectation in the subjective sense in (8). In addition, it instantiates attrition of the element of subjectivity itself. Kranich (2010: 118) maintains that while in the early stages of grammaticalization "the newly emerging constructions are often made use of by speakers to express subjective shades of meanings, such meanings tend to get lost in later stages of grammaticalisation". While I would hesitate to assert that "fail to" is in the later stages of grammaticalization, it certainly exhibits, in sentences like (51)–(53), the sort of loss of subjective shades of meaning to which Kranich is referring.

One reason for asserting that "fail to" is only in the early stages of grammaticalization is the continued existence alongside the negation sense of the other four main senses, the objective effort sense and duty sense, the intersubjective antagonistic sense and the subjective expectation sense. There are also examples, such as (54)–(55), where anaphoric *did* refers to *fail to* rather than the complement clause predicate, as it did in (51)–(53).

(54)  The British **failed to conquer**, and so **did** Russia.
      (http://volokh.com/posts/1235088497.shtml, accessed on 4 January 2010)

(55)  The White House had **failed to notice**. And so **did** CNN.
      (http://www.huffingtonpost.com/richard-grenell/cnn-and-npr-fail-to-quest_b_876848.html, accessed on 1 June 2015)

Just as *neither* in (53) signals a previous negative polarity predication, so in (54) and (55) indicates a previous positive polarity predication (with, of course, in this case a negative meaning). Despite the evidence of the many tokens where it functions as a negation marker, the fact that "fail to" in sentences like (54) and (55) carries primary rather than secondary information in Boye and Harder's (2009) terms, taken together with the fact that it still occurs with the earlier objective, subjective and intersubjective senses, shows clearly that it is still only in the early stages of grammaticalization.

# 9 Summary and conclusions

As indicated in the title of this chapter, both "fail to" and "not fail to" have developed intersubjective senses. Both positive and negative polarity "fail to" were borrowed from French in the 14th century. Whether negated or not, "fail to" was already polysemous with an objective effort sense, a subjective expectation sense and a duty sense, situated somewhere between the other two senses on an objectivity–subjectivity cline. Positive polarity "fail to" seemingly disappeared from the language for a couple of centuries. Intersubjective uses of "not fail to" began to surface in the 15th century, in the first place with second-person subjects, encoding injunctions. From the 17th century, we find first-person "will/shall not fail to" used to encode promises. It soon develops into a fixed formula, which in the 19th century is felt to be archaic. The diachronic development of the intersubjective senses of "not fail to" is shown in (56).

(56)  ca 1400     objective        objective/subjective     subjective
                  effort sense     duty sense               expectation sense
                                        ↓
      ca 1500                      intersubjective
                                   injunction sense
                                        ↓
      ca 1600                      intersubjective
                                   promise sense

Positive polarity "fail to" resurfaces in the late 16th century. It, too, develops an intersubjective sense some two hundred years later. It also comes to be used as a marker of negation pure and simple in the 20th century. Its development is illustrated in (57).

(57)  ca 1600     objective        objective/subjective     subjective
                  effort sense     duty sense               expectation sense
                       ↓                                         |
      ca 1850     intersubjective                                |
                  antagonistic                                   |
                  sense                                          ↓
      ca 1950                                               objective
                                                            negation sense

Although both negative and positive polarity "fail to" developed intersubjective senses, one should note the differences between these developments as sketched in (56) and (57). Firstly, whereas the original three senses of both positive and negative "fail to" are semantic opposites,[6] the intersubjective

---

[6] Semantically they are contrary, rather than contradictory (see Lyons 1977: 772), insofar as the statements *He failed to open the door* and *He did not fail to open the door* may both be true, since the latter may be expanded by *In fact, he did not even try*.

senses are totally unrelated to one another. In (56) they are extensions of the duty sense, in (57) of the effort sense. Note, too, that in neither case are they extensions of the most subjective sense. The second difference worth noting is the absence in (56) of a counterpart to the negation sense in (57). The question here is whether there is any evidence of "not fail to" being used as an emphatic marker. The answer is that there are many examples in which "not fail to" is seemingly bleached of the element of satisfied speaker expectation, where, for example, "never fails to do" seems to be synonymous with "always does". However, the criterion (the identity of the anaphoric referent of *did*) which was applied in the case of positive "fail to" is not applicable in the case of its negated counterpart. The reason is that a contrastive conjunction or conjunct, such as *but* or *however*, would serve in the case of "not fail to" to indicate the cancelation of the most external of two negation markers, of *not/never/seldom* rather than either *fail* or the complement predicate. This is a result of the "not fail to" construction containing two morphemes encoding non-realization of the complement situation. In the absence of historical tokens which could furnish us with syntactic evidence of discursive foregrounding/backgrounding, it is impossible to reach any firm conclusions on the question of the possible grammaticalization of "not fail to". Positive polarity "fail to", on the other hand, does seem to have started on the process of grammaticalizing as a negation marker.

# Acknowledgment

I would like to thank the editors and two anonymous reviewers for their incisive comments and suggestions on an earlier version of this chapter.

# Data sources
## Corpora

ACE: *Australian Corpus of English*. *The ICAME Corpus Collection on CD-ROM*, version 2 (1999). Bergen: Aksis.
BNC: *British National Corpus*, on CD-Rom (2001). Oxford: Oxford University Computing Services.
Brown: *Corpus of Present-Day Edited American English* (1979 [1964]). *The ICAME Corpus Collection on CD-ROM*, version 2 (1999). Bergen: Aksis.
CLMET: *Corpus of Late Modern English Texts*. De Smet, Hendrik (2005). A corpus of Late Modern English texts. *ICAME Journal* 29. 69–82.
CEECS: *Corpus of Early English Correspondence Sampler* (1998). *The ICAME Corpus Collection on CD-ROM*, version 2 (1999). Bergen: Aksis.

COCA: *The Corpus of Contemporary American English*. http://www.americancorpus.org/, accessed on 10.10.2010.
COHA: *The Corpus of Historical American English*. http://corpus.byu.edu/coha/, accessed on 11.10.2010.
FLOB: *The Freiburg – LOB Corpus of British English* (1998). *The ICAME Corpus Collection on CD-ROM*, version 2 (1999). Bergen: Aksis.
Frown: *The Freiburg – Brown Corpus of American English* (1999). *The ICAME Corpus Collection on CD-ROM*, version 2 (1999). Bergen: Aksis.
Helsinki: *Helsinki Corpus of English Texts* (1996). *The ICAME Corpus Collection on CD-ROM*, version 2 (1999). Bergen: Aksis.
Lampeter: *The Lampeter Corpus of Early Modern English Texts*. *The ICAME Corpus Collection on CD-ROM*, version 2 (1999). Bergen: Aksis.
LOB: *Lancaster-Oslo-Bergen Corpus of British English* (1978). *The ICAME CorpusCollection on CD-ROM*, version 2 (1999). Bergen: Aksis.
WebCorp (1999-2009): Birmingham City University. http://www.WebCorp.org.uk/, accessed on 04.01.2010.
Wellington: *Wellington Corpus of Written New Zealand English* (1993). *The ICAME Corpus Collection on CD-ROM*, version 2 (1999). Bergen: Aksis.

## Texts

Chaucer, Geoffrey. 1988. *The Riverside Chaucer* (Benson, Larry D. (ed.)), 3rd edn. Oxford: Oxford University Press.
Gower, John. *Confessio Amantis*. Project Gutenberg, http://www.gutenberg.org/ebooks/266, accessed on 10 January 2010.
Shakepeare, William. 1996 *The Riverside Shakespeare*. (Blakemore Evans, G. & J. J. M. Tobin (eds)), 2nd edn. Boston: Houghton Miffin.

# References

Boye, Kasper & Peter Harder. 2009. Evidentiality: Linguistic categories and grammaticalization. *Functions of Language* 16(1). 9–43.
Boye, Kasper & Peter Harder. 2012. A usage-based theory of grammatical status and grammaticalisation. *Language*. 88(1). 1–44.
Boye, Kasper & Peter Harder. 2014. (Inter)subjectification in a functional theory of grammaticalisation. *Acta Linguistica Hafniensia*. 46(1). 7–24.
De Smet, Hendrik & Jean-Christophe Verstraete. 2006. Coming to terms with subjectivity. *Cognitive Linguistics*. 17(3). 365–392.
Diewald, Gabriele. 2010. On some problem areas in grammaticalization studies. In Katerina Stathi, Elke Gehweiler & Ekkehard König (eds.), *Grammaticalization: Current views and issues*, 17–50. Amsterdam: John Benjamins.
Egan, Thomas. 2010. The *'fail to'* construction in Late Modern and Present-Day English. In Ursula Lenker, Judith Huber & Robert Mailhammer (eds.), *English Historical Linguistics 2008. Selected papers from the fifteenth International Conference on English Historical*

Linguistics. Vol. 1: *The history of English verbal and nominal constructions*, 123–141. Amsterdam: John Benjamins.

Goldberg, Adele. 2006. *Constructions at work: The nature of generalization in language*. Oxford: Oxford University Press.

Gries, Stefan T. 2008. Phraseology and linguistic theory: A brief survey. In Fanny Meunier & Sylviane Granger (eds.), *Phraseology : An interdisciplinary perspective*, 3–25. Amsterdam: John Benjamins.

Hopper, Paul & Elizabeth C. Traugott. 1993. *Grammaticalization*. Cambridge: Cambridge University Press.

Kranich, Svenja. 2010. Grammaticalization, subjectification and objectification. In Katerina Stathi, Elke Gehweiler & Ekkehard König (eds.), *Grammaticalization: Current views and issues*, 101–121. Amsterdam: John Benjamins.

Langacker, Ronald. 1987. *Foundations of Cognitive Grammar: Theoretical prerequisites*. Berlin: Mouton de Gruyter.

Langacker, Ronald. 2008. *Cognitive Grammar: A basic introduction*. Oxford: Oxford University Press.

Lyons, John. 1977. *Semantics*. Cambridge: Cambridge University Press.

Narrog, Heiko. 2010. (Inter)subjectification in the domain of modality and mood – Concepts and cross-linguistic realities. In Kristin Davidse, Lieven Vandelotte & Hubert Cuyckens (eds.), *Subjectification, intersubjectification and grammaticalization*, 385–429. Berlin: De Gruyter Mouton.

OED. 1994. *The Oxford English dictionary*. On compact disc. Oxford: Oxford University Press.

Pearsall, Judy & Patrick Hanks. 1998. *The New Oxford Dictionary of English*. Oxford: Clarendon Press.

Traugott, Elizabeth C. 2007. The concepts of constructional mismatch and type-shifting from the perspective of grammaticalization. *Cognitive Linguisitcs* 18. 523–557.

Traugott, Elizabeth C. 2008. The grammaticalization of *NP of NP* constructions. In Alexander Bergs & Gabriele Diewald (eds.), *Constructions and language change*, 23–45. Berlin: Mouton de Gruyter.

Traugott, Elizabeth C. 2010. (Inter)subjectivity and (inter)subjectification: A reassessment. In Kristin Davidse, Lieven Vandelotte & Hubert Cuyckens (eds.), *Subjectification, intersubjectification and grammaticalization*, 29–71. Berlin: De Gruyter Mouton.

Traugott, Elizabeth C. & Richard B. Dasher. 2002. *Regularity in semantic change*. Cambridge: Cambridge University Press.

Trousdale, Graeme. 2010. Issues in constructional approaches to grammaticalization in English. In Katerina Stathi, Elke Gehweiler & Ekkehard König (eds.), *Grammaticalization: Current views and issues*, 51–71. Amsterdam: John Benjamins.

## II Grammaticalization and directionality

Luisa Brucale and Egle Mocciaro
# 7 Paths of grammaticalization of Early Latin *per/per-*: A cognitive hypothesis

**Abstract:** The paper describes the semantic network of the Early Latin preverb *per-* and its relation with the corresponding preposition *per* 'through'. Making use of the Cognitive Grammar framework, we argue that the basic spatial semantics of both preverb and preposition (here called the "PER relation") can account for the whole set of concrete and abstract meanings *per* and *per-* express. In spite of this common semantic nucleus, however, *per-* and *per* differ as to the mechanisms at work in the development and organization of their semantic continua, thus imposing a differentiated analysis at the semantic as well as the morphosyntactic level. In this respect, the notions of grammaticalization and lexicalization seem to constitute the most adequate analytical tools to describe the different development of preposition and preverb.[1]

## 1 Introduction

This paper aims at describing the semantic network of the Early Latin preverb *per-* and its relationship with the corresponding preposition *per*. To this aim, the entire corpus of comedies by Plautus (ca. 255–184 BCE) and the treatise *De Agri Cultura* by Cato (ca. 234–149 BCE) have been investigated by quering the electronic database Phi5.[2] Drawing upon the insights of Cognitive Grammar (Langacker 1991; Luraghi 2003, Luraghi 2010), as well as on several studies on grammaticalization (e.g. Bybee 1985, Bybee 2003; Heine et al. 1991; Lehmann 2002a, Lehmann 2002b; Hopper and Traugott 2003), it is argued that the schematic content making up the semantic nucleus of both the preposition *per* and the preverb *per-* permits the organization of their semantics along continua ranging from their basic spatial meaning to more abstract values. However, while the development of abstract values in *per* and *per-* is fully consistent with their shared basic semantics, the paths they follow are different. Moreover,

---
[1] Although the entire paper is the result of close cooperation between the authors, Luisa Brucale is responsible for Sections 1, 2, 4 and 5, and Egle Mocciaro for Sections 3, 6, 7 and 8.
[2] Phi5 is an online resource of classical Latin texts, prepared by the Packard Humanities Institute; http://latin.packhum.org/.

different mechanisms are at work in the semantic-functional continua which characterize *per* and *per-*, thus preventing a unified analysis of preposition and preverb, on the semantic as well as on the morphosyntactic level.

The paper is organized as follows. In Section 2, the theoretical assumptions on which the analysis is based are presented, focusing on the processes leading to the formation of prepositions (Section 2.1) and preverbs (Section 2.2). Section 3 provides a schematic description of the semantic nucleus of *per-/per* (the "PER relation"), which constitutes the basis for the analysis of the corpus data. The network of values conveyed by the preposition is described in Section 4, which functions as background to the analysis of the preverb. The spatial values of *per-* are discussed in Section 5, while Sections 6 and 7 deal with its abstract values. Section 8 summarizes the results of the investigation.

# 2 Prepositions and preverbs: Paths of grammaticalization (and lexicalization)

Prepositions and preverbs in Indo-European languages are traditionally argued to have developed from sentence particles or adverbial items (Kuryłowicz 1964; Watkins 1964; Coleman 1991; Nocentini 1992; Pinault 1995; Cuzzolin 1995; Vincent 1999). These items are considered to be free lexemes which could occupy various positions within the sentence, occurring either in a non-fixed position (thus, functioning as adverbs) or optionally modifying a contiguous element, namely a noun or a verb.[3] The regular nature of these positions could have constituted the relevant *locus* of grammaticalization of these items into prepositions and preverbs.[4] The grammaticalization of a preposition consists in the development of a relation of government between the sentence particle and the noun,

---

[3] The generic term "particles" is particularly appropriate as a cover term reflecting the problematic morphosyntactic status of these elements. According to Luraghi (2009: 241), "[h]istorical evidence and the existence of grammaticalization processes itself show that word classes are structured as prototypical categories. Prototypical categories have no clear cut boundaries between each other, but are separated by a continuum, on which items are located that display features of both categories". The so-called particles are located at the boundary of different categories and clear criteria of differentiation are not always easy to determine. We are dealing with multi-functional forms whose behavior is clear only from the context in which they occur.
[4] The development of prepositions and preverbs from adverbial items is anything but unusual in the languages of the world (Heine and Kuteva 2007: 83). As for the Indo-European languages, however, this historical explanation is not universally accepted and other authors argue for the original character of the tripartition adverbs–adpositions–preverbs. As Luraghi

which arises from a previous relation of modification. Lehmann (1985: 95–96) claims that

> [t]he attraction of an NP into the valence of its controller, so that it ceases to be a modifier, and the grammaticalization of the case suffixes are thus two processes that condition each other ... throughout the history of the Latin language, we observe a steadily increasing presence of government. The first step in this direction was the subordination of an NP to the adverb that accompanied it, and thus the creation of prepositional government.

On the other hand, when constrained in a preverbal position, sentence particles may lose their independent status and form a lexical unit with the verb, along a chain of tightness, which, paraphrasing Booij and van Kemenade (2003), can be described as follows: independent particles > left members of verbal compounds > preverbs.[5]

For Latin, we can only observe the outcome of these processes. While in the oldest stages of other Indo-European languages, as in Hittite, Vedic and Homeric Greek, original adverbs were retained, coexisting with corresponding prepositions and preverbs, in Latin (as well as in Classical Greek) prepositions and preverbs replaced adverbs.[6] Moreover, prepositions and preverbs have coexisted

---

(2009: 250, fn. 10) points out, "[t]raditionally it is said that adpositions have been 'added' to cases when the latter were no longer able to express a certain 'concrete' meaning. This interpretation implies the existence of a stage at which Proto-Indo-European had no adpositions, because cases alone could express all semantic functions. That such a stage can be reconstructed is questionable". Dunkel (1990: 169–170) claims that "we must therefore reject attempts to exaggerate the (in itself quite likely) theory that the free adverbial function was at some point original so as to exclude the adnominal and preverbal proper uses from Indo-European itself. ... We must conclude that the partial differentiation of the local adverbs into adnominal and preverbal *sensu stricto* functions had begun already in Indo-European". Since we are concerned with the functions of *per-/per* in Latin, this debate goes beyond the scope of our argumentation.
5 We use "preverb" as a synonym of "verbal prefix", but the two terms may refer to different notions in the relevant literature. For instance, Booij and van Kemenade (2003) distinguish between preverbs and (verbal) prefixes: preverbs are autonomous words which in association with a verb give rise to a verbal compound (what we call "particles"); prefixes are bound morphemes involved in the morphological process of derivation (what we call "preverbs").
6 Cases of sentence-initial particles separated from the verb are only residual and attested in a few archaic examples quoted by the grammarian Festus and analyzed in Cuzzolin (1995: 130): *Sub vos placo, in precibus fere cum dicitur, significat id, quod supplico, ut in legibus (XII, inc. 3): transque dato et (XII, 8, 12) endoque plorato* [When people say, mostly in prayers, *sub vos placo*, it means the same as *supplico* and is like the expressions *transque dato* and *endoque plorato* in the laws; translation in Vincent 1999: 119]. Fruyt (2009) notes that, although there are some examples in which the bond between preverb and verb is broken – mostly by the presence of a conjunction (e.g. *enim* or the enclitic *-que*), a personal pronoun (e.g. *mihi*) or an interjection (e.g. *pol*) – the separation between preverb and verb is no longer productive already at the age of Plautus.

since the earliest attested stages of the language, so that a diachronic relation between them cannot be postulated on the basis of the linguistic data. In the following sections, a more detailed analysis of the grammatical and semantic functions conveyed by prepositions and preverbs will be offered, which suggests considering these categories as different focal areas on a synchronic continuum stretching between lexicon and grammar. Within this continuum, the effects producted by both grammaticalization and lexicalization processes interact in an intriguing way.

## 2.1 Prepositions

As mentioned above, the grammaticalization of a preposition (from a particle contiguous with a noun) consists in the emergence of an integrated syntactic segment – a prepositional phrase (PP) – which shows various syntagmatic constraints. In particular, in contrast to the free position of the adverbial item, the preposition is constrained to prenominal position and governs the noun. In other words, it has come to constitute the head of the PP whose (non-optional) complement is the noun. While an adverb simply modifies the (optional) item placed within its scope, a preposition is not only engaged in a semantic modification relation with its governed complement. In fact, a preposition is endowed with its own argumental structure, both semantically, as it determines the semantic role (or the set of semantic roles) of the argument, and syntactically, as it selects the case form of the argument (Vincent 1999; Lehmann 2002a).[7] At the same time, the preposition is still an autonomous item, whose contribution to the whole phrasal semantics is analytically accessible. More specifically, a preposition expresses an *atemporal relation* (AR) linking two discrete entities: a foregrounded entity, i.e. a *trajector* (TR), and a *landmark* (LM), which constitutes the point of reference of the foregrounded entity and is encoded by the nominal following the preposition (Langacker 1987: 215–243; Lehmann 2002a). This configuration is represented in Figure 1.

---

[7] In this sense, prepositions approximate the function of cases. In Latin, as well as in the other ancient Indo-European languages, cases and prepositions co-operate in expressing grammatical relations and semantic roles. While in some cases prepositions simply reinforce the meaning of a case (e.g. *eo Romam / eo ad Romam* 'I go to Rome'), in other cases the presence of a preposition substantially modifies the function of a case (compare Plautus, *Pseudolus* 463: *per nebulam nosmet scimus* 'we ourselves have found out through a cloud of mist' with the hypothetical \**nebulam nosmet scimus* 'we ourselves found out a cloud').

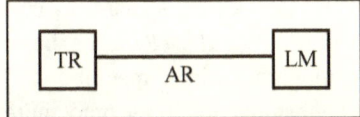

**Figure 1:** Atemporal relation (adapted from Langacker 1987: 215)

The notion of "atemporality" refers to the character of the relation; it is basically conceived as a *spatial location* which does not inherently express a dynamic component (i.e. "TR *at/through/towards* LM").[8] Dynamicity, then, rests on the presence of a verb denoting a *processual relation* (PR), i.e. an event (action, movement etc.) that is necessarily brought about within a time span, and thus expressing *temporal directionality*, i.e. a sequence of sub-events along which a TR metaphorically "moves" (Langacker 1987: 244–274). Figure 2 exemplifies a number of processual sequences: Figure 2a describes an atelic activity, i.e. a series of contiguous locations conceived as homogeneous; Figure 2b represents a change of position, whereby the TR reaches an endpoint; in Figure 2c, the event of *cutting* is a change of state affecting a second participant.

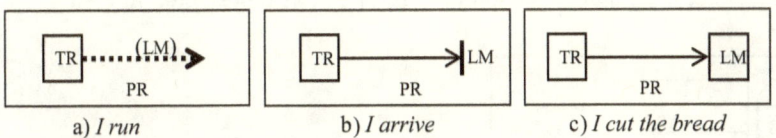

a) *I run*   b) *I arrive*   c) *I cut the bread*

**Figure 2:** Processual relations

With respect to Figure 2, the presence of a prepositional phrase would contribute to specifying the (basically spatial) coordinates of the PR expressed by the verb. In other words, a sentence such as *I run through the city* expresses a

---

**8** As Langacker (1987: 217) points out, "[t]he term trajector suggests motion, and in processual predications describing physical activities (presumably the prototype for relations) the trajector generally does move through a spatial trajectory. Note, however, that the definition makes no reference at all to motion, either physical or abstract, so this schematic description is applicable to both static and dynamic relations". In other words, prepositions basically describe the "place" of a TR in respect to a LM. As we will see in Section 3, the location expressed by Latin *per* (as well as semantic correlates in other languages) is an extended location, frequently a trajectory from one point to another. As a consequence, this preposition is a suitable candidate to occur with motion verbs or to evoke a motion scenario. However, if the verb does not express motion, the preposition does not *per se* express motion, as in Plautus, *Pseudolus* 418: *ita nunc per urbem solus sermoni omnibust* 'for now only he is on evereone's lips throughout the city'. On the notional separation of motion and THROUGH-relation, see also Evans and Tyler (2004).

complex configuration, in which both the TR (*I*) and the PR (*run*, specifically corresponding to Figure 2a) are spatially specified (*through the city*). The basic semantics conveyed by the preposition may undergo various metaphorical-metonymical extensions, projecting the basic conceptual topology onto more abstract domains, so that non-spatial semantic roles can be assigned to the governed noun (see Sections 6 and 7). The internal relation between preposition and governed noun is both semantic (in that a semantic role is assigned, which also depends on the features of the noun) and grammatical (in that the preposition determines the case of the noun). In this respect, prepositions must be considered elements in between lexicon and grammar, rather than unambiguous members of either type.

## 2.2 Preverbs

In forming a lexical unit preverb + verb, preverbation directly attributes an AR to the verb so that the AR is included in the PR. Drawing upon Lehmann (2002a), we can describe this phenomenon as an overlap between two conceptually distinct factors, i.e. a static location (AR) and a PR, as represented in Figure 3.

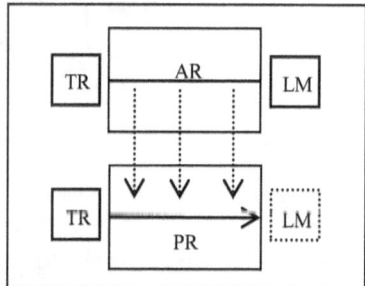

**Figure 3:** Preverbation

The LM of the AR (i.e. its locational scope) becomes part of the PR, that is, the preverb modifies the spatial coordinates of the event denoted by the verb. For Latin, this description fully conforms to the spatial values conveyed by the preverb *per-*. However, a fine-grained analysis of the data provides a more detailed scenario. Apart from the spatial values (which constitute the only semantic area shared by *per-* and *per*), the semantic contribution of the preverb is definitely more abstract compared to that of the preposition, precisely because it concerns the verbal process itself. As we will see in Section 6, *per-* may also affect the internal structure of the verbal process, adding a fully identifiable grammatical value that is aspectual in nature (e.g. *frico* 'to scrub' vs. durative/intensive *perfrico* 'to scrub thoroughly') and constitutes the core of the network of values conveyed by the preverb. Since *per-* has acquired a clear-cut grammatical function in the formation of morphologically more complex items (the preverbed verbs), it may be analyzed in terms of grammaticalization in the spirit of Lehmann (2002b). Sometimes the aspectual value develops a telic nuance which is, however, expressed only by specific verbal lexemes rather than regularly assigned by *per-* (see Section 7). In these cases, the preverb + verb complex has lost compositionality and is stored in the lexicon as a unit. In other words, a different process seems to be at work which involves specific lexemes only and which can be analyzed in terms of lexicalization (e.g. *facio* 'to do' vs. *perficio* 'to complete'). The decrease of compositionality of the preverbed lexemes can be attributed to the overlap AR–PR; it may occur to varying degrees, up to complete unpredictability, sometimes affecting the phonetic shape (e.g. *pergo* 'to hold on, to continue' < *per-* + *rego* 'to lead, direct'). We will return to the complex configuration associated with *per-* in Sections 5 to 7.

## 3 Semantics of the PER relation

The spatial meanings of *per-* largely overlap with the spatial semantics proposed for the corresponding preposition *per* (Brucale and Mocciaro 2011), so we assume that preposition and preverb reflect a unique schematic content, as illustrated in Figure 4.

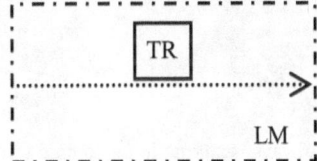

**Figure 4:** PER relation

The spatial configuration associated with the PER relation describes an extended location, consisting of a set of contiguous points that is occupied by the TR through, across or along the LM.⁹ This configuration is fully consistent

---

9 This spatial configuration partially resembles Pottier's (1962: 282) representation of the PER relation, as well as various descriptions proposed for the translational equivalents of Latin *per* in other languages (e.g. Fr. *à travers* and Engl. *through*, see Stosic 2002; Dirven 1993; Taylor

both with the etymologies traditionally proposed[10] and with the various attestations of *per-* and *per* whose interpretation depends on contextual information provided by the features of the LM and the TR, and by the semantics of the verb. In general terms, *per-* and *per* always imply a two- or three-dimensional LM, representing a bounded surface or a volume (e.g. *per urbem* 'through the city', *perfodi parietem* 'I have dug a hole through the party-wall'). The PER relation may define two patterns within this bounded space:

(i) PER denotes a linear Path within LM; this path may include an endpoint within the LM or it may extend beyond the LM, depending on the features of the LM and on the nature of the event denoted by the verb. The LM represents either a two-dimensional entity which may be traversed by a TR, as in Figure 4, or a three-dimensional entity always allowing boundary crossing, as in Figure 5.

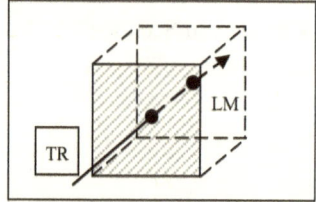

**Figure 5:** "Boundary crossing" trajectory of PER

(ii) a multidirectional and atelic trajectory whose scope is entirely within the LM, which typically consists of an extended and bounded area (e.g. sea, city), as in Figure 6.

---

1993; Evans and Tyler 2004: 267). According to Pottier, *per* always "exprime le parcours d'un bout à l'autre d'une limite double" [expresses the path from one extreme to the other of a double bounded space]. However, in the perspective adopted here, the geometry of the PER-relation depends on the features of the spatial scene, namely the shape of the LM and the semantics of the verb, rather than on the PER relation *per se*, which does not necessarily entail the presence of an endpoint, as the dotted line delimiting the LM in Figure 4 suggests.

**10** See Pokorny (1989 [1959]: 810), who traces *per(-)* back to the IE *\*per(i)* '(to go) over' (cf. Gr. adverbial *perì*, Skr. *pári*, Lith. *per*, Anc. Slav. *prě*, Got. *faír-*), and Ernout and Meillet (2001 [1959]: 497), who link it to the ancient locative case *\*peri/\*per* 'forward', which developed the meaning 'through' in Latin, Slavonic and the Baltic languages (cf. Lat. *pro*, *prae*) and the meaning 'around' in Indo-Aryan languages and Greek.

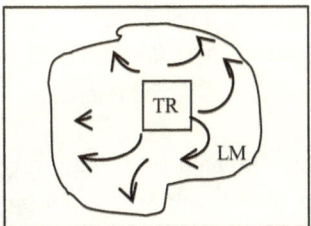

**Figure 6:** Multidirectional trajectory of PER (adapted from Luraghi 2003: 171)

These two patterns, which are both realized by the spatial values of *per(-)*, are described in more detail in the following sections.

## 4 The preposition *per*

The Latin preposition *per* always governs an NP to which it assigns the accusative case, not allowing case variation.[11] The PP *per* + accusative expresses a complex semantic network ranging from the domain of Space to the domain of Causation, but it does not denote any strictly grammatical meaning. Consistent with the schematic import of the PER relation, *per* describes either a multidirectional or a linear Path configuration (Leumann et al. 1965: 239–242; Luraghi 2010: 37), as in (1) and (2) respectively.

(1) *quasi*     **per**   **urb-em**      **tot-am**      *homin-em*
   as though through city-ACC.F.SG all-ACC.F.SG man-ACC.M.SG
   *quaesiveris*
   search.PRF.SUBJ.2SG
   'and thus pretend as though you had been in search of the man throughout the entire city'                                        (Epidicus 195)

---

**11** Strictly speaking, case variation would be indicative of a lower degree of grammaticalization. Building on Lehmann (1983), Luraghi (2010: 89) notes that "one should speak of two groups of prepositions in Latin, depending on the type of relation holding between the preposition and a co-occurring NP: (i) prepositions that do not allow for case variation, and govern their NPs, and (ii) prepositions that can take different cases, and modify their NPs". She also shows, however, that case variation is very limited in Latin and involves only three prepositions, i.e. *in*, *sub* and *super*.

(2) **Per hort-um** nos dom-um trans-ibimus.
through garden-ACC.M.SG we.NOM home-ACC.F.SG over-goFUT.1PL
'We'll go home through the garden.' (Mercator 1009)

The Path configuration represents the source domain of a wide range of abstract meanings conveyed by *per*. This is particularly relevant for the present analysis since the abstract values of the preverb also exclusively originate from the same spatial schema (see Section 6). It is argued that the abstract values conveyed by the preposition *per* belong to the complex semantic domain of Causation. This domain contains causal roles, i.e. "semantic roles taken by the participant(s) that initiate or have a part in bringing about a certain state of affairs. Major causal roles are Agent, Instrument, and Cause, to which Reason, Force, Means, Causee, and Intermediary can be added" (Luraghi 2010: 44). According to Croft (1991: 185), the whole set of semantic roles can be placed along a *causal chain*, depending on their relation with the transmission of force determining a state of affairs. The source domain of the causal chain is Space or, rather, the coordinates defining the organization of Space, namely, Source, Location and Direction (toward an endpoint). Within the causal domain, Croft (1991: 184–192) distinguishes between "antecedent" roles (that is, causal roles properly), which are based on Source, and "subsequent" roles, which are based on Direction. Luraghi (2001: 38) also includes "concomitant" roles, which are based on an intermediate area directly involving the preposition we are dealing with here, that is, Location (Figure 7).

| SOURCE DOMAIN: *SPACE* | SOURCE | LOCATION (trajectory) | DIRECTION (towards an endpoint) |
|---|---|---|---|
| TARGET DOMAIN: *CAUSATION* | *Antecedent roles* (Agent, Cause, Reason) | *Concomitant roles* (Instrument, Means, etc.) | *Subsequent roles* (Purpose, Beneficiary) |

**Figure 7:** Causal chain of events (adapted from Luraghi 2010: 68)

Given the spatial configuration *per* expresses, it is not surprising that it enters the domain of Causation signaling the semantic role Means/Instrument. This central role metaphorically expresses the PATH *through* which an event is realized. More precisely, in Early Latin *per* is stably employed in the expression of Means, a semantic role which differs from concrete and manipulated

Instrument as it refers to abstract and less manipulated entities (Croft 1991: 178).[12] An example of Means is given in (3).

(3) *Ecqu-as        viginti  min-as         **per***
    INT-ACC.F.PL  twenty  minae-ACC.F.PL  through

   ***sycophantiam***    *atque  **per**       **doctos***
    cunning.ACC.F.SG  and    through  artful.ACC.M.PL

   ***dolos***         *paritas            ut*
    trick.ACC.M.PL  be.about.PRS.2SG  so.that

   *aufer-as                   a     me?*
    from.take-PRS.SUBJ.2SG  from  I.ABL

   'So are you about to try to get twenty minæ off me by stealth and artful tricks?' (Pseudolus 485)

Means implies the existence of an Agent who intentionally initiates the state of affairs denoted by the verb. The involvement of an Agent justifies the metonymical shift from Means to Reason, a second semantic role which is strongly associated with *per* in Early Latin (Brucale and Mocciaro 2011). Reason, as in (4), has been described as a sub-specification of Cause: while a Cause enables the realization of a state of affairs not necessarily controlled by an intentional Agent, a Reason represents the motivation for an Agent to act (Pinkster 1990a: 118; Croft 1991: 293). Thus, the difference lies more in the lexical semantics of the verb denoting the caused event, than in the inherent features of the noun following the preposition.[13]

(4) *Ama-ns                   **per**     **amor-em**    si*
    love-PRS.PTCP.NOM.M.SG  through  love-ACC.M.SG  if

   *quid               fec-i,    Milphio,       ignosc-ere*
    something.ACC.N.SG  do-PRF.1SG  Milphio.VOC.SG  forgive-PRS.INF

   *id           te        mi      aequ-om          est.*
    it.ACC.N.SG  you.ACC  I.DAT  right-NOM.N.SG  be.PRS.3SG

   'But if, being in love, I did anything by reason of love, Milphio, it's only reasonable that you should forgive me for it.' (Poenulus 130)

---

**12** The expression of prototypical instruments by means of a PP introduced by *per* represents a rather late development in the history of Latin. In Early and Classical Latin this function was typically performed by the bare Ablative case (see Vester 1983; Pinkster 1990b; Luraghi 2010).
**13** The expression of Cause is only peripheral at this stage and it can be characterized as an incipient generalization, progressively weakening the initial constraint on the agency of the caused event.

We will not discuss in further detail the complex internal relations characterizing the semantic network of *per*. Note, though, that the metonymical extension through which Reason is attracted within the semantic network of *per* determines a shift from the central area (Location) to the initial area (Source) of the causal chain.

## 5 The preverb *per-*

As mentioned in Section 1, Early Latin *per-* is associated with a semantic network comprising both spatial and abstract meanings. In this section, we will discuss these meanings in further detail, showing that preverb and preposition not only differ from each other on the semantic level, but that they also testify to the existence of different mechanisms underlying the process of preverbation in Latin.

### 5.1 Multidirectional trajectory

*Per-* combines with verbal bases expressing motion (or implied motion), resulting in complex forms conveying a scattered trajectory on a two-dimensional surface (Figure 6). With *perambulo* 'to walk around' in (5a), for example, the trajectory inherently expresses non-linearity, while the LM is represented by means of the accusative *aedīs* and the adverbial *qualibet* 'everywhere'. In contrast, *ambulo* 'to walk' frequently occurs in clearly atelic contexts, such as (5b) and (5c), although it may also be accompanied by a PP expressing the direction toward an endpoint, such as *in ius* in (5d).

(5) a. *Qualibet* **per-ambula** *aedīs*[14]
where.please through-walk.PRS.IMP.2SG house.ACC.F.PL

*oppido tamquam tuas.*
precisely as.well.as your.ACC.F.PL

'Walk in every direction, wherever you like, all over the house just as though it were your own.' (Mostellaria 809)

---

[14] This is a special form of the normal plural accusative *-es* ending and is particularly frequent in Plautus, e.g. *omnīs plateas* in (6b) and *aurīs* in (8b).

b. *bene **ambula**  et  red-ambula*
   well walk.PRS.IMP.2SG and back-walk.PRS.IMP.2SG
   'a happy walk there to you, and a happy walk back'  (Captivi 900)

c. *Per  urbem  quom  **ambulent***
   through city.ACC.F.SG when walk.PRS.SBJV.3PL

   *omnibus  os  opturent.*
   all.DAT.M.PL mouth.ACC.N.SG close.PRS.SBJV.3PL

   'When they walk through the city, they should shut the mouths of everyone.'  (Stichus 113)

d. *qui  scis  mercari ...*
   who.NOM.M.SG know.PRS.2SG traffic.PRS.INF.DEP

   *virgines  **ambula**  in ius*
   girl.ACC.F.PL walk.PRS.IMP.2SG in court.ACC.N.SG

   'you, who understand how to traffic ... girls, come before the judge'  (Curculio 620)

A similar distribution is observed for *repto* 'to creep, crawl' and *perrepto* 'to creep, crawl through'. The former occurs with PPs such as *in urbe* in (6a), expressing the delimited space within which the event is brought about. In contrast, the spatial relation in (6b), i.e. the multidirectional trajectory described by the TR, is conveyed by the morphologically complex form *perrepto*; this verb form occurs with a bare accusative *omnīs plateas*, which signals the spatial extension of the TR's trajectory. In (6c), the ablative *omnibus latebris* can be interpreted as conveying a spatial extension as well; in this case, it is the presence of a plural encoding reiterated "crawling through" events (see Talmy's 2000 [1988] notion of a discontinuous LM) that provides the 'extent' reading.

(6) a. *quid in urbe  **reptas**,  vilice?*
     why in city.ABL.F.SG creep.PRS.2SG bailiff.VOC.M.SG
     'why are you creeping about in the city, you bailiff?'  (Casina 98)

  b. *nam omnīs  plateas  **per-reptavi**,*
     for all.ACC.F.PL street.ACC.F.PL through-creep.PRF.1SG

     *gymnasia  et  Myropolia*
     gymnasium.ACC.N.PL and perfumer's.shop.ACC.N.PL

     'for through all the streets have I crawled, the wrestling-rings and the perfumers' shops'  (Amphitruo 1011)

c. *Omnibus     latebris           **per-reptavi***
   all.ABL.F.PL covert.place.ABL.F.PL through-creep.PRF.1SG
   
   *quarere      conservam.*
   seek.PRS.INF fellow-slave.ACC.F.SG
   
   'Through each covert spot have I crawled along, to seek my fellow-slave.'
   (Rudens 223)

Neither in *perambulo* nor in *perrepto* did the univerbation produce complete semantic bleaching of the preverb. Here, the preverb expresses the trajectory followed by the mobile TR, without altering other features of the motion described (manner, atelicity, etc.). At the same time, *per-* does seem to grammatically modify the base, changing the valency of the verb so that it may govern an accusative and, hence, behave like a transitive (Baldi 2006). However, as Lehmann (1983) observes, changes of valency occur sporadically, namely when the preverbs are associated with intransitive verbs belonging to the lexical field 'go'. As a consequence, the accusatives in question seem to express the locational scope of the movement denoted by the verb rather than a real object. More generally, according to Lehmann (1983: 156), "the typical role of a preverb does not consist in changing the argument structure or even the transitivity of a verb, but in bringing the local specification expressed by certain LRs [local relators] nearer to the verb". This claim is reinforced by the examples of preverbs discussed in the following section, which do not show any change of valency.

## 5.2 Linear Path

In many cases, *per-* describes a linear Path. This value can be clearly discerned in *pervenio* 'to arrive' (7), in which the preverb describes the path leading to the endpoint of the motion event. The endpoint is denoted by the telic base *venio* 'to come'.[15]

(7) a. *Postquam tuo           iussu            profectus sum,*
       after.that your.ABL.M.SG order.ABL.M.SG leave.PRF.1SG.DEP
       
       ***per-veni***       *in Cariam.*
       through-come.PRF.1SG in Caria.ACC.F.SG
       
       'After, at your request, I had set out, I arrived in Caria.'     (Curculio 329)

---

**15** What Fillmore (1983 [1972]: 220) defines as "Goal-orientation" is the most significant semantic component of Latin *venio*, which can be hardly considered a deictic verb according to Ricca (1993: 117–127).

b. *Tibi      muni                  viam*
   you.DAT  secure.PRS.IMP.2SG  passage-way.ACC.F.SG

   *qua             cibatus              commeatus=que*
   which.ABL.F.SG  food.NOM.M.SG  provisions.NOM.M.SG=and

   *ad te        tuto    possit              **per-venire**.*
   to you.ACC  safely  can.PRS.SBJV.3SG  through-come.PRS.INF.

   'Secure yourself a passage, by which supplies and provision may be
   enabled in safety to reach yourself.'       (Miles gloriosus 223–225)

With other bases, the spatial meaning of the preverb is less transparent and can only be reconstructed on a historical-comparative basis, as in the case of *pereo* 'to be destroyed, to perish' and *pergo* 'to hold on, to continue'. We will return to *pereo* in Section 7. Suffice it to say here that *pergo* is phonetically opaque (*per + rego*, see Ernout and Meillet 2001 [1959]: 568), and that this may explain why the spatial meaning of *pergo* 'to steer', as in (8c) and (8d), differs substantially from the analogous use of the transitive *rego* 'to keep, lead straight; to guide, conduct', as in (8a). On the other hand, *pergo* more typically covers the grammatical function of a progressive auxiliary (García Hernández 1980: 179), as in (8b).

(8) a. *Hoc              te-cum            oro,         ut    illius*
       this.ACC.N.SG  you.ABL-with  beg.PRS.1SG  that  he.GEN.M.SG

       *animum          atque  ingenium.           **regas***
       mind.ACC.M.SG  and    disposition.ACC.N.S  direct.PRS.SBJV.2SG

       'I beg this of you, that you will influence his feelings and his
       disposition.'                                       (Bacchides 494)

   b. ***Pergi=n              pergere?...      pergi=n***
      hold.on.PRS.2SG=INT  hold.on.PRS.INF  hold.on.PRS.2SG=INT

      *aurīs            tundere?*
      ear.ACC.F.PL  beat.PRS.INF

      'Do you persist in going on this way? ... Do you persist in dinning my
      ears?'                                          (Poenulus 433–434)

   c. ***Pergam***         *in aedīs            nunciam.*
      hold.on.FUT.1SG  in house.ACC.F.PL  just.now
      'I'll steer toward the house immediately.'        (Amphitruo 1052)

d. **Pergo**         ad alios,            venio          ad
   hold.on.PRS.1SG to other.ACC.M.PL come.PRS.1SG to

   alios,          deinde ad alios.
   other.ACC.M.PL then   to other.ACC.M.PL

   'I go to some; then to some others I come; then to some others.'

   (Captivi 488)

The spatial meaning of *per-* is also still accessible in *perfero* 'to carry through' (9a, 9b) and *perduco* 'to lead, bring through' (10b), and it does not alter the basic semantics or the morphosyntactic behavior of the transitive verbs *fero* 'to carry' and *duco* 'to lead' (9b, 10a). Again, *per-* expresses a linear Path, whose endpoint is expressed by the PPs *ad litus* (9a) and *in crucem* (10b). The spatial configuration linear Path sharply differentiates these cases from the type *perambulo* in (5a), and it may also explain the semantic shift toward the so-called intensive meaning, which can be seen in *perfero* 'to suffer' (9b) (see Sections 6 and 7).

Similarly, when *permitto* refers to a spatial configuration, meaning 'to let something go through, to send away' (cf. *mitto* 'to send'), as in (11a) and (11b), *per-* emphasizes the trajectory along which an entity is moved away from a starting point. As we will see in Section 7, when the trajectory achieves an endpoint, the movement can be construed in a resultative way. This resultative value produces an overall semantic shift in *permitto*, which then acquires the non-spatial meaning 'to give permission', as in (11c).

(9) a. Vix     hodie ad litus                **per-tulit**
       hardly today to  sea-shore.ACC.N.SG through-carry.PRF.3SG

       nos    ventus           exanimatas.
       us.ACC wind.NOM.M.SG deprived.of.life.PRF.PTCP.ACC.F.PL

       'Half dead, the wind this day has hardly borne us to the shore.'

       (Rudens 371)

   b. **Feram**       et   **per-feram** ...       abitum
      carry.FUT.1SG and through-carry.FUT.1SG departure.ACC.M.SG

      eius         animo            forti.
      he.GEN.M.SG mind.ABL.M.SG strong.ABL.M.SG

      'I shall bear and endure his absence with mind resolved.'

      (Amphitruo 645)

(10) a. *Tum captivorum      quid         ducunt      secum!*
       then prisoner.GEN.M.PL what.ACC.N.SG lead.PRS.3PL them.with
       'Then, what prisoners they lead with them!'          (Epidicus 210)

   b. *Hic         quidem Pol      summam          in*
      this.NOM.M.SG really  by.Pollux highest.ACC.F.SG to

      *crucem          cena             aut prandio*
      torture.ACC.F.SG dinner.ABL.F.SG or  lunch.ABL.N.SG

      **per-duci**               *potest.*
      through-lead.PRS.INF.PASS be.able.PRS.3SG

      'Really, by Pollux, this fellow might be induced by a dinner or a lunch
      to bear extreme torture.'                             (Stichus 626)

(11) a. *Quid           si ego  impetro       atque*
       what.NOM.N.SG if I.NOM obtain.PRS.1SG and

       *exoro              a    vilico,        causa*
       prevail.upon.PRS.1SG from bailiff.ABL.M.SG sake.ABL.F.SG

       *mea          ut     eam        illi*
       my.ABL.F.SG so.that she.ACC.SG he.DAT.M.SG

       **per-mittat?**
       through-send.PRS.SBJV.3SG

       'What if I prevail upon, and obtain of the bailiff, that for my sake he'll
       give her up to the other one?'                       (Casina 270)

   b. *At  ne  cum argento         protinam*
      but not with money.ABL.N.SG immediately

      **per-mittas**              *domum,         mone          te.*
      through-send.PRS.SBJV.2SG home.ACC.F.SG warn.PRS.1SG you.ACC
      'But don't dash right off home with the money, I'm warning you.'
                                                            (Persa 680)

   c. *Etsi       adversatus              tibi     fui,*
      although oppose.PRF.PTCP.NOM.M.SG you.DAT be.PRF.1SG

      *istac        iudico:         tibi      **per-mitto**.*
      in.that.way decide.PRS.1SG you.DAT through-send.PRS.1SG

      'Although I have been opposed to you, I thus give my decision: I will
      give you permission.'                                 (Trinummus 384)

The semantics of linear extension is transparent in the denominal parasynthetic derivative *pernocto* 'to stay overnight, to pass the night'. Note that the non-linearity reading can be entirely attributed to the preverb, which is added to a non-verbal base (*nox* 'night'). The semantics of time is very often construed by means of spatial metaphors (Lakoff and Johnson 1980) and typically linked to a unidimensional and unidirectional configuration (Haspelmath 1997: 23; Radden 2003). Thus, the metaphor entails the selection of the linear configuration, which is represented as a progression of contiguous points along the temporal axis, as in (12).

(12) *Cum=que ea       noctem        in stramentis*
with=and she.ABL.SG night.ACC.F.SG in straw.ABL.N.SG

***per-noctare                    perpetem.***
through-pass.the.night.PRS.INF uninterrupted.ACC.SG

'And with her spend the full night upon the straw.' (Truculentus 278)

## 5.3 Crossing the boundaries

*Per-* also retains a spatial meaning when it occurs with transitive verbs, such as *fodio* 'to peirce' in (13a) or *tundo* 'to beat, to strike' in (14a), whose LMs correspond to three-dimensional entities which can be crossed by the TR. In *perfodio* 'to pierce through' (13b) and *pertundo* 'to beat through, to make a hole through' (14b), the PER relation signals that the action of the TR crosses boundaries of the LM, i.e. that it may start from a point outside the LM, cross its boundaries from the outside to the inside, extend throughout the LM, and cross its boundaries again from the inside to the outside. The same 'crossing' relation is present in a few intransitive verbs, such as *perluceo* 'to shine through, to be seen through', to be transparent' (15a, 15b) and *perpluo* 'to rain through' (15c, 15d); all these verbs denote physical events "crossing" a multi-dimensional entity (a body, a container, etc.) encoded as the subject.

(13) a. *Miserum              est         opus,        igitur*
miserable.NOM.N.SG be.PRS.3SG work.NOM.N.SG therefore

*demum **fodere**    puteum,      ubi    sitis*
at.last dig.PRS.INF well.ACC.M.SG when thirst.NOM.F.SG

*fauces          tenet.*
throat.ACC.F.PL hold.PRS.3SG

'It's a bad job, to be digging a well at the last moment, just when thirst has gained possession of your throat.' (Mostellaria 379–380)

b. *Ego* **per-fodi** *parietem,     qua*
I.NOM through-dig.PRF.1SG wall.CC.F.SG which.ABL.F.S
*commeatus      clam   esset        hinc*
passage.NOM.M.SG secretly be.IPRF.SBJV.3SG from.this.place
*huc          mulieri.*
to.this.place woman.DAT.F.SG

'I have dug a hole through the party-wall, in order that there may secretly be a passageway for the damsel from the one house to the other.'  (Miles gloriosus 142)

(14) a. *Sed quid        hoc            quod*
but what.NOM.N.SG this.NOM.N.SG what.NOM.N.SG
*picus              ulmum          **tundit**.*
woodpecker.NOM.M.SG elm-tree.ACC.F.SG beat.PRS.3SG

'But what does this mean, that the woodpecker is tapping the elm-tree?'  (Asinaria 262)

b. *I,             puere,        prae;   ne*
go.PRS.IMP.2SG boy.VOC.M.SG before so.that.not
*quisquam          **per-tundat**              cruminam*
anyone.NOM.M.SG through-beat.PRS.SBJV.3SG purse.ACC.F.SG
*cautio=st.*
caution.NOM.F.SG=be.PRS.3SG

'Boy, go you before me; it is necessary that no one makes a hole through my purse.'  (Pseudolus 170)

(15) a. *Ita is          **pellucet**              quasi lanterna*
so it.NOM.M.SG through.shine.PRS.3SG as lantern.NOM.F.SG
*Punica*
Punic.NOM.F.SG

'It's just as transparent as a Punic lantern.'  (Aulularia 566)

b. *Villam         integundam          intellego*
cottage.ACC.F.SG cover.GER.ACC.F.SG understand.PRS.1SG
*totam       mihi, nam    nunc **per-lucet***
all.ACC.F.SG I.DAT in.fact now through-shine.PRS.3SG
*ea         quam cribrum          crebrius.*
it.NOM.F.SG than sieve.NOM.N.SG repeated.COMPR.NOM.N.SG

'I find that the whole of my cottage must be covered; for now it's shining through it, more full of holes than a sieve.'  (Rudens 102)

c. *Venit         imber,          lavit          parietes,*
   come.PRS.3SG rain.NOM.M.SG wash.PRS.3SG wall.ACC.F.PL
   ***per-pluont.***
   through-rain.PRS.3PL
   'The rain comes on and streams down the walls which get waterlogged.'
   (Mostellaria 111)

d. *In uilla,          cum   pluet,              circum-ire*
   in cottage.ABL.F.SG when rain.PRS.SBJV.3SG around-go.PRS.INF
   *oportet,              sicubi    **per-pluat,***
   be.necessary.PRS.3SG wherever through-rain.PRS.SBJV.3SG
   *et    signare        carbone.*
   and mark.PRS.INF coal.ABL.M.SG
   'When it rains, it is necessary to go around into the house and, wherever water is seeping, to mark by means of the coal.'
   (de Agricoltura 155.2.2)

The analysis of the data presented in this section shows that, in the whole set of spatial occurrences, *per-* behaves as a modifier of the meaning of the base. In other words, although its degree of bondedness (and, hence, relevance) to the base is much higher, the behavior of the preverb does not greatly differ, at least on the semantic level, from that of the sentence particle. Moreover, the semantic contribution of the preverb is generally fully identifiable, so that we can assume that *per-* is stored in the lexicon of the language as a lexical formative involved in a derivational process. As we will see in Section 6, the analysis of the abstract meanings of the preverb shows a quite different scenario. Also, occasional deviations from this general description (as in the case of *permitto*, *perfero* and, to a higher extent, *pergo*) require a different explanation. They are restricted to single verbal lexemes which individually developed new values that cannot be attributed directly to the preverb, but rather are conveyed by the preverbed lexeme as a whole. As we will argue in Section 7, these new values are thus lexicalized meanings.

# 6 Abstract and grammatical values of *per-*

As we have already mentioned in relation to *perfero* in (9) (Section 5.2), the abstract value of intensification most frequently develops from the Linear Path configuration. This abstract meaning has been interpreted as an "intensive/

iterative" (Allen and Greenough 1903: 159; Bennet 1908 [1895]: 113) and/or "telic" value of the preverb(s) (e.g. Romagno 2003, 2008). Building on these interpretations, we will analyze the whole range of meanings conveyed by *per-* as different degrees along a continuum moving from spatial to more abstract values.

Often, the contribution of the preverbal constituent to the semantics of the whole verb can be interpreted by means of a synchronic comparison with the non-preverbed correlates, as in (16a) and (16b). The schematic content describing a forward trajectory undergoes a metaphorical extension when applied to verbal bases denoting or containing an activity (i.e. an inherently durative event), such as *permisceo* 'to mix, blend well' in (16b) (cf. also *percoquo* 'to cook thoroughly', *perbibo* 'to soak', *perdoceo* 'to teach, instruct thoroughly', etc.).

(16) a. *Caseum         cum alica         ad eundem*
       cheese.ACC.N.SG with spelt.ABL.F.SG to the.same.ACC.N.SG

   *modum         **misceto**.*
   way.ACC.N.SG  mix.FUT.IMP.2SG

   'Mix the cheese and spelt in the same way.'      (de Agricoltura 79.1.2)

   b. ***Per-misceto**         lentim         aceto*
      through-mix.FUT.IMP.2SG lentil.ACC.F.SG vinegar.ABL.N.SG

   *laserpiciato                  et    ponito          in sole.*
   with.laserpicium.ABL.N.SG and put.FUT.IMP.2SG in sun.ABL.M.SG

   'Soak the lentils in the infusion of vinegar and asafoetida, and expose to the sun.'      (de Agricoltura 116.1.2)

In such cases, the preverb metaphorically "continues/prolongs" the activity denoted by the verb along the linear trajectory it describes. In other words, the spatial semantics of the preverb is bleached and *per-* only expresses a durative (continuative or iterative) value, which is aspectual in nature and from which the meaning of intensification arises.[16] This development can be schematically

---

[16] García Hernández (1985: 521) notes that almost all Latin preverbed verbs may express an intensive modification of the event denoted by the base. He (1989: 153–155) refers to the aspectual value conveyed by the preverb *per-* as *aspect progressif* and claims that spatial and aspectual sequences show parallel structures, namely: (i) a spatial sequence: allative – prosecutive – ablative; (ii) an aspectual sequence: ingressive – progressive – egressive. In other words, verbal aspect can be considered as a space which can be entered (ingressive aspect), passed through (progressive aspect) and exited (egressive aspect). Wood (2007: 15) observes that intensive value is anything but uncommon with categories indicating 'repetition' or a plural event meaning.

described as a quantitative increase along the temporal axis (i.e. "do V again and again > more and more"), which may produce a qualitative improvement (i.e. "do V more and more > well"), based on the metaphor MORE IS BETTER (Lakoff and Johnson 1980: 22). Note that the increase can but need not achieve the highest degree ("do V completely > in the best way").[17] The intensification meaning is represented in Figure 8.

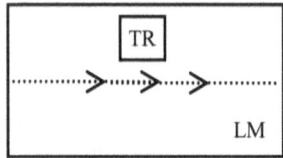

**Figure 8:** Intensification

Qualitative progress also affects verbs implying an extended (two- or three-dimensional) LM, such as *perfrico* 'to scrub thoroughly' in (17b) (see also *perspargo* 'to sprinkle', *perungo* 'to rub with oil thoroughly', *pertego* 'to cover all over', etc.) as well as verbs of seeing behaving as motion verbs (Jackendoff 1983: 150; Slobin 2008); examples of the latter are *perspecto* and *perspicio* 'to look, see thoroughly' in (18) in (19) respectively, which both contain the component 'all around/accurately/completely'. In all these cases, any multi-directional meaning pertains to the lexical semantics of the base, while the preverb only adds the component of intensification.

(17) a. *Ubi     structum                          erit,*
       when  arrange.PRF.PTCP.NOM.N.SG  be.FUT.3SG

   *pavito                      fricato=que                    uti*
   beat.down.FUT.IMP.2SG  scrub.FUT.IMP.2SG=and  so.that

   *pavimentum          bonum              siet.*
   pavement.NOM.N.SG  good.NOM.N.SG  be.PRS.SBJV.3SG

   'When completed, pack and rub down so as to have a smooth surface.'
                                                             (de Agricoltura 18.7.9)

---

**17** Van Laer (2005) suggests explaining some usages of *per-* in light of the concept of *gradation* (Sapir 1944). Assuming that certain lexical domains (e.g. feelings, transmission of knowledge, vision, etc.) are internally structured according to an oriented axis, *per-* acts on the degree of force or duration of a verb causing the achievement of the highest degree of this axis.

b. *Postea lentim          oleo                **per-fricato**,*
   then   lentil.ACC.F.SG  oil.ABL.N.SG  through-scrub.FUT.IMP.2SG

   *sinito              arescat.*
   let.FUT.IMP.2SG  dry.PRS.SBJV.3SG

   'Then rub the lentils with oil, allow them to dry.' (de Agricoltura 116.1.3)

(18) *Sinite              me     prius    **per-spectarem***
     let.PRS.IMP.2PL  I.ACC  before  through-look.PRS.INF

   *ne               uspiam        insidiae              sient.*
   so.that.not  anywhere  ambush.NOM.F.PL  be.PRS.SBJV.3PL

   'Let me first look out, that there may be no ambush anywhere.'
                                                      (Miles gloriosus 597)

(19) a. *Nunc defaecato                         demum animo*
       now   cleanse.PRF.PTCP.ABL.M.SG  at.last  mind.ABL.M.SG

   *e-gredior                    domo,                postquam*
   out-go.PRS.DEP.1SG  home.ABL.F.SG  after.that

   ***per-spexi***              *salva                esse            intus    omnia.*
   through-see.PRF.1SG  safe.ACC.N.PL  be.PRS.INF  inside  all.ACC.N.PL

   'Now, with my mind at ease, at length I go out of my house, after I've
   seen that everything is safe in-doors.'                (Aulularia 80)

   b. *Ad illum              modum                sublitum*
      to  that.ACC.N.SG  way.ACC.N.SG  anoint.PRF.PTCP.NOM.N.SG

   *os                      esse            mi         hodie!  ne=que*
   mouth.NOM.N.SG  be.PRS.INF  I.DAT  today   not=and

   *id                  **per-spicere**            quivi.*
   it.ACC.N.SG  through-see.PRS.INF  be.able.PRF.1SG

   'That I should have been duped in this fashion today! and that I wasn't
   able to see through it!'                                     (Captivi 784)

Example (19b) shows that in *perspicio* the accuracy in observing an object may develop into the ability to fully understand it. Here, the endpoint of the metaphorical Path is focalized, i.e. its result. Thus, the domain of *perspicio* shifts from visual to intellectual perception, expressing an idea of "comprehension" ("to see thoroughly > to see well > to know") (Van Laer 2005: 333) (Section 7).

Sometimes, *per-* denotes a temporally extended path, rather than a spatially extended one. *Perdormisco* 'to sleep on' in (20), for instance, describes the duration of the event "to sleep", in spite of the presence of the inchoative suffix *-sco*. As with *pernocto* in (12), this durative value is made explicit by the preverb.

(20) **Per-dormisci=n** usque ad lucem?
through-sleep.PRS.2SG=INT until to light.ACC.F.SG

*facile=n tu dormis cubans?*
easily=INT you.NOM sleep.PRS.2SG lie.down.PRS.PTCP.NOM.M.SG

'Do you always sleep soundly until daylight? Do you easily fall asleep when in bed?' (Menaechmi 928)

With verbs denoting mental, psychological and physio-perceptive situations, the increase conveyed by the preverb *per-* can be construed as an increase in force (Van Laer 2005: 228–230). This is the case for verbs such as *percrucio* 'to torment greatly' in (21a) (see also *pervolo* 'to wish greatly', *percupio* 'to desire earnestly', *perlubet* 'it is very pleasing', *perplaceo* 'to please greatly', etc.), and inchoative forms such as *peracesco* 'to become thoroughly sour' in the same example (see also *perprurisco* 'to itch all over', *pertimesco* 'to fear greatly', *persentisco* 'to perceive clearly', etc.). In both cases, the increase in degree expressed by *per-* may never achieve the final point of the Path or, in other words, may not produce a change of state, not even when the verb occurs in a perfective tense, as in *peracuit* in (21b).[18]

(21) a. *Hoc est quo <cor>*
this.NOM.N.SG be.PRS.3SG what.ABL.N.SG heart.NOM.N.SG

**per-acescit;** *hoc est demum*
through-become.sour.PRS.3SG this.NOM.N.SG be.PRS.3SG at.last

*quod* **per-crucior.**
what.ACC.N.SG through-torment.PRS.PASS.1SG

'It is this through which my heart becomes embittered; It is this, ultimately, by which I am distracted.' (Bacchides 1099–100)

b. *ita mihi pectus* **per-acuit**
so I.DAT breast.NOM.N.SG through-become.sour.PRF.3SG

'so exasperated were my feelings' (Aulularia 468)

---

**18** The value of 'become' in *peracesco* is already provided by the inchoative suffix *-sco* which, in general terms, adds a dynamic component focusing on the initial part of the event (Haverling 2003). This value is, however, not necessarily present, as with *pertimesco* 'to fear greatly' (vs. *timesco* 'to get frightened'). This also explains why *perdormisco* in (20) maintains a basic durative character ('to sleep') rather than an ingressive one ('to fall asleep'), despite the presence of the inchoative suffix.

The examples discussed in this section differ substantially from the ones in Section 5, where the preverb modifies the lexical semantics of the verb adding spatial information only. In the cases discussed here, *per-* affects the internal structure of the PR denoted by the verb and, in doing so, behaves as a grammatical item that contributes to the formation of morphologically more complex entities, i.e. the preverbed verbs, in a regular and fully compositional way. As such, we are dealing with the result of a grammaticalization process: triggered by a metaphorical abstraction of the basic spatial semantics, the grammaticalization of the aspectual/intensive value of *per-* not only involves semantic bleaching, but it is also characterized by *per-*'s increase in frequency and productivity, as well as its generalization to new contexts. This host-class expansion (Himmelmann 2004) is reflected in the use of intensive *per-* with adjectives and adverbs from Early Latin onward, as in (22)[19] (see also *perpetuus* 'perpetual', Miles gloriosus 1079, adverbs such as *perbene* 'very well', Aulularia 186).[20]

(22) **Per-facile**　　　　　id　　　　　quidem=st.
　　 through-easy.NOM.N.SG it.NOM.N.SG indeed=be.PRS.3SG
　　 'That indeed is a very easy matter.'　　　　　　　　　(Menaechmi 893)

# 7 Telicity and semantic bleaching

The data discussed in Section 6 show that the preverb does not contain a component of telicity, i.e. it does not inherently express an endpoint, and emphasizes only the forward development of the process. Whether or not an endpoint is included in the semantics of the derivative verb rather depends on the base. Besides the case of *pervenio* (Section 5.2), we can distinguish the following preverbed verbs conveying telicity:

---

[19] We are grateful to the one of the anonymous reviewers for pointing out that corresponding prefixes in some Germanic languages also cover an intensive function (e.g. Germ. *durchnässt* and Dutch *doornat* both meaning 'sodden, soaking wet'). That the intensive value is not exclusive to the Latin preverb reinforces the hypothesis that such a value represents an expected (and, in fact, cross-linguistically attested) development of the spatial configuration we are dealing with.
[20] When it conveys aspectual meaning, *per-* can also be used with verbal bases denoting states, to which the preverb then adds a component of intensification. Although no occurrences are found in Plautus, verbs such as *permaneo* 'to linger, to remain' and *persto* 'to stand firmly' are widely attested elsewhere (e.g. Terentius, *Hecyra* 305: *ira ... tam permansit diu* 'anger lingered for a long time'; Cicero, *De Officiis* 3.9.39: *negant enim posse et in eo perstant* 'they deny that this can be possible and persist in this opinion').

(a) In a number of instances, *per-* is added to an inherently telic verb, such as *solvo* 'to dissolve, loosen, untie, release' in (23a) and *vinco* 'to win, defeat' in (24a). In *persolvo* 'to release/discharge completely' in (23b), and in *pervinco* 'to conquer, to gain a complete victory over' in (24b), the verbal meaning is simply intensified by the presence of the preverb, which emphasizes a value 'completely' expressed by the base.

(23) a. *Ille,          decem  minas           dum  **solvit**,*
    he.NOM.M.SG ten    mina.ACC.F.PL while release.PRS.3SG

   *omnis         mensas                    transiit.*
   all.ACC.F.PL money-changer's.counter.ACC.F.PL over-go.PRF.3SG

   'Before he paid me the ten minæ, he went to every banker's counter.'
   (Curculio 682)

   b. *Nunc quod          relicuom                restat*
      now what.ACC.N.SG what.is.left.ACC.N.SG remain.PRS.3SG

      *volo          **per-solvere**,...    ne*
      want.PRS.1SG through-release.PRS.INF so.that.not

      *quid              debeam.*
      what.ACC.N.SG owe.PRS.SBJV.1SG

      'Now, what remains unpaid, I wish to discharge so that I may not remain a debtor.' (Cistellaria 188)

(24) a. *Eum        contra  **vincat**          iureiurando    suo.*
      he.ACC.M against win.PRS.SBJV.3SG oath.ABL.N.SG his.ABL.N.SG
      '(She) has to prevail against him with her oath'    (Miles gloriosus 190)

   b. *Si amas,...    facito              ut       pretio*
      if love.PRS.2SG make.FUT.IMP.2SG so.that price.ABL.N.SG

      ***per-vincas***              *tuo.*
      through-win.PRS.SBJV.2SG your.ABL.N.SG

      'If you love me..., take care to prevail with your offer.'    (Curculio 213)

(b) In causative verbs such as *perterreo* 'to frighten, terrify thoroughly' in (25) or in verbal compounds with the causative component *-facio*, such as *permadefacio* 'to make very wet' in (26) – itself based on a state (i.e. *madeo* 'to be wet'), the preverb expresses only an increase in force affecting the object of the causative verb, which undergoes a change of state at the end of the process (i.e. it becomes "X-*factum*").

(25) *Ad-veniens* **per-terruit** *me.*
 to-come.PRS.PTCP.NOM.M.SG through-frighten.PRF.3SG I.ACC
 'He frightened me on his arrival.' (Mostellaria 1136)

(26) *Amor* *ad-venit* ... **per-madefacit**
 love.NOM.M.SG to-come.PRS.3SG through-make.wet.PRS.3SG

 *cor* *meum.*
 heart.ACC.N.SG my.ACC.N.SG

 'At once passion entered my heart; and seeped through my heart.'
 (Mostellaria 142)

However, the verbal base is not always responsible for the telic nuance of the preverbed lexeme. An explicit telic component is also brought about when the presence of the preverb has already produced a semantic shift in the whole derivative verb. Crucially, this development involves verbal lexemes with a very high token-frequency (of both the base and the derivative) (Bybee 1985, Bybee 2003). Two types can be distinguished:

(c) The first type can be exemplified by the non-spatial instances of *permitto* ('to let go through' > 'to allow/give permission') discussed in Section 5. Similarly, *persequor* can convey the durative meaning 'to follow', either in spatial terms, as in (27a), or in the metaphorical sense 'to follow, to conform to a custom or an order', as in (27b) and (27c). In addition, *persequor* can mean 'to search, to look for' a physical or abstract object, as in (27d). Here the preverb conveys the intensive durative value 'insistently (< 'continuously')'; this durative meaning may develop into 'to try to' when the verb is constructed with an infinitive, as in (27e). Further, the verbal meaning also allows a telic reading, as in (27f), where *persequor* can be interpreted both as 'to search' and 'to find', due to the context describing a suicide plan. This shift is anything but surprising, since the activity of searching typically aims at finding something and, hence, can in fact achieve a final point.

(27) a. *Litus* *hoc*
 seashore.ACC.N.SG this.ACC.N.SG

 **per-sequamur.** **Sequor**
 through-follow.PRS.SBJV.DEP.1PL follow.PRS.DEP.1SG

 *quo* *lubet.*
 wherever please.PRS.3SG

 'Let's keep along this seashore.' 'Wherever you please, I'll follow.'
 (Rudens 250)

b. *meae        orationis          iustam        partem*
my.GEN.F.SG discourse.GEN.F.SG right.ACC.F.SG part.ACC.F.SG

***persequi***
through-follow.PRS.INF.DEP

'to conform to the right part of my discourse/to limit my discourse'
(Miles gloriosus 645)

c. *Non soleo       ego    somniculose eri*
not use.PRS.1SG I.NOM sleepily        master.GEN.M.SG

*imperia          **per-sequi**.*
order.ACC.N.PL through-follow.PRS.INF.DEP

'I am not in the habit of performing the orders of my master in a sleepy fashion.'
(Amphitruo 622)

d. *Ego    mihi   alios           deos*
I.NOM I.DAT other.ACC.M.PL god.ACC.M.PL

*penatis            **per-sequar**.*
Penates.ACC.M.PL through-follow.FUT.1SG.DEP

'I shall now seek other household Gods for myself.' (Mercator 836)

e. *< nec    quam            in > partem          in-gredi*
and.not what.ACC.F.SG in    part.ACC.F.SG in-go.PRS.INF.DEP

***per-sequamur**                  scimus*
through-follow.PRS.SBJV.1PL.DEP know.PRS.1PL

'nor know we in what direction we should try to proceed' (Rudens 667)

f. *Certum         est       mihi  ante    tenebras*
sure.NOM.N.SG be.PRS.3SG I.DAT before darkness.ACC.F.PL

*tenebras            **per-sequi**.*
darkness.ACC.F.PL through-follow.PRS.INF.DEP

'I'm determined, before the dark, I will try to find the dark.'
(Pseudolus 90)

With *persequor* and *permitto*, the preverb seems to focalize the final part of the route metaphorically followed by the TR, thus producing a telic/resultative component. In other words, the extension of the event conveyed by the preverb can be prolonged until a potential endpoint, resulting in the completion of the whole Path and producing a change of state, as is represented in Figure 9.

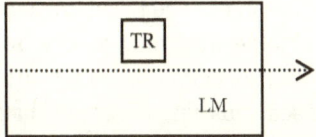

**Figure 9:** Completion (change of state)

The resultative interpretation of *persequor* and *permitto*, however, coexists with the intensive one, and can only be distinguished on the basis of contextual features. This is also the case with *perficio*, which typically expresses the resultative meaning 'to complete', especially in the perfective form (28c), but which can also convey the intensive value 'to do, prepare thoroughly' (28a, 28b).

(28) a. *Curent=que         uti       olea              bene*
     take.care.PRS.SBJV.3PL=and so.that olive.ACC.N.PL well
     ***per-ficiatur***                *siccetur.*
     through-make.PRS.SBJV.PASS.3SG dry.PRS.SBJV.PASS.3SG
     'And see that the olives are thoroughly prepared and that they are well dried.' (de Agricoltura 67.1.2)

   b. *Ut,    si haec         non sint              vera,*
      so.that if this.NOM.N.PL not be.PRS.SBJV.3PL true.NOM.N.PL
      *inceptum                hoc              itiner*
      begin.PRF.PTCP.ACC.N.SG this.ACC.N.SG journey.ACC.N.SG
      ***per-ficere***           *ex-sequar.*
      through-make.PRS.INF out-follow.PRS.SBJV.1SG
      'That, if these things are not true, I may hasten to go upon this intended journey.' (Mercator 913)

   c. *Numquam hodie quiescet       prius quam id*
      never      today rest.FUT.3SG before than it.ACC.N.SG
      *quod          petit        **per-fecerit**.*
      what.ACC.N.SG ask.PRS.3SG through-make.FUTPRF.3SG
      'Never, will he rest today before he has completed that which he is in search of.' (Miles gloriosus 214)

(d) A second type includes verbs which have often been described as conveying a negative or "deviated" sense (Guiraud 1974; García Hernández 1980) (e.g. *periuro* 'to swear falsely, to perjure oneself' in (29)), as well as verbs whose compositional meaning is completely blurred and can only be reconstructed by means of a comparative analysis (e.g. *perdo* 'to destroy, ruin; to lose' in (30a), and *pereo* 'to pass away, to be destroyed, to perish' in (30a) and (30b)). In accordance with the analysis proposed thus far, we argue that the negative value derives from the telic instantiation of the PER relation, which reaches the very final point of the Path and means 'through and until the end'.

(29) *Per-negabo        atque   obdurabo,*
through-deny.FUT.1SG and     persist.FUT.1SG
***per-iurabo***       *denique.*
through-swear.FUT.1SG finally

'I'll persist in my denial, and I'll endure all; finally, I'll perjure myself.'
(Asinaria 322)

(30) a. *Utinam  te       di        prius   **perderent**,*
oh.that! you.ACC god.NOM.PL before destroy.IPRF.SBJV.3PL
*quam  **periisti**   e      patria        tua.*
than  be.lost.PRF.2SG out.of country.ABL.F.SG your.ABL.F.SG

'I wish the Gods had destroyed you, before you were lost to your own country.' (Captivi 537)

b. ***Perii**,         interii.     Pessimus*
be.lost.PRF.1SG be.ruined.PRF.1SG very.bad.NOM.M.SG
*hic        mihi   dies        hodie*
this.NOM.M.SG I.DAT day.NOM.M.SG today
*in-luxit            corruptor.*
in-shine.PRF.3SG corrupter.NOM.M.SG

'I'm undone, ruined quite! Today, this terrible and corrupter day has shone upon me.' (Persa 780)

The metaphorical-metonymical shift Path > Intensive > Telic is generally recognized (Brinton 1988: 187–198; Pompei 2010: 403), and can be analyzed in terms of an extension of the basic configuration of the preverb. The examples in (c) and (d), however, show that the development of the telic component is anything but regular or predictable. It rather affects specific verbal lexemes and produces an overall semantic shift of the preverbed verbs. This shift may involve single segments of the semantics of the preverbed verb, as in the examples discussed in (c), or it may render its compositional accessibility completely opaque, as in the examples in (d). In both cases (although to different degrees), the contribution of the preverb can only be reconstructed, as the telic value is conveyed by the preverb + verb complex as a whole. As such, the component of telicity can be analyzed as an actional value of the verb, which has lost analytical accessibility and which is stored in the lexicon as a unit. In other words, the meaning of telicity is lexicalized (Brinton and Traugott 2005: 144).

# 8 Conclusion

The proposed analysis allows us to locate the whole range of meanings conveyed by *per-* along a continuous scale which starts from spatial values and proceeds along various abstract values, whose most central manifestation is the value of intensification. In Section 3, it has been shown that the schematic import of the PER relation may be instantiated in terms of two patterns, namely a multi-directional configuration and a linear Path. From a theoretical perspective, it is important that the whole set of abstract values conveyed by both preposition and preverb originates from the linear Path configuration only. For the preverb, the existence of a linear interpretation had already been noted (Van Laer 2010), but, to our knowledge, the reason for this interpretation has never been examined.[21] The configurational descriptions provided by Cognitive Grammar have allowed us to provide a possible explanation. PRs are conceived as running along a horizontal path, i.e. they are characterized by inherent directionality (Langacker 1991) (Figure 2). In overlapping with a PR, any AR is somehow forced within this configuration. For the PER relation, the Path schema represents the most suitable candidate for metonymical selection. This hypothesis could explain why the multi-directional configuration is quite marginal in the semantics of *per-* and is limited to the spatial values. Whenever the preverbed verb expresses meanings dealing with the internal structure of the verbal process, the linear Path schema is selected as it is highly compatible with the schematic meaning of the PR.

In our view, the shift from the basic spatial meaning to the abstract value of duration/intensification represents a metaphorical-metonymical process, consisting in the metaphorical mapping of a spatial (i.e. concrete) domain onto an abstract domain as well as entailing the metonymical selection of a specific aspect of the basic meaning (Heine et al. 1991). In some cases a nuance of

---

[21] We are grateful here as well to the anonymous reviewer, who brought this issue to our attention.

telicity develops, which can be interpreted as a metonymical shift focusing on the final part of the metaphorical path.

At the semantic level, the network of meanings expressed by *per-* can be described as a coherent development of values: LOCAL VALUES (PATH) → INTENSIFICATION → COMPLETION/CHANGE OF STATE. A purely semantic analysis, however, cannot explain the different morphosyntactic behavior of the various senses associated with the preverb. In Figure 10, the complex range of meanings of *per-* is illustrated as well as the morphosyntactic status exhibited by each sub-domain.

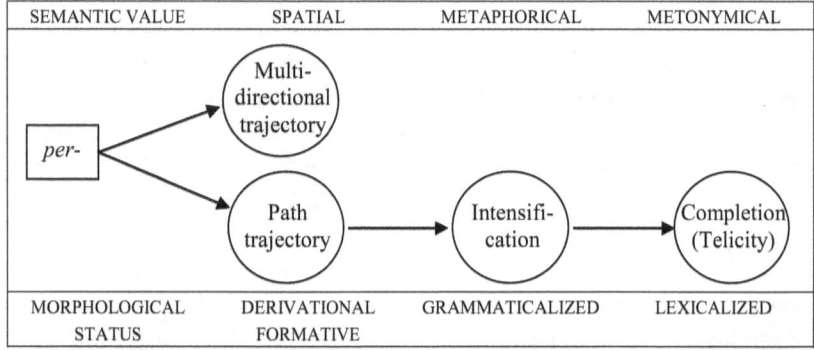

**Figure 10:** The semantic network of *per-*

Figure 10 shows that the results of different mechanisms of language change synchronically coexist within the semantic network of *per-*. As long as *per-* conveys a spatial value, it can be considered a modifier of the verb which regularly contributes in the processes of word formation. The value of durativity/intensification represents a metaphorical shift which projects the basic meaning onto an abstract domain. This abstract domain coincides with a grammatical (aspectual) function, so that *per-* behaves as a grammatical morpheme, whose contribution is fully compositional. The notion of intensification can be further articulated in terms of two patterns, depending on the lexical semantics of the base:

(i) an increase along the horizontal axis consisting of the concrete or metaphorical Path followed by the TR. Since this configuration is inherently directional, the presence of an endpoint is not excluded *a priori*, allowing the possible development of a telic/resultative nuance when the verbal base inherently expresses a telic value;

(ii) an increase in force, involving the manifestations of a psychological state which is incompatible with a telic reading (e.g. *percupio* 'to wish greatly').

The productive character of this gram is testified by its generalization to non-verbal instances (typically adjectives and adverbs), ad hoc uses (e.g. Miles gloriosus 774: *perpurgo* 'to cleanse thoroughly'; Mostellaria 1136: *perterreo* 'to frighten, terrify thoroughly') and *hapax legomena* (e.g. Pseudolus 1215: *perfrigefacio* 'to make very cold'; Stichus 85: *perpavefacio* 'to frighten very much').

The increase of the Path toward and until the end can be metonymically focalized, thus stabilizing as the new relevant value. This metonymical shift typically produces an overall semantic reinterpretation, which is justified by the high token frequency of the derivative verb (*permitto* 'to allow, to permit', *pereo* 'to die', *perdo* 'to destroy, ruin; to lose') and motivates the non-productive character of the 'telic' type. The derivative lexeme is then stored in the lexicon as a unit and the contribution of the preverb can only be reconstructed. Consequently, the aspectual value is better characterized as telic actionality, lexicalized in the meaning of specific verbal lexemes.

The proposed analysis is an attempt to synchronically describe the semantic and morphological status of *per-* in Early Latin. A diachronic extension of the corpus may surely contribute to confirm (or reject) the consistency of the description proposed. This aspect, however, will be food for further research.

## Acknowledgment

We wish to thank the anonymous reviewers for their careful reading of the paper and for providing constructive comments and suggestions.

## List of abbreviations

ABL = ablative; ACC = accusative; Anc. Slav. = Ancient Slavonic; AR = atemporal relation; COMPR = comparative; DAT = dative; DEP = deponent; F = feminine; FUT = future; FUTPRF = future perfect; GEN = genitive; Got. = Gothic; Gr. = Greek; IMP = imperative; IPRF = imperfect; INF = infinitive; INT = interrogative; Lith. = Lithuanian; LM = landmark; M = masculine; N = neuter; NOM = nominative; P = preposition; PASS = passive; PL = plural; PP = prepositional phrase; PR = processual relation; PRF = perfect; PPRF = pluperfect; PRS = present; PTCP = participle; SBJV = subjunctive; SG = singular; Skr. = Sanskrit; SUP = supinum; SUPR = superlative; TR = trajector; VOC = vocative

# References

Allen, Joseph Henry & James Bradstreet Greenough. 1903. *Allen and Greenough's new Latin grammar: Founded on comparative grammar*. Boston & London: Gynn & Company.

Baldi, Philip. 2006. Towards a history of the manner of motion parameter in Greek and Indo-European. In Pierluigi Cuzzolin & Maria Napoli (eds.), *Fonologia e tipologia lessicale nella storia della lingua greca, Atti del VI Incontro Internazionale di Linguistica Greca* (Bergamo, settembre 2005), 13–31. Milano: Franco Angeli.

Bennet, Charles E. 1908 [1895]. *A Latin grammar*. Boston: Allyn & Bacon.

Booij, Geert & Ans van Kemenade. 2003. Preverbs: An introduction. In Geert Booij & Jaap van Marle (eds.), *Yearbook of Morphology 2003*, 1–12. Dordrecht: Kluwer.

Brinton, Laurel J. 1988. *The development of English aspectual systems*. Cambridge: Cambridge University Press.

Brinton, Laurel J. & Elizabeth Closs Traugott. 2005. *Lexicalization and language change*. Cambridge: Cambridge University Press.

Brucale, Luisa & Egle Mocciaro. 2011. Continuity and discontinuity in the semantics of the Latin preposition *per*: A cognitive hypothesis. *STUF – Language Typology and Universals* 64(2). 148–169. [Special issue edited by Johannes Helmbrecht & Elisabeth Verhoeven].

Bybee, Joan L. 1985. *Morphology: A study of the relation between meaning and form*. Amsterdam: John Benjamins.

Bybee, Joan L. 2003. Mechanisms of change in grammaticization: The role of frequency. In Brian D. Joseph & Richard D. Janda (eds.), *The handbook of historical linguistics*, 602–623. Oxford: Blackwell.

Coleman, Robert. 1991. Latin prepositional syntax in Indo-European perspective. In Robert Coleman (ed.), *New studies in Latin linguistics*, 323–338. Amsterdam: John Benjamins.

Cuzzolin, Pierluigi. 1995. A proposito di *sub vos placo* e della grammaticalizzazione delle adposizioni. *Archivio Glottologico Italiano* 80. 122–143.

Croft, William. 1991. *Syntactic categories and grammatical relations*. Chicago: The University of Chicago Press.

Dirven, René. 1993. Dividing up physical and mental space into conceptual categories by means of English prepositions. In Cornelia Zelinski-Wibbelt (ed.), *The semantics of prepositions: From mental processing to natural language processing*, 73–98. Berlin: Mouton de Gruyter.

Dunkel, George. 1990. prae pavore, πρὸ φόβοιο. *Indogermanische Forschungen* 95. 161–170.

Ernout, Alfred & Antoine Meillet. 2001 [1959]. *Dictionnaire étymologique de la langue latine: Histoire des mots*. Paris: Klincksieck.

Evans, Vyv & Andrea Tyler. 2004. Rethinking English 'Prepositions of Movement': The case of *To* and *Through*. *Belgian Journal of Linguistics* 18. 247–270.

Fillmore, Charles S. 1983 [1972]. How to know whether you're coming or going. In Karl Hyldgard-Jensen (ed.), *Linguistik 1971*, 369-379. Frankfurt a M.: Athenäum Verlag. Reprinted in Gisa Rauh. 1983. *Essays on deixis*, 219–227. Tübingen: Narr.

Fruyt, Michelle. 2009. La séparation des constituants de lexèmes en latin : Disjonction entre préverbe et verbe: « tmèse ». Paper presented at the 15th International Colloquium on Latin Linguistics, Innsbruck, 4–9 April.

García Hernández, Benjamín. 1980. *Semántica estructural y lexemática del verbo*. Reus: Ediciones Avesta.

García Hernández, Benjamín. 1985. Le système de l'aspect verbal en latin. In Christian Touratier (ed.), *Syntaxe et Latin : Actes du IIme Congrès International de Linguistique Latine, Aix-en-Provence, 28-31 mars 1983*, 515–536. Aix-en-Provence: Université de Provence.

García Hernández, Benjamín. 1989. Les préverbes latins : Notions latives et aspectuelles. In Marius Lavency & Dominique Longrée (éds.), *Actes du Ve Colloque de Linguistique Latine*, 149–159. Louvain-la-Neuve: Cahiers de l'Institut de Linguistique de Louvain 15.

Guiraud, Charles. 1974. La valeur de *per-* dans *perdo, pereo, perfidus*, etc. *Revue belge de philologie et d'histoire* 52. 29–35.

Haspelmath, Martin. 1997. *From space to time: Temporal adverbials in the world's languages*. Munich: Lincom Europa.

Haverling, Gerd. 2003. On prefixes and actionality in Classical and Late Latin. *Acta Linguistica Hungarica* 50(1–2). 113–135.

Heine, Bernd, Ulrike Claudi & Friederike Hünnemeyer. 1991. *Grammaticalization: A conceptual framework*. Chicago: University of Chicago Press.

Heine, Bernd & Tania Kuteva. 2007. *The genesis of grammar: A reconstruction*. Oxford: Oxford University Press.

Himmelmann, Nikolaus P. 2004. Lexicalization and grammaticalization: Opposite or orthogonal? In Walter Bisang, Nikolaus Himmelmann & Björn Wiemer (eds.), *What makes grammaticalization – A look from its fringes and its components*, 19–40. Berlin: Mouton de Gruyter.

Hopper, Paul J. & Elizabeth Closs Traugott. 2003. *Grammaticalization*, 2nd edn. Cambridge: Cambridge University Press.

Jackendoff, Ray. 1983. *Semantics and cognition*. Cambridge: The MIT Press.

Kuryłowicz, Jerzy. 1964. *The inflectional categories of Indo-European*. Heidelberg: Carl Winter Verlag.

Lakoff, George & Mark Johnson. 1980. *Metaphors we live by*. Chicago: University of Chicago Press.

Langacker, Ronald. 1987. *Foundations of cognitive grammar*. Vol. 1: *Theoretical prerequisites*. Stanford: Stanford University Press.

Langacker, Ronald. 1991. *Foundations of cognitive grammar*. Vol. 2: *Descriptive application*. Stanford: Stanford University Press.

Lehmann, Christian. 1983. Latin preverbs and cases. In Harm Pinkster (ed.), *Latin linguistics and linguistic theory*, 145–165. Amsterdam: John Benjamins.

Lehmann, Christian. 1985. Latin case relations in typological perspective. In Christian Touratier (ed.), *Syntaxe et latin : Actes du IIme Congrès International de Linguistique Latine, Aix-en-Provence, 28–31 mars 1983*, 81–104. Aix-en-Provence: Université de Provence.

Lehmann, Christian. 2002a. *Thoughts on grammaticalization*. Erfurt: Seminar für Sprachwissenschaft der Universität.

Lehmann, Christian. 2002b. New reflections on grammaticalization and lexicalization. In Ilse Wischer & Gabriele Diewald (eds.), *New reflections on grammaticalization*, 1–18. Amsterdam: John Benjamins.

Leumann, Manu, Johann B. Hofmann & Anton Szantyr. 1965. *Lateinische Syntax und Stilistik*. München: Beck.

Luraghi, Silvia. 2001. Syncretism and the classification of semantic roles. *Sprachtypologie und Universalienforschung* 54(1). 35–51.

Luraghi, Silvia. 2003. *On the meaning of prepositions and cases: A study of the expression of semantic roles in Ancient Greek*. Amsterdan: John Benjamins.

Luraghi, Silvia. 2009. The internal structure of prepositional phrases and the notion of government. In Johannes Helmbrecht, Yoko Nishina, Yong-Min Shin, Stavros Skopeteas & Elisabeth Verhoeven (eds.), *Form and function in language research: Papers in honour of Christian Lehmann*, 231–254. Berlin: Mouton de Gruyter.

Luraghi, Silvia. 2010. Adverbial phrases. In Philip Baldi & Pierluigi Cuzzolin (eds), *New perspectives on historical Latin syntax. Vol. 2: Constituent syntax: Adverbial phrases, adverbs, mood, tense*, 19–108. Berlin: De Gruyter Mouton.

Nocentini, Alberto. 1992. Preposizioni e posposizioni in oscoumbro. *Archivio glottologico italiano* 77. 196–242.

Phi5 = Packard Humanities Institut (1991): CD-ROM 5.3: *Latin authors and Bible versions*

Pinault, Georges-Jean. 1995. Le problème du préverbe en indo-européen. In André Rousseau (ed.), *Les préverbes dans les langues d'Europe: Introduction à l'étude de la préverbation*, 35–59. Lille: Presses Universitaires du Septentrion.

Pinkster, Harm. 1990a. *Latin syntax and semantics*. London: Routledge.

Pinkster, Harm. 1990b. The development of cases and adpositions in Latin. In Harm Pinkster and Inge Genee (eds.), *Unity in diversity. Papers presented to Simon C. Dik on his 50th birthday*, 195–209. Dordrecht: Foris.

Pompei, Anna. 2010. Space coding in verb-particle constructions and prefixed verbs. In Marotta Giovanna, Alessandro Lenci, Linda Meini & Francesco Rovai (eds.), *Space in language*: *Proceedings of the Pisa International Conference*, 401–418. Pisa: ETS.

Pottier, Bernard. 1962. *Systématique des éléments de relation*. Paris: Klincksieck.

Pokorny, Julius. 1989 [1959]. *Indogermanisches etymologisches Wörterbuch*. Bern: Francke.

Radden, Günter. 2003. The Metaphor time as space across languages. In Nicole Baumgarten, Claudia Böttger, Markus Motz & Julia Probst (eds.), *Übersetzen, Interkulturelle Kommunikation, Spracherwerb und Sprachvermittlung – das Leben mit mehreren Sprachen: Festschrift für Juliane House zum 60. Geburtstag. Zeitschrift für Interkulturellen Fremdsprachenunterricht* 8(2/3). 226–239. Available online at http://www.ualberta.ca/~german/ejournal/Radden.pdf.

Ricca, Davide. 1993. *I verbi deittici di movimento in Europa: Una ricerca interlinguistica*. Firenze: La Nuova Italia.

Romagno, Domenica. 2003. Azionalità e transitività: Il caso dei preverbi latini. *Archivio Glottologico Italiano* 88(2). 156–170.

Romagno, Domenica. 2008. Applicative and causative: Some further reflections upon verbal prefixation in Greek and Latin. *Archivio Glottologico Italiano* 93. 80–88.

Sapir, Edward. 1944. Grading: A study in Semantics. *Philosophy of Science* 11. 93–116.

Slobin, Dan. 2008. Relations between paths of motion and paths of vision: A crosslinguistic and developmental exploration. In Virginia C. Mueller-Gathercole (ed.), *Routes to language: Studies in honor of Melissa Bowerman*, 197–221. Mahwah, NJ: Lawrence Erlbaum Associates.

Stosic, Dejan. 2002. *Par et à travers dans l'expression des relations spatiales: Comparaison entre le français et le serbo-croate*. France: Université Toulouse 2 dissertation.

Talmy, Leonard. 2000 [1988]. *Toward a cognitive semantics: Typology and process in concept structuring*, Cambridge, MA: The MIT Press.

Taylor, John R. 1993. Prepositions: Patterns of polysemization and strategies of disambiguation. In Cornelia Zelinsky-Wibbelt (ed.), *The semantics of prepositions*, 151–175. Berlin: Mouton de Gruyter.

Van Laer, Sophie. 2005. *Per-* et les procès gradables. In Claude Moussy (éd.), *La composition et la préverbation en latin*, 321–343. Paris: Presses de l'Université Paris-Sorbonne.

Van Laer, Sophie. 2010. *La préverbation en latin: Étude des préverbes ad-, in-, ob- et per- dans la poésie républicaine et augustéenne*. Bruxelles: Latomus.

Vester, Erseline. 1983. *Instrument and manner expressions in Latin*. Assen: Van Gorcum.

Vincent, Nigel. 1999. The evolution of c-structure: prepositions and PPs from Indo-European to Romance. *Linguistics* 37. 1111–1153.

Watkins, Calvert. 1964. Preliminaries to the reconstruction of Indo-European sentence structure. In Horace Lunt (ed.), *Proceedings of the 9th International Congress of Linguists*, 1035–1042. The Hague: Mouton.

Wood, Esther Jane. 2007. *The semantic typology of pluractionality*. Berkelyey, CA: University of California, Berkeley dissertation.

Andrzej M. Łęcki and Jerzy Nykiel
# 8 Grammaticalization of the English adverbial subordinator *in order that*

**Abstract:** This study addresses the development of the English purpose subordinator *in order that*, whose development is intertwined with the rise of a related construction *in order to*. We first trace the meanings with which the lexeme *order* and the prepositional phrase *in order* were used in Middle English and Early Modern English and show how the meanings of this prepositional phrase feed into the rise of the purpose subordinator. The purposive syntagm *in order to* appeared for the first time around 1600 and was followed by *in order that*, which emerged in the second half of the 17th century but did not gain any significant frequency until around 1750. Our data is analysed within the grammaticalization framework. It is argued that the development of *in order that* instantiates the grammaticalization path MANNER to PURPOSE, in that the idea of desired order germane to the prepositional phrase *in order* was crucial to the development of the purpose subordinator *in order that*. We further show how various parameters of grammaticalization such as decatategorialization, reduction of paradigmatic and syntagmatic variability and increase in bondedness pertain to the grammaticalization of *in order that*.

## 1 Introduction

This article deals with the rise and development of the adverbial subordinator *in order that* expressing a purpose relationship in English complex sentences. Even though the history of English linking elements has received a great deal of scholarly attention recently (see, for instance, the papers in Lenker and Meurman-Solin 2007; Rissanen 2009; and Molencki 2012a, Molencki 2012b) English subordinators introducing purpose clauses are somewhat atypical in that their evolution has been to a large extent neglected.[1] The present paper is an attempt to partly fill this gap.

Beside the subordinator *in order that*, this paper will devote considerable attention to the subordinator *in order to*. Although Kortmann (1998: 462) does not include *in order to* in his inventory of adverbial subordinators in (British)

---

1 However, see López-Couso (2007) on the negative purpose marker *lest*.

DOI 10.1515/9783110492347-009

English, mainly because it is not complemented by a finite clause, the semantic and formal congruity between *in order that* and *in order to* is obvious (both express purpose and comprise the *in order* syntagm) and is the effect of historical changes. Analyzing *in order that* and *in order to* together allows us to illustrate and account for these changes in a clearer way.² Thus, a complete picture of the rise of *in order that* cannot be drawn without referring to *in order to*.

Section 2 presents the etymology and the first occurrences of the lexeme *order* with nominal meanings in Middle English (ME). In Section 3, we focus on the ways in which the syntagms *in order to* and *in order that* came to be used as grammatical markers introducing a purpose clause. Section 4 is devoted to a discussion of the development of *in order that* in terms of the grammaticalization mechanisms advanced by Lehmann (2002) [1982], Hopper (1991), Heine and Kuteva (2002) and Heine (2003).

The language data for this study have been collected predominantly from the *Oxford English Dictionary Online* (OED) and the electronic *Middle English Dictionary* (MED) as well as from the electronic corpora of the English language such as the *Penn Parsed Corpora of Historical English* (in particular PPCME and PPCMBE), ARCHER and the ICAME corpora. References to corpus attestations follow the conventions of the corpora's compilers.

## 2 The origins of the English lexeme *order*

The lexeme *order* in English first appeared in the first half of the 13th century as a loan word from Old French *ordre*, earlier *ordene*.³ Specifically, the first occurrences of *order* in English are attested around 1200 in some of the texts

---

**2** Huddleston and Pullum (2002: 727) go as far as to treat both structures as prepositions of purpose with clausal complements, with the difference being that *in order that* is followed by a finite clause while *in order to* by an infinitival one. An anonymous reviewer draws our attention to "[a] major difference between the two combinations [which] concerns the purposive meaning originally inherent in the infinitival marker *to* in English, pointing out that it is likely that this original purposive meaning of the *to* marker provided the convenient link for the reanalysis of structures such as those in (17a–b)".

**3** *A Comprehensive Etymological Dictionary of the English Language* (CEDEL) (s.v. *order*) suggests that *order* is ultimately derived from the Indo-European root *\*ar-* 'to join'. In Italic, this root probably changed to *\*ored(h)-* 'to arrange, arrangement' (*Online Etymological Dictionary* (OEtymD), s.v. *order*), from the Indo-European suffixed form *\*ar-tu-* (*The American Heritage Dictionary of Indo-European Roots* (AHDIER), s.v. *ar-*). In Latin, the base *\*ored(h)-*, in turn, became *ōrdō* 'a straight row, rank, order, regular series, arrangement' and Old French *ordre* is based on the accusative form of Latin *ōrdō*, i.e. *ōrdinem*.

from the Katherine Group, i.e. *Ancrene Wisse* and *Sawles Warde*. The initial nominal senses of *order* in English coincide with those of its French source: one of the earliest meanings in which *order* appears is 'a rank in the hierarchy of God's angels', and it is attested in both Early Middle English (EME) (1a, 1b) and Anglo-Norman (1c).[4]

(1) a. *Engles ... beoð aa biuore godd & seruið him eauer ... Nihe **ordres** [Bod: wordes; Tit: woredes] þer beoð.*[5]
'Angels are always before God and always serve him – nine orders there are.'[6]
(MED, c1225 SWard (Roy 17.A.27) 28/271)

  b. *Þer beoð niene englene **ordes** [Corp-C: weoredes].*
  'There are nine orders (i.e. classes) of angels.'
  (MED, a1250 Ancr.(Nero A.14) 13/11)

  c. *Nof **ordres** d'els trovum.*
  'We find nine orders of them.'
  (AND, *Mirur* 127vb23)

Example (2a) illustrates another early meaning of ME *order*, namely, '(a member of) a religious order, e.g. monks', and it was also borrowed, with *ordre*, from Old French. An Anglo-Norman instance exemplifying this meaning is in (2b):

(2) a. *ʒef ei unweote easkeð ow of hwet **ordre** he beon ... ondswerieð of sein Iames.*
'If any ignorant person asks you to which order you belong, reply that to Saint James.'
(MED, c1230(?a1200) Ancr.(Corp-C 402) 9/28)

---

4 Alongside some of the nominal meanings of OF *ordre*, Early Middle English borrowed a verb *ordren* 'to ordain, arrange' from Anglo-Norman *ordener/ordainer* 'to decree, order':

(i) *Nihe wordes þer beoð, ah hu ha..beoð **iordret** & sunderliche isette, þe an buue þe oðre.*
'There are nine orders, but how they are arranged and separately set, that one above the other.'
(MED, c1225(?c1200) SWard (Bod 34) 28/269)

5 The corpus examples throughout the paper are given in an unaltered form save for the bold forms used to highlight the structures focused on. The square brackets in the MED frequently provide equivalents that can be found in other versions of the same text. Ellipsis used by the editors of the MED is indicated by only two dots.

6 The Modern English translations of the Middle English and Anglo-Norman examples in this article are ours.

b. *ministre general del **ordour** des freres menours*
'minister general of the Order of Friars Minor'
(*The Anglo-Norman Dictionary* (AND), *Anon Chr* 3.36)

*Order* is also recorded in EME in the sense of 'a religious rule, vows' as illustrated in (3a), with (3b) showing an Anglo-Norman semantic counterpart:

(3) a. *He seiþ what is Religiun, hwuch is riht **ordre**.*
'He defines what religion and what the right order is.'
(MED, c1230(?a1200) Ancr.(Corp-C 402) 9/8)

b. *prist e l'**ordre** e les habiz*
'priest and the monastic rule and the habits'
(AND, *S Brend* 31)

Finally, as can be inferred from example (4a), which is not cited in MED (*s.v.* *ordre* (n.)), EME *ordre* was also used with the meaning 'order, sequence, position, rank, status', and this sense was also present in Anglo-Norman (4b).

(4) a. *'munek, preost. oðer clearc. & of þt **ordre**. a weddet mon. a ladles þing; a wummon as ich am'*
'monk, priest, or cleric; and of that order, a wedded man, an innocent thing, a woman as I am'
(MED, c1230(?a1200) Ancr. 5/268)

b. *Or veez par raisuns L'**ordre** des questiuns.*
'Now see properly the order of questions.'
(AND, *Comput* 2518)

In the three centuries following the appearance of *order* in English, other polysemous meanings developed. While MED (*s.v.* *ordre* (n.)) provides as many as twelve different senses of this lexeme, none of them has any grammatical meaning yet.

## 3 The rise of *in order to/that*

In Section 2, it has been shown how and with what meanings the lexeme *order* entered the English language. This section focuses on the development of the grammatical meaning of *order*, or rather the grammatical constructions containing *order* as a building block, i.e. *in order to* and *in order that*.

The syntagm *in order* first appeared in Late Middle English in the sense of 'in order, in sequence', most frequently used with the function of an adverbial of manner, for example:

(5) a. *And suche foules ... makeþ a kyng amongis hem and beþ obedient to hym and fleþ **in ordre** [L ordinate] & in aray.*
 'And such birds make a leader among them and are obedient to it and fly in order and in an orderly arrangement.'
 (MED, a1398 * Trev. Barth.(Add 27944) 141a/b)

 b. *He notyfiyth þe chapituris seriatly, þat is as to sey **in ordyr**, to fynde qwat mater a man wul loke vppon þe more esyly.*
 'He informs the subjects in succession, that is to say, in order, to find what matter a man will look upon more easily.'
 (MED, c1484(a1475) Caritate SSecr.(Tak 38) 115/1)

About the same time, this sense of the prepositional phrase generalized to cover the meaning of 'in proper condition, correctly, properly'; thus, the manner adverbial function of *in order* continued, as in (6):

(6) a. *A child ... may nouht speke noþir sowne his wordes profitabliche, for here teeþ be nouht het parfitliche I-growe and I-sette **in ordere**.*
 'A child cannot speak nor pronounce his words effectively because his teeth are not fully grown and properly set yet.'
 (MED, a1398, * Trev. Barth.(Add 27944) 67a/b)

 b. *I am ... olde, most owgly, Skynned rowh and yrchownly; Myn heer vntressyd and vndyht, And **in Ordre** nat kempt A-ryht.*
 'I am old, very ugly, shaggy-haired and in the likeness of a hedgehog. My hair unbound and also not combed properly.'
 (MED, a1475(?a1430) Lydg. Pilgr.(Vit C.13) 15572)

Note that, originally, the 'properness' meaning of *in order* was not infrequently reinforced by an adjectival phrase modifying the noun, as in (7a), or a determiner and an adjectival phrase preceding the noun, as in (7b):

(7) a. *A dyche is ... place of defence ... whan þe dyche is arayede **in gode ordre** [L ordine congruo] in brede and in lengþe, in hihenesse and in depnesse.*
 'A dike is a place of defence when it is prepared in the right manner in breadth and in length, in height and in depth.'
 (MED, a1398 * Trev. Barth.(Add 27944) 171a/a)

b. *If þou biholde now þe schip of þi fadir, Seynt Domynyk ... þou schalt se how he sett it **in a parfiht ordir**.*
'If you now can see the ship of your father, Saint Dominic, you shall see how he set it in a perfect order.'
(MED, ?a1425 Orch.Syon (Hrl 3432) 388/37)

The various corpora analyzed show that until the second half of the 16th century, hardly any new meanings of the prepositional phrase *in order* could be observed. Some authors, for instance Shakespeare, did not embrace any changes to the use of *in order* even in the early 17th century. In Shakespeare's works, twelve attestations of the *in order* construction could be observed; five of them conveyed the meaning of 'in sequence' and seven the meaning 'in proper condition, properly', as illustrated in (8).

(8) a. GRUMIO: ... *Be the jacks fair within, the jills fair without, the carpets laid, and every thing **in order**?*
(Shakespeare, *The Taming of the Shrew*: 4.1, ?1590–1594)

b. *The thing which is flatter'd, but a spark, To which that blast gives heat and stronger glowing; Whereas reproof, obedient and **in order**, Fits kings, as they are men, for they may err.*
(Shakespeare, *Pericles*: 1.2, 1608)

The overall situation, however, changed at the end of the 16th century when *in order* began to be complemented by *to*. Still, as attested by the language data in our corpora, the construction did not gain frequency until after 1650. At that stage, however, *in order* did not normally introduce an infinitive but a noun phrase, and it was used in the sense of '[w]ith a view to the bringing about of (something), for the purpose of (some desired end). Obs.' (OED, s.v. *order* def. P3†(a)), as illustrated in (9). The mere appearance of the preposition *to* in the syntagm naturally evokes the purposive meaning in the construction, as *to* being an allative marker had developed a purpose function already in Old English (see Los 2007: 37). That allative markers commonly follow that path cross-linguistically has been shown, among others, by Heine and Kuteva (2002: 39–40) and Łęcki and Nykiel (2014: 229). Thus, the syntagm *in order* was part of a complex preposition, which could be followed by either *to* (9) or *for* (19a–b).

(9) a. *There was she faine To call them all **in order to** her ayde.*
(OED, s.v. *order* def. P3†(b): 1590 Spenser *Faerie Queene* iii. viii. sig. Kk2)

b. *Col. Jones and Col. Penruddock are sent downe into the west **in order to** theire tryall.*
(OED *s.v. order* def. P3†(a), 1655 in C. H. Firth *Clarke Papers* (1899) III. 33)

c. *... he intends suddenly for the Spaw, ..., and to cleanse his body from all diseases by the vertue of those Waters, **in order to** his Voyage for Scotland, that so he may not want bodily health to march with his Troops over the lofty Hills, ...*
(ARCHER, 1654mer2.n2b)

Roughly at the same time when *in order to* started being followed by a noun phrase, the construction *in order to* + *inf.* was first attested, with the earliest example in the OED dating back to 1609 (*s.v. order* def. P3†(b)); see (10).

(10) a. *These are they that speak to Pharao king of Egypt, **in order to** bring out the children of Israel from Egypt: these are that Moses and Aaron.*
(1609 Bible (Douay) I. Exod. vi. 27, cited also in Schmidtke-Bode 2009: 174)

b. *if the party that desires it, doe omit for one whole weeke together, to goe on, and doe all and every such Act and Acts as might have been done within the said weeke, **in order to** bring the Cause unto a hearing.*
(Lampeter Corpus, lawa1653)

c. *For this is openly manifest, That whilst some Grandees of this sort sat at the stern, ..., to destroy our fundamentals **in order to** complete their designs, and secure there own empty and pannick fears and jelousies;*
(Lampeter Corpus, polb1660)

It bears stressing, however, that early examples such as (10a) are rather exceptional because the *in order to* + *inf.* structure was not widely attested until the 1680s, as shown in Table 1.

**Table 1:** Frequency of *in order to* expressing purpose between 1650 and 1740, in normalized frequencies per 100,000 words (absolute frequencies are in brackets)

|  | 1650–1659 | 1660–1669 | 1670–1679 | 1680–1689 | 1690–1699 | 1700–1709 | 1710–1719 | 1720–1729 | 1730–1740 |
|---|---|---|---|---|---|---|---|---|---|
| *in order to* + NP | 12.18 (12) | 7.15 (7) | 9.41 (13) | 9.69 (15) | 6.2 (8) | 3.84 (4) | 3.25 (5) | 3.16 (4) | 2.69 (3) |
| *in order to* + inf. | 1.02 (1) | 1.02 (1) | 0 (0) | 1.94 (3) | 9.3 (12) | 6.72 (7) | 20.27 (21) | 11.06 (14) | 19.71 (22) |

Table 1 presents the frequency distribution of the *in order to* construction (both combining with an NP and with an infinitive) in the *Lampeter Corpus* (circa 1.1 million words), which comprises tracts and pamphlets published between 1640 and 1740.[7] The overall number of occurrences of *in order to* in the *Lampeter Corpus* is 167, but 14 were omitted as they encode the meaning 'in reference to, in respect to', as in (11).

(11) a. *For it [discourse] was intended only as a collection of loose Experiments and Observations about the Porosity of the parts of Bodies belonging (as Chymists speak) to the Animal Kingdom, and laid (not to say thrown) together, **in order to** what I had thoughts of offering, toward an Intelligible account of Occult Qualities.*
(Lampeter Corpus, scib1684)

b. *Therefore **in order to** Romes 7th. head or Government was the sixth to be removed, and that it was so accordingly we find it.*
(Lampeter Corpus, rela1679)

An additional example was omitted from Table 1, because it proved to be ambiguous: *farther Incroachments* in (12) could be treated either as a noun phrase with *farther* functioning as a modifier of *Incroachments* or as a verb phrase with *Incroachments* complementing the verb *farther*.

(12) *And as King Charles's departing from the Law in this particular, was one of the first steps towards arbitrary Power, so it was both **in order to** farther Incroachments upon our Laws and Rights, and prepared the way for most of the Tyranny that he exercised afterwards.*
(*Lampeter Corpus*, polb1689)

Then again, the cases in which *in order* is separated from *to* by an adverbial were included in the count. Note, however, that such examples are few and far between: in the Lampeter Corpus there are only three instances of an adverbial tucked between *in order* and *to*, and they are given in (13):

---

[7] The data are presented per period of ten years. The period between 1640 and 1649 is not included in Table 1 as no examples of *in order to* followed by either an NP or a VP are attested in the corpus for that period.

(13) a. *no Reason will appear for bringing Home, or incouraging the Expence of these Goods, if not **in order totally to** Ruin the Manufactury, unless we could be assured that the Falling of Wooll and Manufactures to a low Price, would first Ruin those other Manufactures, and then that ours would certainly Advance in Price again;*
(*Lampeter Corpus*, eca1697)

b. ***In order therefore to** make a Map of some such place, consider both the difference of Longitude and Latitude of the extream parts thereof;*
(*Lampeter Corpus*, scia1698)

c. *I conceive neither Good-nature, nor the Solemnity of Publick Seals shou'd restrain an honest Pen from exploding the Practice, **in order as well to stop** the Progress of its evil Effects, as to prevent the like Attempts for the future.*
(*Lampeter Corpus*, lawb1738)

The Lampeter data in Table 1 confirm that the *in order to* construction appears in English in the mid-17th century and that, at that time, it was normally followed by a noun phrase, as in (14).

(14) a. *Very much more might be said **in order to** this,...*
(*Lampeter Corpus*, scia1653)

b. *For it is not imaginable but that the Prophets of the New Testament instructed others by their inspirations, and that **in order to** their future prophecying.*
(*Lampeter Corpus*, rela1653)

c. *Having thus given my mite of humble Advice **in order to** a good settlement,...*
(*Lampeter Corpus*, lawb1659)

These data also reveal that from 1680 onward, the infinitive became a regular complement of *in order to*. In the last decade of the 17th century, *in order to* was followed roughly equally frequently by an NP and an infinitive. From the beginning of the 18th century onward the infinitive became proportionately increasingly frequent.[8]

---

**8** We have not encountered a single example of the construction *in order for to* in our corpora, which is interesting given the purposive meaning of *for to*.

Despite the early examples (15a-b), the data in the corpora that we have analyzed show that the adverbial subordinator *in order that* only gained ground in terms of frequency from around the middle of the 18th century; see (15c–d):[9]

(15) a. **In order that** we may this deed fulfill, We first will execute th'Impostor's Will.
(OED s.v. order def. P6, 1671 E. Settle Cambyses iv. iv. 64)

b. **In order** therefore **that** the Resemblance in the Ideas be Wit, it is necessary that the Ideas should not lie too near one another in the Nature of things;[10]
(OED s.v. order, def. P6, 1711, Addison Spect. No. 62 (2), cited also in Visser (2002 [1963–1973]: 864), )

c. **In order that** we may, reciprocally, keep up our French,
(ARCHER, 1747ches.x3b)

d. All he now wished was, that she might be possessed of as little warmth of inclination for him as he had known for her, and that the disparity of years between them, might have made her consent to the proposed marriage, intirely on the motive of interest, without any mixture of love, **in order that** the disappointment she was going to receive, might seem the less severe: ...
(Eliza F. Haywood, *Life's Progress Through The Passions*: Ch. IV, 1748)

e. He ... employed a whole army of attorneys and agents, to spirit up and carry on a most virulent prosecution; practised all the unfair methods that could be invented, **in order that** the unhappy gentleman should be transported to Newgate,
(Tobias Smollett, *The Adventures of Peregrine Pickle*, 1751)

From that time onward, *in order* could be complemented either by a finite or non-finite clause, as in (16).

---

[9] It is difficult to establish when exactly the structures *in order to* and *in order that* appear for the first time in American English because of the lack of available corpora of early American English. On the base of the ARCHER corpus, which includes texts in the American English variety from 1750 on, we can say that the earliest example of *in order to* + *inf.* dates back to 1753, while *in order that* appears for the first time in 1797. The first occurrence of the *in order to* construction suggests that actually this structure might have been used before 1750 in American English.

[10] This full quotation has been retrieved from <http://archive.twoaspirinsandacomedy.com/spectator/spectator.php?line=62>

(16) *They are the appointed means, not only of securing to us subsistence and comfort, but also of fitting us to act our part in life with respectability, of making us just, firm, honest, temperate : and that they have been appointed,* **in order that** *the pains we are obliged to take* **in order to** *acquire these tempers, may farther make us self-denying, obedient, faithful, that we may, by degrees, be built up in godliness, and fitted to take our station in another and higher sphere of existence.*
(PPCMBE, FROUDE–1830,2,24.252)

However, infinitival complements of *in order* have always been much more frequent than finite ones: even a cursory search of the ARCHER corpus containing circa 1.8 m words and covering the time span of 1650 till 1997 reveals only 16 instances of *in order that*, compared to as many as 220 cases of the *in order to* + *inf.* structure.

# 4 The grammaticalization of *in order to* and *in order that*

While Section 3 provided an account of the development of the purposive constructions *in order to* and *in order that*, the present section considers the question of how and why *in order to* and *in order that* came to be employed as grammatical markers expressing purpose. We will address this issue by employing the analytical tools provided by the framework of grammaticalization.

As the examples in (5) through (8) illustrate, the prepositional phrase *in order* was originally used as an adverbial expressing manner. It would appear that the emergence of an infinitival complement of *in order* might be attributed to the prepositional phrase appearing in an apokoinu structure, a "[s]yntactic construction in which two sentences share a common element that can be either in the second sentence or on the border between the two sentences. Apokoinu refers to both sentences grammatically and syntactically" (*Routledge Dictionary of Language and Linguistics*, s.v. *apokoinu*). At the time when *in order to* can be assumed to have started grammaticalizing into an adverbial conjunction, i.e. in the middle of the seventeenth century, it could (i) belong to the main clause, where *in order* by itself modified the content of the main clause as an adverbial of manner, and (ii) it could introduce either a *to*-infinitive structure or a *to* + NP structure. This is illustrated in (17).

(17) a. *The building was a spacious Theatre Half round on two main Pillars vaulted high, With seats where all the Lords and each degree Of sort, might sit **in order to** behold, The other side was op'n, where the throng On banks and scaffolds under Skie might stand; I among these aloof obscurely stood.*
(Milton, *Samson Agonistes*, 1671)

b. *Þhis day the Ld Aston mr Howard &c were brought to Westminster **In order to** be tryed but the Atturney Genll moved that it might be put off till ffriday next ...*
(Newdig10, London 22th [sic] June 1680)

c. *Lo. Sir, these People come **in order to** make him a Favourite at Court, they are to establish him with the Ladies.*
(PPCEME, 1696 VANBR–E3–P2,26.45)

The examples in (17) suggest that for some time *in order* might be understood as a simple prepositional phrase and simultaneously invite inferences for a prepositional conjunction expressing purpose. Such examples as those in (17) might have contributed to the change illustrated in (18), which shows that the erstwhile prepositional phrase, which on the surface frequently appears next to purposive *to* (as in *to watch it*), is reinterpreted as part of the expression introducing purposive content.

(18) [$_{CP}$ They sat [$_{PP}$ in order]] [$_{CP}$ φ [$_{TP}$ to watch it]]. >
[$_{CP}$ They sat] [$_{CP}$ in order to watch it].

A puzzling development took place about sixty years after the appearance of *in order to*, namely the rise of the complex subordinator *in order that*. This evolution is somewhat surprising, as one would rather expect the opposite development, especially in the light of what Görlach (1991: 97) states referring to general syntactic changes in Early Modern English: " [...] infinitival clauses increasingly replaced finite adverbial and relative clauses – an economy more apparent than real since it involves the loss of tense and mood marking". However, *in order that* has never fully replaced *in order to* and, what is more, it has never been as popular as the original structure.[11] Even a cursory search of

---

[11] An anonymous reviewer suggests that "the reason for this probably lies in the meaning of purpose originally inherent in the infinitival marker *to* in English". However, also *that* by itself could introduce a clause expressing purpose, cf. OED (s.v. *that, conj.*, def. 3.a.): *Christ.. had prayed that Peter's faith should not fail.* 1847 A.J.CHRISTIE in *Ess.Rel. & Lit.* Ser. III. 50. Hence, it appears that the preponderance of *in order to* over *in order that* has little to do with the semantics of the particle *to*.

the ARCHER corpus turns up 250 tokens of *in order to* (followed by either an infinitive or a noun phrase) and only 16 tokens of *in order that*. A plausible explanation for the appearance of the *in order that* subordinator lies in the fact that the new construction was the effect of the increase in hypotactic sentence structures in Modern English; see, for instance, Görlach (1991: 122). In particular, the demand for the language to be flexible and precise brought about a need on the part of the writers to enrich their inventory of purposive conjunctions and the constructions *in order to* and *in order that* must have seemed good candidates for fulfilling this purpose; see in this respect Molencki (2012b: 198), who claims that "[a]n additional factor favouring the creation of new connectives was the increasing tendency toward the [sic] hypotactic clause combining".

At this point, it needs to be emphasized that both *in order to* and *in order that* exhibit a strong preference for formal text types. These text types naturally impel the writer to a greater exactitude during the production of sentences and, as a result, replenish the inventory of formal expressions with new connectives expressing purpose. This stylistic markedness is especially visible in the case of *in order that*, which is ordinarily employed in highly formal contexts: in the ARCHER corpus, sermons and scientific texts constitute the most typical genres in which the *in order that* subordinator can be found. Similar observations with reference to the emergence of connectives in Late Middle English are offered by Rissanen (2002: 196–197); the emergence of *in order to* and *in order that* seems to corroborate his claim that "this need [for more refined expression of the relations existing between concepts and propositions] would intensify after the revival of English as the written medium from the fourteenth century on" (2002: 191). The subordinators introducing finite clauses of purpose which appeared in English after 1300 and enjoyed a noticeable popularity comprise *to the end that*, *to the effect that*, *to the intent that* and *in order that*.

The rise of the *in order that* subordinator also bears resemblance to the process of "renewal", "a process whereby existing meanings may take on new forms" (Hopper and Traugott 2003: 122), to the extent that *in order that* is a new way of expressing the purpose subordinator function. In the first half of the 18th century, the older purpose subordinators *to the intent that* and *to the end that* are ousted by the new syntagm *in order that* which enters the language at this time; see Nykiel and Łęcki (2013) and Łęcki and Nykiel (2014).[12] What is interesting

---

12 As argued by Nykiel and Łęcki (2013: 78), the use of *to the intent that* as a purpose subordinator was most probably copied from Anglo-Norman *a l'entente que* 'with the intention that, to the end that'. The grammaticalization of the English construction was significantly accelerated by the existence of the Anglo-Norman *a l'entente que* at the end of the 14th century. Even though *order* is also a French loanword, the grammaticalization of *in order* is much more gradual due to the fact that there was no French subordinator employing *ordre* on which *in order that* could be modeled.

is that the renewal process in this case operates on the periphery of purpose subordination, as the most frequent way of introducing purpose clauses since Old English times has been another subordinator (*so*) *that*, while the most common non-finite purposive marker in English has been (*so*) (*as*) *to*.

The change from a prepositional phrase *in order* to a prepositional subordinator *in order to/that* is indicative of decategorialization. The noun *order* in this prepositional subordinator is deprived of its erstwhile nominal properties. A conspicuous sign of decategorialization is the inability of *order* in the *in order to* and *in order that* structures to be marked for plurality (\**in orders to/that*) and the inability to take adjectival modification. These demonstrate that the lexeme *order* has been decategorialized, which is visible in the loss of some morpho-syntactic properties characterizing lexical or less grammaticalised items (see, e.g., Hopper 1991: 22 or Heine (2003 [2005]: 579).

Apart from decategorialization, the process of grammaticalization of *in order to* and *in order that* is visible from the reduction of paradigmatic variability (see Lehmann 2002 [1982]: 123–128) or specialization (see Hopper 1991: 22). While these two notions may not be exactly synonymous, they can both be said to indicate a decrease in autonomy in the use of particular forms.[13] In the case of *in order*, the reduction of paradigmatic variability, or specialization, is noticeable from the loss of particular complements of *in order*, once it proceeded to function as a subordinator of purpose, such as *for* + NP (19a–b) and *to* + NP (19c–e). According to the OED (s.v. *order*, def. P5) the last such example appeared in 1833.

(19) a. *The various stratagems to which she was obliged to have recourse,* **in order for** *this discovery.*
(OED s.v. *order*, def. P5, Eliza Heywood *Female Spect.* No. 24 (1748) IV. 281)

b. *Nottingham had his face taken 3 different ways* **in order for** *a bust.*
(ARCHER, 1720stuk.j3b)

c. *I earnestly recommend his affairs to your favour and patronage; and desire you would stand by him, and appear for him,* **in order to** *his obtaining speedy justice.*
(ARCHER, 1735sim1.m3b)

---

[13] A more detailed discussion of the principles and mechanism of grammaticalization can be found in, for instance, Łęcki (2010: 25–37).

d. **In order to** this, we stretched a cord, as straight as possible, one thousand feet in length; which was measured several times over, in order to avoid mistake.
(ARCHER, 1769west.s4a)

e. Consider then, that as it is absolutely necessary we should become people of a certain sort before we are qualified to fill certain situations here on earth, so even common sense would teach us that, **in order to** our being fitted for acting our part in the other world, some acquirements or other, some sort of character, must be necessary.
(PPCMBE, 1830–FROUDE. 2,22.237)

An additional mark of grammaticalization of *in order that* and *in order to* is that the position of this construction has become fixed at the beginning of the subordinate clause (see, e.g., the examples in (15) and (16)). The original construction, i.e. the prepositional phrase *in order*, was not restricted to one position. For instance, in examples (6b) and (7a) *in order* appears in the middle of the clause, whereas in, e.g., (6a) and (20), this syntagm is used clause finally.

(20) He þat byndiþ him to feiþ of hijs god, mut kepe it al hoole stifly & **in ordre**.
'He who binds himself to the faith of his god, must keep it all completely firmly and in order.'
(MED, a1500(a1400) Wycl.FHC (NC 95) 349)

Finally, mention should be made of the increase in syntagmatic cohesion (see Lehmann 2002 [1982]: 131–140) between the elements constituting the grammaticalized expression. As examples (7a–c) reveal, the lexeme *order* could be modified by an adjectival phrase. In the course of the grammaticalization of *in order*, the bondedness between *in* and *order* increased, rendering formations such as *\*I came here in good order that you could do it* ungrammatical. Even adverbials were rarely inserted between *in order* and the following *to*: apart from three such cases given in (13), only one more unambiguous example has been attested in our corpora (21):

(21) **In order thoroughly to** subdue a scorbutic taint, the physical intentions must be, to keep the outlets and emunctories of the body open and clear, for the gentle evacuation of the scorbutic acrimony viz. the belly, urinary passages, and excretory ducts of the skin:
(PPCEME, LIND–1753,244.37)

What is more, unequivocal examples of any intervening linguistic material between *in order* and *that* are difficult to find, illustration (15b) being a conspicuous exception.[14]

Examples (13) and (21) suggest that the process of the grammaticalization of *in order to* was not completed until the middle of the eighteenth century. Yet such cases are relatively sporadic and what they show at most is that the bondedness between *order* and the following element of the structure was not as strong as between *in* and *order*. As a matter of fact, one cannot expect the same level of bondedness between all the elements of the construction studied because the syntagm *in order* could be followed by either *to* or *that* – thus, naturally, their syntagmatic cohesion could not reach the same degree as that between *in* and *order*, as *order* was never preceded by any other preposition than *in* when it was used as a subordinator. On the face of it, placing an adverbial between *in order* and *to* seems to be comparable to inserting *always* between *provided* and *that* in the development of the conditional subordinator

---

**14** An interesting case, however, is the following example:

(i) *'Tis* **in order thereto that** *they have proposed so many tempting offices, letters of Nobility, and the like, which Bait catches now but very few.*
(ARCHER, 1697pos1.n2b)

Although, at first sight, the above example seems to contradict what we have just said, *in order thereto that* does not function as a subordinator introducing a final clause here. It should rather be analyzed, alongside *in order here(un)to* (iia) and *in order there(un)to* (iib), as just an adverbial paraphrasable by 'to that end'.

(ii) a. *And it is absolutely necessary* **in order hereto**, *that we lay together, and pursue a while, some such Thoughts as these.*
(Lampeter Corpus, rela1711)
b. *We are therefore by invincible necessity obliged to maintain the right of the Banker, and* **in order thereunto** *I will now put his Case, which in short is not more but this.*
(Lampeter Corpus, polb1674)

This analysis can be supported by the very absence of *that* following the adverbial (see examples (iib) and (iii)), the possible occurrence of *in order thereunto* at the end of the sentence (iiic) and finally, a verb form with past tense marking in the subordinate clause ((iiia) and (iiib)) rather than the expected modal verb.

(iii) a. *Hore ... was resolved to prosecute them, and* **in order thereunto**, *took up by Warrant Thomas Wingfield, and Paul Dewey,*
(Lampeter Corpus, lawa 1703)
b. **In order thereunto**, *they form'd a TarCompany, who engross'd the whole;*
(Lampeter Corpus, eca1720)
c. *Therefore His Highness maketh no question, but that you will take these things into your speedy and serious consideration, and that you will think timely of the means of Defence and Offence* **in order thereunto**.
(Lampeter Corpus, pola1659)

*providing/provided (that)* (see Molencki 2012b). However, as Molencki (2012b) observes, "the phrase *provided all-ways that* ... looks like a fossilized expression", while the choice of the adverbial modifier used between *in order* and *to* was not as restricted as it was in the phrase *provided all-ways that*; see (13) and (21).

Let us now turn to the issue the path followed in the grammaticalization of purposive *in order to* and *in order that*. Heine and Kuteva (2002: 335) collected as many as eight different possible sources of grammatical expressions denoting PURPOSE on the basis of an extensive study of the world's languages, i.e. PURPOSE < ALLATIVE, BENEFACTIVE, COME TO, COMPLEMENTIZER, GIVE, GO TO, MATTER, SAY. The meaning expressed by *in order* is not among these possible sources. Hence, the question arises what sort of grammaticalization channel the rise of *in order to/that* shows? It seems that the actual conceptual source of this prepositional subordinator can be labeled MANNER, as *in order* originated as an expression describing the way how items should be placed/ ordered. The element of volition associated with desired order in the prepositional phrase *in order* is also inherent to purpose relations according to Cristofaro (2003) and Verstraete (2008: 761), who argues that "the event in the dependent [purpose] clause is intended by the agent of the main clause". Thus, volition may have been a catalyst in the grammaticalization path from MANNER to PURPOSE in the development of the prepositional subordinator *in order that*.

This proposed development is in line with a more general grammaticalization cline or channel (see Heine et al.'s 1991: 221–229), in which an adverb or a preposition gives rise to a conjunction.[15] Linguistic expressions that have undergone this particular grammaticalization cline in English have been brought together in Brinton (2009). They include adverbs such as *why, now, what, þa* 'then', and the preposition *like* – all of which came to be used as conjunctions in English. The primary example of such a development is the rise of the conjunctive function of *so*: *so*, which was originally used as a manner adverb (*Do not tap your fingers so*), acquired the function of a conjunction (*I left early so that I would not miss my flight*) (Brinton 2009: 312). One cannot escape noticing that there is a parallel between the development of *so* and *in order that* in English although the changes that these items underwent are separated by hundreds of years of the history of the language.

---

15 On the notions "cline", "continuum", "path", "channel" and "chain" referring to grammaticalization, see Łęcki (2010: 41–43).

## 5 Conclusion

Although the rise of the purposive subordinator *in order that* constitutes rather a regular case of grammaticalization, it unveils very interesting facets that accompany this development. First of all, contrary to what might be expected, *in order to*, from the outset, combined with infinitives and NPs (the first occurrence of *in order to* + *inf.* is recorded a little more than 400 years ago); finite clauses introduced by *in order that* followed later. Secondly, even though the noun *order* is a loan word from Old French, this fact did not particularly influence its later development into a grammatical unit as was the case in the evolution of *to the intent that* (see footnote 12). Thirdly, the connective *in order to/that* is rather confined to formal text types, which naturally has led to the expansion of the repertoire of purposive subordinators in the formal style.

The subordinator *in order that* follows a grammaticalization path in which an adverbial of manner becomes a subordinator. On the semantic plane, the prepositional subordinator may have derived from the idea of a desired state of order and gravitated toward purpose. In the development of *in order*, the following processes pertaining to grammaticalisation can be observed: renewal, decategorialization, reduction of paradigmatic variability, specialization, obligatorification, decrease in the syntactic variability and increase in syntagmatic cohesion.

## Acknowledgment

We are grateful to Prof. Rafał Molencki and two anonymous reviewers for their valuable remarks on an earlier version of this paper. Needless to say, all remaining imperfections are only the authors' responsibility.

## Sources of data

ARCHER-3.1 *A Representative Corpus of Historical English Registers* version 3.1. 1990–1993/ 2002/2007/2010/2013/2016. Originally compiled under the supervision of Douglas Biber and Edward Finegan at Northern Arizona University and University of Southern California; modified and expanded by subsequent members of a consortium of universities. Current member universities are Bamberg, Freiburg, Heidelberg, Helsinki, Lancaster, Leicester, Manchester, Michigan, Northern Arizona, Santiago de Compostela, Southern California, Trier, Uppsala, Zurich. Examples of usage taken from ARCHER were obtained under the terms of the ARCHER User Agreement.

CWWS *The Complete Works of William Shakespeare*. 1992. Creative Multimedia Corporation.

Haywood, Eliza 1748. *Life's progress through the passions*. London: T. Gardner.

ICAME. *The International Computer Archive of Modern and Medieval English*, 2nd edition. 1999. Knut Hofland, Anne Lindebjerg, Jørn Thunestvedt et al. (eds.). University of Bergen, Norway: The HIT Centre. <http://icame.uib.no/cd/>

*Lampeter Corpus of Early Modern* English Tracts. 1999. Compiled by Josef Schmied, Claudia Claridge, and Rainer Siemund. See http://www.helsinki.fi/varieng/CoRD/corpora/LC/index.html

Milton, John. 1671. *Samson Agonistes*. London: J.M. for John Starky.

Newdigate newsletters. 1994. Transcribed and edited by Philip Hines, Jr.

PPCEME. *Penn-Helsinki Parsed Corpus of Early Modern English*. 2004. Anthony Kroch, Beatrice Santorini and Ariel Diertani. <http://www.ling.upenn.edu/hist-corpora/PPCEME-RELEASE-2/index.html>

PPCMBE. *The Penn Parsed Corpus of Modern British English*. 2010. Anthony Kroch, Beatrice Santorini and Ariel Diertani. <http://www.ling.upenn.edu/hist-corpora/PPCMBE-RELEASE-1/index.html>

Smollett, Tobias, 1751. *The Adventures of Peregrine Pickle*. London: D. Wilson.

# Dictionaries

AHDIER. *The American Heritage Dictionary of Indo-European Roots*, 2nd edn. 2000. Watkins, Calvert (ed.). Boston: Houghton Mifflin.

AND *The Anglo-Norman Dictionary*. 2001–. Trotter, David A. and William Rothwell et al. (eds.). Electronic Edition. <http://www.anglo-norman.net/>

MED *Middle English Dictionary*. 1956–2001. Hans Kurath and Sherman Kuhn et al. (eds.) Ann Arbor: University of Michigan Press. <http://ets.umdl.umich.edu/m/mec>

CEDEL *A Comprehensive Etymological Dictionary of the English Language*. Vol. I: A–K. 1966. Ernest Klein (ed.). Elsevier Publishing Company: Amsterdam.

OEtymD *Online Etymology Dictionary*. 2001. Harper, Douglas. <http://www.etymonline.com/>

RDLL *Routledge Dictionary of Language and Linguistics*. 2006 [1996]. Hadumod Bussmann. Translated and edited by Gregory P. Trauth & Kerstin Kazzazi. (German original: *Lexikon der Sprachwissenschaft*, 1990). London: Routledge.

OED *The Oxford English Dictionary Online*. June 2015. Oxford University Press. <http://www.oed.com/> Accessed July 2015.

# References

Brinton, Laurel. 2009. Pathways in the development of pragmatic markers in English. In Ans van Kemenade & Bettelou Los (eds.), *The handbook of the history of English*, 307–334. Chichester, West Sussex: Wiley-Blackwell.

Cristofaro, Sonia. 2003. Subordination. Oxford: Oxford University Press.

Görlach, Manfred. 1991. *Introduction to Early Modern English*. Cambridge: Cambridge University Press.

Heine, Bernd. 2003. Grammaticalization. In Brian D. Joseph & Richard D. Janda (eds.), *The handbook of historical linguistics*, 575–601. Chichester, West Sussex: Wiley-Blackwell.

Heine, Bernd, Ulrike Claudi & Friederike Hünnemeyer. 1991. *Grammaticalization: A conceptual framework*. Chicago: University of Chicago Press.

Heine, Bernd & Tania Kuteva. 2002. *World lexicon of grammaticalization*. Cambridge: Cambridge University Press.
Hopper, Paul J. 1991. On some principles of grammaticalization. In Elizabeth Closs Traugott & Bernd Heine (eds.), *Approaches to grammaticalization*. Vol. 1: *Focus on theoretical and methodological issues*, 17–35. Amsterdam: John Benjamins.
Hopper, Paul J. & Elizabeth C. Traugott. 2003. *Grammaticalization*. Cambridge: Cambridge University Press.
Huddleston Rodney & Geoffrey K. Pullum. 2002. *The Cambridge grammar of the English language*. Cambridge: Cambridge University Press.
Kortmann, Bernd. 1998. Adverbial subordinators in the languages of Europe. In Johan van der Auwera (ed.), *Adverbial constructions in the languages of Europe*, 457–561. Berlin: Mouton de Gruyter.
Lehmann, Christian. 2002 [1982]. *Thoughts on grammaticalization*, 2nd edn. (Arbeitspapiere des Seminars für Sprachwissenschaft der Universität Erfurt 9). Erfurt: Seminar für Sprachwissenschaft der Universität.
Lenker, Ursula & Anneli Meurman-Solin (eds.). 2007. *Connectives in the history of English*. Amsterdam: John Benjamins.
Los, Bettelou. 2007. *To* as a connective in the history of English. In Ursula Lenker & Anneli Meurman-Solin (eds.), *Connectives in the history of English*, 31–60. Amsterdam: John Benjamins.
Łęcki, Andrzej M. 2010. *Grammaticalization paths of HAVE in English*. Frankfurt am Main: Peter Lang.
Łęcki, Andrzej M. & Jerzy Nykiel. 2014. All roads lead to purpose: The rise and fall of *to the end that* and *to the effect that* in English. In Michael Bilynsky (ed.), *Studies in Middle English: Words, forms, senses and texts*, 225–251. Frankfurt am Main: Peter Lang.
Molencki, Rafał. 2012a. *Causal conjunctions in mediaeval English: A corpus-based study of grammaticalization*. Katowice: Oficyna Wydawnicza.
Molencki, Rafał. 2012b. *Providing/provided that*: Grammaticalization or loan translation? In Irén Hegedűs & Alexandra Fodor (eds.), *English Historical Linguistics 2010*: *Selected papers from the Sixteenth International Conference on English Historical Linguistics (ICEHL 16), Pécs, 22–27 August 2010*, 197–214. Amsterdam: John Benjamins.
Nykiel, Jerzy & Andrzej M. Łęcki. 2013. Toward a diachronic account of English prepositional subordinators expressing purpose: *to the intent that*. In Marcin Krygier (ed.), *Of fair speche, and of fair answere* (Medieval English Mirror 8), 75–88. Frankfurt am Main: Peter Lang.
Rissanen, Matti. 2002. Despite or notwithstanding? On the development of concessive prepositions in English. In Andreas Fischer, Gunnel Tottie & Hans Martin Lehmann (eds.), *Text types and corpora: Studies in honour of Udo Fries*, 191–203. Tübingen: Gunter Narr.
Rissanen, Matti. 2009. Grammaticalisation, contact and adverbial connectives: The rise and decline of save. In Shinichiro Watanabe & Yukiteru Hosoya (eds.), *English philology and corpus studies: A Festschrift in honour of Mitsunori Imai to celebrate his seventieth birthday*, 135–152. Tokyo: Shohakusha.
Schmidtke-Bode, Karsten. 2009. *A typology of purpose clauses*. Amsterdam: John Benjamins.
Verstraete, Jean-Christophe. 2008. The status of purpose, reason, and intended endpoint in the typology of complex sentences: Implications for layered models of clause structure. *Linguistics* 48(4)/ 757–788.
Visser, Frederikus Theodor. 2002 [1963–1973]. *An historical syntax of the English language*. Leiden: Brill.

Björn Hansen
# 9 What happens after grammaticalization? Post-grammaticalization processes in the area of modality

**Abstract:** This is the first study to present an account of language change following regular grammaticalization. It shows that grammaticalization processes do not have to represent the final stage in the history of a construction. Focusing on the domain of modality, it develops a typology of post-grammaticalization processes that includes at least six types: secondary grammaticalization, marginalization, degrammaticalization, retraction, lexicalization and grammatical word derivation. Whereas secondary grammaticalization, degrammaticalization, retraction and lexicalization can be considered established phenomena which have been discussed by many scholars, marginalization and word derivation have received much less attention. Our typology is based on the empirical analysis of language changes following the rise of modals in five Slavonic languages (Russian, Polish, Czech and Serbian/Croatian).

## 1 Introduction

A large number of studies have been devoted to the description and analysis of what may be called typical grammaticalization processes. Grammaticalization is here understood as a type of language change whereby "lexical items and constructions come in certain linguistic contexts to serve grammatical functions and, once grammaticalized, continue to develop new grammatical functions" (Hopper and Traugott 2003: xv). In this study, the so-called construction-based view of grammaticalization is adopted, which focuses on the role of syntactic constructions (see the discussion in Himmelmann 2004: 31). On this definition, there are two subtypes of grammaticalization, which Norde (2009) calls primary (lexical > grammatical) vs. secondary grammaticalization (grammatical > more grammatical). In recent years, we have seen a growing interest in the distinction between grammaticalization and closely related processes, on the one hand, and in phenomena which seem to contradict the hypothesis that grammaticalization processes are unidirectional and always proceed from less grammatical to more grammatical, on the other. One such closely related process is lexicalization, which has been addressed by scholars as a type of change which seems to

DOI 10.1515/9783110492347-010

share many features with grammaticalization, but which gives rise to new lexical items (see, e.g., Lehmann 2002; Himmelmann 2004; Brinton and Traugott 2005). Changes leading in the direction from a grammatical to a more lexical status have in several recent studies been labeled as degrammaticalization or de-auxiliarization (van der Auwera 2002; Willis 2007; Norde 2009; Nuyts 2013). As Norde points out, token reversal is not attested, but a few cases of type reversal – meaning the development from a grammatical function toward a less grammatical one – do exist.

In this paper, a related question is addressed: What may happen after an element (lexical item or construction) has undergone a grammaticalization process? What I would like to present is a typology of processes following primary or regular grammaticalization processes, a typology of what one might call post-grammaticalization processes. This typology is based on the empirical analysis of all attested language changes following the rise of modals in five Slavonic languages (Russian, Polish, Czech and Serbian/Croatian). The data sample has the following characteristics. First, its point of departure, the rise of modals, is a well-described case of grammaticalization. Second, the sample covers all data from the post-modal domain found in these languages, and it is coherent, coming from a single language family. Third, it has the additional advantage that it can be studied from a historical perspective: sufficient historical data for each language are available and additional historical evidence can be obtained by taking data into account from Old Church Slavonic, the first written Slavonic language dating from the 9th century. This enables us to cover one thousand years of language history, and thus to distinguish between preserved old, i.e. pre-modal, and new post-modal meanings. On the basis of the data analyzed, a typology of post-grammaticalization processes comprising six types is proposed: (i) continuing grammaticalization via expansion into neighboring semantic spaces, (ii) marginalization, (iii) degrammaticalization, (iv) retraction, (v) lexicalization and (vi) grammatical word derivation.

# 2 Exploring post-grammaticalization processes

## 2.1 The post-modal domain

Since the publication of the article by van der Auwera and Plungian (1998), scholars working on modality have generally distinguished between pre-modal, properly modal and post-modal semantic functions. Accordingly, modality's semantic map consists of three subdomains: the modal domain in the proper sense, the pre-modal domain, i.e. the lexical sources from which modals develop, and the post-modal domain which contains the functions that have diachronically developed from modality. To date, the post-modal field has not been very well studied, but we do know that it encompasses more grammatical functions (continuing grammaticalization) as well as lexical functions. The map by van der Auwera and Plungian (1998) is based on a narrow understanding of the notion of modality and, therefore, covers only the semantic primitives, possibility and necessity, and explicitly excludes volition.

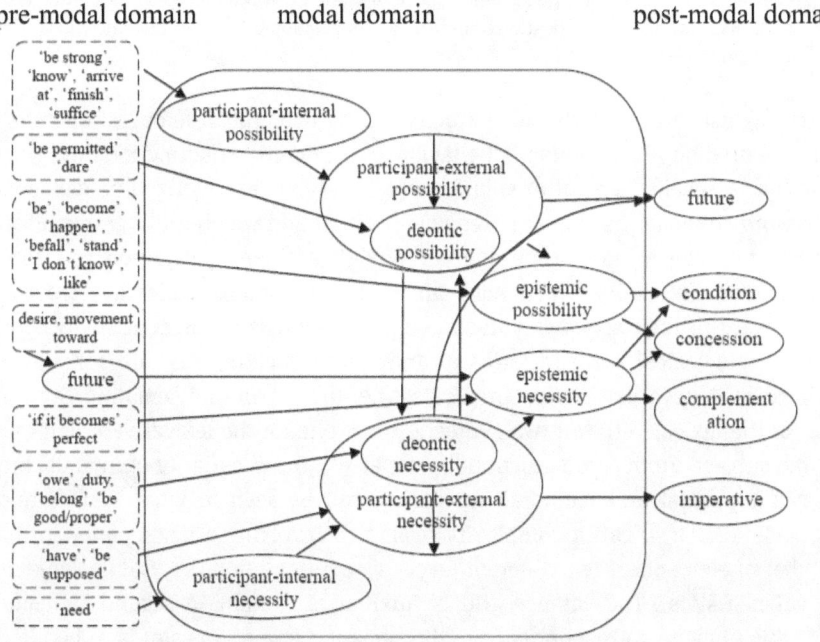

**Figure 1:** Modality's semantic map (taken from van der Auwera and Plungian 1998: 98)

The semantic map in Figure 1, which, according to the authors, does not claim to cover all languages of the world, identifies five post-modal functions: future, condition, concession, complementation and imperative. The focus of mainstream grammaticalization research has mainly been on the transition from pre-modal, i.e. lexical, to modal notions, and the spread within the semantic space of modality, whereas the post-modal field has received much less attention. In the present paper, I would like to discuss the types of changes following up on the established grammaticalization processes, which have resulted in the modals. As was mentioned above, the study investigates all post-modal functions found in five Slavonic languages from a construction-based perspective. Our results will demonstrate that all post-grammaticalization processes are linked to specific syntactic contexts.

## 2.2 The Slavonic data

Our data set is restricted to modals proper. As the term "modals" can be interpreted in a variety of ways, some of their cross-linguistic characteristics will be discussed briefly. Modals are defined in the following way:

> A fully-fledged modal is a polyfunctional, syntactically autonomous expression of modality which shows a certain degree of grammaticalisation. 'Polyfunctional' is understood as covering a domain within the semantic space of modality. A fully-fledged modal functions as an operator on the predicational and/or the propositional level of the clause. (Hansen and de Haan 2009: 512)

Cross-linguistically, modals are characterized by two crucial features: operator-like, i.e. auxiliary-like, syntactic behavior and semantic polyfunctionality. They represent a specific type of auxiliaries which can be characterized as elements with word character used in the predicate position and which fulfill grammatical functions similar to bound morphemes.[1] Modals are here understood as means of expressing modality which have undergone a grammaticalization process. With regard to their specific syntactic behavior, modals are necessarily accompanied by a lexical verb; in terms of argument structure, they are sometimes claimed to behave like raising predicates, i.e. they open one semantic valence slot for the lexical verb but two syntactic slots, one for the lexical verb and one for the subject. From a constructional perspective, the peculiarity of modals, but also of aspectual and temporal auxiliaries, can be seen in what Francis and Michaelis (2003: 4) call a complexity mismatch involving a discrepancy in the number of elements at two different levels of representation (i.e. frame elements vs. valence slots). The valence grid of auxiliaries contains a second syntactic slot which has no correspondence in the semantic frame: this slot is to be filled by the subject of the lexical verb. From a cross-linguistic point of view, modal constructions show variation mainly in the morpho-syntactic encoding of the subject and the morphological make-up of the lexical verb.[2]

From a semantic point of view, modals are characterized by polyfunctionality. They express the basic notions of 'necessity' and 'possibility'. Modal meanings

---

[1] As Hansen and de Haan's (2009) extensive study on modals in the languages of Europe has shown, modals usually have no specific morphological or syntactic markings. The Germanic modals are thus quite exceptional as they have a specific morphological form (preterite-presents).
[2] For an in-depth discussion of the relation between modal polyfunctionality and argument structure, see Hansen (2014). In this work, I propose to distinguish two main types of modal polyfunctionality, and I discuss their relation to the syntactic distinctions between verbs and auxiliaries as well as between raising vs. control predicates, and the coherence of verbal complexes.

include dynamic, deontic and epistemic modality. Typical modal auxiliaries are polyfunctional, in that they express no less than two functions on the map in Figure 1. In contrast, so-called modal content words, i.e. words with modal meaning that have not been subject to an auxiliarization process, have only one modal meaning.

The present study makes use of (i) the data presented in Hansen (2001), which is an in-depth study of the structure and the historical development of the category of modals in Russian, Polish, Serbian/Croatian and Old Church Slavonic; (ii) the results of some additional minor corpus-linguistic studies dedicated to selected modals (Hansen 2009, Hansen 2010; Hansen et al. 2011); and (iii) the survey article by Besters-Dilger et al. (2009). Hansen (2001) contains detailed lexicographic portrayals of each of the modals inspired by the Moscow Semantic School. These portrayals combine the findings of the large number of existing studies on modality[3] with a thorough analysis of the major synchronic and historical dictionaries. All data were checked against the major on-line corpora.[4] In the individual Slavonic languages, the core modals make up a limited set of elements. Table 1 lists all elements which are characterized by the two crucial features: *polyfunctionality* and *auxiliary-like syntactic behavior*. The table does not include monofunctional modal elements (like Russian *prixodit'sja* 'have to', which only has a participant-external reading excluding obligation) or borderline cases, i.e. elements which have not yet fully developed modal polyfunctionality (e.g. Russian *nužno*, which is slowly developing the deontic meaning).

**Table 1:** Core modals in six Slavonic languages

|  | Modals of possibility | Modals of necessity |
|---|---|---|
| Old Church Slavonic | mošti | |
| Polish | móc, można | musieć, mieć, powinien wypada, należy, trzeba |
| Czech | moct | muset, mít, třeba |
| Russian | moč', možno, nel'zja | dolžen, sleduet, nado |
| Serbian/Croatian | moći | morati, trebati, valjati |

---

**3** See, for instance, Kątny (1980) on Polish, Rytel (1982) on Polish and Czech, Šatunovskij (1996) and Vaulina (1988) on Russian, Panevová et al. (1971) on Czech and Kalogjera (1982) on Serbian/Croatian.
**4** *Russian National Corpus* (http://ruscorpora.ru), *Czech National Corpus* (https://ucnk.ff.cuni.cz), *Corpus of the Serbian Standard Language* (http://korpus.matf.bg.ac.rs) and *Polish National Corpus* (http://www.nkjp.pl/).

In addition to these core elements, we will take into consideration elements which used to have the status of a polyfunctional modal, but lost it at a later stage. As shown in previous studies (Hansen 2001, Hansen 2004), only a small number of Slavonic modals are affected by post-grammaticalization processes, which can be understood as changes in the modals' polyfunctionality pattern, whereas the majority of elements remain stable in the sense that their polyfunctionality does not change. Our analysis of post-grammaticalization processes involves the following functional changes:

- impossibility > prohibitive (Serbian/Croatian *nemoj*; ex. (1) and (2))
- weakened necessity > future in the past (Polish *mieć*; ex. (4))
- weakened necessity > avertive (Polish *mieć*; ex. (5))
- weakened necessity > hypothetical subjunctive (Polish *mieć*; ex. (6))
- weakened necessity > hearsay (Polish *mieć*, Czech *mít*; ex. (7))
- general participant-external impossibility > participant-external impossibility excluding deontic impossibility (Polish *niepodobna*; ex. (15)–(17))
- participant external-internal-epistemic necessity > partipant external-internal-necessity (Russian *nado*; ex. (18))
- general participant-external necessity > deontic necessity (Russian *podobat'sja*)
- lack of necessity > dislike (Czech *nemusím*; Section 3.3)
- possibility > actualized possibility (Russian *smoč'*; ex. (26)–(27))
- possibility > to be responsible (Czech *moct*; ex. (23)–(24))
- impossibility > to do no harm (Serbian/Croatian *moći*; ex. (25))
- intersubjective epistemic possibility > subjective epistemic possibility (epistemic sentence adverbs, all languages; ex. (19)–(22))

In Section 3, I propose an initial classification of changes responsible for these functional shifts.

# 3 A typology of post-grammaticalization processes

## 3.1 Secondary grammaticalization: 'prohibitive'

In our sample, several examples were attested of modals developing more abstract functions in other grammatical domains. However, only a single case was found of the development of a fully-fledged grammatical subcategory involving semantic changes, phonological erosion and syntactic fixation: in Serbian/Croatian, the negated modal of possibility *moći* developed into an analytical prohibitive marker. This element, *nemoj*, co-occurs in clause initial or second position either with a verb in the infinitive (Croatian and Serbian) or with a complementizer-headed finite verb phrase (Serbian). It is partly synonymous with the prohibitive formed with the imperative of the modal *moći* with the negator *ne*. *Nemoj* can take the endings *-te* (2PL) or *-mo* (1PL) and expresses a prohibition directed toward any person, as in examples (1) and (2):

(1) Serbian
  *Samo nemoj da se uplaši-š.*
  only PROH COMP REFL to.be.scared-2SG
  'But don't be afraid!'
  (*Corpus of the Serbian Standard Language*, http://korpus.matf.bg.ac.rs, accessed on 5 August 2013)

(2) Serbian
  *Nemoj-mo se zavarava-ti.*
  PROH-1PL REFL betray-INF
  'Let's not be fooled!'
  (*Corpus of the Serbian Standard Language*; http://korpus.matf.bg.ac.rs, accessed on 5 August 2013)

The element *nemoj* is generally assumed to have developed from the negated imperative of the modal verb of possibility *moći* (*Rječnik hrvatskoga ili srpskoga jezika* VI: 884; Havránek 1980: 469–470). The historical data indicate that the transition toward the prohibitive occurred before the rise of Slavonic literacy. The assumed change is therefore the result of a comparative reconstruction based on data from related languages. In the first documents written in Old Church Slavonic, the prohibitive is already attested in the full form *nemozi* + $V_{Inf}$. In Serbian/Croatian, the original form *ne moz'i*, attested for the 13th century, lost a syllable and was contracted to *nèmōi*. It is interesting to note that the form *nemo* is also seen; this is an even more abbreviated form (which, however, is not accepted in the Serbian and Croatian standard languages). The fusion process thus involves the following steps: *ne mog-i* > *ne mozi* > *nemoi* > *nemo*.

All these features show that we are dealing with a typical grammaticalization process which involves not only semantic changes but also phonological erosion and fixation to a certain position within the clause. This language change gives rise to a fully-fledged grammatical operator with maximal host class expansion. The problem with treating this process as a clear-cut case of secondary grammaticalization is that the historical data do not exclude that this change took place simultaneously with the rise of polyfunctionality of the modal *moći*. If this were the case, the development of *nemo* would not be analyzed as a post-grammaticalization process, but as an instance of parallel polygrammaticalization.

## 3.2 Marginalization: 'future in the past', 'avertive', 'hypothetical-subjunctive' and 'hearsay'

As "marginalization" is not an established notion in historical linguistics, I would like to propose distinguishing between regular grammaticalization, which gives rise to fully-fledged grams, on the one hand, and changes which result in marginalized grammatical markers, on the other hand. Marginalization does not lead to the rise of an unmarked, highly frequent grammatical operator, but to elements which occupy a peripheral position in the language system, i.e. which are either stylistically restricted or co-occur with a limited number of verbs. Marginalization, therefore, might be the precursor of actual retraction (see Section 3.4). It is claimed that the basis for the distinction between regular grammaticalization and marginalization lies in differing degrees of what we will call "entrenchment". "Entrenchment refers to the degree to which a given element becomes usual – and eventually unmarked – in a speech community. Therefore, it not only depends on the frequency of activation by individuals, but also applies to speech communities" (Schmid 2007: 119).

A particular "productive" modal giving rise to several post-modal grammatical functions, which might arguably be treated as marginalized grams, is Polish *mieć* and its Czech equivalent *mít* 'should'. These verbs, which can be traced back to a verb of possession 'to have', convey a very particular meaning combining modal with evidential components. Their basic meaning, i.e. *mieć$_1$*, is a sort of weakened necessity based on another person's expressed wish, comparable to German *sollen* (see Hansen 2009; Weiss ms).

(3) a. Polish
   **Ma-sz**  zaraz       **zgłosi-ć**   się   u   dziekan-a!
   have-2SG immediately notify-INF REFL at dean-GEN.SG

   b. German
   Du  **soll-st**   dich        sofort        bei-m
   you shall-2SG you.ACC immediately at-DEF.ART

   Dekan  **meld-en!**
   dean   notify-INF

   'They say you should contact the dean immediately!'      (Weiss ms.)

In particular, *mieć$_1$* characterizes a situation in which the speaker informs the hearer about the fact that someone says that he/she wants the referent of the subject (the hearer *you* in (3a, 3b)) to do something. In Early Modern Polish (turn of the 18th to the 19th century), two new functions associated with the domain of temporality developed. In bookish registers, *mieć* can be used in the past tense to denote a 'future in the past' implying an element of fate (*mieć₂*):

(4) Polish
**Mia-ł** jeszcze wiele **przecierpie-ć**, zanim wyzdrowia-ł.
have-PST still a.lot suffer-INF before recover-PST
'He still had to suffer a lot, before he recovered.' (Weiss ms.)

The link to the modal meaning of a weakened necessity can be seen in a reading where the volitional component is ascribed to God or another supernatural force who wanted the person to suffer. We are, therefore, dealing with a specific combination of temporal and modal features. A further extension of *mieć₁* is the rise of the avertive, a meaning which according to Kuteva (2001: 84) and Drobnjaković (2009) involves three semantic components, namely, imminence, pastness and counterfactuality, and thus relates to no less than three notional categories: aspect, temporality and modality. Without going into detail, I use the label "was on the edge of V-ing, but did not V" as proposed by Kuteva (2001). Here is an early example from the beginning of the 19th century (*mieć₃*):

(5) Polish (19th century)
Już więc **mia-ł-a ujeżdża-ć** [...] Wtem
already so.thus have-PST-F leave-INF suddenly
słycha-ć wrzask srogi.
hear-INF scream awful
'She was about to leave, when all of a sudden an awful scream was heard.'
(Adam Mickiewicz, *Mieszko*, 1817)

A third path gave rise to a function in complex clauses which we could label 'hypothetical-subjunctive' (Hansen 2009; Weiss ms.). Here, the speaker expresses a certain degree of negative commitment to the true state of affairs encoded in the subordinate clause; this meaning comes close to, but does not coincide with a counterfactual reading. The 'hypothetical-subjunctive' contains an epistemic element, i.e. it expresses a high degree of probability that the state of affairs is actually not true or will not become true (*mieć₄*).

(6) Polish
*Inwestor budynk-u zaprzecza, żeby jego obiekt*
investor building-GEN.SG deny.3SG COMP.COND his object
**mia-ł szkodzi-ć** *mniejsz-ym sklep-om.*
have-PST harm-INF smaller-DAT.PL shop-DAT.PL
'The investor denies that his project will cause losses for the smaller shops.' (*Dziennik Polski*, 4 May 2001)

Finally, the same modal *mieć* (like its Czech counterpart *mít*) acquired the meaning 'hearsay' (*mieć₅*). In both languages, this evidential meaning is mainly restricted to journalistic styles, as demonstrated in the following Czech example (Štícha 2003: 118):

(7) Czech
*Liberijec ho* **mě-l** *úmyslně* **udeři-t** *hlav-ou*
Liberian him have-PST on.purpose beat-INF head-INS.SG
*do obličej-e.*
to face-GEN.SG
'The Liberian is said to have deliberately hit him with his head in the face.'

It is important to point out that none of the four post-modal units mentioned developed into a subcategory of an obligatory grammatical paradigm comparable to, for instance, tense or mood and as such display a low degree of paradigmaticization. They have the status of optional markers and are stylistically restricted.

## 3.3 Degrammaticalization

In the introduction, I drew attention to the debate regarding the unidirectionality of grammaticalization processes. Whereas many authors simply deny the existence of degrammaticalization, others claim that it is a rare, but attested phenomenon. In this paper, I have adopted Norde's approach, where degrammaticalization is defined as "a composite change whereby a gram in a specific context gains in autonomy or substance on more than one linguistic level (semantics, morphology, syntax, or phonology)" (Norde 2009: 120). A rare instance of degrammaticalization of a modal can be observed in Czech, as is argued in Hansen et al. (2011). In this article, it is pointed out that the construction *Karla Gotta nemusím* [Karel.ACC Gott.ACC not.must.PRS.1SG] 'I can't stand Karel Gott' developed some ten years ago in the Czech and Slovak youth language, from which it spread to other registers. In a specific constructional context involving negation, the original modal verb of necessity is used as a main verb with the new meaning 'to dislike' and a concomitant change in the complementation pattern. Although this development shows a certain overlap with lexicalization (see Section 3.5.), I would like to argue that we are dealing here with a change from a modal auxiliary to a lexical verb. This could be treated as one of the very rare instances of the subtype of degrammaticalization which Norde calls "degrammation": "a composite change whereby a function word in a specific linguistic context is re-analysed as a member of a major word class, acquiring the morpho-syntactic properties which are typical of that word class, and gaining in semantic substance" (Norde 2009: 135). In this case, we can observe a composite change involving three levels: semantic enrichment, change in the complementation pattern and morphological decategorization. There are no changes on the phonological level.

Let us turn briefly to the linguistic details of this language change following grammaticalization. Czech *muse-t* [must-INF] is a material borrowing of Middle High German *müezen*, attested in the first texts of Old Czech dating from the 13th century (see Hansen 2000). From as early as the 13th/14th centuries, *muset* has functioned as a typical expression of all types of participant-internal and participant-external necessity; consider (8), taken from Hansen 2000: 84):

(8) Old Czech (14th century)
V zakon-u         **mussy-s jmie-ti**   utrpěni-e.
in monastery-LOC.SG must-2.SG have-INF patience-ACC.SG
'In a monastery you have to be patient.'

Later, this form expanded into epistemic modality. It is important to note that Czech *muset* never had any lexical or pre-modal meanings. It functions, therefore, as a "normal" special modal covering the whole domain of necessity. For approximately the last ten years, Czech teenagers have been using *muset* in a new constructional context where the original modal auxiliary is used as a main verb with the new meaning 'to dislike'. In these contexts *muset* changed its complementation pattern: instead of an infinitival phrase, it takes a nominal phrase in the accusative. This lexical construction, as represented in (9) and exemplified in (10)–(11), is currently spreading from youth slang to written registers of Czech where it co-exists with the established modal usages of *muset*. The historical data clearly show that we are dealing with an innovation, and not with the relic of an old pre-modal meaning.

(9) $NP_{ACC}$ + ne + mus- ($NP_{ACC}$ + not + must) > nemus- 'dislike'

(10) Modern Czech
[pojedli u vánočního stolu.] Ryb-a? Tu já
[they had Christmas dinner] fish-NOM that.ACC I

**ne-musí-m**, mě-l jsem kuřecí řízky.
not-must.1SG have.PTCP AUX.1SG chicken schnitzel

'Fish? This is something I don't like, I had chicken schnitzel.'
(*Mladá Fronta DNES*, 20 December 2003)

(11) Modern Czech
Já vlastně podobn-é seriál-y celkově **ne-musí-m**.
I actually similar-ACC series-ACC overall not-must-1SG
'These TV series, I actually don't like them at all.'
(*Deníky Bohemia*, 17 January 2004)

This is the internal make-up of the lexical construction *nemus-* (for more details, see Hansen et al. 2011):

(i) Semantics: *nemuset* expresses a strong aversion to the stimulus encoded in its nominal complement;
(ii) Morphology: *nemuset* is used in present and past tense, but has low acceptability of future tense (by comparison, the modal has no tense restrictions); there is no infinitive and no passive (the modal auxiliary, by contrast, does have an infinitive, but no passive);
(iii) Syntax: negation is obligatory; *nemuset* has two valence slots: (1) the experiencer encoded in the subject position; (2) the stimulus syntactically encoded as an accusative complement (allows for animate and inanimate nouns);
(iv) Pragmatics: *nemuset* has a strong preference for preposing the nominal complement object, i.e. the discourse referent encoded in the complement is topical.

The new construction developed in a bridging context of a preposed infinitival complement yielding two possible readings: the "old" meaning of a negated necessity and the new meaning 'to dislike', as can be seen in (12).

(12) Czech
  a. **Ne-musí-m** cestova-t letadl-em.
     not-must.1SG travel-INF plane-INS.SG
     > 'I don't have to travel by plane.' (the only reading)

  b. Cestova-t letadl-em **ne-musí-m**.
     travel-INF plane-INS.SG not-must.1SG
     > 'I hate traveling by plane.' (preferred reading)
     or 'I don't have to travel by plane.' (possible reading)
     (Hansen et al. 2011: 247)

If the preposed infinitival complement is replaced by a nominal phrase in the accusative, the modal reading of absence of necessity is no longer available. In an analogous development, the modal of possibility *moct* in specific contexts also adopted the same meaning 'to like' (*Karla Gotta můžu* – [Karel Gott I.can] 'I like Karel Gott.').

The transition of a modal of necessity into a verb with the meaning 'to like' is not only found in Czech (and in Slovak), but also in some Germanic languages. The German counterpart *müssen* can have a similar meaning. Here, however, the modal is accompanied by the infinitive of the verb *haben* 'to have' as illustrated by the following Internet example:

(13) German
*Es gib-t so Dinge, die* **muß** *ich* **nicht hab-en**. *Echt nicht.*
it give-3SG so things that must.1SG I not have-INF really not
'There are things I really don't like.'
(www.wunschkinder.net; accessed on 5 August 2013)

Structurally more similar to the Czech construction is the the use of *moeten* in Belgian Dutch, as in (14). Here, the modal governs an accusative complement directly (see Diepeveen et al. 2006: 100).

(14) Belgian Dutch
*[Mag je dat doen, een hond beoordelen op z'n uiterlijk en zeggen]*
"*Ik vind hem niet mooi,* **ik moet** **hem niet**."
I find him not nice I must.1SG him not
'[Can you do that, judge a dog by the way he looks and then say],
I don't find him nice, I can't stand him.'

These parallel structures in the Germanic languages seem to indicate that this is an areal phenomenon involving some sort of contact-induced language change, in this case perhaps "contact-induced degrammaticalization".

## 3.4 Retraction

According to Haspelmath (2004: 33), retraction can in some respects be seen as the opposite of expansion in grammaticalization. As an element $B_1$ develops new grammatical functions ($B_2$, $B_3$, $B_4$) and, thus, forms a grammaticalization chain, some of its earlier manifestations, represented on the left in Figure 2, typically disappear (e.g. $B_1$ in stage 3). Another manifestation of retraction is that the new, more grammatical items in a grammaticalization chain become obsolete ($B_4$ in stage 5; $B_3$, in stage 6), as illustrated in Figure 2:

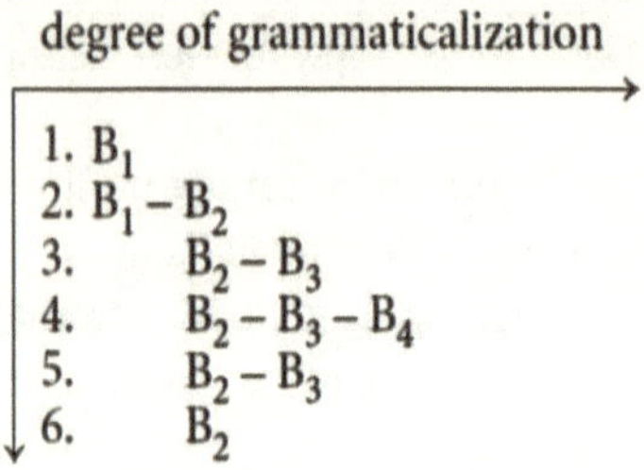

degree of grammaticalization →

1. $B_1$
2. $B_1 - B_2$
3. $\quad B_2 - B_3$
4. $\quad B_2 - B_3 - B_4$
5. $\quad B_2 - B_3$
6. $\quad B_2$

**Figure 2:** Retraction (taken from Haspelmath 2004: 33)

In an earlier study of the diachronic development of Slavonic modals (Hansen 2001), I came across three cases of the loss of modal polyfunctionality which we would treat as retraction. The Polish adjective *podobno*, derived from the lexical source 'similar' (stage 1 in Figure 2) in negated contexts in preliterate times, had gone through a grammaticalization process. In Old Polish, it had the status of a polyfunctional modal covering both objective participant-external possibility (in the sense of possibility based on objective circumstances) and deontic possibility, as illustrated by the examples (15) and (16), dating from 1500 (stages 2 and 3):

(15) Old Polish (ca. 1500)
*Czyrpya-l tako vyelykye vdrączenie yz* **nyepodobn-o**
suffer-PST so great martyrdom COMP not.similar-N.SG

*ktor-emu czlovyek-ovy tego vypoyeda-cz.*
any-DAT.SG man-DAT.SG this.GEN.SG tell.INF

'He suffered such a martyrdom, you cannot tell anybody about it.'
(Anonymous writer, *Rozmyślanie o żywocie Pana Jezusa*, 1500)

(16) Old Polish (ca. 1500)
*Nye yest* **podobn-o** *vzya-cz chleb dzyeczy-om*
not be.3SG similar-N.SG take-INF bread child-DAT.PL

*y da-cz pss-om zye-scz.*
and give-INF dog-DAT.PL eat-INF

'It is not proper to take away bread from the children to feed it to the dogs.'
(Anonymous writer, *Rozmyślanie o żywocie Pana Jezusa*, 1500)

During the 16th century, the modal *podobno* came to be used in the construction *rzecz jest (nie)podobna* + infinitive [thing be.3SG (un)similar.F.SG], where the modal agrees with the dummy subject *rzecz* 'thing'. Later, the subject was omitted leaving the modal with the now unmotivated agreement marker *-a* (feminine singular). From a semantic point of view, it is important to note that this morphosyntactic change was accompanied by the loss of the deontic meaning of prohibition. Since the 16th/17th century, the element has been restricted to objective participant external impossibility and has thus lost its modal polyfunctionality. This would correspond to the transition from stage 5 to 6 in Figure 2. In modern usage, *niepodobna* is an expression of objective impossibility as illustrated by example (17):

(17) Modern Polish
*Dlatego perswazj-ami    demokracj-i    osiągną-ć*
for.this  persuasion-INS.PL democracy-GEN.SG gain-INF

**niepodobna-** *trzeba    ją    wywalczy-ć.*
not.possible  one.should  her   fight-INF

'Therefore, it is impossible to gain democracy by persuasion, one has to fight for it.'         (www.cyfroteka.pl; accessed on 6 August 2013)

Another case of retraction is found in Russian where the polyfunctional modal *nado*, or its precursor *nadobno*, lost its epistemic meaning again. In the 19th century, it could express the notion of probability, but this usage was later lost (Hansen 2001: 378):

(18) Modern Russian (19th century)
*Netrudno    by-l-o    ponja-t'    čto    **nadobno**  by-t'*
not-difficult be-PST-N understand-INF COMP  must        be-INF

*čemu-nibud'         neobyknovenn-omu.*
something.DAT.SG    unusual-DAT.SG

'It was not difficult to see that something unusual must have happened.'
(G.I. Dobrynin, *Istinnoe pověstvovanie*, 1871)

I would like to briefly mention a third example of retraction: in Old and Middle Russian, the verb of Church Slavonic origin *podobati* 'to resemble, to correspond to' was used to express ethical obligation and later expanded into 'participant external objective necessity'. During the 18th century, the Russian modal system underwent considerable restructuring. It involved the replacement of modals of Church Slavonic origin, which led to (i) the retraction of the meaning 'objective necessity' and (ii) the semantic narrowing of 'obligation' which became more specific ('to have the right', 'to be entitled'); for more details, see Hansen (2001: 390–391) and Vaulina (1988).

## 3.5 Lexicalization

Lexicalization can be understood as a "change whereby in certain linguistic contexts speakers use a syntactic construction or a word formation as a new contentful form with formal and semantic properties that are not completely derivable or predictable from the constituents of the construction or the word formation pattern. Over time, there may be further loss of internal constituency and the item may become more lexical" (Brinton and Traugott 2005: 144). Lexicalization, thus, differs from grammaticalization and marginalization in the output of the language change: whereas the former gives rise to a new lexical element, the latter two lead to a grammatical marker.

In the analyzed set of data, two types of lexicalizations were attested. The first involves semantic specialization within the domain of epistemic modality and the second a transition into idiomatic phrases with fully lexical functions.

The first type is found in all Slavonic languages, as in most European ones, where the central modal of possibility (in some languages also of necessity) has split into two elements: the modal itself and an epistemic adverb. A well-known example is the English *maybe*, which is derived from the modal *may* plus the copula verb *to be*. Ramat and Ricca (1998), who analyzed sentence adverbs in a wide range of European languages, found that epistemic adverbs often emerge through the fusion of a modal with a second element; in this case, then, internal constituency is lost (a process also labeled "univerbation"). Our data set revealed the following types of sentence adverbs which involve the lexicalization of modals:

(i) "modal verb.3SG" + "to be": Russian *možet byt'* 'perhaps' (compare English *maybe*)
(ii) "modal verb.3SG" + complementizer: Serbian/Croatian *možda* 'perhaps' (≈ can.that), *valjda* 'probably' (≈ one.should.that)
(iii) "modal verb.3SG": Polish *może*, Colloquial Russian *možet* 'perhaps'
(iv) "modal adverb": Czech *možná*, and *třeba* 'perhaps'

The transition from a lexical verb to a modal of possibility into an epistemic sentence adverb can be illustrated for Modern Russian, which presents both types (i) and (iii) (for the historical reconstruction, see Hansen 2010). In the first stages, we are dealing with the transition from a modal infinitival construction ($NP_{Nom}$ + Modal + $VP_{Inf}$), as in example (19), into a modal governing a complement clause, a construction traditionally called "complex subject sentence" (20):

(19) Russian
*Odin protez **mož-et služi-t'** oporoj dlja trex zubov.*
one implant can-3SG serve-INF support for three teeth
'One of those implanted dentures can function as support for three teeth.'

(20) Russian
***Mož-et by-t'**, čto èto problema ne fizičeskaja,*
can-3SG be-INF COMP this problem not physical

*a psixičeskaja.*
but psychological

'It is possible that this is not a physical, but a psychological problem.'
(*Russian National Corpus*; http://ruscorpora.ru, accessed on 6 August 2013)

In a later stage, speakers start omitting the complementizer *čto*, which leads to syntactic ambiguity. The structure can either be interpreted as a matrix verb governing a complement clause with the elliptical elision of the complementizer, or as a parenthetical insertion into a main clause.

(20') Russian
***Mož-et by-t'**, èto problema ne fizičeskaja,*
can-3SG be-INF this problem not physical

*a psichičeskaja*
but psychological.

'It is possible this is not a physical, but a psychological problem.'
or
'Maybe, this is not a physical, but a psychological problem.' (ibd.)

Finally, the copula verb becomes facultative and can be elided giving rise to sentence adverb type (iii). This final stage has been reached, for instance, in Polish, but is still not accepted in Russian formal speech. The following contexts are non-ambiguously analyzed as adverbial constructions:

(21) Polish
*A **może** siedziba pierwsz-ego biskupstw-a*
and can.3SG seat first-GEN.SG bishopric-GEN.SG

*znalaz-ł-a się na Ostrow-ie.*
situate-PST-F REFL on Ostrowa-LOC.SG

'Perhaps the first bishop's seat was in Ostrawa.'
(Zygmunt Rola, *Tajemnice Ostrowa Tumskiego*, 2000)

(22) Russian
*Minutočkoj by priš-l-i ran'še, to, **može-t**,*
minute COND come-PST-PL earlier then can-3SG
*zasta-l-i by doma.*
meet-PST-PL COND at.home
'Had you arrived one minute earlier, then you might have met him at home.'
(*Russian National Corpus*; http://ruscorpora.ru, accessed on 6 August 2013)

This reanalysis is accompanied by a shift in grounding procedures. In a sentence such as (20), the complex sentence carries a specific focal evaluative component: it expresses a speaker-based evaluation of the state of affairs encoded in the subordinate complement clause. The evaluation is treated as foregrounded, and the state of affairs as backgrounded information (see Nuyts 2001 for West Germanic). In the adverbial construction, however, the figure–ground relation is reversed and the modal statement in relation to the state of affairs is treated as background information. Apart from the reorganization of the grounding procedures, we can observe a specific semantic change when the factor of (inter)subjectivity comes in to play. Whereas the complex subject sentence clearly implies that the speaker shares his/her assumption with a broader group of people, the adverbial construction does not contain any suggestion as to whether the epistemic evaluation is subjective or intersubjective (see Nuyts 2001 for West Germanic). This language change is here treated as lexicalization, because at some point the argument frames of the elements *možet* and *byt'* merge, resulting in a single semantic and syntactic valence frame which leads to the loss of constituency boundaries between them.

Due to lack of space, I will not discuss in detail the development of the types (ii) (modal.3SG + complementizer) and (vi) (adverb). It may suffice to point out that the former is based on the fusion of a modal verb with a complementizer and the second on the lexicalization of a modal adverbial form.

The second type of lexicalization, i.e. the transition into idiomatic phrases with fully lexical functions, is cross-linguistically less common; in our sample we found it only in Czech, Slovak and in Serbian/Croatian. In these languages, the unmarked modal verb of possibility took part in a lexicalization process involving a preposition ('can' + 'for' in Czech) or the negative pronoun 'nothing' (Serbian/Croatian). In Czech, the modal *moct* 'can' can be used with the preposition *za* 'for', in which case it does not take an infinitival verbal complement. In these contexts, the meaning shifts from 'possibility' to 'to be responsible for', as illustrated by the following examples:

(23) Czech
***Za nehod-u*** [...] ***můž-e*** *řidič dodávk-y.*
for accident-ACC.SG can.3SG driver van-GEN.SG

'The driver of the van is responsible for the accident.'
(www.zpravy.aktualne.cz; accessed on 6 August 2013)

(24) Czech
*Růst cen rop-y můž-e **za zdražení***
rise price.GEN.PL oil.GEN.SG can-3SG for price.increase.ACC.SG
*benzin-u.*
petrol-GEN.SG

'The rise in the price of oil is responsible for the price increase of petrol.'
(www.archiv.ihned.cz; accessed on 6 August 2013)

Here, *moct* behaves like a lexical verb with a nominal object: it opens a valence slot for the subject encoded in the nominative case (*řidič, růst*) and a slot for the object instantiated as a prepositional phrase (*za nehodu, za zdražení*). *Moct* plus *za* lacks an infinitival phrase, the typical feature of a modal or auxiliary construction. In line with Brinton and Traugott's definition of lexicalization mentioned above (2005: 144), I would argue that we are dealing with a new lexical construction with formal and semantic properties which are not completely predictable from its constituents.

In Serbian/Croatian colloquial speech, we find a similar lexicalization process, which in contrast to the Czech element just mentioned, leads to the semantic fusion of the modal with the negative pronoun *ništa* 'nothing'. The construction *ne* + *moći* + DAT + *ništa* 'not + can + DAT + nothing' usually occurs with the modal in the third person of the present tense. We are thus dealing with a highly idiomatic phrase which usually occurs as an independent utterance, commenting on a situation mentioned in an earlier context. Its meaning can be paraphrased as 'unable to harm',[5] similar to the German idiom *die können mir nichts*, as in (25):

(25) Serbian
*[fabrikovanjem lažnih afera pokušavaju da me oteraju iz politike]*
*ali, u suštini, nemoćn-i su,* ***ne mog-u mi ništa****.*
but actually not.powerful-PL be.3.PL not can-3PL I.DAT nothing

'[They are trying to squeeze me out of politics by framing me],
but are actually powerless, they can't touch me.'
(www.glas-javnosti.rs; accessed on 6 August 2013)

---

5 See the meaning explanation in Milica Vujanić, *Rečnik srpskoga jezika* [Dictionary of the Serbian Language] (2007, Novi Sad): не може ми ништа – не прети ми никаква опасност од њега.

## 3.6 Grammatical word derivation

Finally, I would like to discuss a specific type of language change which has been suggested by van der Auwera and Plungian (1998). This change (which should be seen in the context of the emerging Slavonic aspect system) is based on grammatical word derivation. It affected the Russian "standard" modal of possibility *moč'* 'can', originally an imperfective verb without a perfective counterpart (as in all Slavonic languages). Under the pressure of the aspectual system at the end of the 18th century, the new derivation *s-moč'* with the perfective prefix *s-* emerged (Hansen 2001: 368–369). In the past tense form (26), it expresses the actualization of a participant-external or internal possibility which comes close to the meaning 'to manage to do something'. In the present tense, it denotes possibility in the future as in example (27).

(26) Russian
*Drug-ogo       gitarist-a        my  **naj-ti***
other-ACC.SG guitarist-ACC.SG we find-INF

*tak i ne  **s-mog-l-i**.*
thus not PFV-can-PST-PL

'We, therefore were unable to find another guitarist.'

(Andrej Astvacaturov, *Ljudi v golom*, 2009)

(27) Russian
***Prokormi-t'*** *140 mln.      naseleni-ja,        tol'ko*
feed-INF    140 million population-GEN.SG only

*prodava-ja neft' i    gaz stran-a          ne  **s-može-t**.*
sell-CVB   oil and gas country-NOM.SG not PFV-can-3SG

'The country will not be able/will not manage to support a population of 140 million by only selling oil and gas.'

(www.zr.ru; accessed on 6 August 2013)

Whereas the locus of change in lexicalization (see Section 3.5) is a specific communicative context, word derivation takes place on the level of the lexicon. The former is gradual and the latter is abrupt. Our set of data revealed some more instances where a modern modal appeared as a building block in a derivation process giving rise to new fully lexical elements; e.g. Polish *zaniemóc* 'to fall ill < *móc* 'can'. The diachronic analysis, however, shows that these derivations are based on the pre-modal lexical meanings. Russian *smoč'*, therefore, is the only instance of word derivation following the grammaticalization of a modal.

## 4 Conclusion and outlook

This is the first study to present an account of language change following regular grammaticalization. It has been demonstrated that grammaticalization processes do not represent the final stage in the history of a construction. In this regard, I have proposed a typology that includes at least six processes: secondary grammaticalization, marginalization, degrammaticalization, retraction, lexicalization and grammatical word derivation. Whereas secondary grammaticalization, degrammaticalization, retraction and lexicalization can be considered established phenomena which have been discussed by many scholars, marginalization and word derivation have received much less attention. I have claimed that marginalization should be distinguished as a process *sui generis* as it does not lead to the rise of unmarked, highly frequent grammatical operators, but to elements with a low degree of entrenchment in the language system. An exception was found in Russian, where a fully-fledged modal was included in a grammatical derivation process. A second result of this explanatory study concerns negative evidence, i.e. types of processes that are not attested. First, it is worth mentioning that there was no evidence of the transition of a modal into an affix. This leads us to the conclusion that the known verb-to-affix cline occurs less frequently than expected. Second, modals do not seem to be suitable for regular lexical word derivation or conversion. In addition, I would like to point out that as this study is limited to modality and a single language family, we can presume that the data do not cover all types of post-grammaticalization processes. In conclusion, I would like to suggest that future research consider both the peculiarities of the functional domain of modality, as well as the specific features of Slavonic languages, for instance, their morphological conservatism. It is clear therefore that we need more systematic cross-linguistic studies on post-grammaticalization-processes covering further domains and languages!

## Abbreviations

1/2/3 = first/second/third person; ACC = accusative; ART = article; AUX = auxiliary; COMP = complementizer; COND = conditional; CVB = converb; DAT = dative; DEF = definite; F = feminine; GEN = genitive; INF = infinitive; INS = instrumental; LOC = locative; N = neuter; NOM = nominative; PFV = perfective; PL = plural; PREP = prepositive; PROH = prohibitive; PST = past; PTCP = participle; REFL = reflexive; SG = singular

# References

Besters-Dilger, Juliane, Ana Drobnjaković & Björn Hansen. 2009. Modals in the Slavonic languages. In Björn Hansen & Ferdinand de Haan (eds.), *Modals in the languages of Europe: A reference work*, 167–199. Berlin: Mouton de Gruyter.

Brinton, Laurel J. & Elizabeth Closs Traugott. 2005. *Lexicalization and language change*. Cambridge: Cambridge University Press.

Diepeveen, Janneke, Ronny Boogaart, Jenneke Brantjes, Pieter Byloo, Theo Janssen & Jan Nuyts. 2006. *Modale uitdrukkingen in Belgisch-Nederlands en Nederlands-Nederlands: Corpusonderzoek en enquête* [Modal expressions in Belgian Dutch and Dutch Dutch: Corpus research and surveys]. Amsterdam: Stichting Neerlandistiek / Münster: Nodus.

Drobnjaković, Ana. 2009. *The grammaticalization of Serbian tense, aspectual and modal auxiliaries*. Leuven: University of Leuven dissertation.

Francis, Elaine J. & Laura A. Michaelis (eds.). 2003. *Mismatch: Form–function incongruity and architecture of grammar*. California, CSLI Publications.

Fried, Mirjam & Jan-Ola Östman. 2004. Construction grammar: A thumbnail sketch. In Mirjam Fried & Jan-Ola Östman (eds.), *Construction grammar in a cross-language perspective*, 11–87. Amsterdam: John Benjamins.

Hansen, Björn. 2000. The German modal verb 'müssen' and the Slavonic Languages – The reconstruction of a success story. In *Scando Slavica* 46, 77–93.

Hansen, Björn. 2001. *Das Modalauxiliar im Slavischen. Grammatikalisierung und Semantik im Russischen, Polnischen, Serbischen/Kroatischen und Altkirchenslavischen* (Slavolinguistica 2). München: Verlag Otto Sagner. (http://epub.uni-regensburg.de/11226/).

Hansen, Björn. 2004. The boundaries of grammaticalization: The case of modals in Russian, Polish and Serbian/Croatian. In Walter Bisang, Nikolaus Himmelmann & Björn Wiemer (eds.), *What makes grammaticalization? A look from its fringes and its components*, 245–271. Berlin: Mouton de Gruyter.

Hansen, Björn. 2009. The hypothetical use of Polish 'mieć plus Infinitive' revisited. In Tilman Berger, Markus Giger, Sibylle Kurt & Imke Mendoza (eds.), Von grammatischen Kategorien und sprachlichen Weltbildern – Die Slavia von der Sprachgeschichte bis zur Politsprache. Festschrift für Daniel Weiss zum 60. Geburtstag (Wiener Slawistischer Almanach – Sonderband 73), 177–185. München: Verlag Otto Sagner.

Hansen, Björn. 2010. A constructional approach to the gradual rise of epistemic sentence adverbs in Russian. In Björn Hansen & Jasmina Grković-Major (eds.), *Diachronic Slavonic syntax: Gradual changes in focus* (Wiener Slawistischer Almanach – Sonderband 74), 75–87. München: Verlag Otto Sagner,.

Hansen, Björn. 2014. The syntax of modal polyfunctionality revisited: Evidence from the languages of Europe. In Elisabeth Leiss & Werner Abraham (eds.), *Modes of modality. Modality, typology, and universal grammar*, 89–126. Amsterdam: John Benjamins.

Hansen, Björn & Ferdinand de Haan (eds.). 2009. *Modals in the languages of Europe: A reference work*. Berlin: Mouton de Gruyter.

Hansen, Björn, Marek Nekula & Monika Banášová. 2011. Nová konstrukce „Karla Gotta nemusím" v češtině a slovenštině: Případ lexikalizace, pragmatikalizace nebo začínající degramatikalizace? [The new construction "Karla Gotta nemusím" in Czech and Slovak: A case of lexicalization, pragmaticalization or incipient degrammaticalization?] *Slovo a slovesnost* 72. 243–267.

Haspelmath, Martin. 2004. On directionality in language change with particular reference to grammaticalization. In Olga Fischer, Muriel Norde & Harry Perridon (eds.), *Up and down the cline: The nature of* grammaticalization, 17–44. Amsterdam: John Benjamins,.
Havránek, Bohuslav (ed.). 1980. *Etymologický slovník slovanských jazyků. Slova gramatická a zájmena* [Etymological dictionary of the Slavonic languages: Grammatical words and pronouns]. Praha: Academia.
Himmelmann, Nikolaus P. 2004. Lexicalization and grammaticalization: Opposite or orthogonal? In Walter Bisang, Nikolaus Himmelmann & Björn Wiemer (eds.), *What makes grammaticalization? A look from its fringes and its* components, 21–44. Berlin: Mouton de Gruyter.
Hopper, Paul J. & Elizabeth Closs Traugott. 2003. *Grammaticalization*. Cambridge: Cambridge University Press.
Kalogjera, Damir. 1982. *The English modals and their equivalents in Serbo-Croatian*. Zagreb: Institute of Linguistics, Faculty of Philosophy, University of Zagreb.
Kątny, Andrzej. 1980. *Die Modalverben und Modaladverben im Deutschen und Polnischen*. Rzeszów: Wydawnictwo Wyższej Szkoły Pedagogicznej.
Kuteva, Tania. 2001. *Auxiliation: An enquiry into the nature of grammaticalization*. Oxford: Oxford University Press.
Lehmann, Christian. 2002. New reflections on grammaticalization and lexicalization. In Ilse Wischer & Gabriele Diewald (eds.), *New reflections on grammaticalization*, 1–18. Amsterdam: John Benjamins.
Norde, Muriel. 2009. *Degrammaticalization*. Oxford: Oxford University Press.
Nuyts, Jan. 2001. *Epistemic modality, language and conceptualization*. Amsterdam: John Benjamins.
Nuyts, Jan. 2013. De-auxiliarization without de-modalization in the Dutch core modals: A case of collective degrammaticalization? *Language Sciences* 36. 124–133.
Panevová, Jarmila, Eva Benešová & Petr Sgall (eds.). 1971. *Čas a modalita v češtině* [Tense and modality in Czech]. Praha: Univ. Karlova.
Ramat, Paolo & Davide Ricca. 1998. Sentence adverbs in the languages of Europe. In Johan van der Auwera (ed.), *Adverbial constructions in the languages of Europe*, 187–277. Berlin: Mouton de Gruyter.
*Rječnik hrvatskoga ili srpskoga jezika* I–XXIII [Dictionary of the Serbian or Croatian language I–XXIII]. 1880–1976. Zagreb: Iugoslavenska Akademija znanosti i umjetnosti.
Rytel, Danuta. 1982. *Leksykalne środki wyrażania modalności w języku czeskim i polskim* [Lexical means of the expression of modality in Czech and Polish]. Wrocław: Zakład narodowy im. Ossolińskich.
Šatunovskij, Ilja B. 1996. *Semantika predloženija i nereferentnye slova: Značenie. Kommunikativnaja perspektiva. Pragmatika* [The semantics of the sentence and non-referential words: Meaning, communicative perspective, pragmatics]. Moskva: Škola "Jazyki Russkoj Kul'tury".
Schmid, Hans-Jörg. 2007. Entrenchment, salience and basic levels. In Dirk Geeraerts & Hubert Cuyckens (eds.), *The Oxford handbook of cognitive linguistics*, 117–138. Oxford: Oxford University Press.
Štícha, František. 2003. *Česko-německá srovnávací gramatika* [Czech-German contrastive Grammar]. Praha: Argo.
van der Auwera, Johan. 2002. More thoughts on degrammaticalization. In Ilse Wischer & Gabriele Diewald (eds.), *New reflections on grammaticalization*, 19–29. Amsterdam: John Benjamins.
van der Auwera, Johan & Vladimir A. Plungian. 1998. Modality's semantic map. *Linguistic Typology* 2(1). 79–124.

Vaulina, Svetlana S. 1988. *Ėvoljucija sredstv vyraženia modal'nosti v russkom jazyke (XI–XVII vv.)* [The historical development of expressions of modality in Russian (11th to 17th century)]. Leningrad: Nauka.

Weiss, Daniel Ms. *Semantyka konstrukcji 'mieć + bezokolicznik': Próba rozstrzygnięcia polisemii* [The semantics of the construction *mieć* + infinitive: A tentative analysis of its polysemy]. Hamburg

Willis, David. 2007. Syntactic lexicalization as a new type of degrammaticalization. *Linguistics* 45. 271–310.

Helle Metslang
# 10 Can a language be forced? The case of Estonian

**Abstract:** This study focuses on forced grammaticalization, in which a new form or construction is introduced into a language on the basis of the material of that same language, but without a prior step-by-step development or bridging contexts. Two types of forced grammaticalization can be distinguished: contact-induced and language-internal forced grammaticalization. In the course of contact-induced forced grammaticalization, the result of a grammaticalization process is adopted from the model language into the replica language without there being a grammaticalization process in the latter. The developers of Old Written Estonian, for whom Estonian was a second language, proceeded in this fashion, introducing, for instance, articles and future constructions into the language. Language-internal forced grammaticalization involves the introduction of innovations which are based on the language's own material, but for which no natural evolution can be observed. Innovations in Estonian brought about through language-internal forced grammaticalization include new morphological verb and adjective forms as well as back-formed verbs. The development of Standard Estonian has seen examples of both types of forced grammaticalization. The mechanisms, causes and scope of these phenomena require further investigation.

## 1 Forced grammaticalization: A result without a gradual process

In addition to traditional gradual grammaticalization, instances of grammaticalization have been attested where a more grammaticalized linguistic unit or structure has been adopted earlier than is to be expected by the natural development of the linguistic material. Usually, these findings concern language change in a contact situation. Three types of contact-induced grammaticalization have been identified: (i) contact-induced "ordinary" grammaticalization, i.e. a grammatical category of the model language is created in the replica language through grammaticalization, on the basis of source material in the replica language for which there is no corresponding structure in the donor language; (ii) replica grammaticalization, i.e. a grammatical category of the model language is created in the replica language from a source structure which has a replica in the model language; (iii) apparent grammaticalization / polysemy copying / selective copying, i.e. the ready-made adoption in the replica language of a corresponding grammatical element or structure from the model language (Heine and Kuteva 2005; Kolehmainen and Nordlund 2011). Note that, in this third type, the innovation (new grammatical category) in the replica language does not emerge from a grammaticalization *process*; it only copies the *result* of a grammaticalization process.

The Estonian language – which, because of its geographical position, has always witnessed multiple contacts and which, during the period of missionary linguistics,[1] was described and standardized by German intellectuals (e.g. Ziegelmann and Winkler 2006: 45; Kilgi 2012: 10) – exhibits all three types of contact-induced grammaticalization. The present article will focus on the last type. Following Nau (1995), this exceptional type of language change will be called "forced grammaticalization" (*Zwangsgrammatikalisierung*). Nau (1995: 121–122) pointed out this type when discussing the adoption of articles in Old Written Estonian and Latvian, but she did not define it. The ethnically German language reformers of Standard Estonian and Latvian introduced as articles – semantically empty noun satellites – the Estonian words *see* 'this' and *üks* 'one' and the Latvian words *tas* 'this' and *viens* 'one'. Thus, they made use of polysemous patterns in their native language German, i.e. the polysemy between the demonstrative 'this' and the definite article, and the polysemy between the numeral 'one' and the indefinite article, whereby the articles represent a late stage of a multi-stage grammaticalization process, while it is likely that, among the native speakers of Estonian and Latvian, the grammaticalization of articles had not yet begun (see also Heine and Kuteva 2005: 252).

Similar abrupt grammaticalization, where only the end product is adopted without going through the process, has been observed in other instances of strong language contact, for example, in pidgin languages, whose grammars are typically formed from the ready-made patterns of the source language (Siegel 2008: 272–273), as well as in some varieties of English (Ziegeler, this volume). In all the above cases, the second language of language developers and speakers adopts categories and patterns grammaticalized in their native language (see Heine and Kuteva 2005: 238–239). In the case of missionary linguistics, the transfer could also have gone from the second language of non-native language developers to the native languages of indigenous people.

---

1 "Missionary linguistics comprises the lexicographic and grammatical studies that have resulted from a cross-cultural and cross-linguistic exchange within the context of missionary work, typically being made in description of a non-native language" (Breitenbach 2008: 58).

The abrupt creation of new structures need not always be contact-induced, however. Standard Estonian, for instance, witnessed such grammatical changes in the 20th and 21st centuries when the language was being developed by native-speaker language reformers. It is likely that the same has occurred in the standardization of other languages. In this paper, we will expand the notion of forced grammaticalization to include such cases and define it more broadly: in forced grammaticalization, a grammatical resource of a language is formed from the material of the language itself straight into its final-stage shape without a natural step-by-step grammaticalization process. In other words, our definition of forced grammaticalization does not specify any particular language-internal or language-external causes or motivating factors, such as polysemy, language contact, or the mother tongue (and the particular variant thereof) spoken by the speech community in question. Such factors are to be identified in the course of the investigation of forced grammaticalization, not to be presumed from the outset.

In this paper, I will discuss some examples of grammatical structures in written and Standard Estonian which, as earlier studies have shown, fall under the definition of forced grammaticalization as described above. These examples belong to different levels and components of grammatical structure: the morphosyntax of the predicate and the noun phrase, the inflectional paradigms of verbs, nouns and adjectives, and conjunctions. I will also present some examples from the closely related language of Finnish, for the purpose of comparison (see also Metslang 2011). The goal is to give a first outline of forced grammaticalization, of some of its mechanisms and background factors and of possible further developments. The study will first focus on some cases of contact-induced forced grammaticalization in Old Written Estonian (Section 3) and then discuss language-internal forced grammaticalization in 20th- and 21st-century Standard Estonian (Section 4). Language-internal forced degrammaticalization will be dealt with briefly in Section 5.

# 2 Developmental history of Standard Estonian: From missionary linguistics to Estonian-medium language development

The Estonian language[2] developed from local tribal dialects between the 13th and 16th centuries. The period of the early development of Estonian coincides

---

[2] An overview of the principal features of Estonian can be found in Erelt (2007) and Metslang (2009). For a comprehensive treatment of the development of Standard Estonian, see Laanekask and Erelt (2007).

with the period of the crusades to the lands surrounding the Baltic Sea, when Estonia fell into the hands of foreign powers. In the 13th to 19th centuries, the Germans constituted the upper class in Estonia and the Estonians the lower class. The language of the rulers and colonists was Low German and later also High German. The history of Standard Estonian started within the context of missionary linguistics. The earliest printed texts made their appearance in the 16th century. In the period of Old Written Estonian (from the early 16th century to the mid-19th century), the language planners and users were Germans for whom Estonian was a second language. German and Latin served as the main models for the description and use of Estonian. The majority of the texts in this old written language were translated from German by sticking closely to the original.

Thus, the Estonian standard as developed by Germans was based on their interlanguage, which displayed many features of an incompletely acquired language (see Makoni and Pennycook 2007: 7; Schlotthauer 2010: 267).[3] Other phenomena characteristic of missionary linguistics are invented categories in the language described and Eurocentric standardization. Indigenous people perceive the written form of the indigenous language as something that is intended for the missionaries rather than for them. This language variety and the knowledge presented in it are regarded as superior to the spoken variety of the indigenous people and what is expressed in it (Nowak 1999: 160; Makoni and Pennycook 2007: 7; Menezes de Souza 2007: 142–143, 165). Written Estonian was the prestigious variety of Estonian during the period of missionary linguistics, i.e. from the early 17th century to the mid-19th century. Presumably, Standard Estonian (and the common Estonian that developed out of it) is based on a number of varieties: native Estonian dialects, non-native written and spoken Estonian varieties as used by Germans, the mixed language of communication between Estonians and Germans that probably existed in towns, and early religious spoken Estonian based on Latin texts (developed by native Estonians) (Ross 2005).

The 19th century witnessed the first native Estonian intellectuals who took over the standardization of Estonian. The first half of the 20th century saw an accelerated development of Standard Estonian, including an increased push for

---

[3] Typical features of interlanguage are the use of mother tongue patterns in the target language and the disproportionate use of target language patterns. Earlier research has found many German-like features in Old Written Estonian, as well as the overuse of analytical constructions (Kask 1970; Habicht 2001).

language reform. Efforts were made to get rid of German-style features, with Finnish being used as a model instead: as the language of the northern neighbors, Finnish is similar to Estonian and intelligible to speakers of the latter language. This change in orientation brought about a change in the typological characteristics of the standard language: German-style analyticity began to be replaced by Finnish-style syntheticity.

A comparison of the developments of Standard Estonian and Standard Finnish (e.g. Habicht et al. 2011) reveals that, while the development of Finnish is impacted by the ruling Swedish language, there is no context of missionary linguistics. Standard Finnish emerged during roughly the same period as Standard Estonian. Finland was part of the Swedish kingdom until 1809 and Finnish was in the sphere of Swedish influence. The developers of Standard Finnish were mostly not native Finns but rather Swedes who used Finnish as a second language. Swedish was the language of education, administration, culture, science and literature, and most scholars were Swedes. Nevertheless, native speakers of Finnish played a slightly more important role in the development of Standard Finnish, even in its earlier stages, than native speakers of Estonian did for the development of Estonian. There were also some Finnish scholars who were bilingual and the standard language was developed by both non-native and native speakers. Presumably, Finnish was the native language of Agricola, the founder of Standard Finnish. Standard Finnish, which was used mostly as a religious language, also had a huge impact on the vernacular (Kolehmainen and Nordlund 2011: 11). The 19th century witnessed puristic language standardization, including the avoidance of Swedishisms. For a long time, the description and development of Finnish was ahead of that of Estonian (thanks to a more democratic state, to the more prestigious status of the language and to linguists who knew Finnish). For this reason, since the 19th century, many Estonian linguists have regarded the description and planning of Finnish as a model for their own work.

# 3 Contact-induced forced grammaticalization

The development of Old Written Estonian with German as its model brought about the introduction of new categories and constructions in descriptions of Estonian and in Estonian texts. In this section, two examples discussed in the literature will be presented: articles and future constructions.

## 3.1 Articles

The use of articles in Old Written Estonian, especially in the 17th century, followed the German use rather closely, as is shown by the Estonian sentence in (1) and its German parallel[4] in (2).[5]

(1) *Esaias pajatap:* **Se** taiwas <u>sah-p</u> kudt **üx** suitz
    Isaiah says ART.DEF heaven FUT-3SG like ART.INDEF smoke

   <u>erra-kaddo-ma</u> / ninck **se** mah kudt
   PFV.PTCL-vanish-mINF and ART.DEF earth like

   **üx** rihd wannax <u>sah-ma:</u> ninck Johannes
   ART.INDEF garment old.TRNSL get-mINF and John

   ütlep; **Se** ilm lehp hucka omma himmo kahs.
   says ART.DEF world go.3SG doom.ILL own desire COM

   'Isaiah says: **the** heavens <u>shall vanish</u> like smoke, and **the** earth <u>will wear out</u> like **a** garment; and John says: **the** world shall perish in its desire.'        (*Corpus of Old Written Estonian* (COWE), 1641)

(2) German (parallel text)
    *Esaias spricht:* **Der** Himmel <u>wird</u> wie **ein** rauch <u>vergehen</u> / vnd **die** Erde wie **ein** kleid <u>veralten</u>; vnd Johannes sagt; **Die** Welt vergehet mit jhrer lust.

   'Isaiah says: **the** heavens <u>shall vanish</u> away like smoke, and **the** earth <u>will wear out</u> like **a** garment; and John says: **the** world shall perish in its desire.'        (COWE, 1641)

Over time, article usage became more creative, as German-speaking reformers of Estonian tried to establish their own rules and did not always copy the article usage in German texts. Some usage types in Estonian reflect different stages of the grammaticalization of articles. The article as a grammatical category clearly existed in the written language of the 17th and 18th centuries, but this usage was discontinued in more recent stages of the language which increasingly focused on mother tongue competence. Contemporary Estonian, especially in its colloquial varieties, has article uses that are typical of initial stages of article development, such as (3), where the word *see* 'this, the' modifies a noun denoting an entity familiar to the discourse participants from the previous context,

---

[4] 17th-century Estonian religious texts were typically accompanied by parallel texts in German, the mother tongue of the writer and the reader.
[5] Unless indicated otherwise, the examples in this paper are from Estonian.

and (4), where the word *üks* 'one, a' indicates that the entity is indefinite for the listener. One cannot rule out the possibility that such uses already existed in native speaker speech in earlier centuries and that more recent language development has simply disregarded them. Similar processes can be observed in the development of Finnish (Laury 1997; Pajusalu 1997; Heine and Kuteva 2006; Habicht et al. 2011; Kolehmainen and Nordlund 2011).

(3) *Irina ütleb, et  tema küll ei  tea,     mis  asi*
    Irina says  that s/he PTCL NEG know.CNG what thing
    ***see***    *abielukriis    on.*
    ART.DEF marriage.crisis is
    'Irina says that she doesn't actually know what **the** marriage crisis is.'
    (Keeleveeb, weekly *Kroonika*, 2000)

(4) *Mul*    ***ühe-l***         *tuttava-l         täpselt sama problem.*
    1SG.ADE ART.INDEF-ADE acquaintance-ADE exactly same problem
    '**An** acquaintance of mine has exactly the same problem.'
    (Keeleveeb, Forum, 1997)

## 3.2 Future constructions

Present-day Estonian, like other Finnic languages, has no regular grammatical future, but there are two main constructions with quasi-auxiliary verbs and infinitives that can be used for future time reference: *hakkama* 'begin' and *saama* 'get, become' (i.e. the auxiliary verb *saama* and the *ma*-infinitive of the main verb).[6] The 'begin' type of future construction is typical of many Finno-Ugric languages. It is probably the result of a long historical development

---

[6] Estonian morphology is rich in infinitive verb forms, including the *da*-infinitive, the *ma*-infinitive or the supine, the *des*-form or the gerund and four participles. The *da*-infinitive (*ela-da*) and the *ma*-infinitive (*ela-ma*) both mean 'to write' but have different usage contexts. The *ma*-infinitive has several case forms and the *ma*-marked form itself is illative in origin. The present personal participle marked by *-v/-va* (nominative *ela-v*/genitive *ela-va* 'living') has given rise to some other forms: the nominative plural of the participle *ela-va-d* yielded the third-person form in *-vad* (*ela-vad* '(they) live'), and the partitive form of the participle *ela-va-t* yielded the *vat*-marked infinitive *ela-vat* 'living'. The latter in turn gave rise to the finite oblique mood form *ela-vat* 'is reported to live'. The past participle markers are *-nud* in the personal and *-tud* in the impersonal and have been used by language reformers to create innovative past forms.

and is unknown in the Indo-European languages that have influenced Estonian. By contrast, the 'become' type, which is most widespread in Old Written Estonian, is likely to have developed by adopting the pattern of the German *werden* 'become' future (Metslang 1994, Metslang 1996a; Dahl 2000), as suggested by the underlined parts in (1) and (2). In Standard High German, the *werden* future has been the predominant type of future since the 16th century. It was promoted especially by Luther (Mägiste 1936). The *saama* future was common in 17th-century texts but, thereafter, its frequency dropped. It is likely that speakers perceived the construction as foreign (Kilgi 2010: 168–169). Nevertheless, it was preserved in the standard language, and it occurs, for example, in texts by Otto Wilhelm Masing, a cultural figure with Estonian roots who is regarded as the best user of the Estonian language in the first half of the 19th century, as in (5).

(5) *Kui needsinnatsed Pühhapäwa wahheluggemised teie*
    if    these        Sunday      readings        you.GEN

   *mele       pärrast peaksid      olle-ma, siis* **saa-b**
   mind.GEN after    shall.COND.PL be-mINF then FUT-3SG

   *peagi teine    ja   kolmas jaggu* **wälja-tulle-ma**,
   soon  second and third   part   out-come-mINF

   *ning siis ka  se  tähhekenne   omma õige*
   and then also this character.DIM own  right.GEN

   *modi        järrele kirjas*    **olle-ma**.
   manner.GEN after   writing.INE be-mINF

   'Should these Sunday readings be to your liking, then also the second and the third part **will soon come out**, and then also this little character **will be** written in the proper manner.'                    (COWE, 1818)

Although 20th-century language planners tried to discourage the use of the *saama* future, it is still used in Contemporary Estonian. It is not a regular grammatical tense form, however, and combines mostly with the verb *olema* 'be' and other static verbs. The language of the 21st century shows some increase in the use of the *saama* future as a pure future without any extra meanings. In addition, although *olema* may be the predominant lexical verb, as in (6), other combinations occur too, such as *saab toimuma* 'will happen, will take place', *saab juhtuma* 'will happen' (7), *saab mängima* 'will play' and *saab levima* 'will spread' (Prass 2011). Also, while the *saama* future was previously used mostly in the written language, in recent times its usage has become increasingly informal.

(6) *Sünnitajate     põlvkond    püsib      suuruses 25 000*
parturient.PL.GEN generation remain.3SG size.INE 25,000

*kuni aastani  2015 [(2020)], pärast seda   **saa-b***
until year.TRM 2015 2020     after this.PRTV FUT-3SG

*see **ole-ma** 13 000.*
this be-mINF 13,000

'The size of the birthing generation **will be** about 25,000 until the year 2015 [(2020)], thereafter it will be 13,000.'

(Keeleveeb, journal *Horisont*, 1998)

(7) *Sama juhtus      ka   aasta tagasi ja   ilmselt    **saa-b***
same happened also year ago    and apparently FUT-3SG

***juhtu-ma**    edaspidigi.*
happen-mINF henceforth.PTCL

'The same happened also a year ago and **will** apparently **happen** also in future.'

(Keeleveeb, diary *Postimees*, 1996)

There is no direct source construction in Estonian which could have served as a basis for the grammaticalization of the *saama* future. The original meaning of the Finnic stem *\*sa-* is 'come'. This meaning developed into 'get, become' in the other Finnic languages too; in the Olonetsian and Finnish dialects (Tauli 1966: 81), for instance, the form with the 'get, become' sense started to be used for future reference in combination with the infinitive of the main verb. These future constructions in genetically related languages and the existence of the construction with the infinitive in Estonian led Mägiste (1936) to doubt the foreign character of the *saama* future. However, in Estonian, *saama* with the infinitive has the rather specific lexical meaning of 'get away, succeed despite difficult circumstances' and is mostly used in the past tense form in narratives, as in (8), which is not a suitable basis for the future use. This meaning is too narrow to serve as a basis for grammaticalization and has not left any traces in the use of the *saama* future. Thus, one cannot establish a link between the possible source structure and the future in Estonian: the future was adopted in a ready-made form by bypassing some stages of the grammaticalization chain.

(8) *Vang    **sa-i**    **põgene-ma**.*[7]
prisoner get-3SG escape-mINF

'The prisoner **managed to escape**.'

---

[7] Unsourced examples are constructed by the author, relying on her native-speaker intuition.

Figure 1 (based on Metslang 1997: 229) shows the the sudden transition to a future auxiliary in the grammaticalization chain of the verb *saama*.[8] Stage I represents the Finnic meaning 'come' of the verb, which is found neither in Contemporary nor in Old Written Estonian (Tragel and Habicht 2012). At stage II, we can distinguish two usages of *saama*: on the one hand, it has the meaning 'become', as in (9), which serves as the source of the future use, but in this meaning, *saama* does not occur with the infinitive of another verb.

(9) Mees **saa-b** vihase-ks.
    man  get-3SG  angry-TRNSL
    'The man **is getting** angry.'

On the other hand, *saama* may be used in a source construction with the infinitive; this construction is formally suitable for the expression of future, but *saama* here means 'manage', and it is therefore semantically unsuitable as a direct source of future. Stage III, i.e. before the grammaticalization into a future marker, is the stage which contains a formally as well as semantically suitable structure, as the verb meaning 'become' combines with the infinitive. However, this stage has not been observed in Estonian. It was skipped in the formation of the future, which started immediately with stage IV. The absence of a direct source structure could be regarded as a reason why the use of the *saama* future was adopted slowly by native speakers of Estonian.

| I → | II → | III (absent) → | IV |
|---|---|---|---|
| saab | saab vihaseks | (BECOME + mINF) | saab olema |
| 'comes' | 'becomes angry' | | 'will be' |
| (COME) | (BECOME) | | saab elama |
| | saab põgenema | | 'will live' |
| | 'manages to escape' | | (FUT + mINF) |
| | (SUCCEED.COME/GO + mINF) | | |

**Figure 1:** Developmental stages of the *saama* future

In the written Estonian of the 17th and 18th centuries, the verbs *tahtma* 'want' and *pidama* 'must, have to' were also used as future auxiliaries, as (10) and (12) show. This use was inspired by the Low German *wollen* and *sollen* futures in (11) and (13). In the model language, these auxiliaries show the natural development from modality to future: intention > future and necessity > future. In Estonian, we are again dealing with a leap in the grammaticalization process: a more abstract

---

**8** In the figure, the central generalized meaning of the verb *saama* is in small caps.

sense than the present use of the modal verbs was adopted in Old Written Estonian through translations. These future constructions are not found in Contemporary Estonian (Habicht 2001; Habicht et al. 2010; Kilgi 2010; cf. Dahl 2000).

(10) *Minna* **taha-n** *sedda* **tegke-ma** / *minna* **taha-n**
I want-1SG this.PRTV do-mINF I want-1SG

**töst-ma** / **kand-ma** / *ninck* **erra-pehst-ma** / *minna*
lift-mINF carry-mINF and PFV.PTCL-save-mINF I

**taha-n** *teid röhmusta-ma* / *kudt öhe*
want-1SG you.PRTV cheer-mINF like ART.INDEF.GEN

*Lapse se Emma tröhstip.*
child.GEN ART.DEF mother consoles

'I **will do** it, I **will lift, carry,** and **save, I will** cheer you like a mother consoles her child.'
(COWE, 1641; example taken from Habicht et al. 2010: 137)

(11) German (parallel text)
*Jch* **wil** *es* **thun** / *ich* **wil heben** / **tragen** *vnd* **erretten** / *Jch* **wil** *euch* **trösten** / *wie einen seine Mutter tröstet.*
'I **will do** it, I **will lift, carry,** and **save, I will** cheer you like a mother consoles her child.'
(COWE, 1641; example taken from Habicht et al. 2010: 137)

(12) *Ollet sinna*/ *ke* **pea-p** **tulle-ma**.
be.2SG you.SG who must-3SG come-mINF
'You are the one who **must / will come.**' (COWE, 1641)

(13) German (parallel text)
*Bistu/der da* **kommen sol**.
'You are the one who **must / will come.**' (COWE, 1641)

## 3.3 Comparison with the future in Finnish

Old Written Finnish too had the future auxiliaries *pitää* 'must' (*pitää tekemän*[9] 'must do') and *tahtoa* 'want' (*tahdon tehdä* 'I want to do'), but they were

---

[9] The Finnish infinitive verb forms are similar to the Estonian ones. Finnish has the *ma/mä*-infinitive (e.g. *tekemään* 'to do') and the *a/ä*-infinitive (e.g. *tehdä* 'to do'), which correspond to the Estonian *ma-* and *da*-infinitives. *Tekemän* is an instructive form of the *ma/mä*-infinitive. The present participle in Finnish has the marker *-va/vä*.

modeled on the Swedish future constructions with *skola* 'intend' and *vilja* 'will'. These modal-based constructions fell into disuse. The archaic and high-style future construction *on tekevä*, by contrast, is still used to a limited extent nowadays. It consists of the present form of the verb *olla* 'be' and the present active participle (suffix *-va/vä*) of the main verb. In other words, none of the components has a future meaning. In some dialects, this construction has probably expressed necessity, but the future interpretation occurs only in the standard language. The construction started to develop into a future marker in the work of Agricola in the 16th century and became established in the 1642 translation of the Bible, following the pattern of the source languages (Swedish *warder görande(s)* and Latin *facturus est*). Its frequent use in the expression *on tuleva* in the Creed, as in (14) – cf. Latin *venturus est* in (15) – acted as a contributing factor to the adoption of the future interpretation. Agricola lived his life surrounded by his texts and in the course of his translation work became accustomed to a foreign pattern, which at least in the Creed had probably been used before his time. However, in Agricola's texts the *on tekevä* future construction acquired a broader usage; in addition to direct translations following the pattern of the original, he began to use it in other situations as well, as a general future construction. (Itkonen-Kaila 1993). Thus, the developers of the standard language initiated the shift from necessity to future, which did not occur in the natural development of the language.

(14) Finnish
*Ja* **on** *sieltä* **tule-va** *tuomitsemaan*
and is from.there come-PRS.PTCP judge.mINF
*eläviä ja kuolleita.*
live.PRS.PTCP.PL.PRTV and die.PST.PTCP.PL.PRTV
'And He **shall come** again with glory to judge both the quick and the dead.'
(Credo, http://www.evl.fi/katekismus/uskontunnustus/uskontunnustus.html; last accessed on 19 January 2012)

(15) Latin
*Et iterum* **venturus est** *cum gloria judicare vivos et mortuos: cujus regni non erit finis.*
'And He **shall come** again with glory to judge both the quick and the dead.'
(Credo, http://gavvie.tripod.com/prayers.html#NC; last accessed on 19 January 2012)

Both in Estonian and Finnish, means of future reference were needed when translating and writing religious texts, and the patterns used are all cases of forced grammaticalization based on patterns of the contact languages. Note that the language-external factors of Finnish *on tekevä* are somewhere between the two types of forced grammaticalization in Estonian: the construction was introduced by a native language reformer under strong influence from another language.

The Estonian *saama* and the Finnish *on tekevä* futures still occur, although their use is restricted and is characteristic of high style. The Estonian *saama*-future even shows some further development, in terms of both its frequency of use and the range of verbs it is used with. However, the question remains why these constructions have survived and the others (with the auxiliaries *pidama/pitää* 'must' and *tahtma/tahtoa* 'want') have disappeared. Could this be due to the fact that the contact language's support of the 'must' and 'want' futures disappeared? Did they not become well-established enough in texts? Or could it be due to the fact that there were other future auxiliaries in the process of grammaticalization in native language use (e.g. Estonian *hakkama* 'begin' and Finnish *tulla* 'come')? Surprisingly, it seems that the survival of the *saama*-future was also supported by its sweeping forced grammaticalization and the gap in the grammaticalization chain: the *saama* construction was not polysemous and there was no influence from other meanings in earlier stages of its development – it was purely an indicator of future meaning. At the same time, the *pidama* and *tahtma* constructions were polysemous, both occurring with a future meaning and with modal meanings, and their use as future markers finally disappeared (Kilgi 2010: 179).

Contact-induced forced grammaticalization occurred in both languages in a situation of multilingualism and is characterized by the adoption of ready-made new forms, categories and functions, by calques and by bypassing some stages of traditional development chains. Forced grammaticalization occurred in the course of the development of the written/standard language when contact-induced and language-internal changes were intertwined. As for the mechanisms of contact-induced influence (Thomason 2001: 129–156), one can find both unconscious negotiation of structural features between the contact languages and conscious decision-making. The innovations were initiated by an influential minority as compared to the native speaker community, and included reformers, users of the literary language and translators. The channels of dissemination of these innovations were influential: the church (e.g. religious texts, the Bible, church services), school, media, fiction and the like. And the innovations were introduced into a prestigious language variety: the written/literary language and the language of religion.

## 4 Language-internal forced grammaticalization: Innovations in Standard Estonian in the 20th and 21st centuries

In the first half of the 20th century, native-speaker language developers laid the foundation for a uniform standardized language, which came to be used in all spheres of society and which served as the basis for the shared language variety – Common Estonian – in both the written and the spoken communication of a relatively small language community. Unlike in the period of missionary linguistics, there was no strong impact of other languages at this point. However, the language reformers of the first decades of the 20th century did suggest some radical innovations that were based on the Estonian material (and which were sometimes inspired by other languages, especially Finnish). The reform, which was led by Johannes Aavik, introduced into Estonian both new vocabulary and several grammatical innovations which were based on Estonian but also added Finnish-like syntheticity to the language. The motivation for such contact-induced innovations was often to fill the gaps that non-native speakers noticed in Estonian, drawing on their experience with other languages. At the same time, the language reformers tried to develop a well-functioning written language that allowed compact expression and elegant style. Their grammatical innovations were often alternatives to existing, longer and more complex expressive means, which they felt to be more cumbersome.

This striving toward a more synthetic mode of expression has been an implicit principle of language planning ever since. This section discusses some examples of innovations suggested by the language reformers as well as of the back-formation of verbs, which is an innovation of recent years.

### 4.1 Synthetic past tense forms in the conditional mood, in the oblique mood and in the *vat*-infinitive

The forms mentioned in the above heading were built on the basis of the existing analytic forms in the language. The synthetic preterite conditional of the verb *tulema* 'come', for example, is *tul-nu-ks* [come-past-COND] 'if somebody had come'. The usual past tense form, by contrast, is analytic: *ole-ks tul-nud* [be-COND come-PST.PTCP]. Similarly, the synthetic oblique mood form of this verb is *tul-nu-vat* [come-past-OBL]. Its analytic counterpart is *ole-vat tul-nud* [be-OBL come-PST.PTCP]. The synthetic forms were proposed in 1922 by Oskar Loorits, an advocate of the language reform. Arguments in favor for his proposals included elegance of form and the example of dialects and genetically related languages, which seemed to exhibit a trend toward synthetic forms.

Like Mägiste for the *saama* future, Loorits looked for support for his radical changes in synthetic preterite forms in similar forms in genetically related languages and dialects, where they had emerged as the result of natural development. He was, however, able to find only one example of a similar synthetic form – the oblique plural form *tei-nu-vad* [make-PST-3PL] in South Estonian (Loorits 1923: 85–86). Contemporary grammars present the synthetic forms as parallels to their analytic counterparts. A study of conditional forms (Jõgi 2008) shows that the synthetic forms began to spread in the 1930s, that their use decreased in the 1950s (due to disapproval of the language reform movement in post-war Soviet Estonia) and that the forms started to spread again in the 1970s and 1990s. Contributing factors are frequency of use, generality of meaning of the verbs and shortness of the innovative forms (e.g. *olnuks* 'would have been', *võinuks* 'could have', *saanuks* 'would have', *pidanuks* 'should have', *tulnuks* 'should come'). Currently, syntheticity is also spreading to longer stems, as (16) shows, and it has also become increasingly common in more colloquial contexts, as in (17).

(16) *Informaatika        õppeaine        kohustuslikuks    muutmine*
information.science.GEN subject.GEN obligatory.TRNSL making
**vähenda-nu-ks** *seda        nappi        mänguruumi*
narrow-PST-COND this.PRTV limited.PRTV playing.room.PRTV
*veel    poole    võrra.*
further half.GEN by
'Making information science an obligatory subject **would have narrowed** this limited playing room further by half.'        (Keeleveeb, IT journal, 2001)

(17) *Kui ta    ole-ks    superstaariks    saa-nud,*
if s/he be-COND superstar.TRNSL become-PST.PTCP
***tul-nu-ks***    *Eesti        muusikasse ka    midagi*
come-PST-COND Estonia.GEN music.ILL also something
*uut    ja    huvitavat.*
new.PRTV and interesting.PRTV
'Had he become a superstar, Estonian music **would have witnessed** something new and interesting.'        (Keeleveeb, Forum, 2008)

The synthetic oblique mood is less common because it is relatively long in terms of the number of syllables and because there are several other forms which, in addition to the *vat*-ending form adopted in Common Estonian, may express referred evidentiality: a single past participle or the indicative past perfect can be used as a preterite form in the oblique mood, as in (18). Yet, the form ending in *-vat* is sometimes used. Web communication seems to help the spread of this innovation, as example (19) from a forum of the homeless shows.

(18) *Itaalias* **sõit-nud /** *ol-i* **sõit-nud** *suur*
Italy.INE drive-PST.PTCP be-PST.3SG drive-PST.PTCP large
*reisilaev karile.*
passenger.ship rock.ALL

'It **is reported** that in Italy a large passenger ship **has/had run** aground on a rock.'

(19) *Aga tegelt* **tul-nu-vat** *välja, et liha*
but actually come-PST-QUOT out that meat.GEN
*söömine / mittesöömine veregrupist sõltub hoopiski*
eating not.eating blood.group.ELA depends altogether
*ja musugused peaksid kõik taimetoitlased olema*
and people.like.me should all vegetarians be.mINF

'But actually **it is said to have appeared** that eating or not eating meat depends on one's blood group, and people like me should all be vegetarians.'

(Forum, 2003; http://www.kodutud.com/viewthread.php?fid=53&tid=1953&action=printable; last accessed on 19 January 2012)

In (20), the *nuvat* forms are used as the past perfect of the oblique mood (in *polnud heitnud*, the auxiliary verb *polnud* is in the preterite participle form).

(20) *Selle jäleda nülgimistööga*
this.GEN disgusting.GEN task.of.skinning.COM
**saa-nu-vat** *hakka-ma kuningas Astüagasese*
get-PST-QUOT begin-mINF king Astyages.GEN
*timukatööspetsialistid Armeeniamaalt; et*
specialists.of.the.executioner's.job Armenia.ABL because
*pühamees aga kohe hinge* **p-ol-nud**
holy.man but at.once soul.PRTV NEG-be-PST.PTCP

| *heit-nud*, | *tul-nu-vat* | tal | veel | ka |
|---|---|---|---|---|
| throw-PST.PTCP | must-PST-QUOT | 3SG.ADE | further | also |

*peanupp maha raiuda.*
noddle   off   chop.dINF

'**It is said that** King Astyages' specialists of the executioner's job from Armenia **were able** to carry out the disgusting task of skinning; however, since the holy man **is reported not to have died** at once, it **was necessary** to chop off his head.' (Keeleveeb, FICT, 2000)

The *vat*-infinitive (and its source, the partitive case form of the *v*-suffixed present participle) has the same form as the oblique mood and is thought to be the source of the finite form of the oblique mood: a sentence like (22) emerged through insubordination of a complement clause as, in (21).[10]

(21) *Isa   ütle-s   ema   **tule-vat**.*
father say-PST.3SG mother.PRTV come-VINF
'Father said that mother **is coming**.'

(22) *Ema   **tule-vat**.*
mother.NOM come-QUOT
'Mother **is said to come**.'

The preterite of the *vat*-infinitive also coincides with the preterite forms of the oblique mood. The usual analytic form here is *olevat tulnud* 'is reported to have come' but Loorits (1923: 86) recommended the synthetic form *tulnuvat*. Authentic usage reveals some examples of synthetic preterite forms of the infinitive, as in (23).

(23) *Kallas mäleta-b Kaugverit   **kahetse-nu-vat**, et*
Kallas recall-3SG Kaugver:PRTV regret-PST-VINF that

*puudub   normaalne ajakirjandus – muidu*
miss.3SG normal   journalism   otherwise

*oleks   ta   meeleldi vinge ajakirjanik.*
be.COND s/he gladly   cool   journalist

'Kallas recalls that Kaugver **is said to have regretted** that there is no normal journalism – otherwise he would love to be a great journalist.'
(Keeleveeb, weekly *Eesti Ekspress*, 2001)

---

**10** According to Evans (2007: 367), insubordination is "the conventionalized main clause use of what, in prima facie grounds, appear as formally subordinate clauses". He gives a number of examples of "evidentializing" insubordination, also from Estonian, Latvian and Lithuanian (Evans 2007: 395–397).

## 4.2 Case forms of the *ma*-infinitive

Aavik also proposed new case forms of the *ma*-infinitive, in addition to the old local and abessive forms such as *tege-ma-st* [do-mINF-ELA] 'from doing' and *tege-ma-ta* [do-mINF-ABE] 'without doing'. The new translative form *tege-ma-ks* [do-mINF-TRNSL] 'in order to do' is a case in point. As (24) makes clear, the form expressing final adverbials was adopted.

(24) *Saksa        telekanal      SAT1   korraldas              testsõidu,*
     German     TV-channel    SAT1   organize.PST.3SG   test.drive.GEN

   ***uuri-ma-ks***              *auto*       *kütusekulu*               *vähendamise*
   explore-mINF-TRNSL   car.GEN   fuel.consumption.GEN   decreasing.GEN

   *võimalusi.*
   possibility.PL.PRTV

   'The German TV channel SAT1 organized a test drive **in order to explore** possibilities of decreasing fuel consumption of cars.'
                                        (Keeleveeb, weekly *Eesti Ekspress*, 2001)

Other proposed forms, namely the comitative and the terminative of the *ma*-infinitive, whose usage possibilities are more restricted syntactically, did not gain ground (Uuspõld 1980).

## 4.3 Invented conjunction *selmet*

Aavik suggested replacing the complex conjunction *selle asemel et* 'instead of' with the abbreviated blend *selmet* (e.g. Raag 2008: 153). In this case, too, he avoided several stages of a possible historical development. *Selle asemel et* is a complex correlative conjunction that emerged on the boundary between a main and a subordinate clause: the pronoun *selle* 'of this', which represents the main clause in a subordinate clause, became part of the conjunction, as in (25a) and (25b). The next plausible step of a normal evolution could be the fusion of this combination into a conjunction, as was the case for the conjunction *nagu* 'like, as': *noin tavoin kuin* > *nõnda kui* 'in the manner of, like' > *nõnna kui* > *nõnnagu* > *nagu* (Uibopuu 1972; Remmelg 2006: 99). This development was skipped in the case of *selmet*. Nevertheless, it is a common subordinator in present-day language use, as in (25c).

(25) a. **Selle      asemel, et**   panna selga     paks džemper,
       this.GEN instead that put      back.ILL thick sweater

   riietu    õhukesse pluusi    ja    kampsunisse.
   dress.IMP thin.ILL   shirt.ILL and sweater.ILL

b. **Selle asemel et** panna selga paks džemper, riietu õhukesse pluusi ja kampsunisse.

c. **Selmet** panna selga paks džemper, riietu õhukesse pluusi ja kampsunisse.
   '**Instead of** putting on a warm sweater, put on a thin shirt and sweater.'
   (Keeleveeb, diary *Eesti Päevaleht*, 2003)

## 4.4 The synthetic superlative

The morphology of the adjective was supplemented with a short superlative formed by means of a new suffix *-im*, as in *noor-im* [young-SUP] 'youngest', *parim* 'best' and *hoolsaim* 'most diligent'. The traditional forms were analytic, as in *kõige suure-m* [most great-COMP] 'greatest'. Here, the language reformers followed the model of the Finnish synthetic superlative with the suffix *-in*, as in *nuor-in* [young-SUP] 'youngest'. Raag's (1999) study of language reform innovations documents the course of the adoption of the synthetic superlative in Estonian. By the end of the 1930s, the short superlative had become common with words whose morphophonological structure allowed its formation. It was consistently used in the 1950s and 1960s, and the 1990s witnessed a new rise in frequency. The short superlative is used with frequent words such as *edukaim* 'the most successful', *parim* 'the best', *kiireim* 'the quickest', *noorim* 'the youngest', *vanim* 'the oldest' and *suurim* 'the greatest'.

The forms discussed in Sections 4.1 to 4.4 gradually took root during the language reform and are now becoming more firmly established not only in the written language but also more generally. Raag (1999) gives the following reasons for the success of the forms initiated by the language reform:
- the innovations came at a suitable point in time, namely, the initial period of standardization and stabilization of Standard Estonian by native linguists;
- there was a desire among Estonians to get rid of the German influence and adopt the example of Finnish;
- the reception of innovations in society was favorable;
- Estonia is a small country and the innovations were promoted all over the country;
- the personalities of language reformers and managers, as well as polemics and compromises about innovations, attracted considerable attention;

- innovations were supported by authoritative language bodies;
- the suggestions of language reformers were put into practice by language managers and editors.

From the perspective of stylistics, the innovative forms made texts more elegant. Grammar, however, became more complicated.

## 4.5 Back-formation of complex verbs

The adoption of complex verbs, formed by back-formation, is an innovation of the past decades. It started in terminology development but is increasingly gaining ground in other registers. In Estonian, phrasal verbs or verb combinations with separable components are common: particle verbs such as *ära pühkima* 'wipe away', *maha raiuma* 'chop off', *läbi vaatama* 'look through' (26) (see Hasselblatt 1990); expression verbs such as *aru saama* 'understand' (lit. 'get sense'), *pead murdma* 'rack one's brains' (lit. 'break one's head') and *korvi andma* 'turn down' (lit. 'give a basket') (27); and verb combinations with support verbs such as *otsust tegema* 'make a decision', *kõnet pidama* 'hold a speech', *rõõmu tegema* 'make happy' (lit. 'make pleasure') (28).

(26) *Õpetaja **vaata-s**    õpilaste      tööd     **läbi**.*
    teacher  look-PST.3SG student.PL.GEN paper.PL through
    'The teacher **looked through** the students' papers.'

(27) *Mari **and-is**    Jürile   **korvi**.*
    Mari give-PST.3SG Jüri.ALL basket.GEN
    'Mari **turned down** Jüri's advances.'

(28) *Lapse     edu    **teg-i**       emale      **rõõmu**.*
    child.GEN success make-PST.3SG mother.ALL pleasure.PRTV
    'The child's success **made** mother **happy**.'

In the past decades, language managers have started to introduce compound verbs with inseparable components such as *helisalvestama* 'sound-record', *pealtharima* 'lit. on-cultivate', *kiirparandama* 'lit. quick-repair', *ülehindama* 'overestimate' and *iluravima* 'lit. beauty-treat'. This process of back-formation of complex verbs from hypothetical deverbal compound nouns as a word formation method is on the rise (Vare 2003). Consider the examples in (29).

(29) a. õhk-jahut-us [air-dry-N$_V$] 'air-drying' > õhk-jahuta-ma [air-dry-mINF] 'to air-dry'

b. sügav-künd [deep-plough] 'deep ploughing' > sügav-künd-ma [deep-plough-mINF] 'to deep-plough'

c. ilu-uisuta-mine [beauty-skate-N$_V$] 'figure-skating' > ilu-uisuta-ma [beauty-skate-mINF] 'to figure-skate'

d. keele-toimeta-mine [language-edit-N$_V$] 'copy editing' > keele-toimeta-ma [language-edit-mINF] 'to copy-edit'

e. paremus-järjest-us [advantage-order-N$_V$] 'ranking' > paremus-järjesta-ma [advantage-order-mINF] 'to rank'

When the predicate of a sentence is a complex verb, the informational load of the verb increases and the word order and rhythm of the sentence change. Compare the analytic construction with the support verb in (30a) to the complex-verb construction in (30b).

(30) a. *Komisjon* **pan-i** *taotlused* **paremusjärjestu-sse**.
committee put-PST.3SG application.PL ranking-ILL

b. *Komisjon* **paremusjärjesta-s** *taotlused*.
committee rank-PST.3SG application.PL
'The committee **ranked** the applications.'

The introduction of the back-formation of complex verbs into Estonian is the result of intentional language development. The situation is different from the one in Finnish, where such verbs emerged naturally (e.g. *peruskorjata* 'give something a complete overhaul' < *peruskorjaus* 'complete overhaul' and *salakuunnella* 'spy' < *salakuuntelu* 'espionage').

Compound verbs have spread with some reluctance in Common Estonian. They emerged first and foremost in cases where no suitable analytic synonym was available – the preferred choices being analytic combinations such as support verb combinations *iluuisutamist tegema* 'do figure skating' and *iluravi tegema* 'do beauty treatment'. Nevertheless, one can observe the gradual adoption of several complex verbs, also in more informal language, as in (31) (Toome 2011), which is a signal of ongoing typological change. Web communication is likely a favorable environment for more synthetic expressions due to the fact that the communication takes place in writing.

(31) *Su         vend     Ilja  Glebov  ka  **iluuisuta-b***
    you.SG.GEN brother Ilya Glebov too figure.skate-3SG
    *ja   on   tippspordis.*
    and  is   top.sports.INE
    'Your brother Ilya Glebov too **does figure skating** and is in top sports.'
                              (example taken from Toome 2011: 79, blog)

## 5 Forced degrammaticalization

There are also some examples of attempts to hinder ongoing developments. The motivation for these is mostly puristic, i.e. to preserve the peculiarities of a language. The Estonian language reform tried, for instance, to revive the instructive case (e.g. *lehvivi hõlmu* 'with flowing flaps', *täisi tiivu* 'with full wings') and preferred the older fusive forms of the partitive plural (e.g. the partitive plural morphemes *maju* 'house', *pesi* 'nest') to the existing parallel forms (e.g. *maja-sid* [house-PRTV.PL], *pesa-sid* [nest-PRTV.PL]). The instructive case can be found in lexicalized expressions but no regular use of this case followed. The shorter partitive plural forms are quite actively used but the more transparent agglutinative forms are gradually replacing them.

Similarly to their Estonian counterparts, the Finnish language reformers tried to direct the language away from presumably "foreign" analyticity toward syntheticity (Kolehmainen and Nordlund 2011: 17). They made efforts, for example, to decrease the use of function words such as adpositions and verb particles. Laitinen (2004) shows how puristic language management tried to stop or redirect some ongoing changes in the 19th century. One successful undertaking was the retention of the negative auxiliary verb: marking negation with a negative auxiliary that inflects in person and number is a Uralic feature that has been preserved in contemporary Standard Finnish, as in (32).

(32) *Minä **e-n**       lue        tätä       kirjaa       tänään.*
     I    NEG-1SG read.CNG this.PRTV book.PRTV today
     'I am not reading this book today.'                           (ISK: 1535)

Texts from the 16th to the 19th century show that agreement of the negative auxiliary verb with the subject was declining and that the personal forms of the negative auxiliary tended to vary freely (e.g. *ei* 'NEG.3SG' + *minä* 'I', *en* 'NEG.1SG' + *me* 'we', *et* 'NEG.2SG' + *te* 'you.PL', *ei* 'NEG.3SG' + *he* 'they'). The negation marker was developing into a non-agreeing particle based on the third-person singular form of the negative auxiliary *ei* for all persons. This type of process had already occurred earlier in Estonian and is typical of the Uralic languages in general. In some Finnish dialects, including the south-western dialects that served as the basis for Early Written Finnish, the negation word is not conjugable (Laitinen 2004: 253; Miestamo 2011: 99). In the 19th century, the use of the non-agreeing particle was already completely conventionalized in certain contexts but "after the public standardization debate, the negation word was placed in the category of verbs with all its syntactic and pragmatic functions" (Laitinen 2004: 259). Present-day usage, however, shows that the process of particlization of the negation auxiliary is underway once again.

# 6 Conclusions

The present study has focused on two groups of innovations, which were introduced into Standard Estonian in the course of its development in a ready-made form without a preceding gradual development.

In the course of contact-induced forced grammaticalization, the result of grammaticalization is adopted from the model language into the replica language without a grammaticalization process in the latter. The reformers of Old Written Estonian proceeded in this way. Old Written Estonian was developed mostly by people who used it as a second language. They brought a product of grammaticalization, which had occurred in the model language, to the replica language by copying the polysemy of the grammaticalized and pre-grammaticalization interpretations of a function word or construction from the model language. The Old Written Estonian examples presented in Section 3 illustrate how some probable stages in the grammaticalization chain were skipped.

The instances of language-internal forced grammaticalization exhibit different degrees of hypothetical evolutionary background. The activities of the native-speaker language reformers in the 20th and 21st centuries have focused on the intentional introduction of innovations without considering any specific developmental chain, though sometimes efforts have been made to find similarities in genetically related languages and dialects. On the one hand, the introduction of complex verbs into contemporary Estonian by native-speaker language managers could be regarded as the forced introduction of a possible change. On the other hand, the language reform of the standard language a century ago included some abrupt innovations for which no natural evolution can be observed (e.g. the synthetic superlative, case forms of the infinitive). One cannot regard these as instances of developmental stages being bypassed.

Rather, language development here is influenced by the subjective creativity of the language reformers.

In both types of forced grammaticalization, the result of the adopted grammatical innovation was based on material of the same language without the prior step-by-step development and bridging contexts that could lead to grammaticalization. In fact, the description in the previous sentence could be regarded as a refined definition of forced grammaticalization, which covers the two groups of changes in Standard Estonian as well as instances of abrupt grammaticalization in pidgin languages and local varieties of internationally used languages.

The factors that generally favor innovations (Metslang 1996b; Heine and Kuteva 2005: 219–259; Aikhenvald 2006) also seem to be valid in the cases discussed in the present paper. The first language-internal factor contributing to the adoption of innovations is the presence of source material. In all of the cases discussed, the linguistic material comes from the native language and its link with the innovative form is recognizable. The link can be based on grammaticalization, in which case the innovation could also have developed naturally (e.g. the articles). Often, though, the link is just associative (e.g. the short superlative). For the forms introduced into Estonian by language reform, such associative links (with existing lexical or grammatical material) have been sufficient to allow them to gain acceptance. A second requirement is the structural suitability of the new form or construction with the language's existing paradigmatics and syntagmatics. The innovative forms studied here (e.g. the case forms of the infinitive and the synthetic preterite forms) all fit well into the existing inflectional paradigms. The innovations also fit into the existing clause structure, though the situation is different with complex verbs, which have started altering the core structure of the clause. Other important factors for the spread of forced grammaticalization forms are usage potential, i.e. the possibility of relatively frequent usage in the clause, and compatibility with the general structural tendencies of a language (transparency, economy, etc.). However, in language, different motivations compete. The forced grammaticalization cases in Old Written Estonian are in line with the principle of transparency and the linguistic innovations brought about by language reform are in accordance with the principle of economy. Present-day Estonian, by contrast, still reveals a conflict between the language's tendency toward analyticity and the intentional syntheticity promoted by the language reformers and standardizers of the 20th and 21st centuries.

When a form or construction fits into a language, there are language-external circumstances that may favor its adoption: expressive needs (e.g. the future constructions), the impact or example of contact languages, the readiness for innovation in society, language attitudes (e.g. the prestige of some language variety, purism, intentional syntheticity in language management), the intensity of communication over different channels and the leveling of register differences in the Internet age, and active campaigning and use. Both types of forced grammaticalization in Estonian have entailed prestigious language use being spread to a wider user population. The second type, that of changes brought about by language reform, has also relied on people's pro-innovation mindset.

A forced grammaticalization innovation may be rather stable for a shorter (e.g. the articles in Old Written Estonian) or longer (e.g. the Finnish *on tekevä* future) time. It may also start a life of its own at some point and be subject to further gradual grammaticalization (e.g. the Estonian *saama* future). The hindering of change (e.g. the Finnish negation marker) will be temporary if the essence of the language remains the same. It seems that both forced grammaticalization and forced de-grammaticalization are deliberate and artificial and occur in the written/standard language. In the case of more widespread use in the standard language, the innovation may reach more informal language use. The spread of these changes to the common language could even shift the typological nature of languages by making both of them increasingly synthetic (first Finnish and then Estonian).

The question posited in the title of the present paper – i.e. whether languages can be forced – can tentatively be answered positively. However, under which conditions, to what extent, in which registers and how permanently remains to be investigated. A more thorough study of the mechanisms of forced grammaticalization and of the distinctions between evolutionary and revolutionary language changes should be carried out through analysis of both modern and centuries-old processes.

# Acknowledgments

The study was funded by the project PUT475 *Integrated model of morphosyntactic variation in written Estonian: A pilot study* of the Estonian Research Council and by the (European Union) European Regional Development Fund (Centre of Excellence in Estonian Studies). I am grateful to two anonymous referees for helpful advice.

# Abbreviations

1/2/3 = 1st/2nd/3rd person; ABE = abessive; ADE = adessive; ALL = allative; ART = article; COM = comitative; COMP = comparative; COND = conditional; CNG = connegative; DEF = definite; DIM = diminutive; dINF = *da*-infinitive; ELA = elative;

FICT = fiction; FUT = future auxiliary; GEN = genitive; GER = gerund; ILL = illative; IMP = imperative; IMPS = impersonal; INDEF = indefinite; INE = inessive; mINF = *ma*-infinitive; N = noun; N$_V$ = deverbal noun; NEG = negation; NOM = nominative; OBL = oblique; PFV = perfective; PL = plural; PRS = present tense; PRTV = partitive; PST = past; PTCL = particle ; PTCP = participle; QUOT = oblique mood; SG = singular; SUP = superlative; SX = suffix; TRM = terminative; TRNSL = translative; V = verb; vINF = *vat*-infinitive.

## Sources of examples

COWE = *Corpus of Old Written Estonian.* http://www.murre.ut.ee/vakkur/Korpused/korpused.htm (accessed 19 June 2011).

Keeleveeb (an online portal collecting a variety of Estonian language corpora, databases, dictionaries, and language processing software) www.keeleveeb.ee (last accessed 19 June 2015)

## References

Aikhenvald, Alexandra Y. 2006. Grammars in contact: A cross-linguistic perspective. In Alexandra Y. Aikhenvald & R. M. W. Dixon (eds.), *Grammars in contact: A cross-linguistic typology*, 1–66. Oxford: Oxford University Press.

Breitenbach, Sandra. 2008. *Missionary linguistics in East Asia: The origins of religious language in the shaping of christianity?* Frankfurt am Main: Peter Lang.

Dahl, Östen. 2000. The grammar of future time reference in European languages. In Östen Dahl (ed.), *Tense and aspect in the languages of Europe*, 309–329. Berlin: Mouton de Gruyter. 309–328.

Erelt, Mati (ed.). 2007. *Estonian language.* Tallinn: Estonian Academy Publishers.

Evans, Nicholas. 2007. Insubordination and its uses. In Irina Nikolaeva (ed.), *Finiteness: Theoretical and empirical foundations*, 366–431. Oxford: Oxford University Press.

Habicht, Külli. 2001. *Eesti vanema kirjakeele leksikaalsest ja morfosüntaktilisest arengust ning Heinrich Stahli keele eripärast selle taustal* [About the lexical and morphosyntactic development of older written Estonian and the background for the peculiar features in the language of Heinrich Stahl]. Tartu: University of Tartu dissertation.

Habicht, Külli, Ritva Laury, Taru Nordlund & Renate Pajusalu. 2011. The marking of definiteness in Old Written Estonian and Finnish: Native or borrowed? In Sandor Csucs, Nora Falk, Vikoria Toth & Gabor Zaicz (eds.), *Congressus XI Internationalis Fenno-Ugristarum, Piliscsaba, Hungary, August 9–14, 2010*, 277–284. Piliscsaba: Reguly Tarsasag,

Habicht, Külli, Pille Penjam & Ilona Tragel. 2010. Kas *tahtma* tahab abiverbiks? [Is *tahtma* becoming an auxiliary?]. *Journal of Estonian and Finno-Ugric Linguistics* 1(2). 115–146.

Hasselblatt, Cornelius. 1990. *Das estnische Partikelverb als Lehnübersetzung aus dem Deutschen.* Wiesbaden: Harrassowitz.

Heine, Bernd & Tania Kuteva. 2005. *Language contact and grammatical change*. Cambridge: Cambridge University Press.
Heine, Bernd & Tania Kuteva. 2006. *The changing languages of Europe*. Oxford: Oxford University Press.
ISK = Hakulinen, Auli, Maria Vilkuna, Riitta Korhonen, Vesa Koivisto, Tarja Riitta Heinonen & Irja Alho. 2004. *Iso suomen kielioppi* [The large grammar of Finnish]. Helsinki: Suomalaisen Kirjallisuuden Seura.
Itkonen-Kaila, Marja. 1993. Miten *on tekevä*-futuuri on tullut suomeen? [How has the *on tekevä* future developed in Finnish?]. *Virittäjä* 42(4). 579–593.
Jõgi, Mirja. 2008. *Konditsionaali minevikuvormide kasutus 1930.–1990. aastatel* [The use of the past conditional forms from 1930s to 1990s]. Tartu: University of Tartu BA thesis.
Kask, Arnold. 1970. *Eesti kirjakeele ajaloost I* [On the history of written Estonian I]. Tartu: Tartu Riiklik Ülikool.
Kilgi, Annika. 2010. Tuleviku tulekust: Tulevikulisuse väljendamisest meie esimestes piiblitõlgetes [The arrival of the future: Expressing futurity in the first bible translations in Estonian.]. *Journal of Estonian and Finno-Ugric Linguistics* 1(2). 163–185.
Kilgi, Annika. 2012. *Tõlkekeele dünaamika Piibli esmaeestinduse käigus: Verbi morfosüntaksi areng ja lõplik toimetamisfaas* [The dynamicity of translation language with the first translation of the Bible into Estonian: The development of the verb's morphosyntax and the final editing stage]. Tallinn: Tallinn University dissertation.
Kolehmainen, Leena & Taru Nordlund. 2011. Kielellinen muutos tutkimuksen kohteena: Kieltenvälinen vertailu, kieliopillistuminen ja kielikontaktien tutkimus [Linguistic change as the subject of research: Language comparison, grammaticalization and contact-induced research]. *Virittäjä* 115(1). 5–35.
Laanekask, Heli & Tiiu Erelt. 2007. Written Estonian. In Mati Erelt (ed.), *Estonian language*, 273–342. Tallinn: Estonian Academy Publishers.
Laitinen, Lea. 2004. Grammaticalization and standardization. In Olga Fischer, Muriel Norde & Harry Peridon (eds.), *Up and down the cline: The nature of grammaticalization*, 247–262. Amsterdam: John Benjamins.
Laury, Ritva. 1997. *Demonstratives in interaction: The emergence of a definite article in Finnish*. Amsterdam: John Benjamins.
Loorits, Oskar. 1923. *Eesti keele grammatika* [Estonian grammar]. Tartu: Odamees.
Mägiste, Julius. 1936. Eesti *saama*-futuuri algupärast ja tarvitamiskõlblikkusest [On the origin of the Estonian *saama*-future and its eligibility of usage]. *Eesti Keel* 3. 65–92.
Makoni, Sinfree & Alastair Pennycook. 2007. Disinventing and reconstituting languages. In Sinfree Makoni & Alastair Pennycook (eds.), *Disinventing and reconstituting languages*, 1–41. Bristol: Multilingual Matters.
Menezes de Souza, Lynn M. T. 2007. Entering a culture quietly: Writing and cultural survival in indigenous education in Brazil. In Sinfree Makoni & Alastair Pennycook (eds.), *Disinventing and reconstituting Languages*, 135–169. Bristol: Multilingual Matters.
Metslang, Helle. 1994. Eesti ja soome: Futuurumita keeled? [Estonian and Finnish: Languages without future tense?] *Keel ja Kirjandus* 38(9/10). 534–547, 603–616.
Metslang, Helle. 1996a. The developments of the futures in the Finno-Ugric languages. In Mati Erelt (ed.), *Estonian: Typological studies I*, 123–144. Tartu: Department of Estonian of the University of Tartu.
Metslang, Helle. 1996b. Evolutsioonilised ja revolutsioonilised uuendused grammatikas [Evolutionary and revolutionary innovations in grammar]. In Heikki Leskinen & Sandor Maticsàk

(eds.), *Congressus Octavus Internationalis Fenno-Ugristarum, Jyväskylä 10.–15.8.1995, Pars IV. Sessiones sectionum: Syntaxis et semantica & contactus linguistici et status hodiernus linguarum & cetera linguistica*, 87–92. Jyväskylä: Moderatus.

Metslang, Helle. 1997. Eesti keele ja teiste soome-ugri keelte futuurumi arenguid [The developments of the future tense in Estonian and other Finno-Ugric langauges]. *Keel ja Kirjandus* 40(4). 226–231.

Metslang, Helle. 2011, Some grammatical innovations in the development of Estonian and Finnish: Forced grammaticalization. *Linguistica Uralica* XLVII(4). 241–256.

Metslang, Helle (ed.). 2009. Estonian in typological perspective [Special issue]. *Language Typology and Universals* 62(1/2).

Miestamo, Matti. 2011. A typological perspective on negation in Finnish dialects. *Nordic Journal of Linguistics* 34(2). 83–104.

Nau, Nicole. 1995. *Möglichkeiten und Mechanismen kontaktbewegten Sprachwandels unter besonderer Berücksichtung des Finnischen*. Munich: Lincom Europa.

Nowak, Elke. 1999. Investigating diversity: Descriptive grammars, empirical research and the science of language. In David Cram, Andrew R. Linn & Elke Nowak (eds.), *History of linguistics 1996*. Volume 1, *Traditions in linguistics worldwide*, 155–164. Amsterdam: John Benjamins.

Pajusalu, Renate. 1997. Is there an article in (spoken) Estonian? In Mati Erelt (ed.), *Estonian: Typological studies II*, 146–177. Tartu: Department of Estonian of the University of Tartu.

Prass, Kerli 2011. *Saama- ja hakkama-tulevik tänapäeva eesti kirjakeeles* [The *saama-* and *hakkama*-futures in contemporary written Estonian]. Tallinn: Tallinn University MA thesis.

Raag, Raimo. 2008. Talupojakeelest rahvakeeleks [From a rustic language to a national language]. Tartu: Atlex.

Raag, Virve. 1999. *The effects of planned change on Estonian morphology*. Uppsala: Uppsala University Library.

Remmelg, Raili. 2006. Korrelaatsidendist eesti keeles: *Sööme selleks, et elada – sööme, selleks et elada* [On correlative conjunctions in Estonian]. In Pille Penjam (ed.), *Lause argumentstruktuur*, 99–107. Tartu: Department of Estonian of the University of Tartu preprints.

Ross, Kristiina. 2005. Keskaegse eesti libakirjakeele põhjendusi ja piirjooni [Arguments and outlines of medieval standard Estonian]. *Emakeele Seltsi aastaraamat* 51. 107–129.

Schlotthauer, Susan. 2010. Kontaktinduzierter Sprachwandel im Bereich der estnischen Verbrektion? Teil I: Verbkomplemente in Formkasusmarkierter Nominalphrasen. *SKY Journal of Linguistics* 23. 265–300.

Siegel, Jeff. 2008. *The emergence of pidgin and creole languages*. Oxford: Oxford University Press.

Tauli, Valter. 1966. *Structural tendencies in Uralic languages*. The Hague: Mouton & Co.

Thomason, Sarah. 2001. *Language contact: An introduction*. Edinburgh: Edinburgh University Press.

Toome, Merli. 2011. Eesti liitverbide ja pöördmoodustiste analüüs ÕS 2006 materjali alusel [The analysis of Estonian compound verbs and back-formations (based on ÕS 2006 material)]. Tartu: University of Tartu MA thesis.

Tragel, Ilona & Külli Habicht 2012. Grammaticalization of the Estonian *saama* 'get'. In Alexandra N. Lenz & Gudrun Rawoens (eds.), The art of getting: GET verbs in European languages from a synchronic and diachronic point of view [Special issue]. *Linguistics* 50(6). 1371–1412.

Uibopuu, Valev. 1972. Nagu: Jooni eesti noorima võrdluskonjunktsiooni ajaloost [The diachronic features of the youngest comparative conjunction in Estonian]. *Tulimuld* (3/4). 134–140, 208–211.

Uuspõld, Ellen. 1980. *Maks*-vorm ja teised finaaladverbiaalid [*Maks*-form and other adverbial clauses of purpose]. *Keel ja Kirjandus* 23(12). 729–736.
Vare, Silvi. 2003. Back-formation of verbs in Estonian. In Helle Metslang & Mart Rannut (eds.), *Languages in development*, 123–132. Munich: Lincom Europa.
Ziegeler, Debra. This volume. Historical replication in contact grammaticalization.
Ziegelmann, Katja & Eberhard Winkler. 2006. Zum Einfluß des Deutschen auf das Estnische. In Anne Arold, Dieter Cherubim, Dagmar Neuendorff & Henrik Nikula (eds.), *Deutsch am Rande Europas*, 43–70. Tartu: Tartu University Press.

Debra Ziegeler
# 11 Historical replication in contact grammaticalization

**Abstract:** The study of replica grammaticalization in contact (Heine and Kuteva 2003, 2005) has not been without its critiques (e.g. Matthews and Yip 2009; Gast and van der Auwera 2012), because it assumes a historical linguistic "awareness" of model language grammaticalization routes. In Heine and Kuteva's studies, the contact "model" language was usually understood to be a substrate or L1. The present study investigates three features observed in more than one contact dialect of English, and proposes instead a replication of diachronic stages in the lexifier observed to have appeared up to 1000 years ago. Replication in such cases is assisted by the identification of co-existing, lexical source meanings recoverable from the grammaticalized meanings in the lexifier.[1]

## 1 Introduction

Contact languages have been the subject of grammaticalization studies for more than a decade now, and it is only recently that such studies have begun to demonstrate interesting theoretical prospects. The considerable range of languages and the data covered in these studies have long provided a commendable contribution to the field of linguistic typology, though mainly in the investigation of contact situations involving established languages. In another area of investigation, that of the sub-varieties of established languages, there is little evidence to date of an extensive research programme into contact grammaticalization or of a theoretical contribution to the study of grammaticalization as a sub-discipline in itself. Perhaps the reason that such "peripheral" fields of study have been overlooked is that much of the variation found in contact dialects has often been left only to sociolinguistics for explanatory support. The restricted nature of such debates has tended to obscure more exciting possibilities for the study of contact typology, which is as valuable and significant for the generation

---

[1] An earlier and shorter version of the present paper has been published as Ziegeler (2014) in the journal *Diachronica* 31(1). 106–141, with the title, "Replica grammaticalisation as recapitulation: The other side of contact". The current paper includes two additional case studies and hence a slightly more elaborated theoretical component.

of theoretical heuristics concerning language change as it is for the study of change in languages with an apparently genetically continuous transmission history.

The term "New English" goes back at least to Platt et al. (1984), who defined it as a variety of English that (i) emerged through the education system where it is spoken, (ii) developed where a native variety of English was not spoken before, (iii) developed an official functional capacity, including a status as a lingua franca and (iv) became indigenized, acquiring its own distinctive morphosyntactic, lexical, discourse and phonological features by which it could be identified. Examples usually included the varieties spoken in countries which had been former colonies of Britain and the United States, such as Singapore, Hong Kong, the Philippines, East Africa, the West Indies and India. As such, these dialects represent sub-varieties of a more established language, having emerged historically since the time of colonization in the countries in which they are spoken. The two varieties under analysis in the present study are (Colloquial) Singaporean English (CSE) and Indian English; they were selected from the *International Corpus of English* for their uniformity of genre and text-type. British English and East African English will be used where necessary, as controls, though the latter spoken corpus varies significantly in form and text-type from the other two corpora.

The study will focus on a three distinctive grammatical features observed in more than one contact dialect of English, which have in common the fact that they appear not to have been affected by the prototypical processes of contact grammaticalization as described in the literature to date (e.g. Hagège 1993; Bruyn 1996, Bruyn 2009; Romaine 1999; Heine and Kuteva 2003, Heine and Kuteva 2005, Matras and Sakel 2007; Mufwene 2008). Rather than replicating the model patterns of their substrates, these features, interestingly, appear to be replicating developmental patterns in their lexifiers[2] and, in some cases, recapitulating stages of development seen to be associated with the lexifier (English) up to a thousand years ago. The study will also attempt to explain, then, what appears on the surface to be mysterious evidence that the contact speakers are assumed to be "aware" of the historical development of the language they are replicating, a phenomenon outlined as highly questionable by (amongst others) Matras and Sakel (2007), Matthews and Yip (2009), Pietsch (2009) and Gast and van der Auwera (2012), who all refer to the process of

---

[2] The term "lexifier" is used only in a general sense in the present paper, to correspond to Weinreich's (1953) earlier use of the term "source" language from which the lexicon is originally derived in contact, as cited in Matras and Sakel (2007) (see Schneider 2003 for an overview of the stages of nativization reached by the various dialects he classes as "new" Englishes).

replica grammaticalization outlined in Heine and Kuteva (2003, 2005). The three items under investigation include the modal verb *will* as a habitual aspect marker, the extended use of the progressive and the use of *one* as a determiner expressing specific noun reference. The items were selected on the basis of previously observed similarities between their frequency in one of the contact dialects, Singapore English, and equivalent functions in historical English data.

Section 2 will review the more recent achievements in the area of contact grammaticalization, as well as some established assumptions of the ways in which superstrate influence has been seen to contribute to creole formation. Section 3 will present examples from present-day variational data involving the three selected grammatical items, as well as discussing any previous research on the same items. In Section 4, a comparison will be made with the historical data; this section will discuss the possibility of parallels with historical developments, offering possible reasons for such parallels, while taking into consideration accounts of current research on contact grammaticalization. It is hypothesized that there may be historical recapitulation in contact, influenced by universal grammaticalization processes, in which certain forms will tend to follow an almost pre-determined functional pathway of development defined by cross-linguistic cognitive principles operating in any new systemic context in which the same lexical source data is selected for development, rather than by the modeling patterns of the substrate. This may also give rise to the appearance of (contact) degrammaticalization, and layering (Hopper 1991) across contact boundaries.

# 2 Contact grammaticalization

## 2.1 Relative rates across contact

Research into contact grammaticalization has been regenerated in recent years by the contributions of, for example, Heine and Kuteva (2003, 2005), who have provided a wealth of examples coming from different contact situations (not just those relating to pidgins and creoles). This study has been influenced by close observations of the nature of general processes of universal grammaticalization, and it has been convincingly demonstrated that contact grammaticalization offers a platform of description that is relatively parallel to any prototypical case of ordinary grammaticalization, whatever the circumstances. In addition, Heine and Kuteva's studies deny any recorded cases of degrammaticalization (Heine and Kuteva 2005: 108), as does Mufwene (2008: 169), and they concur with claims made, for instance, by Mufwene (2008: 166) that it would be very difficult to find any language that had shown no evidence of contact at any stage of its history.

This would mean, though, that there is little justification to regard contact grammaticalization as a separate sub-discipline. In many ways, there are superficial similarities between contact grammaticalization and "ordinary" grammaticalization (i.e. where contact situations are not so readily perceivable), but one factor that distinguishes them has been said to be the one of timing: what normally takes many generations to accomplish in terms of ordinary grammaticalization situations, taking often up to three or four centuries, will happen very suddenly, perhaps over only one or two generations, in a contact situation (Heine and Reh 1984: 87–90). The reason is that a contact situation in linguistic terms is a situation of communicative urgency, where there is a greater need to move to advanced levels of automation of the language system in as short a time period as possible, a situation labeled *Communicative Pressure* (CP) according to Hagège (1993: 130). It is such communicative pressure which is the driving force behind the use of certain forms in an over-extended sense: they may come to be used preemptively in environments which are not yet part of the distributional range of older varieties of the language (see Mufwene (1996: 87); an example is the use of auxiliaries with inanimate subjects. Although it is anticipated that a grammaticalizing form will eventually extend its range of uses to such environments, the time taken in older varieties of the language will generally be much longer. One example of such preemptive generalization was described in Ziegeler (2000: 12) as *Hypergrammaticalization*, a phenomenon analyzed within the context of relative grammaticalization, that is, the study of comparative grammaticalization developments across varieties of the same language or different languages undergoing the same grammaticalization developments. Hypergrammaticalization was illustrated in the use of the modal verb *would* in hypothetical predicates in Colloquial Singapore English: it was shown to have been extended to grammatical environments in which it would be less likely to appear in non-contact varieties, for instance, with inanimate subjects and with stative verbs over which the subject may have no volitional control (Ziegeler 1996, Ziegeler 2000), as in (1):

(1)  *I wish the Porsche would belong to me.*

The use of *would* with a stative verb in such contexts was rated as acceptable by 36.3% of the student speakers of Singapore English, while only 24.3% of student speakers of British English found the example acceptable. These differences led to the hypothesis that the Singaporean speakers accepted a function that was more grammaticalized than that found in British English usage, which was otherwise constrained in its distributional range by the continued adherence of its lexical source meanings of volition from which it originally grammaticalized.

On the other side of the coin, however, CP may motivate a greater transparency of function, and there is equal evidence that grammaticalization levels in contact may be progressing at a slower rate than in non-contact situations, a situation described in Ziegeler (2000: 12) as *Hypo-grammaticalization*. The reasons for such a lag in development may be traced to the pressures of substrate or L1 influences in contact. One notable example is observed in Ho and Platt (1993), who provided quantitative evidence that past tense marking in Colloquial Singapore English (CSE) is predominantly associated with the lexical aspect of the verb; if the verb is non-stative, it is likely to receive past tense marking more frequently than if it is stative or imperfective, and if the grammatical aspect is imperfective, as with habituals and progressives, there will be less frequent use of the past tense than if it is perfective. This is shown in example (2) (Ziegeler 2000: 114), in which the stative verb *was* is marked for past, though past habituals are expressed in the present tense:

(2) *When I was a child my mother goes to work and my father looks after us.*

The reasons offered by Ho and Platt related mainly to substrate effects, but the patterns of distribution they observed, incidentally, also reflect the pathways of grammaticalization laid down by Bybee et al. (1994), in which past tense is hypothesized to be a further generalization from grammatical perfective marking, which is, in turn, conditioned by the lexical aspect of the verb. In the absence of substrate evidence, then, we are left with the universal pathways of tense, aspect and modality outlined by Bybee et al. (1994) as equally viable explanations (though nothing, of course, need diminish the possibility of a diagnosis pertaining to both substrate and universal reasons).

At least from the time of Bickerton (1981), efforts have been pressed into studying the genetic origins of creoles and mixed contact languages, though not always with the theoretical application of grammaticalization. Mufwene (1998: 325) cites Labov's (1994) "Uniformitarian Principle" by which the same processes that have produced creoles historically have produced new varieties of other languages; it is plausible, then, to consider the study of grammaticalization in new language varieties as following similar lines of argument to those that discuss creoles. However, even older varieties may reveal contact in their histories. Mufwene (1998) emphasizes the fact that English has experienced a number of contact stages in its history: for example, at the time of the introduction of the languages brought over by the Angles, Jutes and Saxons, not to mention later contact stages such as the time of the Scandinavian settlement in the northeast of Britain before the 10th century, as well as the role of Norman French a century later. The same questions of the historical contact of English have been raised on more than one occasion by McWhorter (2002), who discusses the question of "grammaticalization overkill" of languages that are not creoles. He also suggests that creoles lack, for example, overt marking for categories such as reflexivity simply because they have not existed for long enough for the function to start grammaticalizing (see also Heine 2005). In this way, his suggestions concur with the assumptions of the present study that new varieties of languages, along with creoles (which are unavoidably new languages), start grammaticalizing features from first principles; that is, for certain items at least, they may begin anew the same grammaticalization paths of the lexifiers. For example, the presence of grammatical triggers for marking the topic in Philippine languages is not found in creoles, because they require long periods of time in which lexical items can develop into such particles, and the lifetime of a creole language is relatively short by comparison (McWhorter 2002: 28). It would seem, then, that the contact language situation may be typically represented by grammaticalizing forms in their early developmental stages.

Quite apart from this, Mufwene considers that creoles are likely to co-opt the morphosyntactic behavior that is already part of the extant grammar of the lexifier languages (2008: 162), citing the example of *be going to* in Atlantic creoles. Significant amongst Mufwene's claims is that creoles have not developed from pidgins, but from basilectal varieties approximating their lexifiers (2008: 164), a view previously adopted by Chaudenson (1992). The same socio-historical approach has been applied to the study of the Irish English medial-object perfect by Siemund (2004) and Pietsch (2009), who demonstrate that transfer of a particular construction-type was reflective of the stage of English at the time it came into contact with Irish (an approach known as the "retentionist" view of contact). While such studies do not engage a specifically grammaticalization-theoretical point of departure, the data they provide realistically informs contact grammaticalization studies to a significant degree.

## 2.2 Models of replication

Heine and Kuteva (2003) discuss the process of replica grammaticalization as one in which an entire grammaticalization process is transferred from the M(odel)-language to the R(eplica)-language, the M-language generally being associated in creolistic terms with the substrate, and the R-language being the language replicating the M-language, usually a contact variety. The process is modeled using the following strategies (see Heine and Kuteva 2003: 539; Heine and Kuteva 2005: 92):

(3) Replica grammaticalization
   a. Speakers of language R notice that in language M there is a grammatical category Mx.
   b. They develop an equivalent category Rx, using material available in their own language (R).
   c. To this end, they replicate a grammaticalization process they assume to have taken place in language M, using an analogical formula of the kind [My > Mx] = [Ry > Rx].
   d. They grammaticalize category Ry to Rx.

In ordinary contact-induced grammaticalization (see Heine and Kuteva 2005: 81), Ry involves the use of any available material – it need not have any conceptual relation to the parallel function in My. In replica grammaticalization, however, Ry and My share similar lexical source concepts. The most frequently cited example comes from Irish English, which has as its substrate (M) the Irish language. Irish employs as its "hot-news" perfect a form instantiating the schema [X is after Y]; it is described by Heine and Kuteva as the Location Schema and expresses events which have just been completed. In other words, this particular usage of the perfect employs a spatial or temporal schema suggesting that something is just "after" happening, i.e. has just recently happened. The model process in the substrate Irish language, the Location Schema (My), is grammaticalized into a perfect aspect marker [Mx]. In Irish English in the late 17th century, the same process was replicated (Ry > Rx). The fact that no other language in the world is known to have undergone a similar process indicates that it is not a universal strategy but a replication of the entire process of grammaticalization in the model language. The examples are given by Heine and Kuteva (2003: 540):

(4) Irish
   *Tá     sí   tréis  an   bád   a dhíol.*
   be.NPST she  after  the  boat  selling
   'She has just sold the boat.'                    (Harris 1991: 205)

(5) Irish English
   She's after selling the boat.
   'She has just sold the boat.'                    (Harris 1991: 205)

Irish English also has the construction with a NP following the *after*-expression: *He's after the flu* 'He's just had the flu' (Heine and Kuteva 2005: 102). The presence of a NP complement suggests an intermediate stage of development, as NP complements usually precede VP ones diachronically, and offers evidence for the fact that the entire grammaticalization process was copied, not just the beginning and the end of it.

Many accounts that followed Heine and Kuteva's work (e.g. Matras and Sakel 2007, Matthews and Yip 2009, as mentioned earlier, as well as Pietsch 2009 and Gast and van der Auwera 2012) had problems with the subprocess conveyed in (3c), suggesting that it implies that speakers of the replicator language had access to the historical processes known to be associated with the grammaticalization of a certain replicated feature in the lexifier. It is not certain that that was what was intended by Heine and Kuteva, as their data appear often to take recourse to what are apparently universal paths of grammaticalization, whether also adopted by the lexifier or not. However, as Pietsch (2009) notes, the statement is misleading if understood literally, as it seems to assume that the speakers are intentionally creating the grammaticalization process, as well as having knowledge of the diachronically preceding stages of development. In his study of the Irish English (medial-object) perfect, though, Pietsch demonstrates that the framework in (3) has a usefulness as long as the older and newer stages of grammaticalization can be seen to co-exist synchronically. Such a panchronic view of grammaticalization has always been at the heart of much of Heine's and his colleagues' earlier work (e.g. Heine 1992, Heine 1993 and Heine 1997), and is also indispensable for explaining the results of the present study, as will be seen below.

The synchronic co-existence of older and newer stages of grammaticalization also served as the basis for Matras and Sakel's (2007) theoretical approach to grammaticalization in contact, which builds on earlier research by Nau (1995), who suggests that loan translations involve the recognition of a certain polysemy between concrete and abstract senses in words in the model language for correspondences to be made in the replica language. They also cite Keesing's (1991) studies on Melanesian Pidgin, which suggest that speakers of the replica language are able to identify lexemes in the lexifier that carry the same grammatical meanings as functionally parallel lexemes in the model languages (Matras and Sakel 2007: 833–834). Keesing's studies had highlighted the importance of a polysemous grammatical function in the replica language which was perceivable by its speakers in order for them to create new functions. This meant, though, that the trigger in most cases was a grammaticalizing form that had retained co-occurring lexical functions, which would allow the transparency required to match it with a similar item in the model language, as it would not be possible for the replica language to re-grammaticalize forms that had become too conceptually abstract and too distant from their concrete lexical sources in the lexifier language. The co-existence of the original lexical functions is also noted in Pietsch's (2009) study, and it is characteristic of many Southeast Asian languages (Matthews and Yip 2009: 381) which tend towards polyfunctionality (see also Ansaldo and Lim 2004). Such co-existence represents a situation of intense layering of the kind discussed by Hopper (1991), suggesting an essential factor in the process of contact re-grammaticalization. These factors will be taken into account in the light of contact data from the New Englishes.

## 3 The New Englishes study

As noted in the Introduction, earlier research on the topic of grammaticalization in the New Englishes (NEs) is not widely available. Ziegeler (2000), for instance, discussed relative rates of grammaticalization in data from Singapore English and non-contact varieties such as Australian and British English. Part of the reason for such a paucity of research is that the data from New Englishes lacks adequate evidence from diachronic stages of development, and the advice cautioned by Bruyn (2009: 332) not to rely too heavily on the appearance of synchronic data for making diachronic claims seems to stand in the way of many research efforts as diachronic data are often difficult to obtain.[3] However, there has been a noticeable increase in the number of synchronic, comparative studies of the New Englishes since corpora such as the *International Corpus of English* (ICE) have become freely available, and the field is developing a typology of its own.

It should be noted from the outset that a range of grammatical features have been observed as shared, to some extent, by the new varieties of English. Many of these features are comprehensively summed up in a study by Sand (2005), who refers to them as Angloversals (citing Mair's 2003: 84 original use of the term). Other studies that have discussed Angloversals include those of Kortmann et al. (2004) and Szmrecsanyi and Kortmann (2009a), who show that the relationships between a range of universals apply not just to L2 varieties of English, but to all varieties, pidgins and creoles included. Szmrecsanyi and Kortmann (2009b) distinguish Anglo/Franco-versals (referring to shared vernacular features of a specific language) from "Varioversals", referring to features of language varieties of a similar historical background (e.g. resumptive pronouns in relative clauses). As such, Varioversals may be considered to be a sub-type of Angloversals.

---

[3] It should be noted that there are few, if any, diachronic resources obtainable for the new English dialects, though Hoffmann and Tan (2011) present a preliminary overview, and a corpus based on Oral History Interviews available from the National Archives in Singapore is currently being constructed (Bao Zhiming, p.c.).

Szmrecsanyi and Kortmann (2009b) also include classifications such as Typoversals (in which a distinction is made on the basis of shared typological features), Phyloversals (in which the distinctions are made on the basis of shared family features), Areoversals (common areal distinctions amongst languages) and Vernacular Universals (universals of common vernacular usage, e.g. double negation). There has been little research, though, to present knowledge, on the possibility of a grammaticalization explanation for the prevalence of such features.

While it may be difficult to access details on the historical backgrounds of the new Englishes, it is clear that the varieties under discussion share a similar general background in having been introduced during periods of colonization, and thus the items to be discussed could qualify as Varioversals. There are some accounts which provide a clear picture of the type of input provided by the lexifiers at the time of colonization. Gupta (1998: 111) makes it clear that the model language of transmission in the case of Singapore (mainly in the late 19th century) was Standard English used by the teachers in the English-medium schools, but not necessarily by British speakers of English. Most of the teachers, it seems, were of Eurasian or Indian descent, often with Portuguese names, indicating either Portuguese or Indian origins; the variety they spoke was already a new English at the time.[4] However, it was the lingua francas of the time that provided the principal substrates: Baba Malay (the Malay of the Straits Chinese), Bazaar Malay (now almost obsolete), as well as southern Chinese dialects, especially Hokkien (Southern Min). As such, the situation of language contact was extremely volatile, determined by the enormous mix of languages and ethnicities concentrated in a small and dense population community (now more than 4 million inhabitants). In the case of India, Kachru (1994), Sharma (2012) and Coelho (1997) provide comprehensive summaries of the historical contact periods, while not emphasizing in any great detail the nature of the transmission variety, though Kachru does note that it was taught by Europeans, and missionaries in the first instance, which would have meant that a literary variety was being transmitted in the colonial situation, from the 17th century onward. In all cases, though, it was a foreign language variety that was in use, which, according to Kachru, became indigenized over time. In the case of Indian English, the principal substrates according to Sharma (2009a) are Hindi, Punjabi and Gujarati, with Tamil and Kannada in South India.

---

4 Gupta (1998) uses the term "standard English" to refer to any international variety used in formal and educational contexts; hence her estimations of its correlation with a "new" English.

## 3.1 The corpora

Synchronic data were initially extracted from the *Flowerpod Corpus*, an internet forum corpus of over 700,000 words taken from a range of internet chat forums in Singapore. The corpus is named after its principal site, the Flowerpod site, which comprises approximately half of the corpus.[5] The advantages of the *Flowerpod Corpus* over other, more generalized corpora are that the data are completely unedited, and the speakers are not aware at all that their contributions are being used as a data source for linguistic analysis. The data, as a result, tend to be more colloquial than their counterparts in the ICE corpora: there is a large amount of elision, text-speak, creative re-spellings and abbreviations, though this is not felt to be a disadvantage; the authenticity of the language far outweighs the disadvantages of such features from the point of view of linguistic analysis. By using a diversity of topics selected from the internet sites, efforts were made also to control for biases of gender, age and cultural background.

The remainder of the data has been taken from the ICE corpora of Singapore English and of Indian English, since, as Sharma (2009a) also observed, these two corpora are strictly parallel in terms of genre distribution. For the data on the stative progressive aspect, the ICE-East Africa (ICE-EA) has been added as a control, as Sharma (2009b) makes strong claims for a substrate cause for the presence of stative progressives in both Indian English and Singapore English. However, only the sections from S1a-001 to S1b-020 are used in both the ICE-Singapore and the ICE-India (ICE-EA is structured differently), since they contain the files of spoken usage which are the likely to represent the most colloquial sub-varieties in either case (according to the text-type listings in Sand's 2005 appendix). As a result, they would most closely correspond to the more haphazard data found in the *Flowerpod Corpus*, which, although representative of a wide range of speakers, ages and with no gender bias, is not controlled for genre parallels in the same way as in the ICE Corpora.

In the case of habitual *will*, the ICE-GB Corpus has been used as a control, since the modal appears as a marker of habitual aspect in older, non-contact varieties as well, though, as will be seen below, with a different frequency. The other two features under discussion do not show up in non-contact varieties. It could be argued that the progressive has a limited usage in some non-contact varieties with stative verbs, though, it will be seen, not generally with the same

---

5 Acknowledgements are due to the National University of Singapore Staff Research Support Scheme (2008) and Amelyn Thompson for assistance in compiling the corpus. The original Flowerpod forums are now no longer accessible.

verbs that co-occur with it in the new varieties. The specific determiner *one* is not found in non-contact varieties, thus precluding the need to supply control data where that is concerned. The three target grammatical features will now be investigated in turn.

## 3.2 Grammatical features

### 3.2.1 Habitual *will*

The relatively frequent appearance of the modal verb *will* to mark habitual aspect in Singapore English has been observed for some time: Deterding (2003) discusses its prominence as attributable to the use of the Chinese (Mandarin) modal verb *hui* in the substrate. However, a substrate explanation is not so easy to retrieve in the case of *hui*, as its meaning is closer to that of ability, not volition, as habitual *will* would suggest. The frequency of habitual *will* relative to British English usage has also been observed by Deuber (2010) for Trinidadian English, and it was noted in Guerti (2009) for Singaporean English that habitual functions of *will* are unusually frequent. Deuber's study attributes the use of habitual *will* to a need to develop a functional parallel with habitual *does/(dez)* in Trinidadian Creole, though it is not explained why Trinidadian English did not just employ *does* for habituals instead. The need to investigate the modal became obvious in a study which looked at the distribution of forms used to mark present habitual aspect in Singapore English (Ziegeler 2012). The study showed that in one portion of the *Flowerpod Corpus* more than 24% of habituals were marked by *will*. The data were extracted from the corpus in a particular thread which naturalistically elicited multiple responses in the habitual aspect in answer to a question about the time taken by participants to have a shower in the morning. The total number of responses using a finite verb form came to 129; the breakdown of the responses is presented in Table 1 (PFP – "past for present" – is a category in which past tense is used to express present habitual aspect).

**Table 1:** Responses using habitual aspect in answer to the lead posting: *How long do you take for shower? What's the first thing that you will mostly do in the bathroom?*

| Present tense forms | Will + V | PFPs | Total |
|---|---|---|---|
| 84.5 (65.5%) | 32 (24.8%) | 12.5 (9.7%) | 129[6] |

---

[6] The absolute scores of 84.5 and 12.5 in Table 1 represent tokens from participants who used both *will* and one of the other forms in the same response: they have been weighted as half values.

Examples of the responses included:

(6) *on average before work every morning is 15 min.*
*but on days i dont have to rush, eg, weekends... I **will** take half an hour and scrub etc shiok.*[7]
(Posted by Princessa, 6 November 2006, 10:07 AM)

(7) *In the morning, about 15–20 mins. Night **will** be longer, about half hour to wash hair and sometimes scrub. Being in the shower is very relaxing after working for a long day...*[8]
(Posted by clloud, 11 November 2006, 10:07 PM)

Interestingly, lexical sources with the meaning of volitional modality functioning to express habitual aspect are infrequent in the crosslinguistic literature. Bybee et al. (1994: 154) list sources derived from lexemes meaning 'know', but also a few sources with the meanings 'live' or 'see' (e.g. Yagara). Heine and Kuteva (2002: 331) list habitual aspect sources crosslinguistically as derived from lexemes with the meanings 'go', 'know', 'live', 'remain', 'sit' and 'use', and from other grammatical aspects such as continuous and iterative, suggesting that habitual aspect may be considered as an imperfective aspect of a different type from that of the progressive aspect. With regard to (English-based) creole data, the most frequently cited source for habituals is that of *do* (see Rickford 1980; Holm 1988), especially in Atlantic creoles (though this has been attributed to the use of the form *do* at the specific historical period of transmission; see, for instance, Mufwene 2001: 32, who notes its frequency in Southwestern English and Irish dialects during the 17th century). It is noteworthy that many creoles seem to require habitual aspect marking whereas their lexifiers often do not, and that the use of *will* to express habitual aspect does not appear to be following any universal grammaticalization pattern. The only contact data that may be of interest to the present study are those of Singler (1990), who refers to Kru, a West African, English-based creole, in which the forms *ken* and *we*, derived from English *can* and *will*, have not only irrealis functions but habitual ones as well (e.g. Singler 1990: 211):

(8) *Das     hem   wok    hi    **we**   du.*
    that.COP  his    work    he    IRR    do
    'That's the work that he (a tailor) will do/does.'

---

[7] *Shiok* is a discourse particle in CSE, meaning 'very nice'.
[8] Note the use of adverbial topicalization in (7); *night* is not a subject in this example – according to Bao (2001) almost any grammatical element may be topicalized in CSE.

It has been long claimed that habitual aspect represents a hybrid categorial position between realis and irrealis meaning (see Givón 1994; Cristofaro 2004). To find a marker expressing both irrealis as well as habitual aspect would, therefore, not be surprising. *Will*, then, as a habitual aspect marker, is not un-prototypical; moreover, from a comparative point of view, its use in CSE may later be seen to be relevant to the development of irrealis meaning.

The relation between generics and habituals has frequently been noted. Langacker (1997: 191) described generics as "expressions that ascribe a general property to all members of a class", and habituals as expressions referring to customary and repeated events. Bybee (1994: 237) described habituals and generics as carrying the same aspectual meanings, discriminated only by the nature of the subject, e.g. generic *Dogs pant to cool off* vs. habitual *My dog pants to cool off*. In their cross-linguistic study of 76 unrelated languages, Bybee et al. (1994) found no clear distinctions in the grammatical expression of generic and habitual. Because of this, Ziegeler (2006a: 91) defined generics and habituals as interlocking categories: generics referring to multiple participants for which a single event or property may hold, and habituals referring to a single participant to which multiple events may be attributed. Thus, in discussing habitual aspect, we are essentially discussing generic aspect in reverse, and examples of either classification were included in the totals.

The results of the surveys of habitual *will* in the present study are presented in Table 2, with total scores including the forms *will*, *'ll* (in all persons) and *won't*, *wun*. *Wun* (CSE *won't*) was also searched in the Flowerpod Corpus (no examples of this form were obtained from the ICE-Singapore corpus).

**Table 2:** Results of the multi-corpora searches for habitual uses of *will* (*'ll*, *won't*, *wun*) showing comparisons between data from new varieties of English and those of British English

| Corpus | Habituals | % of total | Total no. of tokens |
| --- | --- | --- | --- |
| Flowerpod | 418 | 20.93% | 1997 |
| ICE – Singapore | 186 | 11.67% | 1593 |
| ICE – India | 224 | 12.22% | 1833 |
| ICE – GB | 28 | 3.13% | 893 |

The data from British English were included for this particular feature, as the use of habitual aspect *will* (and *would*, for past time reference) is not unknown in older varieties of English, as shown by Deuber's (2010) comprehensive survey of similar features in the ICE corpora. (It is also worth noting that since the form appears in British English, though to a lesser extent, it cannot be considered a distinctive feature of Colloquial Singapore English only, but may just as readily belong to Standard Singapore English as well.) Nevertheless, it is clear that its frequency is up to seven times higher in the Flowerpod Corpus than in ICE-GB, and up to four times higher in the other two corpora. The figures in Table 2 also show that there is a large difference between the ICE corpora statistics for this feature and those of the Flowerpod Corpus. This may be due to the nature of the topics of discussion, frequently about regular habits, possessions and activities, thus providing more opportunity for any form of habitual (or generic; see below) aspect to be used than in any of the ICE corpora.[9] However, it is for this reason that the ICE-Corpora, with their relatively balanced uniformity of genres, may act as a control on the more spontaneously occurring data in the Flowerpod Corpus.

Examples of the *will* data included the following:

(9)  Flowerpod Corpus, Health file
*... but usually I **will** just eat it straight from the cup ... don't really bother to add some more fruits.*
(Posted by jadedollie, 25 July 2008)

(10) Flowerpod Corpus, Hardwarezone
*Btw has anyone manage [sic.] to get any fine nib Waterman fountain pen in Sg ? A few places I ask here and in Malaysia all only have M or B. The salesperson usually **will** say it's good for signature.*
(Posted by Lehnsherr, 3 October 2008)

(11) Flowerpod Corpus, Health file
*but once i get home, alone, i'll start all my nonsense. I treasure life alot, so i **won't** think of death.*
(Posted by jess82, 13 December 2006)

(12) ICE-Singapore
*Now dienes **will** react with certain reagents uhm which are called dienophile.*
(ICE- SIN S1B005#81:1:A)

(13) ICE-India
*Everyday I **will** have rice then curry then uh
... one word ... when I go to sleep I **will** have a glass of milk ...*
(ICE-IND:S1A-072#214:1:A)

---

**9** It could be argued that the statistics may be skewed by the presence of paradigmatic alternatives expressing the same functions as *will* (e.g. *be going to*, for future uses), thus creating the appearance of greater or lesser frequency of habitual uses in opposition. However, it should be noted that prediction is not the only function for *will*, and a complete survey of all the possible paradigmatic substitutes would be necessary to eliminate this possibility. Such a survey is beyond the scope of the present study.

(14) ICE-India
*Uh you know ... in Karnataka no ... usually people **will** prefer ... that roti what we'll call roti it's prepared of jowar ... and chapati rarely once in a week they **will** do it ...*
(ICE-IND:S1A-072#115:1:A)

(15) ICE Great Britain
*From about the age of one children speak uh a child **will** speak one or two words not actually in a sentence or anything like that ...*
(ICE-GB:S1B-003 #47:1:B)

Note that example (15) in the British data is more representative of a generic usage than the other examples, since it does not have a specific subject. It should also be noted that usage with first-person subjects in CSE appears to be quite frequent. This could be claimed as an over-extension of the habitual uses elsewhere; while it would appear to be redundant in non-contact varieties, giving a sense that the speaker is indulging in self-observation, in contact varieties modal habitual marking is seen to apply to all subject persons. The facility with which habitual *will* co-occurs with first-person subjects may also be ascribed to the presence of topic-comment information structure in some dialects (especially CSE), since topic-comment information structure demonstrates a weaker relationship between the verb and the first argument than subject-predicate structure (see Ziegeler 2008 for more details).

### 3.2.2 The progressive aspect

The extension of the progressive to stative contexts (only found in restricted uses in non-contact varieties of English) has long been the subject of discussion in descriptive studies of the New Englishes (see, for instance, Platt et al. 1984: 83, who attribute its usage to "over-teaching" of the standard use of the progressive). The feature is listed in Platt et al. (1984) as occurring in Indian English, Singapore English, Papua New Guinean English and East and West African English. The feature is certainly a candidate for an Angloversal, and one of Sand's (2005) "breaking points" of the grammar. While Sand (2005) finds no clear correlation between substratum features and the extended use of the progressive in any of the contact varieties she has surveyed (including Jamaican English, Singapore English, Indian English and East African English), Sharma (2009b) attributes differences between contact varieties in the use of the progressive to differences in the substrate usage. In Sharma's data (2009a: 176), Indian substrate languages such as Hindi have an obligatory imperfective marker -*ta*, which alternates with another progressive marker -*rahna*, according to the verb type used, while the Chinese substrates do not have such a close correspondence, since the Chinese markers for progressive aspect are somewhat restricted compared with those of English and Hindi. In both cases, though, it is difficult to reason from the substrate point of view. In the case of Indian English, there is a far greater number of possible substrate languages than in the case of Singaporean English, and since part of Sharma's (2009a) account was based on data from a selection of twelve speakers sharing only three principal substrate languages, it was therefore not parallel with the Singaporean data, which came from various secondary sources as well as the ICE corpus. Nevertheless, the twelve individuals' responses were backed by data from the ICE corpus of Indian English, which was compared with the ICE-Singapore corpus. Sharma (2009a: 192) found a total of 141 non-standard uses of the progressive *be + having* in the ICE-India against 2 non-standard uses of the same progressive verb in the Singapore English corpus. Sharma did not specify how much of the ICE corpora was used in either sample, but the results of the present study offer a slightly different picture, as seen below.

In terms of grammaticalization universals, there does not seem to be evidence of an association between stative progressives and lexical source forms. Heine (1994) suggests that schemas rather than isolated lexemes provide the most common source in the crosslinguistic grammaticalization of progressives. (1994: 269). In particular, the English progressive was claimed to have developed from the Location Schema, according to Heine (1994) and Bybee et al (1994), see Section 4.

As noted above, the present survey examined data taken from the *Flowerpod Corpus*, the ICE-SG and the ICE-India; extra data were taken from the ICE-EA (East Africa) corpus to be used as a control measure on the evidence of substratist explanations provided by Sharma (2009a, 2009b). Since a survey of the progressive aspect requires a survey of open class items, which would be impractical under the circumstances, the range of lexical verbs selected was restricted to those observed in historical texts (see Section 4), i.e. *have, contain, believe* and *belong*. Only *(be) having* was found to occur across all four dialects, *belonging* occurring only in ICE-India. *Containing* occurred only twice in the ICE-EA, as did *believing* (though the latter example appeared ambiguous, on re-examination of the contexts, between a finite stative progressive and a non-finite usage, and thus was not included in the totals); another, *remaining*, appeared in both ICE-India (2 tokens) and ICE-EA (1 token). *Owning* (Flowerpod, 1 token), *smelling* (ICE-EA, 1 token), *hearing* (ICE-EA, 1 token) and *seeing* (ICE-EA, 6 tokens) were also found, after observation of their appearance in the corpora during the data-gathering process. The data are presented in Table 3.

**Table 3:** Data from the progressive stative survey across 4 NE dialects, showing occurrence of the lexical verbs *have*, *contain*, and *belong* in the extended stative progressive as a percentage of the total number of progressive uses overall

|  | Flowerpod | ICE-SG | ICE-India | ICE-EA |
|---|---|---|---|---|
| *(be) having* | 42/232 = 18.1% | 12/76 = 15.7% | 62/153 = 40.5% | 66/216 = 30.5% |
| *(be) containing* | – | – | – | 2/5 |
| *(be) belonging* | – | – | 4/15 = 26.6% | – |

It can be seen in Table 3 that the use of the stative progressive extends beyond Singaporean and Indian English. Although a further study of the substrate languages of East African English might be needed to exhaust all possible substratist accounts, it can be fairly confidently claimed that the appearance of the feature across so many NE dialects cannot be attributed to substratum language influence alone. Uses in which the progressive expresses limited duration of a holding state were not included in the totals, as in the following: *JL **is having** 20% off now* ('John Lewis [a department store] is having 20% off [the price of certain items]' – Flowerpod Corpus Health thread, Oct 3, 2005). Similar exclusions included *having problems* and *having trouble*, which are standardly expressed using the progressive in non-contact English dialects. The figures are therefore slightly different from Sharma's (2009a) totals of only 2 (non-standard uses) for the entire ICE-SG, and Bao's (2005) attestations that the stative progressive is not used at all in the ICE-SG corpus. The *Flowerpod Corpus* shows that it is alive and well in CSE, though lexically restricted mainly to *have*; this could be due to the fact that *have* would score higher on frequency whatever aspect it appears with, since it is a "light" verb.

Amongst the 12 extended uses of *having* in the Singaporean data were found the following examples:

(16)  *Flowerpod Corpus,* Cosmetics forum:
*Just my 2 cents worth. I saw Sasa **having** alot of colour palettes (brown/bronze/nude/cream & the likes & also colourful 1s) Mb u can take a look too if u r on a budget!* ['Maybe you can take a look too if you are on a budget'][10]
(Posted by wen_kitty 17 December 2005, 12:27 PM)

---

**10** *Sasa* is the name of a shop selling cosmetics. Note that although (16) does not contain a finite stative progressive, the participle *having* nevertheless refers to possession of a state, as do the finite uses in ICE-SG.

(17) *Oh maybe I'm not **having** migraine then.*
(ICE-SIN:S1A-028#286:1:B)

(18) *In fact at the moment only one school is is **having** the the system running so there there are three more actually.*
(ICE-SIN:S1A-045#47:1:A)

(19) *But I still think that it's it's still nicer than what we are **having** here in Singapore you know.*
(ICE-SIN:S1A-003#250:1:C)

The uses in (16)–(19) can be idiomatically replaced by the non-progressive. Examples found in the ICE-India corpus included the following:

(20) *For example okay we have done our MA and all that ... suppose we do get married with someone who is not **having** any education.*
(ICE-IND:S1A-024#179:1:A)

(21) *Almost every year because uh every year we are **having** two vacations.*
(ICE-IND:S1A-047#106:1:B)

(22) *And the key the key of that basati is given to one of the persons who is not **belonging** to that sect uhm I mean Jain.*
(ICE-IND:S1A-063#95:1:B)

An example in the ICE-EA is (23):

(23) *Therefore in Tanzania we have two document documents. The Our constitution is **containing** that is in the act two documents the nineteen seventy-seven and the nineteen sixty-six act of union.*
(Conversation T)[11]

The *Flowerpod* data were then restricted to cover a specific, topic-focused, subset of the corpus, in which the same semantic environment, a discussion on health problems, was expected to provide a natural means of elicitation of the item searched. Using this method of delimiting the productivity of the item, it was possible to arrive at an estimation of the frequency of the stative progressive

---

[11] It should be noted that the ICE-EA corpus appears in a different file format from that of ICE-SG and ICE-IND.

*be having* relative to the non-progressive *have*. Table 4 shows that in the Health-thread environment, stative progressive forms expressing possession alone showed a probable usage frequency of over 11%.

**Table 4:** Relative probability of stative progressive *have* (expressing possession of a physical condition) occurring in a restricted portion of the *Flowerpod Corpus* (Health thread)

| Stative progressive *have* | Non-progressive (finite) *have* | Total |
|---|---|---|
| 23 = 11.4% | 179 = 88.6% | 202 |

Examples included:

(24) *Flowerpod Corpus*, Health forum
 *my gf is **having** depression now. seen the doc and doc has confirmed and prescribe her some med*
 (Posted by zhiz22, 25 June 2007, 01:01 AM)

(25) *and my frenz too ... one of them **have** depression ... another one keep saying wanna suicide....*
 (Posted by aliciagal, 26 November 2005, 04:56 PM)

It can be seen from the data that the uses of the stative progressive in the four contact dialects most noticeable as being "indigenized" are those that refer to possession, either of states of a physical condition or of concrete objects. Such uses would be less likely to be found in non-contact varieties, since they refer to stable or indefinite lapses of time, not characteristic of the use of the progressive as a marker of continuous imperfectivity. As noted earlier, the ICE-GB was not set aside as a Control, since the particular usage for which the contact dialects are noted was not expected to be found. Nevertheless, it could be argued that the finite stative progressive is found in more established varieties of English as well. Amongst the uses that were observed in the ICE-GB (spanning the same file range as the other ICE corpora) were the frequent use of *having* with the function of expressing the present or future progressive, as in *We're having a party*; in such cases, the meaning is one of a (caused) present or future event, rather than a possessed current state; also observed were uses such as *I'm having problems* (these uses were also found in the contact data, but not included since they refer to a function that is not unique to the contact dialects). Only three examples describing physical conditions that could be rated as similar to the uses found in the new varieties data were found in the ICE-GB:

(26) *So that's not the problem,*
*Are you still **having** the tremor?*
(ICE-GB:S1A-051 #256:4:A)

(27) *Is she still **having** hallucinations?*
(ICE-GB:S1A-080 #285:1:A)

(28) *Now I saw you was it a year ago when you were **having** back pain?*
(ICE-GB:S1A-089 #218:4:A)

None of these uses carries the same meaning as the caused events that are often found in combination with the progressive *have* in standard usage; they carry instead a meaning of adversity, as do many of the examples in the NE data, where the subject is a (malefactive) patient, rather than a causative agent (as in examples like *We're having a party*). However, both uses of the progressive in (26)–(27) are reinforced with the adverb *still*, which increases the sense of continuity required for the use of an aspectual marker of a temporary process; the use in (28) is reinforced by the backgrounding frame of a temporal subordinate clause. It may be the case that such adverbials are triggering the use of the progressive here, but these are only three examples, and further research would be required to verify such possibilities using a wider data-base than is obtainable within the scope of the present paper.

### 3.2.3 The specific determiner *one*

Platt et al (1984: 53–58) explain the usage of the determiner *one/wan* as related to the difference between the definite and the indefinite (which, according to them, refers to what is known or unknown) and specific or non-specific (terms which they use to refer to particular or non-particular nouns). With regard to cases in which the nominal referent is specific and known, they discuss the use of demonstratives such as *this*. Their distinctions reflect those that Bickerton (1981) used for creoles, and they exemplify such distinctions in examples from Indian English, West African English, East African English, Papua New Guinean English, Hong Kong English, Philippine English, Malaysian English and Singapore English.

Since then, there has not been a great deal of research into the use of the specific/non-specific distinction with indefinite nominals in the New Englishes, though this referential distinction is discussed by Ziegeler (2003a 2010) in relation to the presence or absence of plural marking in CSE, and by Gil (2003) in relation to the absence of count–mass categories in Singapore English (transnumerality). One study that has discussed the distinction for singular nouns is that of Sharma (2005), who concludes that it is a combination of substratum and universalist effects that influence the presence or absence of articles in general in Indian English. Sand (2005) provides a very minimal token count of specific *one*, which she claims appears only in ICE-India and ICE-Singapore. Her tagged results reveal six tokens in the former corpus and four in the latter, in co-occurrence with *get*.

In terms of universal grammaticalization strategies, it is not unusual to find in many of the world's languages indefinite determiners derived from forms expressing the numeral 'one': Heine and Kuteva (2002: 220–221) list Albanian, Turkish, German, French, Ewe, Moré, Hungarian, Lezgian, Tamil, and Easter Island as languages in which this grammaticalization path is found. However, in their (2002) data, the numeral marks both specific as well as non-specific indefinites, just as the English indefinite article does today. In Heine (1997: 72–74), a five stage-sequence of changes is observed to be involved in the grammaticalization of the indefinite article from the numeral 'one' crosslinguistically. The following stages are distinguished (1997: 72-4):

**Stage 1:** the numeral, in which specific indefinite reference may be left unmarked;

**Stage 2:** the presentative marker, introducing a new participant into the discourse;

**Stage 3:** the specific marker, when the form develops a discourse function in marking any nominal participant that is known to the speaker but presumably not to the addressee (this means that in many cases non-specific reference is marked in opposition to specific by bare nominals);

**Stage 4:** the non-specific marker, no longer restricted to marking specific reference, but used whenever an indefinite singular nominal is referred to;[12]

**Stage 5:** the generalized article, not restricted to determining singular count nouns but possible with plural and mass nouns as well; see, for instance, Spanish *unos hombres* [one.M.PL men] 'some men'.

The following survey will examine whether such stages may apply to the development of articles in the New Englishes.

---

[12] At this stage, it may be said that the indefinite article marks not only actual reference, but *potential* reference.

For this study, the corpora were searched for instances of specific uses of *one* (the *Flowerpod Corpus*, and the first 120 files of the spoken sections of the ICE-SG and the ICE-India). Again, the ICE-GB was not needed as a control, since the item under investigation is not attested as appearing in more established, non-contact varieties. Because the data were not audio files, it was in some cases difficult to discern whether the use of *one* was to express specificity or merely numerical contrast, the latter being found in non-contact varieties as well (though specificity would not be excluded from such meanings). Ambiguous examples were therefore not included in the counts; in other words, the only figures that were obtained came from indisputably specific or referential uses of *one*. The counts may therefore represent a smaller proportion of use than was actually the case. Forms searched were *one, wan, wun* and *1* (the latter often being used as an abbreviation in the *Flowerpod Corpus*). The data are presented in Table 5, as frequencies per 10,000 words, in order to provide a more salient standard of comparison, since expressing the data as a proportion of the total counts of *one* would be a fairly meaningless exercise given the high overall frequencies and the differences in the size of the corpora.

Table 5: Frequency of occurrence per 10,000 words, of specific *one* across three NE corpora

| Corpus | Raw frequency | Frequency per 10,000 wds |
|---|---|---|
| Flowerpod | 66 | 1 |
| ICE-SG | 28 | 1.16 |
| ICE-India | 39 | 1.625 |

The data in Table 5 show that specific *one* is 16% more frequent in the ICE-SG than in the *Flowerpod Corpus* and 62.5% more frequent in the ICE-India than in the *Flowerpod*. Examples from the *Flowerpod Corpus* are in (29)–(30), showing evidence of Heine's Stages 2 and 3 above:

(29)  *Flowerpod Corpus*, Hardwarezone 2 file,
      bought the shampoo nia ... $9.90 for the small bottle ... amk ntuc got **one**
      table specially for this brand one[13]
      (Posted by Pepperthrow, 7 June 2007)

---

[13] *amk ntuc* = "Ang Mo Kio NTUC", the name of a shop at Ang Mo Kio in suburban Singapore. Note the use of the emphatic function of *one* appearing at the end of the sentence; this is a nominalizing use, and has nothing to do with the specific determiner use under investigation (comprehensive accounts of its use may be found in, for instance, Bao 2009).

(30) *Flowerpod Corpus*, Hardwarezone
Hi guys, i have two BRAND NEW unopen LONGSHOT from HASBRO US for sale. got sabo [sabotaged] *by* **one** *chap here.*
(Posted by Benttw, 22 November 2008)

Examples from ICE-SG included (31)–(32):

(31) *do this blur you know that day* **one one** *lecturer came and ask uh uh ask me to help him lah so I went then*[14]
(ICE-SIN:S1A-001#219:1:A)

(32) *but Kallang got* **one** *Fun world or what lah*
('But there is a Fun World in Kallang')
(ICE-SIN:S1A-085#281:1:A)

Examples from ICE-India included (33)–(34):

(33) *Like uh District Industries Corporation ... industries ... there is uh* **one** *corporation called uh Karnataka State Financial Corporation.*
(ICE-IND:S1A-020#32:1:A)

(34) *And I know* **one** *professor uh ... in Selam who was our professor also.*
(ICE-IND:S1A-027#215:1:B)

In both the Singaporean as well as the Indian data, the use of specific *one* appeared to be relatively frequent in presentative constructions, such as (29), (32) and (33). In CSE, the verb *got* is used with an existential meaning 'there is' (as in (32)), an example of predicative possession being used to express existence. This construction is considered a case of replica grammaticalization in Heine and Kuteva (2005: 93), copying a similar grammaticalization process in Chinese. Whether it could be an instance of replica grammaticalization is not out of the question, but the possibility of a universalist explanation for the use of *one* should also be considered, given that the use of specific *one* does not appear to be restricted to the existential constructions alone, as seen in (30) and (34). The reasons for such a possibility will be explained below.

In order to provide an estimate of the relative frequency of this feature, a token count was taken of the occurrence of *one* alongside the specific indefinite article in one selected discussion thread in the *Flowerpod Corpus*, the Pen Club

---

[14] *Blur* = 'stupid' in CSE; *lah* is a frequently used discourse particle expressing emphasis or certainty (see, e.g., Lim 2007 for more details).

thread, an optimal enviroment for the use of specific determiners qualifying nominal referents that are known to the speaker, but not necessarily to the addressee, the reader. The results are presented in Table 6:

**Table 6:** Probability of the occurrence of the specific determiner *one* relative to indefinite article use in a restricted portion of the *Flowerpod Corpus* (the Pen Club thread)

| Specific *one* | Specific indefinite article | Total token no. |
| --- | --- | --- |
| 19 = 11.17% | 151 = 88.82% | 170 |

Examples of specific use of the indefinite article include:

(35) *Flowerpod Corpus*, Hardwarezone file
*I got them from **a** shop in Bras Basah Complex.*
(Posted by Lehnsherr, 4 October 2008)

Table 6 shows that the relative frequency of the specific determiner *one* in the *Flowerpod Corpus* is not high, though it is present, and has the same relative frequency in selected environments as the stative progressive *have* in Table 4. Thus, although the two features are distinctive in CSE, their frequency is lower than that of habitual *will*, as seen in Table 1. Clearly, there is a case, though, for such items to be still listed as Varioversals; whether their presence is due to substratum influence or universal grammaticalization processes is a question to be addressed below.

# 4 Interim summary

From the above surveys, it can be seen that in each instance the selected form for analysis is found to a greater or lesser extent in more than one NE variety: habitual *will* is found in Singapore English, Indian English and Trinidad and Tobego English; the stative progressive in CSE, Indian English and East African English; and specific *one* in CSE and Indian English, as well as in the other new Englishes mentioned by Platt et al. (1984) and English-based creoles, as explained above. Such findings, of course, need not rule out a substratist explanation, but they do make a strong case for Varioversals, as discussed above. In other ways, it does not appear that speakers of language R are resorting to universal grammaticalization strategies to grammaticalize habitual aspect using *will* or the progressive aspect in the case of stative progressives; specific *one*, however, does appear to be following a universal grammaticalization strategy in that it is a common source for the grammaticalization of the indefinite article. However, the universality of the strategies lies mainly in the means of replication, as will be seen below. Thus, there is not necessarily a case for ordinary contact-induced grammaticalization, nor is there any evidence for replica grammaticalization of the kind discussed by Heine and Kuteva (2005), since substratist explanations do not appear in every case to provide the model on which the features are structured. The ever-increasing awareness of Angloversals, and in particular those arising in contact New Englishes, together with the absence of a model in the substrate languages in the case of habitual *will* or the stative progressive, raise the question of the source of the model system, whether from the substrate or from the lexifier. An alternative explanation may be obtained by investigating the historical development of the features, as discussed below.

### 4.1 Habitual *will*

In a previous diachronic survey of the emergence of the modal meanings in *will* (Ziegeler 2006a), it was seen that a large proportion of the Old English and some of the Middle English functions were clustered around the core meanings of not just volition (as had been assumed in most earlier historical accounts; see, for instance, Aijmer 1985, Bybee and Pagliuca 1987 and Hopper and Traugott 1993), but of volition attributable to a generic subject (e.g. 37–38). This created a sense of proclivity of action, rather than the "intention" meanings previously thought to have contributed to the future meanings associated with the modal. The data surveyed were minimal, but a total of 32.7% of purely generic meanings were found in selected texts of the Helsinki Corpus, with only 21.8% of purely volitional meanings and 16.3% of what could be described as future prediction (the remaining attestations were ambiguous between the categories). Generic functions were determined by the presence of generic or non-referential subject or object participants; occurrences in the scope of a conditional construction were also regarded as generic but under the restriction of their conditional clauses.

By Middle English, the generic functions were beginning to give way to future-oriented meanings, the proportion of generics remaining at 32.3% but future predictive meanings increasing to 38.2%. At this stage, very few purely volitional meanings appeared to be present, and a gradual shifting through generic to future modality was evidenced, suggesting that generic meanings formed the source constructions for the development of future predictive meanings, through the adoption of volitional senses by non-specific participants. Thus, the semantic grammaticalization path to future meanings for *will* was hypothesized to follow the course in (36) (Ziegeler 2006a: 110):

(36) VOLITION > PROCLIVITY > PROBABILITY > PREDICTION

This path enabled the more plausible analysis of the development of predictive meanings, which could be seen to have arisen by the speaker's reporting on the observed tendencies and characteristic behaviour of the subject, rather than reporting the subject's intentions (something which could not be so readily observed, and would need to be communicated by the speaker).[15] In this way, there is semantic continuity between observed volition and prediction which is an inference already present in the generic uses of *will*. Examples appearing in the texts included the following, in which the habitual tendencies of plants and farm animals are referred to:

(37) *Hu ne meaht þu gesion þæt ælc wyrt & ælc wudu **wile** weaxan on þæm lande selest þe him betst gerist & him gecynde bið & gewunlic...?*
'Can you not see that each plant and each tree **will** grow best on the land which suits it best, and is natural and habitual to it...?'[16]
(*Helsinki Corpus of English Texts*, 850–950, Alfred's *Boethius*; ed. Sedgefield; p. 91)[17]

(38) *Be ðæm is awriten ðæt se hund **wille** etan ðæt he ær aspaw, & sio sugu hi **wille** sylian on hire sole æfterðæm ðe hio aðwægen bið.*
'Therefore it is written that the dog **will** eat what he formerly vomited, and the sow **will** wallow in her mire after being washed.'
(*Helsinki Corpus of English Texts*, 850–950, Alfred's *Cura Pastoralis*; ed. Sweet; p. 419)

Examples of generics with overtones of volition included the following, in which a negative appears:

(39) *Sua is cynn ðæt sio halige gesomnung tæle ælces ðara god ðe hit him anum **wile** to gode habban, & **nyle** oðera mid helpan.*
'In the same way it is proper for the holy assembly to blame the advantages of those who **will** appropriate them to themselves alone, and will not help others with them.'
(*Helsinki Corpus of English Texts*, 850–950, Alfred's *Cura Pastoralis*; ed. Sweet; p. 45)

---

15 I am grateful to Pierre Cotte (p.c.) for this insightful suggestion.
16 Unless otherwise stated, the glosses for the Old English and Middle English examples are taken from the Early English Text Society's parallel translations.
17 The page numbers are as they appear in the Helsinki Corpus. The editor's name is the editor of the version found in the Early English Text Society volume which was used in compiling the corpus.

Similar habitual or generic uses have been isolated by Wischer (2006), who discusses a "timeless" sense mentioned by Visser (1963–72, III: 1582), by which future meanings first arose. It was hypothesized in Ziegeler (2006a) that such aspectual contexts would lend themselves most easily to the development of modal meanings, since they have no anchorage in space or time, and that *will* was not the only case of a generic source modality – *be supposed to* and the ability modals also shared similar generic functional origins (see Ziegeler 2001, 2003b).

It is for this reason that the data showing relatively high proportions of habitual aspect uses of *will* appeared to be so revealing in the New English data: habituals are also aspectually generic. Although the proportions in the New Englishes do not exceed 21% in any given corpus in the present study, the relatively minimal usage of habitual *will* in the ICE-GB is surprising by comparison. If the new Englishes, then, are, as defined, new varieties of an old language, then there is no reason why they should not follow in their early development directions similar to those of their historical predecessors. The other two features, the stative progressive and the specific determiner *one*, may now be examined under the same analysis.

## 4.2 The stative progressive

In Ziegeler (1999, 2006b) the historical development of the progressive participle in English was accounted for as a reanalysis along the Noun–Verb continuum (e.g. Haspelmath 1994). The reanalysis is believed to have begun in Old English, when a predicate form with the grammatical morphology of the agent noun was reinterpreted as an adjectival predicate, developing gradually into a participle by Middle English, and then in Early Modern English acquiring the characteristics of a main verb (including extension to passive contexts). The reanalysis is in accord with diachronic accounts of the progressive that place its origins in Old English times (e.g. Nickel 1966; Scheffer 1975; Mitchell 1976, Mitchell 1985; Traugott 1992; Nuñez-Pertejo 2004; and Brinton and Traugott 2005). Such accounts conflict with other, more typological studies that refer to the source of the progressive as a locative prepositional construction with origins in Middle English constructions such as *he wæs on huntyng/huntunge* (e.g. Bybee et al. 1994). Ziegeler (1999, 2006b) refers to the frequently cited "merger", due to phonological neutralization, of the *-ende* participial suffix and the verbal noun suffix *-ing* around the 14th century (see Nehls 1988). However, the evidence for the adoption of the locative construction is not clear, as noted, for instance, by Nuñez-Pertejo (2004: 99–100). De Groot (2007) attributes the use of the locative prepositional construction to a quite different function: the absentive (meaning roughly 'he was away hunting'), which eventually led to a coalescence with the existing progressive.

Thus, there is alternative evidence in the diachronic accounts suggesting that the progressive had its origins in a form in Old English, (*be* + *V-ende*), which expressed aspectual uses of a more permanent nature than those that were associated with prepositional constructions. Many of the early examples were noted by Traugott (1992) as referring to activities with an inherent duration and others were shown (as in the example below) to be expressing permanent states; because of this, these early examples were believed to have had little to do with the present-day progressive. An example of such a use appears in Traugott (1992: 187):

(40) | Europe | hio | onginð | ... | of | Danai | þære | ie, |
|---|---|---|---|---|---|---|---|
| Europe | she | begins | | from | Don | that | river, |

| seo | **is** | **irnende** | of |
|---|---|---|---|
| that | is | running | from |

| norþdæle | & | seo | ea | Danai | irnð | þonan | suðryhte |
|---|---|---|---|---|---|---|---|
| northern.part | and | that | river | Don | runs | thence | due.south |

| on | westhealfe | Alexandres | herga. |
|---|---|---|---|
| into | western.part | Alexander's | kingdom |

'Europe begins at the river Don, which **runs** from the North ... and the river Don **runs** thence due South into the Western part of Alexander's kingdom.' (*Orosius* 1 1.8.14)

The use of the Old English form to express habitual or recurrent action was also noted in Mitchell (1985: 275). Clearly, its use in (40) describes generic or habitual aspect, rather than progressive.[18] Such examples indicate that the ancestor of the progressive was employed as a general imperfective, covering the broader aspectual dimensions of both temporary and permanent duration, and that the progressive's restriction in Present-day English to mainly non-stative verbs is an indication of its current location on the Noun–Verb continuum (i.e. closest to the more dynamic, verbal end of the continuum). If the progressive had started out as a predicate construction with agent nouns and adjectival functions, it would not be surprising to find more time-stable imperfective functions with activity verb predicates expressing duration within its distribution range. This may be

---

[18] Traugott (1992: 187) also claims that there is no syntactic or semantic motivation for the switch to the simple form in the same text; it may be illustrative of a change in progress.

the reason that examples of stative progressives are still observable in Middle English (Mustanoja 1960: 595):

(41)   ... *we holden on the Crysten feyth and **are bylevyng** in Jhesu Cryste*
       '... we hold onto the Christian faith and **believe** in Jesus Christ'
       (Caxton, *Blanchardyn and Eglantine*)

(42)   *They sayd thre men ansuerd them with grete fere that the paleyce and the ysle **was belongynge** unto the Kynge of Fryse.*
       'They said three men answered them with great fear (saying that) the palace and the isle **belonged** to the King of Fresia.'
       (Caxton, *Blanchardyn and Eglantine*)

Another one comes from Visser (1973: 2011) dated c. 1475:

(43)   *He cosyn vnto the hy king of fraunce, By the which branche honour **is hauing**.*
       'He, being cousin to the noble king of France, by which connection he **has** honour.'
       (*The Romans of Partenay*, 6266.)

It is not known, of course, whether such uses were widespread at the time: a more extensive survey would need to be undertaken to investigate the frequency of such verbs in the ME period. However, their occurrence is sufficient to suggest that today's progressive, with its range of functions restricted to non-stative, agentive verbs, is not necessarily reflective of the situation of its earlier development. As a marker of imperfective aspect, it is anticipated that the progressive would have been most prototypically used, in the first instance, with lexically imperfective verb types, including statives (see Bybee (1985: 13–15) on the Principle of Relevance, a principle explaining the semantic harmony of lexical and grammatical aspect). Thus, what we may be seeing in the data from the New Englishes, is not so much an overgeneralization of function, but an undergeneralization, a return to the functions associated with the early aspectual prototype. As such, it may explain why stative progressives in the New Englishes cannot be attributed to substrate influence alone, as Sand (2005) maintains.

## 4.3 The specific determiner *one*

Heine (1997: 74–75), citing Hopper and Martin's (1987) study, discusses the grammaticalization of the indefinite article, *an(e)*, in English. At the time of Old English, *(an)e* shared the function of marking specific reference with the determiner *sum*. However, since it was less restricted in distribution than *sum*, it was, in Heine's view, already grammaticalized at that time beyond Stage 2 of the stages discussed in Section 3.2.3. An example of its earlier presentational uses (Stage 2) appears in Quirk and Wrenn (1957: 71):

(44) *þær is mid Estum **an** mægð.*
'Among the Estonians there is **a** (**certain**) tribe.' (lit. 'Among the Estonians there is **one** tribe')[19]

By Middle English, Stage 4 (the indefinite marker) appears to have been reached, but this period may have been marked by an intermediate stage when the indefinite article served both the function of marking specificity and unrestricted indefiniteness at the same time. This overlap stage is illustrated in the following examples, both co-occurring in the same text of the Helsinki Corpus:

(45) a. *For ðat it ilimpð ofte ðat godd sant **ane** man an oðer to helpe.*
'For it often happens that God sends **a** man to help another man.'

b. *aif [Ø] rihtwis mann habbe swo aedon te-fore ðe, aif ðat holi writ ne wiðseið ðe naht...*
'If **a** righteous man has done so before thee, and if that holy Writ does not contradict thee...'
(1150–1250, *Vices and Virtues*, Ed. Holthausen, p. 101)

Example (45a), then, may represent an instance of a Stage 4 NP, where *ane* is used to mark non-specific referentiality, while in (45b), reference to a non-specific man is left unmarked, as it would have been in Old English.[20] In the same period, examples were found in which the phonologically reduced form of the indefinite article was used:

(46) *þulke ymage he weddede with **a** ring: ase **a** man dotþ is wif*
'the same image he wedded with **a** ring, as **a** man does his wife'
(1130–1250, *Kentish Sermons*, Ed. Hall, p. 433)

The use of the indefinite article in (46) has no specific reference in the discourse, and can be said to have reached Stage 4 by this time, but co-occurring alongside its non-use, as in (45b).

---

[19] Quirk and Wrenn do not supply the text sources for their examples.
[20] The possibility of (45a) expressing emphasis as in *one man* cannot be ruled out of course, without a parallel corpus of audio data.

Thus, in the history of English, as well as in the New Englishes, there is evidence of the grammaticalization of indefinite articles from the numeral 'one'. The same grammaticalization paths are shown for languages such as Chinese and Punjabi, as pointed out by Heine (1997), languages which are substrates in Singapore and India respectively. This could mean that it would be difficult to disprove this as a case of replica grammaticalization; similarly, the same grammaticalization paths are frequently attested crosslinguistically, so the question of whether there is even a model language being replicated remains to be answered as well. Furthermore, if similar patterns of grammaticalization also appear in the diachronic stages of the lexical source, the problem of what type of contact grammaticalization we are witnessing becomes an issue. It is highly likely, then, that such grammaticalization processes will come into play in any situation wherever a numeral 'one' is taken up to grammaticalize presentative constructions. If so, the exhaustive search for substratum correlations is futile. This has nothing to do with Bickertonian-style bioprograms, in which grammatical categories are presumed to be created *ex nihilo*, but has more to do with what uses of certain lexemes are universally exploited by speakers to automate the code and reduce processing time in the creation of grammatical formatives, whatever the situation. New language situations invite new cycles of grammaticalization, and universals should not be taken at face value, but linked to what is already observed in the repetition of the same grammaticalization paths both crosslinguistically and historically.

## 5 Discussion

As shown in the evidence from habitual *will*, the stative progressive and the use of *one* as a specific determiner, there are strong similarities between the frequency of use of these functions in the new varieties surveyed and their relative frequency in particular grammaticalization stages in the history of the source language itself. It could not be argued, it might be emphasized, that the frequencies follow exact, sequential correlations with diachronic grammaticalization paths (the statistics provided above are not strong enough to show this, for a start). Rather, clear resemblances were found to exist between historical stages in the grammaticalization in English and certain distinctive features shared by the New Englishes. However, this leaves open one or two important questions. First, is this situation one of replication of the historical paths shown, and second, if the grammatical features are associated mainly with contact languages, then why could it not have been the case that they are replicating similar features of *contact* from the history of English itself?

The answer to the latter question is simple: even if the historical data also reflect a situation of contact (and, as discussed above, there is adequate evidence to suggest such a possibility from studies such as Mufwene 1998), this is not to deny the fact that as a historical contact language English may have been just as much a new language variety as are present-day new varieties. The likelihood of historical contact cannot be ruled out, but it does not affect the hypothesis.

The answer to the former question requires a plausible account of the nature of actuation in the transfer of such features. This question may be answered with reference to the findings of Matthews and Yip (2009). They suggested, along with a number of other researchers (e.g. Matras and Sakel 2007; Pietsch 2009; Gast and van der Auwera 2012), that there was a weak point in the replica grammaticalization model, in that speakers of the contact language could not plausibly have access to the history of the model language in order to replicate the same grammaticalization processes that they assume to have taken place in it. Such assumptions may seem naïve, but Matthews and Yip (2009: 384) have shed some light on the way in which replica grammaticalization might work in such situations. In their study of the bilingual child's developmental model of the verb 'give' in his/her dialect, they find that children have access to an implicational hierarchy representing the stages of grammaticalization of the verb 'give'; the earlier stages are found to exist on the basis of implication in later stages: lexical 'give' < permissive < passive. The implications are formed in the replica situation, given the presence of "bridging contexts" (Evans and Wilkins 2000; Heine 2002) or areas of overlap where two stages of development are possible. Alternatively, the presence of the lexical source form in the input is sufficient for the child to generalize it to the more abstract functions in expressing permission and later the passive (stages which are relatively less represented in comparison to the lexical stages). The presence of an implicational hierarchy does not imply that the contact speaker has access to historical sources of a grammaticalizing item, only that the historical sources are often comparable with lexical roots of forms that may, at a particular time, still be visibly co-existing with the more grammaticalized form. This produces a situation of polysemy enabling grammaticalization pathways to be reconstructed by the speaker in contact.

The same proposal has been supported by Matras and Sakel's (2007) study in which it is maintained that the speaker of the contact language has access to residual lexical senses in the form–function correspondences used to replicate the functions in the model language. On the surface, such a situation carries the appearance in the examples discussed above (Sections 4.1–4.3) of a form of functional devolution, a momentary degrammaticalization. Matras and Sakel

(2007: 851) claim that unlike grammaticalization, degrammaticalization in contact is abrupt and spontaneous. However, more data collected over a longer time period would be required in order to verify whether the recovery of functions resembling those of historically earlier stages of grammaticalization, as shown in the present data sample, can actually predict a reversal of the general direction of change across contact.[21]

What is fairly perspicuous, according to the present study, is the presence of a type of contact layering, as noted above. Hopper (1991) described layering with reference to either the co-existence of different forms grammaticalizing the same function (e.g. the past tense in English is expressed by vowel changes in strong verbs as well as the -*ed* suffix on weak verbs), or the overlap of earlier and later functional stages in the same grammaticalizing form (e.g. spatial movement meanings as well as "empty" future functions for the *going to*-form in English). In some cases, the older layers may be only marginally used, relative to the newer layers. In the use of *will*, the function of expressing habitual aspect is present in the lexifier model language, but not necessarily to a significant degree, as shown in the data from the ICE-GB. The speakers of language R are then retrieving a marginal function in the source grammar (habituality) and regrammaticalizing it to a frequency exceeding that of the source language. As noted above, this requires a context of polysemy in which both the earlier and later stages may co-exist, but what is not so clear is the reason for the relatively increased usage of these habituals in the new English dialects. This is not a case of hypergrammaticalization, but a reflection of earlier developmental stages that once held more salience than they do today.

The situation with the progressive is less complex, as the progressive participle was claimed above to represent diachronically an example of a reanalysis rather than of grammaticalization, in its early stages. Reanalysis is not unidirectional (Heine and Reh 1984: 95; Heine et al. 1991: 215) and if the Noun–Verb continuum is the explanation for the progressive's development historically, then it may be hypothesized that in some varieties the progressive appears to be reanalyzing back to be used with verbs with more time-stable, aspectual meanings. From the point of view of the New English varieties, such a reversal accords with the hypothesis that contact speakers, using the more restricted imperfective aspect associated with mainly dynamic verb types in the present-day source language, are simply generalizing the need for a broader imperfective

---

[21] What is also questionable is whether speakers would actually be motivated to degrammaticalize forms in contact, when, according to Hagège (1993), Communicative Pressure predicts the need for a faster pace of grammaticalization, as discussed in 2.1. A similar suggestion was made by Tania Kuteva (p.c.).

distribution, covering both stative and dynamic situations and reflecting that of the Old English usage. The transparency by which speakers in contact may identify such aspectual meanings in the present-day, more restricted use of the progressive could be associated with the search for an aspectual prototype in the regrammaticalization of this category: it has been noted in studies such as Shirai and Anderson (1995) that L1 learners of many languages acquire the most prototypical uses of certain grammatical categories earlier than those which are less prototypical punctual verbs, for instance, are used first with past tense morphology. It would not be too speculative to suggest that in a new language setting, as in a context of contact, speakers are likely to readily associate durative grammatical aspectual categories with verbs expressing durative lexical aspect.

Specific *one* is re-grammaticalized in contact via similar principles. The process follows a universal pathway of grammaticalization (see, e.g., Heine and Kuteva 2002) as well as a language-specific one, and there is no question of the availability of a polysemy in the present-day indefinite article, since it is significantly reduced in form from its original numeral form, which co-exists with it. However, since the numeral *one* co-exists with specific *one* in the same dialect, it is not surprising that the former is co-opted to re-create the distinctions of specific referentiality that have become "grammaticalized over" (i.e. are no longer formally distinct), in the use of the indefinite article, which nevertheless still entails the meaning of the singular numeral. The relation between the indefinite article and the numeral *one* is optimized, from the functional point of view of the speakers in contact, in order to recover the specificity of reference needed to provide the speakers with greater communicative effectiveness in a situation of communicative pressure: specificity is not distinguished at all in the use of the English present-day indefinite article. The replication of the grammaticalization path is thus not only cognitively motivated, but also functionally driven in the mixed language situation. The deductive mechanisms that trigger the retrieval of lexical source polysemies are, in turn, motivated by the need for greater conceptual transparency of expression and communication in a sociolinguistic situation in which a vast range of diverse language backgrounds is exposed to constant contact, hence justifying the recycling of inherent lexical polysemies in the contact languages as well.

# 6 Conclusions

The present study has endeavored to explain a number of problems arising from the field of contact grammaticalization. In the first instance, it has attempted to explain why speakers in contact situations may appear to be replicating grammaticalization pathways of their model languages with little awareness of the diachronic stages through which the model language items have passed. In Pietsch (2009), one solution was offered in that the contact periods were found to correlate with an earlier diachronic time period in which the feature under investigation was found to be current. In the present study, a kind of cognitive leveling across time and across dialects of the same language is seen to operate to create universal pathways of development, which is relevant, both diachronically and synchronically, whatever the linguistic situation under investigation.

However, many mechanisms are found to be in operation. The study has examined three distinctive features found in more than one New English variety, habitual *will*, the stative progressive and the specific determiner *one*, and pitched the question of universals against the alternative possibility of substratum influences. It was seen that, although substratum forces need not be ignored, the sheer prevalence of these three features recurring repeatedly in a range of New English dialects leads to the conclusion that their presence is more likely the effect of a new language situation than the effect of specific features in the substrate model languages. This hypothesis has been backed up by data from historically earlier stages of English itself, revealing a reflection of earlier historical stages in the use of these forms. On the surface, the data also resemble a momentary degrammaticalization, relative to the stages of the same items in the source language, but it is not clear from the available data whether the processes observed will continue to become a counter-directional shift. It was also shown that not every case could be interpreted as replica grammaticalization of this kind: habitual *will* reflects the generic sources of its Old English origins; it frequently occurs with a first-person subject, though, which would be unlikely to provide the ideal source contexts for future predictive meanings, since it carries stronger volitional senses. The progressive participle is hypothesized to have developed via reanalysis (Ziegeler 1999, 2006), from a marker of imperfective grammatical aspect often with a stative or durative main verb. The case of specific *one* is found crosslinguistically as a universal means of grammaticalizing indefinite articles, and thus it is not so easy to determine whether universal strategies operating under alternative motivations or historical replication are the true reasons for its reappearance in the New English data. Nevertheless, in spite of such considerations, the observations shown also appear to reflect in each case historical patterns pertinent to the lexifier language, and should not be ignored as explanations for what have been described as Varioversals.

While the New English data shown in the present study are not substantial, and some of the patterns are represented to a lesser extent in British English, it is still challenging to question their presence and the almost eery correlations with historical equivalents. In order to strengthen the claims made above, then, the hypotheses need to be extended to the study of new varieties of other languages with contact histories, for example, French or Portuguese. There is also an obvious need for a much wider range of data than the three token examples shown in the above study. It remains an open door for much future research to explore such initiatives and to support or disprove whatever claims have been made so far.

# Abbreviations

COP = copula; IRR = irrealis; M = masculine; PL = plural; NPST = non-past; PFP = past-for-present (tense forms)

# References

Aijmer, Karen. 1985. The semantic development of *will*. In Jacek Fisiak (ed.), *Historical semantics and historical word-formation*, 11–21. Berlin: Mouton de Gruyter.

Ansaldo, Umberto & Lisa Lim. 2004. Phonetic absence as syntactic prominence: Grammaticalization in isolating tonal languages. In Olga Fischer, Muriel Norde & Harry Perridon (eds.), *Up and down the cline: The nature of grammaticalization*, 345–362. Amsterdam: John Benjamins.

Bao, Zhiming. 2001. The origin of empty categories in Singapore English. *Journal of Pidgin and Creole Languages* 16. 275–319.

Bao, Zhiming. 2005. The aspectual system of Singapore English and the systemic substratist explanation. *Journal of Linguistics* 41. 237–267.

Bao, Zhiming. 2009. *One* in Singapore English. *Studies in Language* 33. 338–365.

Bickerton, Derek. 1981. *Roots of language*. Ann Arbor: Karoma Publishers.

Brinton, Laurel J. & Elizabeth Closs Traugott. 2005. *Lexicalization and language change*. Cambridge: Cambridge University Press.

Bruyn, Adrienne. 1996. On identifying instances of grammaticalization in Creole languages. In Philip Baker & Anand Syea (eds.), *Changing meanings, changing functions: Papers relating to grammaticalization in contact languages*, 29–46. London: University of Westminster Press.

Bruyn, Adrienne. 2009. Grammaticalization in creoles: Ordinary and not-so-ordinary cases. *Studies in Language* 33. 312–337.

Bybee, Joan. 1985. *Morphology: A study of the relation between meaning and form*. Amsterdam:: John Benjamins.

Bybee, Joan. 1994. The grammaticalisation of zero: Asymmetries in tense and aspect systems. In William Pagliuca (ed.), *Perspectives on grammaticalization*, 235–254. Amsterdam: John Benjamins.

Bybee, Joan & William Pagliuca. 1987. The evolution of future meaning. In Anna Giacalone Ramat, Onofrio Carruba & Giuliano Bernini (eds.), *Papers from the Seventh International Conference on Historical Linguistics*, 527–570. Amsterdam: John Benjamins.

Bybee, Joan, Revere D. Perkins & William Pagliuca. 1994. *The evolution of grammar: Tense, aspect and modality in the languages of the world*. Chicago: University of Chicago Press.

Chaudenson, Robert. 1992. *Des îles, des hommes, des langues: Essais sur la créolisation linguistique et culturelle*. Paris: L'Harmattan.

Coelho, Gail M. 1997. Anglo-Indian English: A nativized variety of Indian English. *Language in Society* 26. 561–589.

Cristofaro, Sonia. 2004. Past habituals and irrealis. In Yuri A. Lander, Vladimir A. Plungian & Anna Yu Urmanchieva (eds.), *Irrealis and irreality*, 256–272. Moscow: Gnosis.

De Groot, Casper. 2007. *The king is on huntunge*: On the relation between progressive and absentive in Old and Early Modern English. In Mike Hannay and Gerard Steen (eds.), *Structural-functional studies in English language*, 175–190. Amsterdam: John Benjamins.

Deterding, David. 2003. Tenses and *will/would* in a corpus of Singapore English. In David Deterding, Adam Brown & Low Ee Ling (eds.), *English in Singapore: Research on grammar*, 31–38. Singapore: McGraw Hill.

Deuber, Dagmar. 2010. Modal verb usage at the interface of English and a related creole: A corpus-based study of *can/could* and *will/would* in Trinidadian English. *Journal of English Linguistics* 38(2). 105–142.

Evans, Nicholas & David Wilkins. 2000. In the mind's ear: The semantic extensions of perception verbs in Australian languages. *Language* 76. 546–592.

Gast, Volker & Johan van der Auwera. 2012. What is 'contact-induced grammaticalization'? Evidence from Mayan and Mixe-Zoquean languages. In Björn Wiemer, Bernard Wälchli & Björn Hansen (eds.), *Grammaticalization and language contact*, 381–426. Berlin: De Gruyter Mouton.

Gil, David. 2003. English goes Asian: Number and (in)definiteness in the Singlish noun phrase. In Frans Plank (ed.), *Noun phrase structure in the languages of Europe* (Empirical Approaches to Language Typology 20–7), 467–514. Berlin: Mouton de Gruyter.

Givón, Talmy. 1994. Irrealis and the subjunctive. *Studies in Language* 18(2). 265–337.

Guerti, Anissa. 2009. Colloquial Singapore English: A theoretical and corpus-based study. Contribution to the study of 'New Englishes'. University of Antwerp MA thesis.

Gupta, Anthea Fraser. 1998. The situation of English in Singapore. In Joseph A. Foley, Thiru Kandiah, Bao Zhiming, Anthea F. Gupta, Lubna Alsagoff, Ho Chee Lick, Lionel Wee, Ismail S. Talib & Wendy Bokhorst-Heng (eds.), *English in new cultural contexts: Reflections from Singapore*, 106–126. Singapore: Singapore Institute of Management.

Hagège, Claude. 1993. *The language builder: An essay on the human signature in linguistic morphogenesis*. Amsterdam: John Benjamins.

Harris, John. 1991. Conservatism versus substratal transfer in Irish English. In Peter Trudgill & J. K. Chambers (eds.), *Dialects of English: Studies in grammatical variation*, 191–212. New York: Longman.

Haspelmath, Martin. 1994. Passive participles across languages. In Barbara Fox & Paul J. Hopper (eds.), *Voice: Form and function*, 151–177. Amsterdam: John Benjamins.

Heine, Bernd. 1992. Grammaticalization chains. *Studies in Language* 16(2). 335–368.

Heine, Bernd. 1993. *Auxiliaries: Cognitive forces and grammaticalization*. New York: Oxford University Press.

Heine, Bernd. 1994. Grammaticalization as an explanatory parameter. In William Pagliuca (ed.), *Perspectives on grammaticalization*, 255–287. Amsterdam: John Benjamins.
Heine, Bernd. 1997. *Cognitive foundations of grammar*. Oxford: Oxford University Press.
Heine, Bernd. 2002. On the role of context in grammaticalization. In Ilse Wischer & Gabriele Diewald (eds.), New reflections on grammaticalization, 83–101. Amsterdam: John Benjamins.
Heine, Bernd. 2005. On reflexive forms in creoles. *Lingua* 115. 201–257.
Heine, Bernd, Ulrike Claudi & Friederike Hünnemeyer. 1991. *Grammaticalization: A conceptual framework*. Chicago: University of Chicago Press.
Heine, Bernd & Tania Kuteva. 2002. *World lexicon of grammaticalization*. Cambridge: Cambridge University Press.
Heine, Bernd & Tania Kuteva. 2003. On contact-induced grammaticalization. *Studies in Language* 27. 529–572.
Heine, Bernd & Tania Kuteva. 2005. *Language contact and grammatical change*. Cambridge: Cambridge University Press.
Heine, Bernd & Mechthild Reh. 1984. *Grammaticalization and reanalysis in African languages*. Hamburg: Helmut Buske.
*The Helsinki Corpus of English Texts*. 1991. Department of Modern Languages, University of Helsinki. Compiled by Matti Rissanen (Project leader), Merja Kytö (Project secretary); Leena Kahlas-Tarkka, Matti Kilpiö (Old English); Saara Nevanlinna, Irma Taavitsainen (Middle English); Terttu Nevalainen, Helena Raumolin-Brunberg (Early Modern English). See http://www.helsinki.fi/varieng/CoRD/corpora/HelsinkiCorpus/.
Ho, Mian Lian & John. T. Platt. 1993. *Dynamics of a contact continuum: Singaporean English*. Oxford: Clarendon Press.
Hoffmann, Sebastian & Peter Tan. 2011. The historical corpus of post-colonial Englishes: Aims and first steps. Paper presented at the Helsinki Corpus Festival, University of Helsinki, 28 September–2 October.
Holm, John A. 1988. *Pidgins and creoles*. Vol. 1: *Theory and structure*. Cambridge: Cambridge University Press.
Hopper, Paul J. 1991. On some principles of grammaticization. In Elizabeth C. Traugott & Bernd Heine (eds.), *Approaches to grammaticalization*, Vol. 1, 17–35. Amsterdam: John Benjamins.
Hopper, Paul J. & Janice Martin. 1987. Structuralism and diachrony: The development of the indefinite article in English. In Anna Giacalone Ramat, Onofrio Carruba & Giuliano Bernini (eds.), *Papers from the Seventh International Conference on Historical Linguistics*, 295–304. Amsterdam: John Benjamins.
Hopper, Paul J. & Elizabeth Closs Traugott. 1993[2003]. *Grammaticalization*. Cambridge: Cambridge University Press.
The ICE Corpus: The International Corpus of English: http://ice-corpora.net/ ice/avail.htm.
Kachru, Braj. 1994. English in South Asia. In Robert Burchfield (ed.), *The Cambridge history of the English language*. Vol. 5: *English in Britain and overseas: Origins and development*, 497–553. Cambridge: Cambridge University Press.
Keesing, Roger M. 1991. Substrates, calquing and grammaticalization in Melanesian pidgin. In Elizabeth C. Traugott & Bernd Heine (eds.), *Approaches to grammaticalization*, Vol. 1: 315–342. Amsterdam: John Benjamins.
Kortmann, Bernd, Edgar Schneider, Kate Burridge, Rajend Mesthrie & Clive Upton (eds.). 2004. *A handbook of varieties of English*, 2 vols. Berlin: Mouton de Gruyter.
Labov, William. 1994. *Principles of language change: Internal factors*. Oxford: Blackwell.

Langacker, Ronald W. 1997. Generics and habituals. In Angeliki Athanasiadou & René Dirven (eds.), *On conditionals again*, 191–122. Amsterdam: John Benjamins.

Lim, Lisa. 2007. Mergers and acquisitions: On the ages and origins of Singapore English particles. *World Englishes* 26. 446–473.

Mair, Christian. 2003. Kreolismen und verbales Identitätsmanagement im geschriebenen jamaikanischen English. In Elisabeth Vogel, Antonia Napp & Wolfram Lutterer (eds.), *Zwischen Ausgrenzung und Hybridisierung*, 79–96. Würzburg: Ergon.

Matras, Yaron & Jeanette Sakel. 2007. Investigating the mechanisms of pattern replication in language convergence. *Studies in Language* 31. 829–865.

Matthews, Stephen & Virginia Yip. 2009. Contact-induced grammaticalization: Evidence from bilingual acquisition. *Studies in Language* 33. 366–395.

McWhorter, John. 2002. The rest of the story: Restoring pidginization to creole genesis theory. *Journal of Pidgin and Creole Languages* 17(1). 1–48.

Mitchell, Bruce. 1976. Some problems involving Old English periphrases with *beon/wesan* and the present participle. *Neuphilologische Mitteilungen* 77. 478–491.

Mitchell, Bruce. 1985. *Old English Syntax*, Vol. I. Oxford: Clarendon.

Mufwene, Salikoko. 1996. Creolization and grammaticization: What creolistics could contribute to research on grammaticization. In Philip Baker & Anand Syea (eds.), *Changing meanings, Changing functions*, 5–28. London: University of Westminster Press.

Mufwene, Salikoko. 1998. What research on creole genesis can contribute to historical linguistics. In Monika Schmid, Jenifer R. Austin & Dieter Stein (eds.), *Historical linguistics 1997: Selected papers from the 13th International Conference on Historical Linguistics*, 315–338. Amsterdam: John Benjamins.

Mufwene, Salikoko. 2001. *The ecology of language evolution*. Cambridge: Cambridge University Press.

Mufwene, Salikoko. 2008. *Language evolution, contact, competition and change*. London: Continuum.

Mustanoja, Tauno F. 1960. *A Middle English syntax*. Helsinki: Société Néophilologique.

Nau, Nicole. 1995. *Möglichkeiten und Mechanismen kontakbewegten Sprachwandekls unter besonderer Berücksichtigung des Finnischen*. München: Lincom Europa.

Nehls, Dietrich. 1988. On the development of the grammatical category of aspect in English. In Josef Klegraf & Dietrich Nehls (eds.), *Essays on the English language and applied linguistics on the occasion of Gerhard Nickel's 60th birthday*, 173–198. Heidelberg: Julius Groos.

Nickel, Gerhard. 1966. *Die Expanded Form in Altenglischen: Vorkommen, Funktion und Herkunft den Umschreibung 'Beon/Wesan + Partizip Präsens'*. Neumünster: Wachholtz.

Núñez-Pertejo, Paloma. 2004. *The progressive in the history of English*. Münich: Lincom Europa.

Pietsch, Lukas. 2009. Hiberno-English medial-object perfects reconsidered: A case of contact-induced grammaticalisation. *Studies in Language* 33. 528–568.

Platt, John T., Heidi Weber & Mian Lian Ho. 1984. *The new Englishes*. London: Routledge & Kegan Paul.

Quirk, Randolph & C. L. Wrenn. 1957. *An Old English Grammar*. London: Methuen.

Rickford, John R. 1980. How does *doz* disappear? In Richard R. Day (ed.), *Issues in English creoles: Papers from the 1975 Hawaii Conference*, 77–96. Heidelberg: Groos.

Romaine, Suzanne. 1999. The grammaticalization of the proximative in Tok Pisin. *Language* 75(2). 322–346.

Sand, Andrea. 2005. *Angloversals? Shared morphosyntactic features in contact varieties of English*. Freiburg, Germany: University of Freiburg postdoctoral thesis.

Scheffer, Johannes. 1975. *The progressive in English*. Amsterdam: North Holland Publishing Co.

Schneider, Edgar W. 2003. The dynamics of New Englishes: From identity construction to dialect birth. *Language* 79(2). 233–281.

Sharma, Devyani. 2005. Language transfer and discourse universals in Indian English article use. *Studies in Second Language Acquisition* 27. 535–566.

Sharma, Devyani. 2009a. Typological diversity in New Englishes. *English World-Wide* 30. 170–195.

Sharma, Devyani. 2009b. Contact-based aspectual restructuring: A critique of the Aspect Hypothesis. *Queen Mary's Opal* 12 (Occasional Papers Advancing Linguistics).

Sharma, Devyani. 2012. Second-language varieties: English in India. In Alexander Bergs & Laurel Brinton (eds.), *English historical linguistics: An international handbook*, 2077–2091. Berlin: De Gruyter Mouton.

Shirai, Yasuhiro & Roger W. Andersen. 1995. The acquisition of tense-aspect morphology: A prototype account. *Language* 71(4). 743–762.

Siemund, Peter. 2004. Substrate, superstrate and universals: Perfect constructions in Irish English. In Bernd Kortmann (ed.), *Dialectology meets typology*, 401–433. Berlin: Mouton de Gruyter.

Singler, John. 1990. The impact of decreolization upon T-M-A: Tenselessness. mood and aspect in Kru Pidgin English. In John Victor Singler (ed.), *Pidgin and creole Tense-Mood-Aspect systems*, 203–230. Amsterdam: John Benjamins.

Szmrecsanyi, Benedikt & Bernd Kortmann. 2009a. The morphosyntax of varieties of English worldwide: A quantitative perspective. *Lingua* 119. 1643 R. Hogg (ed.), 1663.

Szmrecsanyi, Benedikt & Bernd Kortmann. 2009b. Vernacular universals and angloversals in a typological perspective. In M. Filppula, J. Klemola & H. Paulasto (eds.), *Vernacular universals and language contact: Evidence from varieties of English and beyond*, 33–53. London: Routledge.

Traugott, Elizabeth Closs. 1992. Syntax. In R. Hogg (ed.), *The Cambridge history of the English language*, Vol. 1, 168–289. Cambridge: Cambridge University Press.

Visser, F. Th. 1969–1972. *An historical syntax of the English language. Part 3.a., Syntactical units with two verbs*. Leiden: Brill.

Weinreich, Uriel. 1953. *Languages in contact*. The Hague: Mouton.

Wischer, Ilse. 2006. *Will* and *Shall* as markers of modality and/or futurity in Middle English. Paper presented at the 14th International Conference on English Historical Linguistics, University of Bergamo, Italy, 21–25 August.

Ziegeler, Debra P. 1996. A synchronic perspective on the grammaticalisation of *WILL* in hypothetical predicates. *Studies in Language* 20(3). 411–442.

Ziegeler, Debra P. 1999. Agentivity and the history of the English progressive. *Transactions of the Philological Society* 97(1). 53–101.

Ziegeler, Debra. P. 2000. *Hypothetical modality. Grammaticalisation in an L2 dialect*. Amsterdam: John Benjamins.

Ziegeler, Debra P. 2001. Past ability modality and the derivation of complementary inferences. *Journal of Historical Pragmatics* 2. 273–316.

Ziegeler, Debra P. 2003a. On the zero-plural in commercial Singaporean English. In David Deterding, Adam Brown & Low Ee Ling (eds.), *English in Singapore: Research on grammar*, 48–57. Singapore: McGraw Hill.

Ziegeler, Debra P. 2003b. On the generic origins of modality in English. In David Hart (ed.), *English modality in context: Diachronic perspectives*, 33–69. Bern: Peter Lang.

Ziegeler, Debra P. 2006a. Omnitemporal *will*. *Language Sciences* 28. 76–119.
Ziegeler, Debra P. 2006b. *Interfaces with English aspect: Diachronic and empirical etudies*. Amsterdam: John Benjamins.
Ziegeler, Debra P. 2008. Grammaticalisation under control: Towards a functional analysis of same-subject identity-sharing. *Folia Linguistica* 42(2). 401–451.
Ziegeler, Debra P. 2010. Count-mass coercion, and the perspective of time and variation. *Constructions and Frames* 2(1). 33–73.
Ziegeler, Debra P. 2012. On the interaction of past tense and potentiality in Singaporean Colloquial English. *Language Sciences* 34. 229–251.
Ziegeler, Debra P. 2014. Replica grammaticalisation as recapitulation: The other side of contact. *Diachronica* 31. 106–141.

Freek Van de Velde and Béatrice Lamiroy

# 12 External possessors in West Germanic and Romance: Differential speed in the drift toward NP configurationality

**Abstract:** This paper inquires into the external possessor in West Germanic and Romance. Against other accounts in the literature, it argues that the distribution of the dative external possessor can be explained neither by reference to Standard Average European nor by direct substrate influence. Instead, it argues that its diachronic decline is better explained as the result of increased configurationality or a tighter structure of the noun phrase. Although the emergence of a tight NP structure may itself be traced back to language contact factors, substrate influence on the diachrony of the external possessor is shown to be more indirect than what is suggested in the literature. The increase in configurationality can be considered a case of constructional grammaticalization (i.e. constructionalization), as the slots for determination and modification become progressively more fixed. One of the main claims here is that this grammaticalization process proceeds at different rates in cognate languages.

## 1 Introduction

This paper is concerned with external possessors of the type presented in (1) and (2), which are often referred to as "dative external possessors". As the construction also occurs in languages that have given up the morphological distinction between accusative and dative, the term "indirect object external possessor" is more apt.

(1) German
    *Die Mutter wäscht dem Kind die Haare.*
    the mother washes the.DAT child the hair
    'The mother is washing the child's hair.'    (König and Haspelmath 1998: 526)

(2) Spanish
    *No le he visto la cara.*
    not 3SG.DAT have.1SG seen the face
    'I have not seen his face.'    (Lamiroy and Delbecque 1998: 29)

The construction can be safely reconstructed for Proto-Germanic, but it has been losing ground both in West Germanic and in Romance, especially in English, which is often claimed to have lost it almost completely (e.g. Haspelmath 1999: 124). The distribution of the construction in West Germanic, and its absence in English in particular, is often explained as follows: the external possessor is an areal feature of a Sprachbund commonly called Standard Average European (SAE) and since English, as opposed to German, is outside the nucleus of the SAE Sprachbund, the feature is better entrenched in German than in English. In such an analysis, the Romance data are normally not taken into consideration at all. As will be shown in the present paper, this explanation does not hold up under closer scrutiny, nor do accounts which attribute the near-absence of the external possessor in English to substrate influence. An alternative explanation will be proposed: the distribution of the construction, both in West Germanic and in Romance, is the outcome of the differential speed at which the languages have changed. More specifically, we will claim that the retention of the external possessive inversely correlates with the increased configurationality of the NP. An important caveat here is that we do not consider increased grammaticalization of the NP as the only factor at play, nor language contact as totally irrelevant. Indeed, the increased configurationality of the NP itself is likely to be due to language contact effects. What we do claim, however, is that extant language contact explanations for the diachrony of the external possessor are naïvely simple, in that they often have a myopic interest in English and fail to take into consideration the situation in Romance, on the one hand, and because they do not take sufficiently into account the internal structure of the NP, on the other.

The paper is organized as follows. In Section 2, we introduce the difference between internal and external possession. Section 3 discusses the distribution of external possessors in West Germanic and Romance. Section 4 presents earlier explanations for the distribution of the external possessor and offers arguments against them. In Section 5, an alternative explanation is proposed. Section 6 presents the conclusions.

## 2 Internal and external possessors

The semantic relation between a possessee and its possessor can be encoded in various ways. A major distinction is that between external and internal possessor constructions (König and Haspelmath 1998).

Let us start with the latter. The following four constructions can be distinguished for non-pronominal possessors in the West Germanic languages:[1] (i) the *s*-possessive or – in the English tradition – Saxon genitive, exemplified in (3) and (4); (ii), the concordial genitive, exemplified in (5); (iii) the post-modifying possessor or PP possessor, exemplified in (6) to (8); and (iv) the prenominal periphrastic possessive (also called resumptive possessive pronoun or possessor doubling construction), exemplified in (9) to (11).[2] For Romance the situation is simpler. The internal possessor can be expressed by a possessive adjective or pronoun in all three languages studied, but non-pronominal possessors have to be expressed by post-modifying PPs, as in (12) to (14). Historically, there was also a morphological genitive in Latin, as in (15), which already started to decrease in Late Latin, and Old French also had a prepositionless possessive as in (16), which survives only in a few totally lexicalized expressions such as *l'hôtel Dieu* (lit. 'God's hostel') 'the hospital' in Modern French, and has been replaced by *de* + NP (for more examples see Ramat 1986: 586 and for a detailed analysis see Carlier et al. 2013).

(3) *my father's book*[3]

(4) Dutch
 *mijn vaders boek*
 my father.POSS book
 'my father's book'

---

[1] In this article, we focus on English, Dutch, German, French, Italian and Spanish, ignoring other West Germanic (e.g. Afrikaans, Frisian, Yiddish) and Romance languages (e.g. Portuguese, Romanian).

[2] A few remarks are in order here. Following Weerman and De Wit (1999), we make a distinction between the *s*-possessive and the genitive, though, historically, the former has evolved from the latter. As regards the s-possessive, its syntactic behavior varies across the West Germanic languages, especially with respect to the NP to which it attaches as a phrasal clitic, which can appear with post-modifiers or without. Though it is not regularly found in Standard German, it does occur in informal communication (e.g. *mein Vaters Buch*, see Scott 2014). As regards the resumptive possessive pronoun construction, it is absent from Present-day English, but earlier stages of the language still had it (pace Allen 2008, who doubts that the English construction is cognate to the German one). Finally, we will not discuss the distribution of these constructions, as it is subject to many factors, including animacy, information status and syntactic weight (see Wolk et al. 2013).

[3] All examples without explicit source indication are constructed examples. We only use constructed examples for straightforward structures, i.e. where there is no discussion about their grammaticality.

(5) German
*meines Vaters    Buch*
my.GEN father.GEN book
'my father's book'

(6) *the book of my father*

(7) Dutch
*het boek van mijn vader*
the book of  my   father
'the book of my father'

(8) German
*das Buch von meinem Vater*
the book of  my    father
'the book of my father'

(9) Dutch
*mijn vader zijn fiets*
my   father his  bike
'my father's bike'

(10) German
*meinem Vater sein Buch*
my    father his  book
'my father's book'

(11) Middle English
*Æthelstan his tente*
Æthelstan his tent
'Æthelstan's tent'                                    (Allen 2008: 187)

(12) French
*le  livre de mon père*
the book of my  father
'the book of my father'

(13) Italian
*il  libro di mio padre*
the book of my father
'the book of my father'

(14) Spanish
   *el libro de mi padre*
   the book of my father
   'the book of my father'

(15) Latin
   *in fīnes Bellovacōrum*
   in territory Bellovaci.GEN
   'in the territory of the Bellovaci'          (Iulius Caesar, *De Bello Gallico*)

(16) Old French
   *la fille son oste*
   the daughter his guest
   'the guest's daughter'          (Chrétien de Troyes, *Erec* 744, 12th century)

Pronouns can be used "internally" as well, either in pronominal position or in the PP post-modification construction, as illustrated in (17) to (22). The former are called possessive pronouns or possessive adjectives. The latter are personal pronouns (or possessive pronouns in the case of English).

(17) German
   *mein Buch / das Buch von mir*
   my book / that book of me
   'my book'

(18) Dutch
   *mijn boek / dat boek van mij*
   my book / that book of me
   'my book'

(19) *my book / that book of me*[4] */ that book of mine*

(20) French
   *mon livre / ce livre à moi*
   my book / that book to me
   'my book'

---

[4] The use of the personal pronoun in a post-modifying PP to mark possession is unidiomatic. The grammaticality of such uses is multifactorially driven.

(21) Italian
*il   mio libro / questo mio libro*
the my book / that   my book
'my book'

(22) Spanish
*mi libro / este libro mío*
my book / this book my
'my book'

External possessor constructions, on the other hand, are those in which the possessor is not expressed in the same constituent as the possessee, but functions as a separate constituent at clause level. In (1) and (2), the possessor *dem Kind/le* and the possessee *die Haare/la cara* are encoded as indirect object and direct object respectively. The range of constructions that fall under this heading depends on the definition, however. Some scholars, such as Payne and Barshi (1999: 22 fn. 5), would hesitate to qualify (23) to (28) as external possessor constructions on the grounds that the clauses are also grammatical without the expression of the possessee and that the external possessor is thus not encoded as an otherwise unlicensed, extra-thematic argument, which they consider a definitional criterion (Payne and Barshi 1999: 3). In Payne and Barshi (1999), the construction in (23) to (28) goes under the name "possessor splitting" (König 2001: 971).

(23) ... *a school of aggressive, seven-foot bull sharks, one of which bit him in the foot.* (COCA)

(24) Dutch
*Een van hen   beet haar in het been.*
one of  them bit  her  in the leg
'One of them bit her in her leg.' (Internet example)[5]

---

5 The source indication "Internet example" refers to examples taken from the Internet, used as a corpus (all examples were gathered through Google; date of access: May–June 2011 and February 2013). We are of course aware of the fact that using internet examples may be dangerous, in that one cannot control for the regional or social background of the language user, and if external possessors are subject to lectal/diatopic variation, these dimensions remain hidden in data retrieval via Google. However, this increased variation in fact only strengthens our main point here, namely that categorizing languages into "having external possessors" (e.g. German) and "not having external possessors" (English), is not a clear dichotomy. Moreover, newspaper corpora usually do not mention their writers' regional provenance either.

(25) German
   *Er hat ihn    in den Hals gebissen.*
   he has 3SG.M.ACC in the neck bitten
   'He bit him in his neck.' (Internet example)

(26) French
   *On l'     a blessé à la jambe.*
   one 3SG.M.ACC has injured at the leg
   'They injured his leg.'

(27) Italian
   *L'    hanno   ferito  alla  gamba.*
   3SG.M.ACC have.3PL injured to.the leg
   'They injured his leg.'

(28) Spanish
   *Lo      han      herido en la pierna.*
   3SG.M.ACC have.3PL injured in the leg
   'They injured his leg.'

There is also some debate about whether (29) to (33) really count as external possessors. This type, which is sometimes called "implicit possessor" construction (see König and Haspelmath 1998: 526–527, 573–581; König 2001: 971; König and Gast 2009: 119–120), can be analyzed as an external possessor that collapses with the subject (see Lamiroy and Delbecque 1998: 32 and Payne and Barshi 1999: 23 fn. 5, referring to work by Velázquez-Castillo). However, they are different from other cases of external possessors, as the coreferentiality of the subject and the possessor is of a pragmatic nature: in (30), the hands are not necessarily the subject's own body parts.[6]

(29) Dutch
   *Bestuurders hieven de handen in onmacht.*
   directors    raised  the hands in impotence
   'Directors threw their hands in the air in helplessness.' (Internet example)

(30) German
   *Ich zeigte  ihm die Hände.*
   I    showed him the hands
   'I showed him my hands.' (Internet example)

---

6 We owe this observation to Volker Gast (p.c.).

(31) French
*Les enfants lèvent la main.*
the children raise the hand
'The children raise their hands.'

(32) Italian
*I bambini alzano la mano.*
the children raise the hand
'The children raise their hands.'

(33) Spanish
*Los niños levantan la mano.*
the children raise the hand
'The children raise their hands.'

While taking a restrictive approach to external possession may be adequate for wide-ranging typological surveys (as in Payne and Barshi 1999), we see no principled reason to leave examples like (23) to (28) out of consideration. The close connection between "proper" external possessors, with an (unlicensed) dative possessor, and "improper" external possessors of the type exemplified in (23) to (28), with a (licensed) accusative possessor, is clear from the fact that, in German and Spanish, the pronoun occurs in the dative as well as in the accusative:

(34) German
*Er hat ihm in den Hals gebissen.*
he has 3SG.M.DAT in the neck bitten
'He bit him in his neck.' (Internet example)

(35) Spanish
*... que la víbora le había mordido en la pierna izquierda.*
... that the snake 3SG.M.DAT had bitten in the leg left
'That the snake had bitten him in the left leg.' (Internet example)

Moreover, the split between internal and external constructions is not as clear-cut as the above examples suggest. The prenominal periphrastic possessive in (9) and (10) in particular is actually less internal than the constructions in (3) to (5). It probably developed from a *dativus commodi* construction (Havers 1911:

296; König and Haspelmath 1998: 586).⁷ "Bridging contexts", allowing both readings (see Heine 2002 for this term), are exemplified in (36) and (37), with data from Dutch (see De Vooys 1967: 317–318 and Ramat 1986).

(36) 17th-century Dutch
*En ried      de ridderschap en  al de groote steên*
and advised the knighthood and all the big    cities

*te roepen om den vorst zijn' moedwil te besnoeien.*
to call    to  the king  his   fickleness to prune
'And advised to gather the knighthood and all the big cities to curtail the king's fickleness.'

(37) Present-day Dutch
*Ze    hebben mijn broer   z'n fiets afgenomen.*
they have    my   brother his bike  taken
'They took my brother's bike.' / 'They took the bike from my brother.'

Both in German and in Dutch, the *dativus commodi* left a visible trace. In German, the prenominal periphrastic possessor still requires dative case marking in many varieties:

(38) German
*kennengelernt habe ich sie durch meinem kumpel   seine freundin.*
acquainted     have I   her by    my.DAT  friend.DAT his  girlfriend
'I met her through my friend's girlfriend.'
(Van de Velde 2009a: 69, Internet example, *Kleinschreibung* in original)

Persistence of the old *dativus commodi* construction is still visible in Dutch as well, as illustrated in the following examples, where the possessor is separated from the possessee. Separation is not normally allowed for premodifiers in the NP. Yet, although the construction in (41) is generally considered ungrammatical in Standard Dutch, Van der Lubbe (1958: 125) did find an example in a small

---

7 Some scholars have doubts about this diachronic account (see Allen 2008: 187–189 and Hendriks 2012 for references), although they cannot really disprove the *dativus commodi* origin. What may have happened is that the reanalysis of the *dativus commodi* was strengthened by the phonetic similarity between the genitive *-es* suffix and the possessive pronoun (see Fischer 1992: 231). Such issues of "multiple source constructions" are fairly common (see De Smet et al. 2013). In this paper, we adhere to the traditional view that the resumptive prenominal possessor developed out of the *dativus commodi*.

written corpus, and it is perfectly normal in some dialects (e.g. Haegeman 2003: 222). The possibilities for separation of possessor and possessee in Dutch are of course limited, but note that, in the other internal possessor construction, separation is completely ungrammatical, as (42) shows.[8]

(39) Dutch
*Die werkgever van de OM,     die Tonino's vrijsprak ...*
that employer of the prosecutor who Toninos acquitted
*die moeten ze   ook z'n pc nakijken.*
that must they also his pc check
'They should also check the PC of that employer of the prosecutor who acquitted T.' (Van de Velde 2009a: 71)

(40) Dutch
*die collega van mn vader die zn vrouw*
that colleague of my father that his wife
'that colleague of my father's wife' (Van de Velde 2009a: 72)

(41) Dutch
*vader al z'n sigaren*
father all his cigars
'all of father's cigars' (Van der Lubbe 1958: 125)

(42) Dutch
*\*de auteur wiens de autoriteiten (het) boek uit de*
the author whose the authorities the book out the
*handel genomen hebben*
store withdrawn have
'the author whose book the authorities have withdrawn'

In sum, the West Germanic prenominal periphrastic possessive seems to occupy a middle position, in between the external and internal possessor constructions, although, in Present-day West Germanic, it is closer to the internal possessor construction than to the external one.

---

**8** Separation of the post-modifying possessor PP from its possessee is also possible, but this is true for all post-modifiers of the NP. The phenomenon goes under the term of extraction (leftward) or extraposition (rightward). For a discussion of what this means for the dependency/constituency relations in the NP, see Van de Velde (2009a: Ch. 3, 2012).

# 3 The different status of the external possessors in West Germanic and Romance languages

This section takes a closer look at the distribution of the external possessor in the West Germanic languages English, Dutch and German and the Romance languages French, Italian and Spanish. It gives a more fine-grained picture of the situation than the categorical black and white picture that is sometimes sketched in comparative work. The literature, for instance, disagrees on the existence of an external possessor in Dutch (see Haspelmath 1999 versus Van Pottelberge 2001), but this disagreement can be resolved if we accept the gradient nature of this syntactic feature.

## 3.1 West Germanic

At least since Van Haeringen dedicated a lengthy publication on the topic in 1956, it has been recognized that Dutch occupies a position in between its West Germanic neighbors, English and German, both geographically and linguistically. His line of work has been extended in recent publications such as Hüning et al. (2006) and Vismans et al. (2010). Van Haeringen (1956) and the papers in the aforementioned volumes discuss a wide range of topics, from lexical over morphological to syntactic matters, but – with the exception of Lamiroy (2003) – possessor constructions have never been examined from this perspective. Yet, a look at the facts clearly shows that there is a telling correspondence between the internal/external possessor division and the areal and linguistic configuration of the languages. The external possessor is well established in German, less so in Dutch and least so in English whereas the best established internal possessor constructions can be found in English (ignoring the problematic status of the concordial genitive for the moment).[9] Interestingly, as we will show in Section 3.2, a similar cline holds for Romance: the external possessor is well-established in Spanish, less so in Italian and least of all in French. Moreover, in West Germanic, the "mid-position" prenominal periphrastic possessive is the default construction for (animate) premodifying possessors in Dutch – though eschewed in formal written Dutch – while it seems to be used less often

---

[9] The concordial genitive is strongest in German, but note that it is acquired late in child L1 acquisition and can be argued to be obsolescent.

in (Standard) German (e.g. the surprisingly low number of attestations in informal German, see Scott 2014: Ch. 6) and it is absent in Present-day English.

In what follows, we will present examples that show that Dutch indeed takes up a position in-between English and German (see also Lamiroy 2003).

The absence of external possessors in English is not absolute. First of all, the possessor splitting constructions exemplified in (23) to (25) are widely attested in Dutch and in English, as (43) and (44) show, and so are implicit possessors, as in (45) and (46).[10] Still, for reasons mentioned earlier, one could reject them as "improper" external possessor constructions. König and Gast (2009: 114), for example, do not immediately dismiss them, but argue that they are "very different from the German constructions".

(43) *He kissed her on the forehead.* (Haspelmath 1999: 121)

(44) Dutch
*Hij kust haar op het voorhoofd.*
he kisses her on the forehead
'He kisses her on the forehead.' (Internet example)

(45) *She was sick at heart.* (Haspelmath 1999: 121)

(46) Dutch
*Hij haalde zich de woede op de hals van de*
he got himself the anger on the neck of the
*China Daily door een artikel in Foreign Affairs.*
China Daily by an article in Foreign Affairs
'China Daily got furious with him because of an article in Foreign Affairs.'
(Internet example)

While it is true that the possessor argument in (23) to (25), (43) and (44) is licensed by the verb, there are other examples where such an analysis cannot be maintained. Consider (47) and (48), for example. The corresponding sentence without the possessee PP is ungrammatical (*She looked him*, *She yelled him*). This suggests that the possessor does occupy an unlicensed slot here, which would make it a real external possessor by the strict standards put forward in Payne and Barshi (1999) (see also König and Haspelmath 1998: 554).

---

**10** If, for (46), one argues that not the subject (*hij*) but rather the indirect object reflexive (*zich*) is the possessor, then (46) is a regular indirect object external possessor.

(47) *She looked him in the eyes.* (Internet example)

(48) *She yelled him in the face, her voice shaking. "Wake up!"*
(Internet example)

The same goes for Dutch. In (49), the verb *kijken* 'look' is used, which, like English *look*, does not normally combine with a non-prepositional object (\**Ze keek hem*, literally 'she looked him'). Interestingly, the Dutch verb *bekijken* (literally 'be-look', i.e. 'examine') does combine with a non-prepositional object (*ze bekijkt hem* 'she examines him'), but it does not occur in the possessor-splitting construction, as (50) shows.

(49) Dutch
   Ze keek hem in de ogen.
   she looked him in the eyes
   'She looked him in the eyes.' (Internet example)

(50) Dutch
   \**Ze bekeek hem in de ogen.*
   she be-looked him in the eyes
   'She looked him in the eyes.'

Dutch also has external possessors with non-prepositional object possessees in sentences with particle verbs, as in (51). According to Vandeweghe (1987: 149), such particle verbs are often historically related to prepositional possessees, as in (24). Presumably, the preposition drifted away from its complement and became associated with the verb. Thus, *de keel doorgesneden* (lit. 'the throat through-cut') derives from *door de keel gesneden* (lit. 'through the throat cut').

(51) Dutch
   Ik heb hem de keel door-gesneden.
   I have him the throat through-cut
   'I cut his throat.' (Internet example)

Note that not all external possessors in Dutch occur with particle verbs, as (52) to (54) show (the last example with a reflexive).

(52) Dutch
   Ik schudde hem de hand.
   I shook him the hand
   'I shook his hand.' (Internet example)

(53) Dutch
   *Zij rukten hem de kleren van het lijf.*
   they tore him the clothes off the body
   'They tore his clothes of his body.' (Internet example)

(54) Dutch
   *Poes heeft zich het hoofd gestoten.*
   cat has itself the head banged
   'The cat has banged its head.' (Internet example)

Moreover, the existence of subject-possessee external possessors as in (55) suggests that the direct object construction should also be possible, as there is a universal (or at least European) implicational scale by which the existence of subject-possessee external possessors entails that of direct-object-possessee external possessors (see Haspelmath 1999: 113; König 2001: 976).

(55) Dutch
   *Ma het is puur die kaak die me zo'n pijn doet.*
   but it is purely this cheek that me so pain does
   'But it is only my cheek that really hurts so badly.' (Internet example)

Another construction that can be regarded as an instance of an external possessor involves verbs with noun-incorporation, as in (56) to (59), which do involve possessor splitting as well.

(56) *They brainwashed him.* (Haspelmath 1999: 122)

(57) Dutch
   *Dan kan ik hem hersenspoelen.*
   then can I him brainwash
   'Then I can brainwash him.' (Internet example)

(58) *And I earmarked a page.* (COCA)

(59) Dutch
   *Hij oormerkt de koeien.*
   he earmarks the cows
   'He earmarks the cows.' (Internet example)

As pointed out by Vandeweghe (1986) and Lamiroy and Delbecque (1998: 50), the Dutch external possessor is very frequent in figurative expressions. It is commonly assumed that such idiomatic constructions are calcified relics from a time when the external possessor construction was still productive. Consider the examples in (60) to (65).

(60) Dutch
  iemand op de vingers tikken
  someone on the fingers tap
  'to rebuke someone'

(61) Dutch
  iemand de mantel uitvegen
  someone the coat wipe.out
  'scold someone'

(62) Dutch
  iemand iets op het hart drukken
  someone something on the heart press
  'insist on something (with someone)'

(63) Dutch
  iemand een pad in de korf zetten
  someone a toad in the basket put
  'saddle someone with a problem, get someone in difficulties'

(64) Dutch
  iemand in het verkeerde keelgat schieten
  someone in the wrong throat.pipe shoot
  'upset someone'

(65) Dutch
  iemand iets in de maag splitsen
  someone something in the stomach split
  'to thrust something upon a person'

In English too, external possessors occur in constructions with a figurative meaning and in idioms, such as (66), though not as frequently as in Dutch. The figurative expression in (67) is marked, as the normal construction would involve an internal possessor (i.e. *getting on my nerves*).

(66) *Don't look a gift horse in the mouth.*      (König and Haspelmath 1998: 537)

(67) *Truly, anything goes in the world, but I really dare to see the shocking things getting me on the nerves.*      (Internet example)

In sum, what the above data show is that the distribution of external possessor constructions is not an all-or-nothing matter but that it has fuzzy boundaries. Any purely synchronic explanation that hinges on the observation that the external possessor is categorically absent in English or totally unproductive with non-PP possessees in Dutch is thus bound to be inadequate. In contrast, we adopt a diachronic perspective (see also Vandeweghe 1986: 125) and view the fluid synchronic boundaries as the result of diachronic change – or, put differently, as "gradience" due to "gradualness" (Lamiroy 2007; Traugott and Trousdale 2010; Carlier et al. 2012).

## 3.2 Romance

The dative external possessor is well-attested in Romance, both historically and in the present-day languages. Still, the individual languages differ considerably in the extent to which the construction is productive (see Lamiroy 2003 for a detailed investigation). Spanish is the least restrictive language in its use of dative external possessors while French is the most restrictive. Italian is in the middle, with some contexts allowing it and others not.

That dative external possessors are by far more productive in Spanish than in the other two languages is shown, for example, by the fact that the construction can be used with non-human possessors – the dative clitic *le* is coreferential with 'the table' in (68) – and with kinship possessees, as in (69).

(68) Spanish
*Le        fregué      las manchas     al        tablero.*
3SG.DAT wiped.1SG the stains      to.the table
'I wiped the stains off the table.'      (Demonte 1995: 23)

(69) Spanish
*Se         les        casa      la     hija      mañana.*
REFL.3SG 3PL.DAT marries the daughter tomorrow
'Their daughter is getting married tomorrow.'      (Lamiroy 2003: 268)

French does not allow the external possessor construction in either of these cases, as (70) to (73) show.[11]

(70) French
    *La table, je l'    ai    astiquée sur toute la surface.*
    the table I 3SG.ACC have polished on whole the surface
    'I polished the whole surface of the table.'    (Leclère 1995: 183)

(71) French
    *\*La table, je lui    ai    astiquée toute la surface.*
    the table I 3SG.DAT have polished whole the surface
    'I polished the whole surface of the table.'

(72) French
    *\*La fille    se    leur    marie demain.*
    the daughter REFL.3SG 3PL.DAT marries tomorrow
    'Their daughter is getting married tomorrow.'    (Lamiroy 2003: 268)

(73) French
    *\*La mère    lui    est morte il y    a    peu.*
    the mother 3SG.DAT is dead it there has little
    'His mother died not long ago.'    (Lamiroy 2003: 268)

Italian seems to be more restrictive than Spanish, in that part-whole relations with inanimate possessors as in (74) do not allow the dative construction, but it is less restrictive than French, where kinship terms as in (75) and (76) are allowed in certain contexts.

(74) Italian
    *\*Gli    ho    pulito le macchie al    tavolo.*
    3SG.DAT have.1SG wiped the stains to.the table
    'I wiped the stains off the table.'

(75) Italian
    *?Gli    si    sposa la figlia    domani.*
    3sg.dat refl.3sg marries the daughter tomorrow
    'Their daughter is getting married tomorrow.'    (Lamiroy 2003: 268)

---

**11** Not surprisingly, the only possibility to express the equivalent of (69) in French is the internal possessor construction *Leur fille* ('their daughter') *se marie demain*. Also compare (73) to *Sa mère* ('his/her mother') *est morte il y a peu*.

(76) Italian
   *Gli    è mancata la   mamma poco fa.*
   3SG.DAT is missed the mother little ago
   'His mother died not long ago.'            (Lamiroy 2003: 268)

The contrast between Spanish and the other two languages with respect to the external dative construction is all the more striking in view of the fact that the three languages share the construction with an implicit possessor illustrated in (31) to (33) and, more crucially, that, as already shown by (26) to (28) and (35), all three make use of the possessor splitting construction:

(77) French
   *Il la         baisait au    front,   dans ses cheveux,*
   he 3SG.F.ACC kissed at.the forehead in  her hair

   *en sanglotant.*
   in weeping

   'He kissed her on the forehead, in her hair, while he was weeping.'
                                              (Maupassant, *L'enfant*)

(78) Spanish
   *Delincuentes golpearon en la  cara a  un párroco en*
   criminals    beat      in the face to a priest  in

   *Caracas para robarlo.*
   Caracas to   rob.him

   'Criminals hit a priest in the face in Caracas to rob him.'
                                              (Internet example)

(79) Italian
   *I   miei suoceri        hanno il  vizio     di baciare*
   the my   parents-in-law have the bad.habit of kiss

   *sulla   bocca la  mia bimba    di due anni.*
   on.the mouth the my  little.girl of two years

   'My parents-in-law have the bad habit of kissing my two-year-old little girl on her mouth.'            (Internet example)

Note that, in Spanish, as in German, the productivity of the external dative possessive construction parallels that of two other productive "unlicensed" dative constructions, viz. the *dativus commodi/incommodi*, as in (80), and the ethical dative, as in (82). Both may contribute to the vitality of the external dative possessor structure. As expected, these two types of datives are not entirely absent from the other Germanic or Romance languages, but they are far less common, as shown by the following contrasts with French in (81) and English in (83).

(80) Spanish
    Nos     han   entrado  ladrones  en  casa.
    1PL.DAT have  entered  thieves   in  house
    'Thieves entered our house.'

(81) French
    *Des       voleurs  nous    sont entrés  dans  la  maison.
    INDEF.PL   thieves  1PL.DAT are  entered in    the house
    'Thieves entered our house.'

(82) German
    Mir      ekelt     vor fetten Speisen.
    1SG.DAT  nauseate  for fat    food
    'I hate high-fat foods.'                              (Draye 1996: 193)

(83) ?*High-fat foods are disgusting to me.*

A final observation we want to make with respect to French is similar to what we saw for Dutch in Section 3.1: the dative possessor construction may be receding in everyday language (Spanoghe 1995), but it is still widely attested in French idiomatic expressions, i.e. in fossilized remnants of older stages of the language. Consider the examples in (84) to (89).

(84) French
    *casser les pieds à quelqu'un*
    break  the feet  to someone
    'to bother someone'

(85) French
    *tirer les vers du     nez  à  quelqu'un*
    pull  the worms from.the nose to someone
    'to ask someone delicate questions'

(86) French
    *la moutarde monte    au    nez  à  quelqu'un*
    the mustard goes.up  to.the nose to someone
    'to get very upset'

(87) French
*rire au nez et à la barbe à quelqu'un*
laugh to.the nose and to the beard to someone
'to laugh at someone'

(88) French
*donner froid dans le dos à quelqu'un*
give cold in the back to someone
'to give the shivers'

(89) French
*fendre le coeur à quelqu'un*
split the heart to someone
'to be heartbreaking'

In the following section, we discuss existing accounts of the possessor construction in West Germanic and Romance as it has been sketched so far.

# 4 Previous accounts of the distribution of the external possessor construction in West Germanic and Romance

The conundrum in the distribution of the external possessor in West Germanic is its conspicuous near-absence in English, as pointed out by Haspelmath (1999), McWhorter (2002), Vennemann (2002) and König and Gast (2009: 112–121). It has not escaped the attention of these scholars that there is a striking areal pattern in the presence or absence of the external possessor illustrated in (1) and (2): the external possessor is a feature of continental Europe. It is found in a continuous area on the continent, including non-Indo-European languages like Basque, Hungarian and Maltese while it is, at the same time, absent in geographically peripheral Indo-European languages such as the Celtic languages, English and the Scandinavian languages. This has led to the idea that external possessors are a feature of what is often referred to as Standard Average European.

Standard Average European (SAE) is a term coined by Whorf (1956: 138) and revived in a number of recent publications on the topic, most notably in Haspelmath (1998a, 2001a), to label the remarkably homogeneous linguistic area to which most languages of the old continent belong.[12] Several features that these languages share are typologically not very common, and their fading distribution – ranging from a geographically contiguous group of languages forming the "nucleus" over languages forming the "core" to languages at the periphery – is indeed consistent with a wave-like spread due to language contact. The language contact spread resulted in a Sprachbund, as this distribution cross-cuts the genetic relationships between the European languages. French, for instance shares more SAE features with German, a neighboring nuclear SAE language, than with its Romance sister Spanish, which does not belong to the SAE nucleus. Similarly, Hungarian, though not an Indo-European language, occupies a position in the periphery of the SAE Sprachbund, together with Indo-European languages like Russian, in contrast to the Indo-European Celtic languages and the non-Indo-European languages Turkish and Lezgian. It is no coincidence that Hungarian is surrounded by Indo-European languages. There is some discussion about the exact features which can be attributed to SAE (see Haspelmath 1998a, 2001a; Heine and Kuteva 2006: 23–27), but definite and indefinite articles, *have*-perfects, participial passives and verbal negation with a negative indefinite, for instance, are generally assumed to be SAE features. Dative external possessors also appear in all lists of SAE features (see Haspelmath 1998a: 277–278, 2001a: 1498; Heine and Kuteva 2006: 24; Harbert 2007: 11; van der Auwera 2011). In view of its near non-existence outside Europe, Haspelmath (1998a: 278) calls them "a very robust example of an SAE feature".

There are a number of hypotheses on what exactly gave rise to the remarkable homogeneity in SAE. Haspelmath (2001a: 1506–1507) considers various explanations, and concludes that the most likely one is language contact at the time of the great migrations at the transition from Antiquity to the Middle Ages. Van der Auwera (2011) basically concurs, but adds Charlemagne's reign to the equation, and the later use of French and German in a cultural homogenous region. Whatever exactly happened in the early Middle Ages that ultimately gave rise to the Sprachbund, scholars seem to agree that it is the result of language contact (see also Heine and Kuteva 2006).

If the SAE features spread through language contact, the absence of the external possessor in English can be ascribed to the fact that the English-speaking community was less involved in this contact situation, which in turn is at least partly connected with the fact that Britain is an island.

There are, however, a number of serious problems with the analysis of the dative external possessor as an SAE feature. The first problem is that, in contrast

---

[12] Haspelmath's notion of SAE overlaps to a large extent with van der Auwera's (1998) "Charlemagne Sprachbund". See van der Auwera (2011) for a recent overview.

to other SAE features, it has a venerable tradition in the European languages (see Havers 1911). It is well-attested in old Indo-European daughter languages like Greek, Latin, Sanskrit and Old Church Slavonic, as (90) to (93) show. This in itself sets it apart from other SAE features, as they are all of much more recent date (Haspelmath 1998a: 282; Harbert 2007: 11).

(90). Vedic Sanskrit
*ā́ te vájraṃ jaritā́ bāhvór dhāt*
PT 2SG.DAT bolt.of.lightning singer arm.DU.LOC put
'The singer put the lightning bolt in your arms.'
(König and Haspelmath 1998: 551)

(91) Homeric Greek
*enéplēsthen dé hoi ámphō haímatos ophthalmoí*
were.filled PT 3SG.M.DAT both blood.GEN eyes
'Both his eyes were filled with blood.' (König and Haspelmath 1998: 551)

(92) Latin
*Cornix cornice numquam ocellum effodit*
crow.NOM crow.DAT never eye guts
'A crow never guts another crow's eye.' (König and Haspelmath 1998: 552)

(93) Old Church Slavonic
*brъnьe položi mъně na očiju*
clay.ACC.SG put.AOR.3SG 1SG.DAT on eye.LOC.DU
'He put clay on my eyes.' (Havers 1911: 306)[13]

It is not only the timing that sets apart the external possessor construction from the other SAE features. The distribution of the construction over the linguistic area is also somewhat suspect. Dutch, for instance, does not have a fully productive possessive dative (at least if the construction with possessee PPs is not considered a genuine external possessor construction), although the language is according to Haspelmath (1998a) part of the SAE nucleus in other respects.[14]

---

[13] We would like to thank Jaap Kamphuis for helping us with the glosses for this example.
[14] In Haspelmath (2001a), the nucleus is reduced to just two languages, German and French. Dutch is pushed to the core because it has one feature less than the nuclear languages. The feature that Dutch is said to lack is the differentiation of reflexives and intensifiers. In actual fact, Dutch does make a difference between the two: reflexive *zich* versus intensifier *zelf*, just like German *sich* versus *selbst*.

Furthermore, the external possessors in the non-Indo-European languages Hungarian and Maltese are not pure instances either, as Haspelmath (1999: 117) himself notes: the possession relation is also marked NP-internally by a pronominal affix, as in (94).

(94) Hungarian
 A  kutya beleharapott a   szomszéd-nak a   lálá-ba.
 the dog  bit.into     the neighbor-DAT the leg.3SG-LOC
 'The dog bit (into) the neighbor's leg.'         (Haspelmath 1999: 117)

In addition, the external possessors in the European languages seem to have been in recession since ancient times (see Havers 1911; König and Haspelmath 1998: 583–584). Their use along the implicational hierarchies mentioned in Haspelmath (1999) has been severely curtailed, whereas other SAE features have become stronger and have spread over a larger area (e.g. Heine and Kuteva 2006: 97–182 on the rise and spread of articles and *have*-perfects). In other words, the use of the external possessor lost ground at the time that other SAE features were thriving.

The problem is even clearer if we take the Romance languages into account. French and the Northern Italian dialects belong to the SAE nucleus, whereas the Southern Italian Dialects and Spanish merely belong to the SAE core (the region just around the nucleus) (Haspelmath 1998a: 273). Consequently, one would expect France and Northern Italy to have a more established external possessor than Southern Italy and Spain, especially in view of the fact that external possessors are well preserved in the other nuclear SAE member, German. We have shown in Section 3.2 that the opposite is true.

Another problem with the SAE account of external possessors pertains to their absence in Indo-European languages like Celtic and English. The geographically peripheral position of these languages can be argued to support the areal SAE account of the dative external possessor construction: their remote position precluded them from adopting the feature. This view, however, is at odds with the fact that, in earlier stages, the Celtic languages and English did have a dative external possessor (see Havers 1911: 240 for Celtic examples and Traugott 1992: 205–206 for Old English examples).

Moreover, in all other major features of SAE listed in Haspelmath (2001a), English behaves exactly like its continental neighbor Dutch. Whether one looks at the presence of articles, relative clauses with a relative pronoun, *have*-perfects, nominative experiencers, participial passives, anti-causative prominence, negative pronouns and lack of verbal negation, particles in comparative constructions, relative-based equative constructions or subject person affixes as strict agreement markers, English is just as much a nuclear member of SAE as Dutch or German.[15] In some respects, English is even *more* of a well-behaved SAE language than the exemplar language German: it has a higher nominative experiencer ratio, for instance (Haspelmath 2001b: 62).

Another explanation for the (near-)absence of indirect object external possessives in English – though not necessarily incompatible with the SAE account – is provided by Vennemann (2002). He ascribes the absence of external possessors to substrate influence from Celtic. The immediate objection that Celtic did have external possessors at some point in its history (see Havers 1911) is countered by Vennemann by assuming that insular Celtic was itself influenced by a (Hamito-)Semitic substrate. This assumption remains controversial (see Baldi and Page 2006), however, and even if it is accepted, the account remains problematic. First, Vennemann has to come up with an explanation why there was an external possessor in Old English. Indeed, the demise of the external possessor dates back to late medieval times, long after the Anglo-Saxon invasion of the 5th century.[16] Second, Vennemann does not consider the situation in Romance at all. If the absence of the external possessor in English and its weaker position in coastal ("Ingvaeonic") Dutch are the result of early colonization of the Atlantic coast, it begs the question why the same did not happen in Spain, which is the logical first stop on the Semitic route to North-Western Europe.[17] Third, Vennemann's account does not explain why the dative external possessor changed radically in North Germanic (see Section 5) and why it receded throughout the entire European area – even in those languages where it is still alive, like the Slavic languages (König and Haspelmath 1998: 583–584). Of course, it is not impossible that the continental recession of the external possessor is due to one factor, and the recession in English to another. By Occam's razor and given the controversial status of Vennemann's claims, it would however be preferable to attribute the fate of the external possessor in the whole of Europe to the same factor.

Some of the objections against Vennemann's account of the demise of the external possessor also apply to McWhorter's (2002) account. He too argues for language contact, not through a Semitic/Celtic substrate but through imperfect transmission after the Viking settlements. The advantage of this hypothesis is

---

[15] The only feature in which English, just like Dutch, deviates from the SAE norm is the intensifier/reflexive differentiation. But this feature is rather spurious (see fn. 14).

[16] Vennemann rescues his theory by assuming that substrate influence can make itself felt in delayed relay.

[17] This problem is all the more pressing in view of the Phoenician settlements that are archaeologically attested on the Iberian peninsula.

that it is less controversial in its archaeological assumptions. Yet, McWhorter also fails to take into account the continental European development in Romance, and his analysis consequently suffers from English bias as well. A case could be made for Viking influence in France to account for the geographically differentiated demise of the external possessor in Romance, but in light of McWhorter's central claim that English is sharply distinct from continental West Germanic, it would be hard to maintain.

In short, most current explanations for the distribution of the external possessor – i.e. SAE, Celtic and Semitic substrate, and imperfect language acquisition by the Vikings – are problematic. One recurring problem is a bias toward English or, in other words, the disregard of the distribution in Romance. In Section 5, we provide an alternative hypothesis of the distribution of the external possessor.

# 5 An alternative account of the distribution of the external possessor in West Germanic and Romance

The absence of the external possessor in English is unlikely to be due merely to the language's peripheral geographical position with regard to the SAE nucleus, and the previous section has shown that the evidence for treating it as a Celtic, Semitic or North Germanic substrate effect is not very strong either. In this section, we want to propose an alternative account. We argue that the absence of external possessors in English and their significant recession in French is due to an increase in noun phrase configurationality, with the emergence of specialized slots for determination and modification. Combining Haspelmath's (1998b: 318) broad definition of grammaticalization as "the gradual drift in all parts of the grammar toward tighter structures, toward less freedom in the use of linguistic expressions at all levels" with a constructional view on grammaticalization, which encompasses the rise of abstract, lexically underspecified constructions (see Bybee 2003: 146, 2007; Traugott 2008; Trousdale 2008, 2010; Traugott and Trousdale 2013), we regard the rise in NP configurationality as the result of a grammaticalization process (see also Van de Velde 2009a; Carlier and Lamiroy 2014), sometimes termed in current linguistic theorizing as 'constructionalization' (Traugott and Trousdale 2013). This process has progressed further in English than in German, and Dutch occupies a middle position in-between its West Germanic neighbors. In Romance, French is ahead of Spanish, and Italian occupies a middle position. The advantage of this account is that it works both for Germanic and for Romance, as opposed to the accounts presented above.

As noted in Section 4, the indirect object external possessor is attested in the ancient Indo-European daughter languages. As (95) shows, it is also attested in Gothic (König and Haspelmath 1998: 552), suggesting a continuous line of transmission with the construction still being in productive use in Present-day German.

(95) Gothic
*Fani         galagida      mis         ana    augona.*
clay.ACC.SG   put.PST.3SG   1SG.DAT     on     eye.ACC.PL
'He put clay into my eyes.'                                         (John 9, 15)[18]

It is also attested in the old West Germanic languages, including Old English, as (96) to (99) make clear.

(96) Old High German
*So     riuzit    thir       thaz    herza.*
then    mourns    2SG.DAT    the     heart
'Then your heart will mourn'                                        (Havers 1911: 285)

(97) Old Saxon
*Thiu   hlust   uuarð   imu          farhauuan.*
the     ear     was     3SG.M.DAT    hewn
'His ear was cut off.'                                              (Havers 1911: 293)

(98) Old Dutch
*Tho     bat       her   that    min    imo          an    themo   cruce   up*
then     asked     he    that    they   3SG.M.DAT    on    the     cross   up
*kerde        the    uóze.*
turned       the    feet
'Then he asked that they would turn his feet up on the cross.'
                                                                    (ONW s.v. *fuot*)

(99) Old English
*... him            mon   aslog       þæt    heafod   of.*
... 3SG.M.DAT       they  cut         the    head     off
'They cut his head off.'                                            (Traugott 1992: 205–206)

---

**18** The Greek original uses the genitive of the personal pronoun here. The use of the possessive dative in this construction is, in other words, authentically Germanic, not just a translation interference.

It seems that all West Germanic languages inherited the construction from the Germanic parental language. Subsequently, there was a long period during which the external possessor dwindled. According to Mustanoja (1960: 98), external possessors were common in Old English but comparatively infrequent in Middle English, when the construction steadily lost ground (see also Visser 1963: 633; McWhorter 2002: 226). External possessors persisted in Middle Dutch, as in (100), but judging from the situation in Present-day Dutch, they were declining there as well.[19]

(100) Middle Dutch
    *Mi        is den buuc     so gheladen.*
    1SG.OBL is the  stomach so loaded
    'My stomach is so full.'                    (Burridge 1996: 691)

The situation in Present-day West Germanic is a snapshot of a diachronic process in which English is the most progressive language and German is the most conservative one. The situation is summarized in Table 1.

**Table 1:** Diachrony of external possessors in West Germanic

|         | German | Dutch | English |
|---------|--------|-------|---------|
| Old     | +      | +     | +       |
| Middle  | +      | +     | ±       |
| Modern  | +      | ±     | −       |

This differential speed of language change[20] in the West Germanic languages has been noted in the literature (Van Haeringen 1956; Weerman 2006; König and Gast 2009: 14; Lamiroy and De Mulder 2011). As Faarlund (2001: 1718) puts it: "The differences between the Germanic languages can to a large extent be ascribed to their different stages on a continuous line of development."

This type of situation is also found in Romance, where French is ahead of Italian, which itself is ahead of Spanish (Lamiroy 1999, 2001; Lamiroy and De

---

[19] With regard to the situation in English, Van Bree (1981: 386) even posits that the dative external possessor had disappeared already in Middle English, but this seems contrary to the facts.
[20] The idea that languages change at different rates is sometimes objected to on the grounds that it glosses over subsystems or individual constructions and treats languages as holistic entities. Still, note that even Darwin (1859: 422) already argued that languages change at different paces.

Mulder 2011; Carlier et al. 2012, and references cited therein; De Mulder and Lamiroy 2012). For the Romance language family, Posner (1996: 185) posits the idea that "each language is tracking at different speeds along tramlines that lead in the same direction from the same starting point". As mentioned in Section 4, French is far more restrictive in the use of external possessors than Italian and Spanish: when we take a diachronic perspective, this suggests that French has progressed farther from the common origin. Havers (1911: 235) and Lamiroy (2003) point out that, in older stages of the language, French had less restrictions on the use of external possessors, as illustrated by the following examples from the 16th and 17th centuries, in which the possessee occupies the subject position, and which are ungrammatical in Present-day French (but still possible in Spanish and Italian!):

(101) French
*Le visage leur reluisoit.*
the face 3PL.DAT sparkled
'Their faces shone.' (Rabelais, *Pantagruel*, prologue)

(102) French
*Hélas! Notre pauvre Péronne, il faudra bien*
Alas our poor Péronne it will.be.necessary well
*la renvoyer si le mal lui continue.*
3SG.F.ACC fire if the evil 3SG.DAT continues
'Alas! We will have to fire our poor Péronne if she keeps being ill.'
(Lamiroy 2003: 272)

Carlier et al. (2012) assume that the cline French > Italian > Spanish and its West Germanic parallel English > Dutch > German are due to the extent to which these languages have carried through an overhaul in their macro-grammatical structure. In this light, retention of the external possessor is a sign of conservatism. The idea of attributing the absence of external possessors in English to its faster rate of grammatical change, rather than to the influence of a substrate, is supported by looking at overall changes in the noun phrase.

At first sight, the general shift from external to internal possessors seems to be a direct effect of deflection, i.e. the loss of morphological categories and their markers (see Weerman and De Wit 1999). As the distinct marking of the dative case is lost, the dative external possessor comes under pressure. This account is supported by the fact that English and Dutch display accusative/dative syncretism, i.e. they have no distinctive form for the dative pronoun, unlike German.

This line of reasoning has been suggested by Havers (1911: 284–285), Van Bree (1981: 386–388), König (2001: 973) and König and Gast (2009: 253), but there are several reasons to doubt that the demise of external possessors is directly due to the loss of distinctive dative desinences (see also Haspelmath 1999: 124–125; McWhorter 2002: 226–228; Vennemann 2002: 213–215).

First, languages such as Icelandic have preserved the dative case, but have nevertheless lost their dative external possessor (König and Haspelmath 1998: 583). Second, conversely, in languages like Spanish with a meaningful case of dative/accusative syncretism in the pronominal system (the so-called *acusativo* or *complemento directo preposicional*, which is used to mark specific (mostly human) direct objects, see Torrego 1999: 1779), the external possessor is holding up very well. Third, distinctive dative morphology is not really necessary to construe a recognizable external possessor. There are indeed several other options to mark the external possessor:

(i) by word order – Dutch, for instance, has lost its dative/accusative distinction in pronouns, but makes a distinction between direct objects and indirect objects by word order, and the external possessor behaves like an indirect object in this respect (see Haspelmath 1999: 111–112);

(ii) by using a preposition – in French, for example, the morphological dative/accusative distinction is only preserved in third-person pronouns, not in nouns, but the external possessor with nouns can still be marked by means of the preposition *à* (Lamiroy 2003: 257);[21]

(iii) by relegating the possessor argument to a locative PP – Scandinavian languages, for instance, have grammaticalized a new external possessor with a superessive preposition, as in (105) and (106). In Icelandic, as in (107), and Russian, similar constructions have arisen with an adessive preposition (König and Haspelmath 1998: 584).

(103) French
*Max a tordu le bras à Luc.*
Max has twisted the arm to Luc
'Max has twisted Luc's arm.'

(104) French
*Max lui a tordu le bras.*
Max 3SG.DAT has twisted the arm
'Max has twisted his arm.'

---

[21] The construction with the clitic dative is less marked than the PP construction, though (Lamiroy 2003: 258).

(105) Swedish
*Någon bröt armen på honom.*
someone broke the.arm on him
'Someone broke his arm.'  (König and Haspelmath 1998: 559)

(106) Norwegian
*Legen røntgenfotograferte magen på dei.*
the.doctor radiographed the.stomach on them
'The doctor radiographed their stomach.'
 (König and Haspelmath 1998: 559)

(107) Icelandic
*Han nuddaði á henni fæturna*
he massages on her the.legs
'He massaged her legs.'  (König and Haspelmath 1998: 559)

In principle, English could have made use of any of these options. Thus, it could have developed an external possessive construction with an oblique pronoun, as in *They broke him the arm* (like Dutch after its loss of a formally marked dative). After all, the lack of a dative has not prevented English from still having an indirect object. It could also have used its recipient preposition *to* for marking the external possessor, as in *They broke the arm to him* (like French). Haspelmath (1999: 125–131) argues that this is not possible because the range of the preposition *to* on the semantic map of "dative" functions does not extend to the benefactive and the *dativus iudicantis*. This does not seem to be true, as *to* in (108) to (110) does mark a *dativus iudicantis*.

(108)  *It is too ugly to us.*  (COCA)

(109)  *It is too real to me.*  (COCA)

(110)  *The AT is too important to me.*  (COCA)

Another alternative would be for English to grammaticalize the Scandinavian-type external possessor in a locative PP. In fact, English marginally allows this construction, as (111) shows.[22] Note that English's close neighbor Dutch uses this construction as an alternative to its dative external possessor more extensively, as in (112) and (113) (Van Belle and Van Langendonck 1996: 233–234).

---

[22] The construction occurs with other verbs as well (e.g. *he walked out on me*).

(111)  *The rest of the children died on me.*     (König and Haspelmath 1998: 560)

(112)  Dutch
*De tranen stonden (bij) hem in de ogen.*
the tears  stood   by  him  in the eyes
'The tears were in his eyes.'

(113)  Dutch
*Dan rijzen (bij) mij de haren te berge.*
then rise  by  me the hair  to mountain
'This makes my hair stand on end.'

The fact that English did not select any of these options – with the marginal exception of (111), which is not really productive in Standard English – is still in want of a good explanation. But what the data described thus far crucially show is that the mere loss of dative case, which did not only occur in English but was part of an overall deflection process that had been raging through the West Germanic and Romance languages alike, is unlikely to be the ultimate cause for the decline of the external possessor. This leaves room for another explanation.

The hypothesis that we want to put forward is that the West Germanic and Romance languages are moving toward greater configurationality in the noun phrase, the hierarchical syntactic structure of the NP being the result of a long-term process of expanding the modification structures of the noun. Integral NPs with a hierarchical constituency structure are a typical feature of European languages (see Rijkhoff 1998: 322–325, 362–363). A close look at the nominal syntax of ancient Indo-European languages suggests that Proto-Indo-European probably lacked tightly structured NPs. The rise of configurationality in the Indo-European NP has been argued for at length in Van de Velde (2009a, 2009b), and has been defended for both Germanic and Romance languages by Himmelmann (1997), Faarlund (2001: 1713), Luraghi (2010), Ledgeway (2011), Perridon and Sleeman (2011) and Carlier and Lamiroy (2014). Looking at a range of Indo-European languages and old Germanic in particular, Van de Velde (2009a) shows that there has been a massive shift of clause-level elements getting absorbed in the NP, in particular as modifiers of all kinds (adjectives, quantifiers, pronouns, etc.) show a tendency to lose their "floating" capacities. Discontinuous structures like (114) and (115) (see Van de Velde 2009a: Ch. 6 for further examples) are no longer possible in Present-day English, Dutch or German.

(114) Gothic
*dauns sijum woþi*
odor be.1PL sweet
'We are a sweet odor.' (Behaghel 1932: 241)

(115) Old Saxon
*hiet that hie is suerd dedi scarp an scethia*
ordered that he his sword did sharp in sheath
'ordered that he sheathed his sharp sword' (Van de Velde 2009a: 193)

These observations concur with findings by Admoni (1967), who shows that the proportion of NP-internal to NP-external material per clause is growing over time in German (see also Weber 1971; Ebert 1978: 49–50). In other words, over the centuries, Germanic has been putting less weight on the clause and more weight on the NP. For Romance, Ledgeway (2011) similarly argues that, in the transition from Latin to Romance, the NP has emerged as a structural template with dedicated positions for the expression of definiteness and modification. Discontinuous structures which were common in Latin, like (116) and (117), are no longer grammatical in Romance.

(116) Latin
*magno cum dolore*
great with grief
'with great grief' (Ledgeway 2011: 393)

(117) Latin
*nostram ridebant inuidiam*
our laugh.PST.3PL unpopularity
'They mocked at our unpopularity.' (Ledgeway 2011: 394)

In our view, possessor constructions are a good example of this long-term drift towards NP constituency. The strategy of expressing possessors externally, as a direct argument of the predicate, can be seen as a tendency to highlight the relation between the verb and the relevant participants, downplaying their mutual relations. In contrast, the strategy of expressing possessors internally in one constituent highlights the relations that exist between the participants, irrespective of the predicate (König 2001: 973). Extending this idea, one could argue that in languages with external possessors, the verbal predicate plays a more central role as the pivot which inter-connects all the participants, whereas languages with internal possessors have a stronger noun pivot. The distinction between predicate vs. noun pivots should be conceived of as a cline, rather than as a strict dichotomy, and Germanic and Romance languages vary with regard to how far they have evolved on this cline.

Note that the emphasis on the noun and, hence, the tighter organization of NPs in the Indo-European languages are supported by other syntactic changes in the nominal domain besides the loss of discontinuous modifiers. The rise in NP configurationality is intimately connected to the development of a determiner slot, as marked by the rise of articles (see Himmelmann 1997: 133; Lyons 1999: 323; Luraghi 2010; Ledgeway 2011; Perridon and Sleeman 2011; Carlier 2007; Carlier and Lamiroy 2014). Definite articles did not exist in the ancient Germanic period, and first signs of a budding article occur in the Old English, Old Dutch and Old High German period (Lehmann 1994: 28; Heine and Kuteva 2006: 99–100).[23] The same is true for Romance, where the first definite[24] articles emerge between the 3rd and the 8th centuries (Ledgeway 2011: 388, 409–415 and references cited there), a full-fledged article being a 9th-century innovation (Goyens 1994; De Mulder and Carlier 2011).[25] In the long run, the rise of determiners often led to a decrease in external possessors. That the two tendencies are indeed related is supported by the observation that the modern West Germanic and Romance languages show slight differences in the extent of grammaticalization of the article, which correlate inversely with the retention of the external possessor.

In West Germanic, the grammaticalization of the definite article has progressed further in English than in Dutch, in which the definite article is in turn more grammaticalized than in German. On the phonetic level, this is clear from the distinction between the demonstrative and the article. Phonetic erosion has separated the definite article from its demonstrative origin in English and Dutch, with the full vowels having become a schwa. This is not the case in German, where the vowels have been largely preserved in *der, die, das* (see Van Haeringen 1956: 40). The same holds, to some extent, for the indefinite article. In English, the article and the numeral from which it derives have different vowels (<a> [eɪ]/[ə]) versus <one> [wʌn]). This is true for Dutch as well (<een> [ən] versus <één> [en]). German, however, preserves the same diphthong for both (<ein> [aɪn]), at

---

[23] The precise date of the emergence of the article is a moot point; see Crisma (2011) and Sommerer (2012) for recent surveys.
[24] The indefinite article did not emerge until the Old French period (Goyens 1994: 277) while the partitive appeared in Middle French (Carlier 2007).
[25] Goyens (1994: 276) provides the following figures for French: whereas her Latin corpus contains 86.66% of NPs with zero marking for the determiner slot, the percentage of NPs with zero marking is down to 40.76% in Old French and 15.98% in Modern French.

least when pronounced in full in the standard language.[26] On the morphological level too, there is evidence that English is ahead of its continental sister languages. The English definite article does not agree in gender or number with its noun and has become an invariant particle whose surface form is conditioned only by phonological factors. In Dutch and German, however, the article still has gender and number agreement with the following noun. Hence, the English definite article can be considered as more "specialized" in the expression of definiteness than the Dutch article – which, in addition to definiteness, expresses information about gender and number – and much more so than the German article – which even expresses case. The one-to-one mapping between the expression of definiteness (function) and the article (form) is violated in two ways in German: the article expresses more than just definiteness and the expression of definiteness is partly encoded on the adjective as well, by the alternation between strong and weak inflection (pace Demske 2001). Similarly, in Dutch, the inflectional schwa is absent on attributive adjectives with indefinite singular neuter nouns (e.g. *een mooi huis* 'a beautiful house'), but present in all other cases (e.g. *het mooie huis* 'the beautiful house'). Still, there are indications that the adjective is currently losing this function in Dutch and that the schwa is increasingly used as an attributive marker, irrespective of gender, number, or definiteness (Weerman 2003; Van de Velde and Weerman 2014).

Additional evidence for the hypothesis that the grammaticalization of the determiner as part of NP configurationality follows an English > Dutch > German cline comes from the distribution of the resumptive prenominal possessive construction discussed above (Sections 2 and 3.1, see examples (9), (10), (38)). As mentioned, this construction stands midway between internal and external possession. What we see is that German explicitly marks the external nature by a dative, which is reminiscent of its *dativus commodi* origin. Dutch does not do this, and English eschews this semi-external construction altogether.

The rise of the determiner as part of NP configurationality is not only responsible for the switch from dative external possessors to internal possessors but, arguably, also affected genitive possessors. It is clear from (118) and (119) that the genitive used to be a lot freer, and could easily be separated from its head noun.

---

[26] Note that, in spoken German, the article is often reduced to the form we find in Dutch. However, in English and Dutch, the pronunciation of the numeral cannot be used for the indefinite article, not even in its unreduced form.

(118) Middle Dutch
*Maer ic sal   offerande doen minen            Gode,    die*
but    I   shall   offer      do   1SG.POSS.DAT god.DAT who

*mechtich es boven al, die sceppere es hemelrijcx    ende*
mighty   is above all and creator  is heaven.GEN and

*eerterijcx ende alles datter     in es.*
earth.GEN  and  all   that.there in is

'But I shall bring an offer to my god who is almighty, and who is the creator of heaven and earth and all that is in it.'
(Van de Velde 2009a: 289)

(119) Early Modern Dutch
*Wy hebben ... sommige monstren gezien der       Kinderen van*
we  have       some    monsters  seen  the.GEN children  of

*Enac, vander      reusengeslachte, by de  welcke wy gheleken,*
Enac of.the.GEN   giants.breed     by the  which  we compared

*schenen sprinchanen  te wesen.*
seemed  grasshoppers to be

'We have seen some monsters of the children of Enac, of giants' breed, compared by which we seemed like grasshoppers.'
(Van de Velde 2009a: 289)

This separability could well be taken as a relic of the former autonomous status of genitive modifiers, which were not configurationally integrated in the NP (see Van de Velde 2009a: 104–105, 285–291 for a more extensive discussion).[27]

In Romance as well, the versatility of the external possessor seems to correlate inversely with the grammaticalization of the article. Examples (120) to (122) show a dissociation between the article and the demonstrative in French and Italian which does not hold for Spanish. The article cannot license NP ellipsis in French or Italian, but it can in Spanish. Put differently, contrary to the demonstrative, the article in French and Italian has lost part of its autonomy. Interestingly, Spanish also has the widest range of external possessors.

---

[27] Separation is also used as a criterion to distinguish internal and external possessors in König and Haspelmath (1998: 584–586), who argue that the separation of the Greek genitive involves a switch to external possessors.

(120) French
 *la voiture de Jean* / *\*la de Jean* / *celle de Jean*
 the car     of John / the of John / that of John
 'John's car' / 'the of John' / 'that of John'

(121) Italian
 *la machina di Gianni* / *\*la di Gianni* / *quella di Gianni*
 the car     of John  / the of John   / that   of John
 'John's car' / 'the of John' / 'that of John'

(122) Spanish
 *el coche de Juan* / *el de Juan*
 the car  of John  / the of John
 'John's car' / 'the (one) of John'

Furthermore, French has gone furthest in the grammaticalization of the so-called partitive article, which has become a full-fledged indefinite article for plural and mass nouns in Modern French (Carlier 2007; De Mulder and Carlier 2011; Carlier and Lamiroy 2014). As shown in (123), where the partitive is used with an abstract noun, the original partitive interpretation is of course no longer available.

(123) French
 *Il a fait ça avec de l' amour.*
 He has done that with of the love
 'He did this with love.'                (Carlier and Lamiroy 2014: 482)

Carlier and Lamiroy (2014) show that the grammaticalization of the partitive article has progressed further in French than in Italian, as (124) to (126) make clear. Spanish has simply not developed a partitive article at all, as illustrated in (127). The partitive construction is possible, but not with the indefinite reading intended here, only with the literal partitive meaning in a deictic context.

(124) French
 *Pierre mange du pain.* / *\*Pierre mange pain.*
 Pierre eats of.the bread / Pierre eats bread
 'Peter eats bread.'

(125) North Italian
 *Piero mangia del pane*
 Piero eats of.the bread
 'Peter eats bread.'

(126) South Italian
*Piero mangia pane.*
Piero eats    bread
'Peter eats bread.'

(127) Spanish
*\*Pedro come del    pan. / Pedro come pan.*
Pedro eats of.the bread / Pedro eats    bread
'Peter eats bread.'

In addition, French behaves differently from Italian and Spanish with regard to the possessive pronoun. In Old and Middle French, possessives could be combined with the article within the same NP (e.g. *un mien filz* 'a son of mine', Chanson de Roland). In Modern French, the possessive adjective is mutually exclusive with the article or demonstrative, which suggests that it is itself a determiner (see Lyons 1999), as in (128). In Italian and Spanish, however, they still co-occur, as in (129) and (130). This again shows that French is ahead in the grammaticalization of the determiner.

(128) French
*(\*ce/\*le) mon livre*
this/the my book
'my book/this book of mine'

(129) Italian
*il    mio libro*
the my book
'my book'

(130) Spanish
*el libro mio*
the book my
'my book'

Yet other aspects of NP configurationality pattern according to the English > Dutch > German and French > Italian > Spanish clines. According to Ledgeway (2011), for instance, agreement morphology on adjectives is typical of non-configurational NPs. The loss of agreement in West Germanic and Romance, which has progressed furthest in English and French and least in German and Spanish, does indeed straightforwardly follow the suggested clines.

Now, if we look beyond the West Germanic and Romance languages, we find further support for the association between the shift to internal possessors and the rise of definite articles, both being the result of an increase in NP configurationality. The external possessor is best preserved in the Balto-Slavic languages (König and Haspelmath 1998: 552), which are precisely the European languages lacking a definite article (see Haspelmath 2001a: 1494).[28] Note that the Slavic languages also have less configurationality in the NP, as they allow adjectives to occur outside of the determiner–noun brace, for example (Corver 1989: 38).[29]

All of the above observations point to a clear historical inverse correlation between NP configurationality (decrease of floating modifiers and emergence of an article and determiner phrase in general) on the one hand and retention of the external possessor on the other hand.

Obviously, the relation between the grammaticalization of the determiner and the decrease of external possessors should be seen not as a law but as a robust tendency. Otherwise, we would expect French to lack an external possessor altogether, just like English, which is not the case.[30] Similarly, the retention of the external possessor in German would be at odds with the NP configurationality that German undeniably displays. However, the main claim stands: if we look at closely related languages, i.e. members of one and the same family, the differences in both domains of syntax are correlated, i.e. the more grammaticalized the determiner slot, the less common the external possessor.[31]

Let us now return to the question of whether there is a relation between deflection and the loss of the external possessor in English. As argued in Section 5, a simple causal connection between these two tendencies does not stand up to scrutiny. Yet, to the extent that the rise in NP configurationality is connected

---

**28** The article in Bulgarian and Macedonian is an exception, possibly influenced by the Balkan Sprachbund: the two languages are near the language that boasts the oldest definite article, i.e. Greek, and we see that Romanian has grammaticalized a postposed article as well, contrary to what happened in the western Romance languages.

**29** External possessors also occur in Kalkatungu (König 2001: 975), the standard example of a language that lacks NP configurationality (Blake 1983).

**30** A large corpus study (Spanoghe 1995) does show that the external possessor (dative) structure is receding in Modern French.

**31** It remains to be seen to what extent all aspects of NP configurationality pattern alike. German and Dutch, for instance, have a richer internal branching of premodifying adjective phrases than English. If this is also part of NP configurationality, we see an inverse patterning of what we have observed for determiners or adjectival inflection. For the time being, we focus on the correlation between the grammaticalization of the determiner slot and the loss of the external possessor.

with the deflection tendency, the decline of the external possessor construction can indeed be analyzed as a consequence of the morphological erosion of the dative, albeit an indirect one.

A similar indirect causal relationship may hold between the external possessor and SAE. As argued above, the dative external possessor is unlikely to be a feature of SAE. However, NP configurationality could be an SAE feature: it is strongest in the SAE nucleus and fades out to the east (Balto-Slavic), where articles and a configurational position for adjectives are either absent, or less developed. Furthermore, NP configurationality is comparatively rare in languages across the world (Rijkhoff 1998). If the loss of the external possessor is due to an increase in NP configurationality, and if the latter is an SAE feature, then the external possessor is ultimately linked to SAE.

If the SAE Sprachbund is a result of language contact during the early Middle Ages, as is not implausible (see also Haspelmath 2001a: 1506–1507), then the differential demise of the external possessor as the result of increased NP configurationality in West Germanic and Romance is ultimately still due to language contact. Indeed, we believe that Indo-European as a spread-zone, to use Nichols' (1992) term, is characterized by intense language contact and late L2 learners' effects and concomitant deflection (see Kusters 2003, Lupyan and Dale 2010, Trudgill 2011, and Bentz and Winter 2013 on the effect of L2 learners). This in turn gave rise to increased NP structure. Which itself bled the external possessor.

We believe that the decline of external possessors was favored by the fact that the determiner slot was increasingly used for the expression of possessors that formerly operated at clause level. Although the internal possessor construction subsequently drained the external possessor construction, the latter did not become totally unsustainable. As shown above, the external possessor construction could have survived in English in one guise or another. On a more general level, the idea that a change in constructions is brought about by an old construction becoming "worn out" or "deficient" is not very likely. As Hopper and Traugott (2003: 124) put it:

> Rather than replace a lost or almost lost distinction, newly innovated forms compete with older ones because they are felt to be more expressive than what was available before. This competition allows, even encourages, the recession or loss of older forms. Textual evidence provides a strong support for this view of coexisting competing forms and constructions, rather than a cycle of loss and renewal.

In this view of syntactic change, there is no automatic trade-off between the rise of determiners and the loss of dative external possessors. German and Spanish have a well-developed determiner, but the dative external possessor is holding up quite well. Thus, the new determiner-possessive structure has not wiped out external possessors. It merely offered a new opportunity to express them NP-internally. All languages have taken up the offer, though some more reluctantly so than others.[32]

# 6 Conclusions

We have argued in this paper that previous accounts of the distribution of the indirect object external possessor face numerous problems. Contrary to what has often been claimed, we have shown that the indirect object external possessor is not a straightforward feature of Standard Average European and that its debated near-absence in English, ascribed to either Sprachbund or substrate influences, is not the direct result of the less central position of the language in comparison to its continental West Germanic sisters. Nor is it likely, in our view, that the external possessor has been eradicated from English as a result of exposure to a Semitic, Celtic or North Germanic substrate. In our opinion, all previous accounts are problematic in two respects. First, they fail to sufficiently take into account the gradual distribution of the external possessor in the different languages. The literature is equivocal with regard to the presence of an external possessor in Dutch, and vestigial constructions in English (e.g. in idioms and with the verb *look*) are underplayed as well. Furthermore, the fact that the dative external possessor has partly receded in many languages, including those in which it still is a productive construction, is not always recognized. Second, the focus on English has often led scholars to ignore data from the Romance languages. As shown in this paper, the differential retention of the external possessor in the Romance languages is relevant to discriminate between the various explanations suggested for West Germanic.

In order to solve the abovementioned problems, we have argued that the distribution of the dative external possessor in West Germanic and Romance is better explained by the rise in NP configurationality. Both language families have seen the emergence of syntactic structures to accommodate determination and modification slots (see Van de Velde 2009a, 2009b and Ledgeway 2011, respectively), and exactly these structures have attracted the possessor. In other

---

[32] Interestingly, and not coincidentally, German shows conservatism in its NP-internal genitives (Scott 2014).

words, all languages under consideration have undergone a process of "possessor descending": free dative possessors that used to operate at the level of the clause have moved down to the level of the NP. The extent to which this has happened in the West Germanic languages corresponds to the language constellation that has been described by Van Haeringen (1956), in which Dutch occupies a middle position between English and German, both geographically and linguistically. A similar constellation holds for Romance, with Italian being in-between French and Spanish (see Lamiroy 2007, Lamiroy and De Mulder 2011; Carlier et al. 2012; De Mulder and Lamiroy 2012). The *raison d'être* of these clines is that some languages are ahead of others in the overhaul of their grammatical system.

The explanation that we have proposed here raises the question as to what determines the differential rates of change in the individual languages: *why* is English ahead of Dutch, and Dutch ahead of German, and *why* is French ahead of Italian, and Italian ahead of Spanish? For Germanic, McWhorter (2002) argues that the explanation lies in the extremely high level of language contact that English had when Scandinavians learned Anglo-Saxon as a second language from the 8th century onward. A similar argument can be put forward for Dutch. Buccini (1995, 2010), for instance, argues that the Dutch language is a result of Ingvaeonic speakers learning Frankish as a second language in the early Middle Ages. While these accounts are well-taken, one may wonder whether the differential speed of language change in West Germanic can really be attributed to one specific period in time. As argued above, McWhorter's story is difficult to link to the demise of the external possessor directly. Of course, a major breakdown in the transmission of a language can have long-term effects, but some changes in West Germanic seem to have started only in the late Middle Ages or later. The loss of adjectival inflection, for instance, follows the English > Dutch > German cline, but both Old English and Old Dutch still exhibited complex adjectival agreement. The same applies to the external possessor. Moreover, McWhorter's account leaves unexplained why we find a similar cline in Romance.

Preliminary work on demographic data shows that one can establish a correlation between the rate of language change in the West Germanic and Romance languages and the urbanization (and concomitant immigration) in the areas where these languages are spoken (see Breitbarth 2008 for a close look at the speed of Jespersen's cycle in Middle Low German; Lodge 1996: 142–143, 2004 on French). Although the preliminary data on the relation between demography and language change seem promising, this is obviously a matter for further research.

## Acknowledgments

We would like to express our gratitude to the anonymous reviewers for helpful comments on an earlier draft of the paper. Special thanks also go to the editors of this volume for their meticulous work both on the formal and on the content level. We also appreciate the discussion with the series editor Volker Gast, who has a decidedly different view on the topic at hand, but: "Du choc des idées jaillit la lumière" (Nicolas Boileau, 1636–1711).

## List of abbreviations

1/2/3 = person; ACC = accusative; AOR = aorist; DAT = dative; DU = dual; F = feminine; GEN = genitive; INDEF = indefinite; LOC = locative; M = masculine; NOM = nominative; OBL = oblique; P = particle; PL = plural; POSS = possessive; PST = past; REFL = reflexive; SG = singular

## Corpora

COCA. *Corpus of comtemporary American English.* http://corpus.byu.edu/coca
ONW. *Oudnederlands woordenboek* [Old Dutch dictionary]. http://gtb.inl.nl

## References

Admoni, Wladimir G. 1967. Der Umfang und die Gestaltungsmittel des Satzes in der deutschen Literatursprache bis zum Ende des 18. Jahrhunderts. *Beiträge zur Geschichte der deutschen Sprache und Literatur* 89. 144–199.
Allen, Cynthia L. 2008. *Genitives in Early English: Typology and evidence.* Oxford: Oxford University Press.
Baldi, Philip & Richard Page. 2006. Review of Theo Vennemann, 2003, *Europa Vasconica – Europa Semitica. Lingua* 116. 2183–2220.
Behaghel, Otto. 1932. *Deutsche Syntax: Eine geschichtliche Darstellung. Band IV, Worstellung. Periodenbau.* Heidelberg: Winter.
Blake, Barry J. 1983. Structure and word order in Kalkatungu: The anatomy of a flat language. *Australian Journal of Linguistics* 3. 143–175.
Breitbarth, Anne. 2008. The development of negation in Middle Low German. Paper presented at the Annual meeting of the Linguistics Association of Great Britain, University of Essex, 10–13 September.

Bentz, Christian and Bodo Winter, Languages with More Second Language Learners Tend to Lose Nominal Case', *Language Dynamics and Change* 3. 1–27.
Buccini, Anthony F. 1995. Ontstaan en vroegste ontwikkeling van het Nederlandse taallandschap [Origin and earliest evolution of the Dutch linguistic landscape]. *Taal & Tongval* 8. 8–66.
Buccini, Anthony F. 2010. Between pre-German and pre-English: The origin of Dutch. *Journal of Germanic Linguistics* 22. 301–314.
Burridge, Kate. 1996. Degenerate cases of body parts in Middle Dutch. In Hilary Chappell & William McGregor (eds.), *The grammar of inalienability*, 679–710. Berlin & New York: Mouton de Gruyter.
Bybee, Joan. 2003. Cognitive processes in grammaticalization. In Michael Tomasello (ed.), *The new psychology of language: Cognitive and functional approaches to language structure*, Vol. 2, 145–167. Mahwah: Lawrence Erlbaum Associates.
Bybee, Joan. 2007. Diachronic linguistics. In: Dirk Geeraerts and Hubert Cuyckens (eds.), *The handbook of Cognitive Linguistics*, 945–987. Oxford: Oxford University Press.
Carlier, Anne. 2007. From preposition to article. The grammaticalization of the French partitive. *Studies in Language* 31. 1–49.
Carlier, Anne, Walter De Mulder & Béatrice Lamiroy. 2012. Introduction: The pace of grammaticalization in a typological perspective. *Folia Linguistica* 46. 287–301.
Carlier, Anne, Michèle Goyens & Béatrice Lamiroy. 2013. *De*: A genitive marker in French? Its grammaticalization path from Latin to French. In Anne Carlier and Jean-Christophe Verstraete (eds.), *Case and grammatical relations across languages: The genitive*, 141–216. Amsterdam: John Benjamins.
Carlier, Anne & Béatrice Lamiroy. 2014. The grammaticalization of the prepositional partitive in Romance. In Tuomas Huumo & Silvia Luraghi (eds.), *Partitive Cases and Related Categories*, 477–523. Berlin: De Gruyter Mouton.
Corver, Norbert. 1989. Left branch extractions and DP. In Hans Bennis & Ans van Kemade (eds.), *Linguistics in the Netherlands 1989*, 31–40. Dordrecht: Foris.
Crisma, Paola. 2011. The emergence of the definite article in English. In Petra Sleeman & Harry Perridon (eds.), *The noun phrase in Romance and Germanic: Structure, variation, and change*, 175–192. Amsterdam: John Benjamins.
Darwin, Charles. 1859. *On the origin of species by means of natural selection, or the preservation of favoured races in the struggle for life*. London: John Murray.
Demonte, Violeta. 1995. Dative alternation in Spanish. *Probus* 7. 5–30.
Demske, Ulrike. 2001. *Merkmale und Relationen: Diachrone Studien zur Nominalphrase des Deutschen*. Berlin: Mouton de Gruyter.
De Mulder, Walter & Anne Carlier. 2011. The grammaticalization of definite articles. In Heiko Narrog & Bernd Heine (eds.), *The Oxford handbook of grammaticalization*, 522–535. Oxford: Oxford University Press.
De Mulder, Walter & Béatrice Lamiroy. 2012. Gradualness of grammaticalization in Romance: The position of French, Spanish and Italian. In Kristin Davidse, Tine Breban, Lieselotte Brems & Tanja Mortelmans (eds.), *Grammaticalization and language change: New reflections*, 199–226. Amsterdam: John Benjamins.
De Smet, Hendrik, Lobke Ghesquière & Freek Van de Velde (eds.). 2013. Multiple source constructions in language change [Special issue]. *Studies in Language* 37(3).
De Vooys, C.G.N. 1967. *Nederlandse spraakkunst* [Dutch grammar]. Groningen: Wolters.
Draye, Luk. 1996. The German dative. In William Van Belle & Willy Van Langendonck (eds.), *The dative*. Vol. 1: *Descriptive studies*, 155–215. Amsterdam: John Benjamins.

Ebert, Robert P. 1978. *Historische Syntax des Deutschen*. Stuttgart: Metzler.
Faarlund, Jan Terje. 2001. From ancient Germanic to modern Germanic languages. In Martin Haspelmath, Ekkehard König, Wulf Österreicher & Wolfgang Reible (eds.), *Language typology and language universals*, Vol. 2, 1706–1719. Berlin: Mouton de Gruyter.
Fischer, Olga C.M. 1992. Syntax. In Norman Blake (ed.), *The Cambridge history of the English language*. Vol. 2: *1066–1476*, 207–408. Cambridge: Cambridge University Press.
Goyens, Michèle. 1994. *Emergence et évolution du syntagme nominal en français*. Bern: Peter Lang.
Haegeman, Liliane. 2003. The external possessor construction in West Flemish. In Martine Coene & Yves D'hulst (eds.), *From NP to DP.* Vol. 2: *The expression of possession in noun phrases*, 221–256. Amsterdam: John Benjamins.
Harbert, Wayne. 2007. *The Germanic languages*. Cambridge: Cambridge University Press.
Haspelmath, Martin. 1998a. How young is Standard Average European? *Language Sciences* 20. 271–287.
Haspelmath, Martin. 1998b. Does grammaticalization need reanalysis? *Studies in Language* 22. 315–351.
Haspelmath, Martin. 1999. External possession in a European areal perspective. In Doris L. Payne & Immanuel Barshi (eds.), *External possession*, 109–135. Amsterdam: John Benjamins.
Haspelmath, Martin. 2001a. The European linguistic area: Standard Average European. In Martin Haspelmath, Ekkehard König, Wulf Oesterreicher & Wolfgang Raible (eds.), *Language typology and language universals*, Vol. 2, 1492–1510. Berlin: Mouton de Gruyter.
Haspelmath, Martin. 2001b. Non-canonical marking of core arguments in European languages. In Alexandra Y. Aikhenvald, R.M.W. Dixon & Masayki Onishi (eds), *Non-canonical marking of subjects and objects*, 53–83. Amsterdam: John Benjamins.
Havers, Wilhelm. 1911. *Untersuchungen zur Kasussyntax der indogermanischen Sprachen*. Strasbourg: Karl J. Trübner.
Heine, Bernd. 2002. On the role of context in grammaticalization. In Ilse Wischer & Gabriele Diewald (eds.), *New reflections on grammaticalization*, 83–101. Amsterdam: John Benjamins.
Heine, Bernd. & Tania Kuteva. 2006. *The changing languages of Europe*. Oxford: Oxford University Press.
Hendriks, Jennifer. 2012. Re-examining the 'origins' of the prenominal periphrastic possessive construction *Jan z'n boek* in Dutch: An empirical approach. *Diachronica* 29. 28–71.
Himmelmann, Nikolaus P. 1997. *Deiktikon, Artikel, Nominalphrase: Zur Emergenz syntaktischer Struktur*. Tübingen: Max Niemeyer Verlag.
Hopper, Paul J. & Elizabeth Closs Traugott. 2003. *Grammaticalization*. Cambridge: Cambridge University Press.
Hüning, Matthias, Ulrike Vogl, Ton van der Wouden & Arie Verhagen (eds.). 2006. *Nederlands tussen Duits en Engels* [Dutch between German and English]. Leiden: Stichting Neerlandistiek Leiden.
König, Ekkehard. 2001. Internal and external possessors. In Martin Haspelmath, Ekkehard König, Wulf Österreicher & Wolfgang Reible (eds.), *Language typology and language universals*, Vol. 2, 970–978. Berlin: Mouton de Gruyter.
König, Ekkehard & Volker Gast. 2009. *Understanding English-German contrasts*. Berlin: Erich Schmidt.
König, Ekkehard & Martin Haspelmath. 1998. Les constructions à possesseur externe dans les langues d'Europe. In Jack Feuillet (ed.), *Actance et valence dans les langues de l'Europe*, 525–606. Berlin: Mouton de Gruyter.

Kusters, Christiaan Wouter. 2003. *Linguistic complexity: the influence of social change on verbal inflection*. Utrecht: LOT.
Lamiroy, Béatrice. 1999. Auxiliaires, langues romanes et grammaticalisation. *Langages* 135. 33–45.
Lamiroy, Béatrice. 2001. Le syntagme prépositionnel en français et en espagnol: Une question de grammaticalisation? *Langages* 143. 91–106.
Lamiroy, Béatrice. 2003. Grammaticalization and external possessor structures in Romance and Germanic languages. In Martine Coene & Yves D'hulst (eds.), *From NP to DP*. Vol. 2: *The expression of possession in noun phrases*, 257–280. Amsterdam: John Benjamins.
Lamiroy, Béatrice. 2007. Gradation, grammaire et grammaticalisation. In Michel Charolles, Nathalie Fournier, Catherine Fuchs & Florence Lefeuvre (eds.), *Parcours de la phrase: Mélanges offerts à Pierre Le Goffic*, 29–42. Paris: Ophrys.
Lamiroy, Béatrice & Nicole Delbecque. 1998. The possessive dative in Romance and Germanic languages. In William Van Belle & Willy Van Langendonck (eds.), *The dative*. Vol. 2: *Theoretical and contrastive studies*, 29–74. Amsterdam: John Benjamins.
Lamiroy, Béatrice & Walter De Mulder. 2011. Degrees of grammaticalization across languages. In Heiko Narrog & Bernd Heine (eds.), *The Oxford handbook of grammaticalization*, 302–318. Oxford: Oxford University Press.
Leclère, Christian. 1995. Sur une restructuration dative. *Language Research Institute Seoul National University* 31. 179–198.
Ledgeway, Adam. 2011. Syntactic and morphosyntactic typology and change. In Adam Ledgeway, Martin Maiden & John-Charles Smith (eds), *The Cambridge history of the Romance languages*, 382–471. Cambridge: Cambridge University Press.
Lehmann, Winfred P. 1994. Gothic and the reconstruction of Proto-Germanic. In Ekkehard König & Johan van der Auwera (eds.), *The Germanic languages*, 19–37. London: Routledge.
Lodge, Anthony. 1996. *Le français: Histoire d'un dialecte devenu langue*. Paris: Fayard.
Lodge, Anthony. 2004. *A sociolinguistic history of Parisian French*. Cambridge: Cambridge University Press.
Luraghi, Silvia. 2010. The rise (and possible downfall) of configurationality. In Silvia Luraghi & Vit Bubenik (eds.), *A companion to historical linguistics*, 212–229. London: Continuum.
Lupyan, Gary & Rick Dale. 2010. Language structure is partly determined by social structure. *PLoS ONE* 5(1).
Lyons, Christopher. 1999. *Definiteness*. Cambridge: Cambridge University Press.
McWhorter, John H. 2002. What happened to English? *Diachronica* 19. 217–272.
Mustanoja, Tauno F. 1960. *Middle English syntax*. Part I, *Parts of speech*. Helsinki: Société Néophilologique.
Nichols, J. 1992. *Linguistic diversity in space and time*. Chicago: University of Chicago Press.
Payne, Doris L. & Immanuel Barshi. 1999. External possession: What, where, how, and why? In Doris L. Payne & Immanuel Barshi (eds.), *External possession*, 3–29. Amsterdam: John Benjamins.
Perridon, Harry & Petra Sleeman. 2011. The noun phrase in Germanic and Romance: Common developments and differences. In Petra Sleeman & Harry Perridon (eds.), *The noun phrase in Romance and Germanic: Structure, variation, and change*, 1–21. Amsterdam: John Benjamins.
Posner, Rebecca. 1996. *The Romance languages*. Cambridge: Cambridge University Press.
Ramat, Paolo. 1986. The Germanic possessive type *dem Vater sein Haus*. In Dieter Kastovksy & Aleksander Szwedek (eds.), *Linguistics across historical and geographical boundaries: In*

honour of Jacek Fisiak on the occasion of his fiftieth birthday. Vol. 1: *Linguistic theory and historical linguistics*, 579–590. Berlin: Mouton de Gruyter.

Rijkhoff, Jan. 1998. Order in the noun phrase of the languages of Europe. In Anna Siewierska (ed.), *Constituent order in the languages of Europe*, 321–382. Berlin: Mouton de Gruyter.

Scott, Alan K. 2014. *The genitive case in Dutch and German: A study of morphosyntactic change in codified languages*. Leiden: Brill.

Sommerer, Lotte. 2012. Investigating article development in Old English: About categorization, gradualness and constructions. *Folia Linguistica Historica* 33. 175–213.

Spanoghe, Anne-Marie. 1995. *La syntaxe de l'appartenance inalienable en français, en espagnol et en portugais*. Frankfurt am Main: Peter Lang.

Torrego, Esther. 1999. El complemento directo preposicional. In Ignacio Bosque & Violeta Demonte (eds.), *Gramática descriptiva de la lengua española*, Vol. 2, 1779–1807. Madrid: Espasa-Calpe.

Traugott, Elizabeth Closs. 1992. Syntax. In Richard M. Hogg (ed.), *The Cambridge history of the English language*. Vol. 1: *The beginnings to 1066*, 168–289. Cambridge: Cambridge University Press.

Traugott, Elizabeth Closs. 2008. Grammaticalization, constructions and the incremental development of language: Suggestions from the development of degree modifiers in English. In Regine Eckardt, Gerhard Jäger & Tonjes Veenstra (eds.), *Variation, selection, development: Probing the evolutionary model of language change*, 219–250. Berlin: Mouton de Gruyter.

Traugott, Elizabeth Closs & Graeme Trousdale (eds.). 2010. *Gradience, gradualness and grammaticalization*. Amsterdam: John Benjamins.

Traugott, Elizabeth Closs & Graeme Trousdale. 2013. *Constructionalization and constructional change*. Oxford: Oxford University Press.

Trousdale, Graeme. 2008. Words and constructions in grammaticalization: The end of the English impersonal construction. In Susan M. Fitzmaurice & Donka Minkova (eds.), *Studies in the history of the English Language 4: Empirical and analytical advances in the study of English language change*, 301–326. Berlin: Mouton de Gruyter.

Trousdale, Graeme. 2010. Issues in constructional approaches to grammaticalization. In Katerina Stathi, Elke Gehweiler & Ekkehard König (eds.), *Grammaticalization: Current views and issues*, 51–71. Amsterdam: John Benjamins.

Trudgill, Peter. 2011. *Sociolinguistic typology: social determinants of linguistic complexity*. Oxford: Oxford University Press.

Van Belle, William & Willy Van Langendonck. 1996. The indirect object in Dutch. In William Van Belle & Willy Van Langendonck (eds.), *The dative*. Vol. 1: *Descriptive studies*, 217–250. Amsterdam: John Benjamins.

Van Bree, Cor. 1981. *Hebben-constructies en datiefconstructies binnen het Nederlandse taalgebied: Een taalgeografisch onderzoek*. [*Have*-constructions and dative constructions in the Dutch-speaking region: A language-geographic study]. Leiden: Leiden University dissertation.

van der Auwera, Johan. 1998. Phasal adverbials in the languages of Europe. In Johan van der Auwera (ed.) *Adverbial constructions in the languages of Europe*, 25–145. Berlin: Mouton de Gruyter.

van der Auwera, Johan. 2011. Standard Average European. In Bernd Kortmann & Johan van der Auwera (eds.), *The languages and linguistics of Europe: A comprehensive guide*, 291–306. Berlin: de Gruyter Mouton.

Van der Lubbe, H.F.A. 1958. *Woordvolgorde in het Nederlands: Een synchrone structurele beschouwing* [Word order in Dutch: A synchronic structural outlook]. Assen: Van Gorcum.

Van de Velde, Freek. 2009a. *De nominale constituent: Structuur en geschiedenis* [The nominal constituent: Structure and history]. Leuven: Leuven University Press.
Van de Velde, Freek. 2009b. The emergence of modification patterns in the Dutch noun phrase. *Linguistics* 47. 1021–1049.
Van de Velde, Freek. 2012. PP extraction and extraposition in Functional Discourse Grammar. *Language Sciences* 34. 433–454.
Van de Velde, Freek & Fred Weerman. 2014. The resilient nature of adjectival inflection in Dutch. In Petra Sleeman, Freek Van de Velde & Harry Perridon (eds.), *Adjectives in Germanic and Romance*, 113–146. Amsterdam: John Benjamins.
Vandeweghe, Willy. 1986. De zogenaamde possessieve datief en configuratieherschikking [The so-called possessive dative and configuration rearrangement]. In Cor Hoppenbrouwers, Ineke Schuurman, Ron van Zonneveld & Frans Zwarts (eds), *Syntaxis en lexicon: Veertien artikelen bij gelegenheid van het emeritaat van Albert Sassen* [Syntax and lexicon: Fourteen articles on the occasion of Albert Sassen's retirement], 117–131. Dordrecht: Foris.
Vandeweghe, Willy. 1987. The possessive dative in Dutch: Syntactic reanalysis and predicate formation. In Johan van der Auwera & Louis Goossens (eds.), *Ins and outs of the predication*, 137–151. Dordrecht: Foris.
Van Haeringen, C.B. 1956. *Nederlands tussen Duits en Engels* [Dutch between German and English]. The Hague: Servire.
Van Pottelberge, Jeroen. 2001. Sprachbünde: Beschreiben sie Sprachen oder Linguisten? *Linguistik Online* 8(1). http://www.linguistik-online.de/1_01/VanPottelberge.html
Vennemann, Theo. 2002. On the rise of 'Celtic' syntax in Middle English. In Peter J. Lucas & Angela M. Lucas (eds.), *Middle English from tongue to text. Selected papers from the Third International Conference on Middle English: Language and Text, held at Dublin, Ireland, 1–4 July 1999*, 203–234. Bern: Peter Lang.
Vismans, Roel, Matthias Hüning & Fred Weerman. 2010. Guest editors' preface [To special issue on Dutch between English and German]. *Journal of Germanic Linguistics* 22. 297–299.
Visser, F.T. 1963. *An historical syntax of the English language*, Vol. 1. Leiden: Brill.
Weber, Heinrich 1971. *Das erweiterte Adjektiv- und Partizipialattribut im Deutschen*. Munich: Max Hüber.
Weerman, Fred. 2003. Een mooie verhaal: Veranderingen in uitgangen [Een mooie verhaal: Changes in endings]. In Jan Stroop (ed.), *Waar gaat het Nederlands naartoe? Panorama van een taal* [Where is Dutch going? Panorama of a language], 249–260. Amsterdam: Bert Bakker.
Weerman, Fred. 2006. It's the economy, stupid: Een vergelijkende blik op *men* en *man*. [It's the economy, stupid: A comparative look at *men* and *man*]. In Matthias Hüning, Ulrike Vogl, Ton van der Wouden & Arie Verhagen (eds.), *Nederlands tussen Duits en Engels* [Dutch between German and English], 19–47. Leiden: Stichting Neerlandistiek Leiden.
Weerman, Fred & Petra de Wit. 1999. The decline of the genitive in Dutch. *Linguistics* 37. 1155–1192.
Whorf, Benjamin L. 1956. *Language, thought and reality: Selected writings of B.L. Whorf*. Edited by John B. Carroll. Cambridge, MA: MIT Press.
Wolk, Christoph, Joan Bresnan, Anette Rosenbach, and Benedikt Szmrecsányi. 2013. Dative and genitive variability in Late Modern English: Exploring cross-constructional variation and change. *Diachronica* 30. 382–419.

# Index

actionality 88, 231
- telicity 223–229
adaptation hypothesis 116
agency 184, 209fn
agent 101fn, 104, 208–209, 338–339
agentive 168, 184–185, 340
apokoinu 247
argument structure 89, 101, 260
article 282, 286–287, 332–335, 340–342, 346, 385–391
assertion 147–150
auxiliation/auxiliarization 6, 47–49, 67–70, 258, 261

back-formation 294, 300–302
bleaching (see semantic attrition)
bondedness (see syntagmatic cohesion)

Cantonese 143–144
coalescence 71–72, 339
Cognitive Grammar 24–28, 199
comparative adverb 82–83, 102–104
comparative modal (see modals)
composite change 68, 76, 266–267
compositionality 71–72, 104, 205
concessive 37, 40, 48, 50–54, 58, 62–64, 66–67, 73, 76–77
condensation 73
conditional 40, 53, 87–88, 97–99, 101, 152, 159–160, 294–295, 336
configurationality 377, 383, 385–386, 389–392
conjunction 126, 142, 159, 194, 247–249, 253, 298
contact degrammaticalization
    (see degrammaticalization)
contact grammaticalization
    (see grammaticalization)
continuative relative clause 114, 121–136
Czech 261–262, 264, 266–269, 272, 274–275

decategorialization/decategorization 39, 82, 87, 99, 101, 250, 267

degrammaticalization 4, 74fn, 258, 266–269, 277, 302–303, 313
- contact degrammaticalization 343–344
deontic modality (see modality)
desemanticization (see semantic attrition)
direct speech 86, 173, 187, 189
directionality 2–5, 35, 41, 229–230, 346
- linear path 206–207, 212–216
- multidirectional path 206–207, 210–212
- unidirectionality 2–5, 58, 216, 257, 266, 344
directive meaning 60, 76–77, 88, 102–105, 150–151, 158–160
discourse continuity 130–133
discourse marker 37, 40, 139, 149–161
discourse-orientation 36–38, 41
divergence 73–74, 77
Dutch 24, 26, 113–135, 223fn, 269, 355–368, 374–383, 385–387
dynamic modality (see modality)

East African English (see English)
echo question 142–144
English 28, 35, 114, 167–194, 237–254, 311–347, 354–358, 363–368, 372–380, 382–383, 385–386, 389–393
- East African English 326, 328, 331, 335
- Indian English 312, 320–321, 326–328, 331–334
- New English 312, 319–320, 326
- Singapore English 312, 314–315, 319, 321–322, 327–328, 334
- West African English 323, 326, 331
entrenchment 27, 97, 101, 108, 169, 175, 182, 186–187, 264, 277, 354
epistemic modality (see modality)
Estonian 281–305
evaluative meaning 88, 102–105, 274
evolutionary perspective 115–117, 135–136, 303–305
external possessor 353–393

Finnish 285, 289–294, 299, 301–303, 305
forced grammaticalization
    (see grammaticalization)

French 81–108, 173–174, 316, 332, 347, 355–357, 359–360, 369–375, 377, 379–381, 387–390
frequency 73, 82, 85, 93–95, 135, 146, 169, 223, 225, 231, 264, 293, 295, 299, 313, 321, 342
functional load 121, 170, 191
future (*see* tense)

German 264, 269, 282, 284–286, 290–291, 353, 356–357, 359–361, 363–364, 371, 373, 375–380, 385–386, 389–390, 393
grammatical aspect
– progressive 213, 219fn, 326–331, 338–340, 344–345
– habitual 315, 322–326, 335–339, 344, 346
grammaticalization 38–41, 68–75, 101, 115–121, 133–135, 157–160, 170, 190–192, 200–205, 247–253, 263–264, 377–392
– contact grammaticalization 313–319
– forced grammaticalization 281–285, 293–294, 303–305
– replica grammaticalization 281–282, 313, 317, 342–343, 346

habitual (*see* grammatical aspect)
Hakka 143–145
hearer-orientation 33, 35–37, 39, 139, 188
historical fiction 176–177
hypotaxis 115–116, 133, 249

imperative 40, 103, 140–141, 144, 147, 150–155, 259, 263
impersonal construction 83–84, 89, 96–97, 174
Indian English (*see* English)
indirect speech 86, 158
infinitive 89–93, 169, 242, 244, 247–249, 297–298
information focus 168
injunction 174–175, 177, 185–186, 193
insubordination 132–133, 297
intensification 218–220, 229–230
intersubjectification 35–41, 49, 71, 75–77, 133–135, 142, 169–170, 185–188
intersubjectivity 23–25, 30–34, 134–135, 139–140, 150, 155, 157, 183, 186, 188

invited inference (*see* pragmatic inferencing)
irrealis 88, 97, 99, 323–324
Italian 356, 358–360, 368–370, 375, 380, 387–389, 393

language reform 294–295, 299–300, 302–305
Latin 199–231, 292, 355, 357, 374, 384
layering 73–74, 108, 313, 319, 344
lexicalization 187, 189, 205, 229, 257, 272–275
linear path (*see* directionality)

marginalization 264–266
missionary linguistics 282–285, 294
modality 19–42, 47–77, 81–109, 140–142, 147, 258–277, 322–326, 336–338
– deontic modality 29, 35, 50–52, 59–60, 64–65, 88, 102–105, 174, 262, 270–271
– dynamic modality 50
– epistemic modality 21, 31–32, 35, 50–51, 60–61, 65, 76–77, 143, 262, 272
modals 47–77, 258–277, 314, 322–326, 336–338
– comparative modal 81–109
– semi-modal 81–109
multidirectional path (*see* directionality)

negation 116, 173–177, 190–194, 302–303
New English (*see* English)
noun phrase 41, 377, 380, 383–392

obligatorification 73, 101, 158, 254
optative meaning 61–62, 66, 76–77, 103–105

paradigmatic variability 73, 109, 250
paradigmaticity 73
paradigmaticization 73, 109, 266
parataxis 115–116, 133
past (*see* tense)
performativity 20–23, 25–30, 33–34
persistence 73–75, 105, 107, 361, 379
phonetic attrition/erosion/reduction 39, 70–71, 158, 160, 205, 213, 262–263, 341, 385
phraseologism 169, 173

Polish 261–262, 264–266, 270–273, 276
post-grammaticalization 258–276
post-modal meaning 47–49, 51, 58, 70, 73–77, 258–259, 264, 266
pragmatic inferencing 50, 51fn, 104–105, 134, 139–140, 154–155, 158, 181, 187–188, 248, 337
preposition 202–204, 207–210, 243, 381–382
preverb 204–205, 210–218
primitive change 68, 70–72
private letters 122
progressive (*see* grammatical aspect)
promise 174–177, 185–187, 193
purpose subordinator 237–254

reanalysis 68–72, 76, 99–100, 160, 238fn, 274, 338, 344, 361fn
rebuttal 155–157
relative adverb 113, 117, 119, 134
relative pronominal adverb 113, 117, 131, 134
relative pronoun 113, 117
relativization 113–115, 117, 119, 133, 135
renewal 249–250, 391
replica grammaticalization (*see* grammaticalization)
represented speech 86
retention 26, 89, 96–97, 107, 216, 302, 318, 380, 385, 390
retraction 269–271
rhetorical reconstruction 140, 157, 159
Romance 81, 353–362, 368–392
Russian 261–262, 271–274, 276–277

'say' verb 141–142, 145, 157, 160–161
semantic attrition/bleaching/desemanticization 2fn, 4, 39, 70–71, 82, 105, 107–108, 190–194, 212, 219, 223–229
semanticity 82
semi-modal (*see* modals)
Serbian/Croatian 261–263, 272, 274–275
simplification 98, 116
Singapore English (*see* English)
Sinitic 140–145
Southern Min 146–160

Spanish 353, 357–360, 368–371, 380–381, 387–389
speaker-orientation 26–30, 33–35, 37–42, 53, 139
specialization 73–74, 104, 109, 121, 250, 272, 386
speech-act orientation 38–40
speed of language change 379–380, 393
spoken language 86, 122
Sprachbund 354, 373, 390–392
Standard Average European 354, 372–376, 391
standard of comparison 105–107
structural scope 73
subjectification 20, 34–36, 38–41, 48–49, 67, 71, 75–77, 133, 135, 158, 160–161, 183–184
subjectivity 20–35, 75, 88, 124–125, 129–134, 139–140, 147, 150, 156–157, 172–173, 183–185, 190, 192–193, 274
subordination 115–116, 132–133, 201, 250
suggestion 150–153
superlative 299–300
Swedish 47–77, 285, 292, 382
syntacticization 115–116, 135
syntagmatic cohesion 218, 251–252
syntagmatic fixation 71, 82, 84, 86, 91, 93, 99, 101, 263
syntagmatic variability 82, 84, 86, 92–93, 101, 237

telicity (*see* actionality)
tense 86–88, 265, 288–289, 294
– future 87, 99, 264–265, 287–293, 336
– past 294–297, 315

unidirectionality (*see* directionality)
univerbation 212, 272

warning 153–155
West African English (*see* English)
West Germanic 353–368, 372–392
written language 114, 117, 122, 284, 286, 288, 294, 299,
Wu 145